THE CONSTITUTION

OF THE

UNITED STATES OF AMERICA.

VOL. I.

"As the British Constitution is the most subtle organism which has preceded from progressive history, so the American Constitution is the most wonderful work ever struck off at a given time by the brain and purpose of man." — *William E. Gladstorne*

REPUBLISHERS' NOTES.

This volume (I of II) is a republish of the SIXTH EDITION published in 1886 which incorporates all inaccuracies or additional information discovered by Mr. Bancroft since the FIRST EDITION was published in 1882.

We have attempted to accurately duplicate the original publisher's format, language, phrasing and spelling. However, differences in older linotype layup and newer word processing formatting made an exact duplication in publishing next to impossible to accomplish.

The two historical periods involved, the late eighteenth century when most of the quotes and letters were written, and the middle nineteenth century when the original author's narrative text of this volume was written, the phraseology and spelling were sometimes different.

We have also been careful to accurately reproduce each and every character of the original interior text. The cover was designed to reflect modern paperback standards. We also added the watermark text in all original blank pages.

The page count and sequence have been left unchanged.

ushistoricaltruth.org

ISBN-13: 978-1452843926
ISBN-10: 1452843929

HISTORY

OF THE

FORMATION OF THE CONSTITUTION

OF THE

UNITED STATES OF AMERICA.

BY
GEORGE BANCROFT.

IN TWO VOLUMES.

VOL. I.

SIXTH EDITION.

NEW YORK:
D. APPLETON AND COMPANY,
1, 3, AND 5 BOND STREET.
1889.

COPYRIGHT BY

GEORGE BANCROFT,

1882.

PREFACE.

Very many years have gone by since I conceived a hope of one day writing a history of the formation of our federal constitution. The congress of the confederation and the federal convention having sat with closed doors and under injunctions of secrecy, materials for the work lay almost exclusively in manuscripts widely dispersed. I have visited the archives of more than half the thirteen states, and have never neglected an opportunity of taking copies of papers relating to the subject wherever I could find them.

In New Hampshire members of the family of Langdon-Elwy, of more than one generation, placed their rich collection of letters at my disposition. Papers of John Sullivan, the rival of John Langdon for public honors, and his equal in zeal for the acceptance of the constitution, were entrusted to me by Mr. Thomas C. Amory, of Boston.

In turning to the rich materials that are preserved in the archives of Massachusetts, I have had most friendly and beneficial assistance from Mr. Henry B. Peirce, the present secretary of that commonwealth; and the cordial co-operation of those employed in his office. The descendants of John Adams for three generations have unfailingly been ready to further my researches. The papers of Samuel Adams came into my possession through the late Samuel Adams Wells. From Mr. John A. King; I have received reports of debates in the federal convention of 1787, taken by Rufus King, who was at that time still in the public service of Massachusetts.

From Connecticut valuable papers of Roger Sherman came to me through Professor Simeon E. Baldwin, of New Haven; though nothing equal in importance to the document which embodies nine articles of amendments of the confederation, and which is preserved only in Sherman's Life, by Jeremiah Evarts. Through the kindness of Mr. Oliver Ellsworth Wood, of New York, I was able to examine what remains of the manuscripts of Chief-Justice Ellsworth. The large collections left by William Samuel Johnson have been open to me through three generations of their possessors. The proceedings of the convention held at Hartford in November, 1780, a convention which was the starting-point of the regularly continued efforts for new articles of union,

PREFACE vii

were long inquired for, but in vain. Recently I discovered them in the archives of the old congress. I have since learned that Mr. C. J. Hoadly has a copy from the offices of Rhode Island.

The papers of each of the two great rival states men of New York, devoted fiends in their college life, though afterwards divided, were equally open to me. Accompanying my contemporary and constant friend Dr. Alonzo Potter, who was wishing to find time to write the life of Robert R. Livingston, we ransacked masses of papers preserved at the manor; of which the choicest were kept apart, bound in four folio volumes. The papers of Jay, which are very extensive and reserved in perfect order, were confided to me without the least restriction by the courtesy of my friend Mr. John Jay. Of Hamilton I have taken extracts from interesting letters not as yet published. For knowledge of his personality in his riper years, I sought the conversation of his friend President Eliphalet Nott. Copies of the most important papers of Governor George Clinton I owe to the long-continued aid of Mr. George R. Howell, one of the state librarians at Albany. Manuscripts of Gouverneur Morris were unreservedly communicated by his widow.

Of William Paterson, the foremost member of the federal convention from New Jersey, many papers are till preserved. His descendant, Mr. William Paterson, of Perth Amboy, had the exceeding kindness to examine them and to send to me all which seemed of public interest. In this way great help was gained in tracing the currents of thought that prevailed in the years between the peace and the institution of the government of the United States, and precious instruction received on the movements in the federal convention.

I cannot be grateful enough for the aid furnished me from Pennsylvania, alike from Harrisburg and from Philadelphia. Every one who had letters seemed willing, nay desirous, that I should have the benefit of them. I must specially acknowledge the untiring zeal in my behalf of Mr. John William Wallace and Mr. Frederick D. Stone. Letter-books and papers of Robert Morris were in trusted to me by Captain Morris of our navy.

The notes made by Mr. Thomas Rodney, of Delaware, of proceedings in congress in 1786, were communicated to me by Mr. Cesar A. Rodney, of Wilmington; and they throw light on the early efforts in congress for a federal convention.

My collections relating to Maryland at the crisis of the constitution are ample. Mr. J. T. Briscoe, its secretary of state, most promptly aided me by researches in answer to my inquiries. The notes of Samuel Chase on the new constitution were imparted to me by one of his descendants.

Of the very able and warm-hearted enthusiast George Mason, I obtained, in 1857, exceedingly instructive documents and family letters from his son, the late James M. Mason.

The most interesting incident connected with these researches was a visit to Madison in the last days of March and the first of April, 1836, a few weeks only before his death. His health was still so firm that he could pass the whole day and evening in conversation. He had taken pains to recover the letters written by him in his earlier public life; these he set before me, as well as his manuscripts of the debates in congress and in the convention. At my departure he assured me that he had carried his confidence with me further than he had done with any one.

All the time that I was with him he spoke not one harsh word of any opponent of younger or later days, nor one that could bias the judgment of a listener respecting any of his contemporaries. He was a man of peace striving for peace. Still less did he take the opportunity of bringing into view his own public service, though I could discern a regret that more ample materials were not before the world of the part which he took in promoting the union, when the rule of rotation drove him from congress and for three years he occupied a seat in the legislature of Virginia.

There rested upon his mind an obvious anxiety about the destiny of the United States. The divisions between the North and the South were already tending to greater divergences; and, while he had painful apprehensions for the future, he knew no hope except in mutual moderation and forbearance.

As to the division of the country on the questions involved in that of slavery, he pointed out to me that they began very much earlier than was usually supposed. The different hues of color seen in the South, he observed, did not all spring from the intermixture of blacks and whites: the slaves imported from Africa were of different races; some of them of light complexion. To the question whether the negro was in natural capacity equal to the white man, he said that he could not give an answer; he himself was old enough to have seen imported Africans just after their arrival, and during the generations of his period of observation their transformation from an almost brutal condition had been so great that he could not set a limit to their further improvement.

The character of his mind was essentially that of a mediator, careful to study thoroughly the ground of difference between conflicting opinions, and find a share of truth in each of them.

The thought nearest to the affections of Madison was the union. He loved everything that helped

PREFACE   xi

to bind the states together in new bonds. For this special reason he took delight in anticipating the multiplication of railroads and canals, saying, "they will dove-tail the states"; and to manifest visibly his meaning he interlaced his thin, wan fingers as he spoke.

With the recognition of our independence the European nations who most sought commercial connections with us sent ministers, consuls, or agents, to reside with us. Their reports of the course of events form continuous and most instructive narratives of four contemporary witnesses from different European powers, giving special accounts each to his own sovereign.

When Joseph II. attempted to open the river Scheldt, he designed to establish commerce between Belgium and the United States, and to promote that end he sent the Baron de Beelen Bertholff to reside in Philadelphia, not as an accredited minister, but as an observer and correspondent. I possess an ample selection from his careful reports, extending from March, 1785, to the end of September, 1788.

From 1783 the republic of the United Netherlands maintained near congress Mr. P. J. Van Berckel as its minister. Of his voluminous reports, which particularly abound in information on all that relates to commerce, full copies were made for me.

The two most important kingdoms in their relations to the United States were France and England. The political mind of England was displayed in its greatness in the debates of the two houses of its parliament; in France, before the revolution, the political genius of the government showed itself very remarkably in its diplomacy. It is to Mr. Guizot that I was, in the first instance, obliged for free admission to the French archives. Nothing was refused me for examination, nor was one line of which I desired a copy withheld. I made the very long and laborious examination in person, and was assured that I had obtained everything. Every one who represented France in the United States, from 1782 to 1790, was a man of great ability; the reports of Luzerne, of Marbois, of Otto, of the Count de Moustier, and the instructions given them, first by Vergennes, then by Montmorin, are of income parable value.

Till after the middle, of this century, the British government was loath to suffer its diplomatic papers to be examined by Americans for any period later than the year 1782, the epoch of peace between England and its former colonies. A few years ago Lord Granville was so good as to give me leave to send an agent, to examine papers extending even later than the formation of our constitution, and I availed myself of the privilege. When, in 1874, I chanced to be in England, I was allowed by Lord Granville the freest access to the papers which I needed to see, and the principle was laid down by those who overlooked the copies taken for me, that no restricttion should be put upon historical research after truth. Since then I am told this liberality has been still further extended in point of time. Indeed, with the pacification of our domestic troubles in 1865 America has opened *novæ tabulæ*, and the relations of England with us from 1789 to 1865 belong as much to ancient history as those of the time of the house of Hanover. The number of persons employed to gather information for the British ministry in the United States from 1783 to 1790 was very great, but no one of them had a diplomatic character.

Meantime Mr. Jared Sparks brought out a part of the writings of Washington, amply elucidated by the fruits of his own wide research at home and abroad, as well as a series of grave and weighty letters addressed to Washington on public affairs. A large and most instructive selection from the manuscripts and published works of John Adams was laid before the world by his grandson. The journal of the federal convention, the reports of its debates by Madison and by Yates, the diplomatic correspondence of congress between 1783 and March, 1789, the writings of Jefferson, of Madison, of Hamilton, were published by congress. These, though of the greatest possible value, were far from including all the materials served in the public archives. Happily for me, at the time when it as most convenient to me to examine them, there was at the head of the department of state Mr. William M. Evarts, lover of historic truth and perfectly acquainted with the necessity of exhaustive research for its attainment. He gave me that opportunity for thorough examination which Mr. Guizot had granted me at Paris. The additional materials which were brought to light were in part dispersed through a couple of hundred folio volumes, which had been preserved by Charles Thomson. Then there are very many unpublished letters of Monroe and of Washington, and innumerable unpublished letters written in unreserved familiarity and confidence by members of congress or of the state legislatures and others to Washington, Jefferson, Madison, and Monroe. From these, with the materials which I already possessed, I have been able to trace step by step the march of the people of the United States, from the Hartford convention of the New England states and New York in 1780, to the federal convention of 1787; and to show the origin, progress, and completion of the ordinance of 1787 for governing the North-west.

Jackson, the secretary of the federal convention, left its journal unfinished, and passed hours of its last day in burning its papers. The journal of that convention, as published by congress, was injured by its editors, who, in their zeal to complete what is but a fragment, made various interpolations, alike of documents and of words in the text. The paper which purports to be from Charles Pinckney has no right to be there, and is not worth printing anywhere. He himself never said that it was the motion which he offered in congress; its want of genuineness is proved by a contemporary publication of his own; and the internal evidence against it is absolutely conclusive. I was therefore obliged to have a thorough comparison made of the whole printed journal and the manuscript; and on one point at least to collate the papers of Madison, as edited, with the original text in his own clear hand.

Nine volumes of selections relating to America, cut from London journals by William Vaughan, a friend of Franklin, and extending through the period of which I am writing, came to me as the gift of my friend the late Mr. William H. Russell. Mr. Fauntleroy, the secretary of state of Virginia, and in his absence his assistant, Mr. McKae, have readily and most promptly aided my inquiries. On an important point I have derived instruction from my friend Mr. Joseph W. Harper, Junior. For unremitting and most important attention I may not omit to thank Mr. Ainsworth K. Spofford, who combines the highest executive ability of a librarian with a comprehensive knowledge of what is contained in our national collection.

That which I attempt to do is to trace the formation of the federal constitution from its origin to its establishment by the inauguration of its president. The subject has perfect unity, and falls of itself into five epochs or acts. I have spared no pains to compress the narrative within the narrowest limits consistent with clearness. In weighing my authorities, I have striven to follow with strict severity the laws of historical criticism; ever careful to discriminate between those materials which are sources, and those which are but helps or aids.

Large extracts from my collections are printed at the end of each volume. The selection has been strictly confined to those of which I have authentic copies in manuscript. Unless my knowledge or memory fails me, not more than a half dozen of them all have been printed heretofore, and those are inserted for some special purpose. They are so numerous and so different that I cannot but hope every one will find something of interest, as well as assistance in watching the movement of the mind of the people and of congress from a league of states to a perfected union.

Having finished what I had undertaken, I dismiss it with the hope that it may find the most lenient reception from those who are the most perfect masters of the subject.

Washington D.C, January 1882

CONTENTS.

BOOK I.

THE CONFEDERATION.

CHAPTER I.

A RETROSPECT. MOVMENTS TOWARDS UNION.

Progress of the world by mastery over the forces of nature, 4 — By a better knowledge of the nature of justice, 5 — The laws of morals may be proved by inductions from experience, 5 — First American union, 6 — Concert of the colonies in action, 1684, 6 — Consolidation of colonies attempted by an absolute king, 7 — Effect of the revolution of 1688, 7 — Proposal of a federal union by William Penn, 7 — Plan of union of Lord Stairs, 7 — Of Franklin in 1754, 8 — Of Lord Halifax, 8 — The colonies as the allies of England, 8 — Plan of unity through the supreme power of the British parliament, 9 — First American congress, 9 — The elder Pitt and colonial liberty, 9 — The American congress of 1774, 10 — Independence and a continental convention and charter, 10 — Question at issue between Great Britain and the colonies, 11 — The confederation imperfect from jealousy of central power, 11 — Rutledge proposes a constituent congress, 11 — New England convention at Boston, August, 1780, 12 — Measures of New York of September, 1780, 12 — Effort of Hamilton, 13 — Thomas Paine and a continental convention, 13 — Greene's opinion, 14 — Convention of New York and New England at Hartford, 14 — Reception of its proceedings in congress, 15 — New Jersey and the federal republic, 15 — Cession of western lands by New York and Virginia, 16 — Washington explains the imperfection of the confederation, 17 — The confederation adopted, 17 — Washington discriminates between the functions of the individual state and the power of the whole, 18 — He appeals to the statesmen of Virginia, 19 — His decisive letter for a stronger government, 20, 21 — His instructions to Custis and to Jones, 22 — Madison's report of March, 1781, 23 — Madison receives a copy of Washington's letter, 23 — The French minister reports the effort to reform the constitution, 24 — Pamphlet by William Barton, 24 — Report of the grand committee of congress, 25 — Appeals of Hamilton through the press, 25 — The committee of three on the confederation and their report, 25-27 — Coercion impossible, 28 — Washington desires a new constitution, 28.

CHAPTER II.

THE STRUGGLE FOR REVENUE.

Schuyler proposes the union of New England and New York, 29 — Congress establishes departments, 30 — The minister of war, 30 — Of finance, 31 — Hamilton on a national debt and a national bank, 31 — Robert Morris and a national bank, 32 — Congress and a national bank, 33 — New Jersey demands for congress the power to regulate commerce, 33 — Protection of American industries, 34 — Congress asks power to levy an impost, 34 — The answers of the states, 34, 35 — How Morris started the bank, 36 — Hamilton on regulating trade, 37 — Becomes a receiver of the United States' revenue, 37 — Schuyler in the New York legislature, 38 — New York sanctions a federal convention, 39 — Indifference of Clinton, 39 — Hamilton elected to congress, 39 — Morris entreats a loan from France, 39 — Embarkation of the French troops, 40 — What befell their officers, 40-42 — Pennsylvania and the public debt, 42 — Rhode Island refuses the impost, 43 — Hamilton's reply to Rhode Island, 43 — Richard Henry Lee divides Virginia, 44 — Congress by its judicial powers reconciles states, 45.

CHAPTER III.

AMERICA AND GREAT BRITAIN. 1782, 1783.

Peace between America and Great Britain, 46 — Moderation of Vergennes and Shelburne, 47 — Cessation of hostilities, 48 — The king of England invites a cordial understanding with France, 49 — Commercial relations between America and England, 49 — Fox refuses an invitation to join the ministry, 49 — Coalition of Lord North and Fox, 50 — Debate in the peers, 51 — Shelburne's defence, 52 — The ministry tottering, 53 — Pitt retires with dignity, 54 — Shelburne's modification of the navigation act, 55 — Liberal opinion of Burke, 56 — Ministry of Fox and the Duke of Portland, 57 — The king against the ministry, 58 — Fox and the navigation act, 59 — The unfair offers of Fox to America, 60 — Jay and the slave-trade, 61 — The American commissionersoffer mutual unconditional free trade, 62 — Debate in the house of lords, 62 — England excludes American shipping from the British West Indies, 63 — Re-nounces the right to purchase American-built ships, 64 — Creates a national spirit in America, 64 — England believes American union impossible, 65 — Lord Sheffield on American commerce, 66 — The king sure that America could estab-lish no stable government, 67 — Regret in England that the treaty of peace had been made with the collective states, 68 — The British fur-traders induce Lord North to retain the interior American posts, 68 — Pitt, Fox, and reform, 69 — The new colonial system of Great Britain, 69.

CONTENTS. xix

CHAPTER IV.

AMERICA AND CONTINENTAL EUROPE. 1783.

Sweden, 70 — Prussia, 71 — Joseph II. and Belgium, 72 — Denmark, 73 — The free city of Hamburg, 73 — Portugal, 73 — Russia, 73 — Holland, 74 — Spain, 74 — France, 75.

CHAPTER V.

A PLAN TO FORCE A STRONGER GOVERNMENT. JANUARY — MARCH, 1783.

The army at Newburg, 76 — Its appeal to congress, 76 — Financial scheme concerted between Morris and the grand committee of congress, 78 — Interview of the grand committee with the deputies of the army, 78 — Disinterested conduct of Hamilton, 79 — Plan of Morris to coerce congress into bolder measures, 80 — The debt to the army and half pay, 81 — Debate on revenue, 82 — Virginia repeals her grant of the impost, 82 — Debate in congress, 83 — Madison speaks, 84 — Methods of general revenue, 85 — Pamphlet of Pelatiah Webster, 86 — Robert and Gouverneur Morris aim at new powers to the government through the army, 87 — Hamilton to Washington, 87 — Gouverneur Morris to Greene, 88 — Opinions of Knox and Washington, 89 — The news of peace, 90 — Rutledge proposes different treatment of military and civil creditors, 90 — Mercer and Arthur Lee combat Madison, 91 — Robert Morris publishes his letter of resignation, 91.

CHAPTER VI.

THE ARMY AND ITS CHIEF. MARCH, 1783.

Washington's meditations, 92 — His appeal to the governor of Virginia, 93 — Conduct of Gates, 93 — His plan of action, 94 — Armstrong's anonymous address, 95 — Washington's reply in general orders, 95 — Meeting of officers of the army, 96 — Washington's address to them, 97 — Their resolutions, 98 — Result of the meeting, 99 — What congress did for the army, 100 — News of peace, 100 — Proclamation of congress, 101.

CHAPTER VII.

DISBANDING THE ARMY. MARCH — JULY, 1783.

The rightful claims of the army, 102 — Madison proposes a plan for revenue, 103 — Debt and resources of the United States, 103 — Slaves rated as five to three, 104 — Hamilton wishes to propose a federal convention, 104 — The financial report adopted, 104 — The appeal of congress to the states, 105 — Committee on the New York resolutions favor a general convention, 105 — Rufus Putnam plans colonizing Ohio, 106 — Timothy Pickering advises the exclusion of slavery, 106 — The ordinance of Bland, 107 — Discharging the army, 107 — Society of the Cincinnati, 107 — How the army was disbanded and how it was paid, 108 — Washington's legacy to the people, 109 — The opportunity of the citizens of America, 111 — The necessity of a supreme power, 112 — The choice of union or anarchy followed by arbitrary power, 113 — Washington wished reform through a convention of the people, 113.

BOOK II.

ON THE WAY TO A FEDERAL CONVENTION. 1783—1787.

CHAPTER I.

HOW THE LAND RECEIVED THE LEGACY OF WASHINGTON. JUNE — DECEMBER, 1783.

The universal love of union, 117 — Inter-citizenship, 118 — How Washington's legacy was received in Connecticut, 119 — In Delaware, 120 — In Pennsylvania, 120, 121 — In South Carolina, 121, 122 — In New York, 122 — In Massachusetts, 123-125 — In Virginia, 125-128 — In Maryland, 128 — In congress, 128 — Riot in Philadelphia, 128 — Congress adjourns to Princeton, 129 — Rivalry for the site of the federal government, 129 — Coalition in favor of its present site, 130 — Hamilton on the defects of the confederation, 131 — Ellsworth on national existence, 132 — Forebodings of Hamilton, 132 — He retires from congress, 133 — Connecticut delays its adhesion to a federal convention, 133 — Forced emigration of royalists, 134 — Washington examines the inland water communications of New York, 135 — Haldimand refuses to surrender the interior posts, 135 — Congress votes Washington a statue, 136 — It receives him publicly, 136 — Follows his counsels on the army and navy, 137 — On interior trade, 137 — On the state of Ohio, 138- On doing honor to Kosciuszko, 138 — An envoy from the Dutch republic, 138 — Madison forced to retire by the rule of rotation, 139 — Washington calls on his old soldiers to promote union, 140 — The city of New York restored, 141 —The officers of the army bid farewell to Washington, 141, 142 — His journey through New Jersey, 142 — Through Philadelphia, 143 — He resigns his commission, 143-145 — He returns to Mount Vernon, 145.

CHAPTER II.

VIRGINIA STATESMEN LEAD TOWARD A BETTER UNION. 1784.

Four motives to union, 146 — Congress declines to lead the way, 147 — England compels union, 147 — The views of Virginia, 148 — Jefferson describes the United States as one nation, 149 — Congress vote them to be one nation,

CONTENTS. xxi

150 — Jefferson's plan for international commerce, 150 — Accepted by congress, 151 — Jefferson and Washington on commerce with the West, 151, 152 — Honors decreed to Washington by Virginia, 152 — Washington pleads with Virginia statesmen for a national constitution, 153 — The great West to form an empire of republics, 154 — Jefferson's ordinance, 155 — Against slavery in the West, 156 — How it was lost, 157 — Jefferson's life-long opinion on slavery, 158 — His ordinance for disposing of the public lands, 158 — The mint and American coinage, 159 — The cost of the war, 159 — Holland and John Adams, 160 — Generosity of France, 161 — Jefferson's financial plan, 161 — Patrick Henry disposed to increase the power of congress, 162 — National measures of Virginia, 163 — Jefferson enforces union, 164 — The committee of states, 164 — Retirement of Robert Morris, 165 — Lee and Madison on a federal convention, 166 — France sees the tendency of the confederation to dissolution, 167.

CHAPTER III.

THE WEST. 1784, 1785.

Washington's tour to the West, 168 — His scheme of internal navigation, 169 — His report to Governor Harrison, 170 — Lafayette in the United States, 171 — Washington negotiates between Virginia and Maryland, 172 — He refuses gifts, 173 — Virginia appoints commissioners to treat with Maryland, 174 — The fifth congress and Richard Henry Lee as its president, 174 — Samuel Adams for a firm government, 175 — The politics of New York corrupted by its custom-house, 175 — Washington's western policy, 176 — He lays it before the president of congress, 177 — William Grayson, 177 — Pickering against slavery in the West, 178 — King revives Jefferson's anti-slavery clause, 179 — The proposal committed, 179 — King's report, 180 — Grayson favors the prohibition of slavery, 180 — His ordinance for the disposal of western lands, 180-182 — Can congress levy armed men? 182, 183.

CHAPTER IV.

THE REGULATION OF COMMERCE, THE FIFTH CONGRESS. 1784, 1785.

Connecticut and Maryland, but not Virginia, propose reform of the confederacy by less than a unanimous vote, 184 — Tract by Noah Webster, 185 — Excessive importations of British goods, 185 — The consequent distress, 186 — Remedies proposed in New York, 186 —Pennsylvania proposes a protective system, 187 — Movements in Boston noted by Grayson, 188 — Boston demands more powers for congress and a protective tariff, 189 — Bowdoin recommends a federal convention, 190 — Instructions to the Massachusetts delegates, 190 — Movements in New Hampshire and Rhode Island, 191 — In Pennsylvania, 191 — John Adams applauds a navigation act, 191 — James Monroe, 192 — His compromise proposal for a revenue, 192, 193 — His report, 193 — His procrastination, 194

— Is puzzled by Adam Smith on the wealth of nations, 195 — The extreme South afraid of a navigation act, 195 — The objections of Richard Henry Lee, 196 — Monroe wishes his measure delayed, 197 — Congress regrets Madison, 197 — The Massachusetts delegates disobey their instructions, 198 — Their reasons, 198, 199 — Bowdoin's reply, 199 — The effect, 199 — The American commissioners for treaties meet with a rebuff from England, 200 — John Adams and King George, 201 — England will not treat except on the condition of a preference, 202 — Adams proposes retaliation, 203 — Interview of Adams with Pitt, 203-206 — The United States agree with France for a perfect reciprocity, 207 — France reduces the duty on American fish-oil, 207 — Treaty with Prussia, 207, 208 — Spain reserved, 208 — Noble spirit of South Carolina, 208 — Treaty with Morocco, 208 — A new constitution cannot spring from congress, 209.

CHAPTER V.

OBSTACLES TO UNION KEMOVED OR QUIETED. 1783—1787.

State of religion in the colonies, 210 — Virginia disestablishes the church, 211 — Hawley and the inquisition into faith by the temporal power, 212 — Decline of the Anglican church in Virginia, 212 — Does religion need compulsory support ? 213 — Opinions o the Presbyterians, 213 — Of the Baptists, 213 — Patrick Henry proposes a legal support for Christianity, 214 — Madison opposes, 214 — Opinion of Washington, 215 — Of the Baptists, 215 — Of the convention of the Presbyterian church, 216 — Jefferson's bill for religious freedom adopted, 216 — Other states follow, 217 — The statute in French and Italian, 217 — The Protestant Episcopal church of the United States, 217, 218 — The Methodists, 218 — Their missionaries in America, 219 — Their superintendents, 220 — Their liturgy, 221 — Their first general conference, 222 — The superintendent defined to be a bishop, 223 — The Methodists and slavery, 223 — Rapid increase of the Methodists, 224 — Roman Catholics in the United States, 224, 225 — Cession of claims to land by Massachusetts, Connecticut, New York, South Carolina, Virginia, 226 — Enlargement of Pennsylvania, 226 — New York yields to temptation, 227 — Slavery and freedom never reconciled, 227.

CHAPTER VI.

STATE LAWS IMPAIRING THE OBLIGATION OF CONTRACTS PROVE THE NEED OF AN OVERRULING UNION. BEFORE MAY, 1787.

Paper money in the American states, 228 — Laws of Connecticut, 229 — Of Massachusetts, 230 — Of New Hampshire, 231 — Rhode Island, 231 — The court and the legislature of Rhode Island in conflict, 232 — The laws of New York, 232 — Of New Jersey, 233, 234 — Of Pennsylvania, 234, 235 — Of Delaware, 235 — Of Maryland, 235 — Of Georgia, 235 — Of South Carolina, 236 — Of North Carolina, 236, 237 — Of Virginia, 237-239 — Inflexibility of Washington, 239 — Public opinion on paper money, 240 — Opinions of Madison and Roger Sherman, 241.

CHAPTER VII.

CONGRESS CONFESSES ITS HELPLESSNESS. 1785, 1786.

Washington in private life, 242 — The visit of Houdon, 242, 243 — Invitations to France by its king and queen, 243 — Situation and value of Mount Vernon, 243 — The house and grounds, 244 — The lands, negroes, and produce, 244 — Washington embarrassed for income, 245 — A gradual abolitionist, 245, 246 — His love of hunting, 246— He arranges his papers, 246 — His perfect amiability, 247 — His exemplary life, 247 — His religion, 247, 248 — His hatred of war, 248 — His sympathy for the Irish and the Greeks, 248 — His enthusiasm at the beginning of the French revolution, 249 — He enjoins moderation on Lafayette, 249 — In politics an impartial American, 249 — The commissioners of Maryland and Virginia meet at Mount Vernon, 249, 250 — The results, 250 — States divided on granting power overtrade to congress, 250 — Opinion of Madison, 251 — Of Washington, 251 —Hesitation of Virginia, 251, 252 — Maryland suggests a politico-commercial commission, 252 — The wisdom of Madison, 253 — Calling a convention at Annapolis, 253 — The sixth congress, 253 — More strength to the confederacy, or an end to the union, 254, 255 — Plans for a federal convention, 256 — Strife between New Jersey and New York, 256 — Congress interposes, 256, 257 — New Jersey leads the way to a general convention, 257 — What was written by Monroe, 258 — By Grayson, 258 — The views of South Carolina, 258, 259 — Monroe opposes a general convention, 259 — Grayson's proposal, 260 — Proposal of Charles Pinckney, 260, 261 — His committee offer seven new articles of confederation, 261-263 — Congress rests its hopes on the system of April, 1783, 263 — Discussions in New York city, 263, 264 — New York retains the collecting of the revenue, 264 — Pennsylvania recedes from the revenue plan of congress, 264 — Does not heed a delegation from congress, 264 — Congress expostulates with the governor of New York, 265 — Clinton will not yield, 265 — Congress fails, 265 — Why it could not but fail, 265, 266.

CHAPTER VIII.

VIRGINIA INVITES DEPUTIES OF THE SEVERAL LEGISLATURES OF THE STATES TO MEET IN CONVENTION. 1786.

The convention at Annapolis, 267 — Only five states appear, 268 — Their extreme caution in their report, 268 — They fix the time and place of a federal convention, 268, 269 — King prevents the recommendation of the measure by congress, 269 — Clinton condemns the commissioners from New York, 269 — King before the legislature of Massachusetts, 269 —Followed by Nathan Dane, 269 — Massachusetts declines the suggestions from Annapolis, 270 — Madison and Virginia, 270 — The assembly unanimous, 270 — Its declaratory preamble, 270-272 — Virginia selects its delegates, 272 — Decision of New Jersey, 272 — Of Pennsylvania, 272 — North Carolina and Delaware, 272 — The conciliatory movement of King in congress succeeds, 272-274 — The decision of New York, 274 — The insurrection in Massachusetts, 274, 275 — Its legislature accepts the invitation from Annapolis, 275 — So do South Carolina and Georgia, 275 — Connecticut, 275, 276 — New Hampshire, 276 — Expectation of the British ministry, 277 — Jefferson's advice, 277 — Madison prepares a complete plan of a constitution, 277 — Conciliates Randolph, governor of Virginia, 277 — Principles that governed Madison, 278 — The preparation of Washington for the convention, 278.

APPENDIX.

LETTERS AND PAPERS.

(For Index to Letters and Papers, see page 513.)

BOOK I.

THE CONFEDERATION.

This Page Intentionally Left Blank

CHAPTER I.

A RETROSPECT. MOVEMENTS TOWARD UNION.

1643—1781.

The order of time brings us to the most cheering act in the political history of mankind, when thirteen republics, of which at least three reached from the sea to the Mississippi, formed themselves into one federal commonwealth. There was no revolt against the past, but a persistent and healthy progress. The sublime achievement was the work of a people led by statesmen of earnestness, perseverance, and public spirit, instructed by the widest experience in the forms of representative government, and warmed by that mutual love which proceeds from ancient connection, harmonious effort in perils, and common aspirations.

Scarcely one who wished me good speed when I first essayed to trace the history of America remains to greet me with a welcome as I near the goal. Deeply grateful as I am for the friends who rise up to gladden my old age, their encouragement must renew my grief for those who have gone before me.

CHAP. VI.

While so much is changed in the living objects of personal respect and affection, infinitely greater are the transformations in the condition of the world. Power has come to dwell with every people, from the Arctic sea to the Mediterranean, from Portugal to the borders of Russia. From end to end of the United States, the slave has become a freeman; and the various forms of bondage have disappeared from European Christendom. Abounding harests of scientific discovery have been garnered by numberless inquisitive minds, and the wildest forces of nature have been taught to become the docile helpmates of man. The application of steam to the purposes of travel on land and on water, the employment of a spark of light as the carrier of thought across continents and beneath oceans, have made of all the inhabitants of the earth one society. A journey round the world has become the pastime of a holiday vacation. The morning newspaper gathers up and brings us the noteworthy events of the last four-and-twenty hours in every quarter of the globe. All states are beginning to form parts of one system. The "new nations," which Shakespeare's prophetic eye saw rising on our eastern shore, dwell securely along two oceans, midway between their kin in Great Britain on the one side and the oldest surviving empire on the other.

More than two thousand years ago it was truly said that the nature of justice can be more easily discerned in a state than in one man.[1] It may now be

---

[1] Plato in the Republic, Book ii. Bekker, III. i. 78.

studied in the collective states. The ignorance and prejudices that come from isolation are worn away in the conflict of the forms of culture. We learn to think the thought, to hope the hope of mankind. Former times spoke of the dawn of civilization in some one land; we live in the morning of the world. Day by day the men who guide public affairs are arraigned before the judgment-seat of the race. A government which adopts a merely selfish policy is pronounced to be the foe of the human family. The statesman who founds and builds up the well-being of his country on justice has all the nations for a cloud of witnesses, and, as one of our own poets[1] has said, "The linked hemispheres attest his deed." He thrills the world with joy; and man becomes of a nobler spirit as he learns to gauge his opinions and his acts by a scale commensurate with his nature.

History carries forward the study of ethics by following the footsteps of states from the earliest times of which there is a record. The individual who undertakes to capture truth by solitary thought loses his way in the mazes of speculation, or involves himself in mystic visions, so that the arms which he extends to embrace what are but formless shadows return empty to his own breast. To find moral truth, he must study man in action. The laws of which reason is conscious can be tested best by experience; and inductions will be the more sure, the larger the experience from which they are drawn. However great may be the number of those who persuade themselves

---

[1] Emerson: The Adirondacks, 248.

that there is in man nothing superior to himself, history interposes with evidence that tyranny and wrong lead inevitably to decay; that freedom and right, however hard may be the struggle, always prove resistless. Through this assurance ancient nations learn to renew their youth; the rising generation is incited to take a generous part in the grand drama of time; and old age, staying itself upon sweet Hope as its companion and cherisher,[1] not bating a jot of courage, nor seeing cause to argue against the hand or the will of a higher power, stands waiting in the tranquil conviction that the path of humanity is still fresh with the dews of morning, that the Redeemer of the nations liveth.

The colonies, which became one federal republic, were founded by rival powers. That difference of origin and the consequent antagonism of interest were the motives to the first American union. In 1643 three New England colonies joined in a short-lived "confederacy" for mutual protection, especially against the Dutch; each member reserving its peculiar jurisdiction and government, and an equal vote in the general council.

Common danger gave the next impulse to collective action. Rivers, which were the convenient war-paths of the natives, flowed in every direction from the land of the Five Nations; against whom, in 1684, measures of defence, extending from North Carolina to the northern boundary of New England, were con-

---

[1] γλυκεῖά οἱ καρδίαν ἀτάλλοιθα γη- Ροτρόφος ὀυναορέι ἐλπίς. Pindar in Plato, Republic, Book i. Bekker, III. i. 10.

certed. Later, in 1751, South Carolina joined northern colonies in a treaty with the same tribes.

On the side of England, James II., using the simple method of the prerogative of an absolute king, began the suppression of colonial legislatures, and the consolidation of colonies under the rule of one governor. After the English revolution of 1688 had gained consistency, the responsible government which it established would gladly have devised one uniform system of colonial administration; and in 1696 the newly created board of trade, of which John Locke was a member, suggested the appointment of a captain-general of all the forces on the continent of North America, with such power as could be exercised through the prerogative of a constitutional king.

In 1697 William Penn appeared before the board and advised an annual "congress" of two delegates from each one of the American provinces, to determine by plurality of voices the ways and means for supporting their union, providing for their safety, and regulating their commerce.

In 1721, to ensure the needed co-operation of the colonies in the rivalry of England with France for North American territory, the plan attributed to Lord Stairs provided for a lord-lieutenant or captain-general over them all; and for a general council to which each provincial assembly should send two of its members, electing one of the two in alternate years. The lord-lieutenant of the king, in conjunction with the general council on behalf of the colonies, was then to allot the quotas of men and money which the several assemblies were to raise by laws of

8   THE CONFEDERATION.

CHAP.
I.

their own. All these projects slumbered among heaps of neglected papers.

On the final struggle between England and France, the zeal of the colonists surpassed that of the mother country. A union, proposed by Franklin in 1754, would have preserved the domestic institutions of the several colonies; for the affairs of the whole, a governor-general was to be appointed from England, and a legislature, in which the representation would have borne some proportion to population, was to be chosen triennially by the colonies. This plan, which foreshadowed the present constitution of the Dominion of Canada and the federation which with hope and applause was lately offered by rival ministries to South Africa, was at that day rejected by the British government with abhorrence and disdain.

1 7 5 4.

The English administration confined itself next to methods for obtaining a colonial revenue. For this end Lord Halifax, in 1754, advised that the commander-in-chief, attended by one commissioner from each colony, whose election should be subject to one negative of the king by the royal council and another by the royal governor, should adjust the quotas of each colony, which were then to be enforced by the authority of parliament. This plan was suppressed by impending war.

1 7 5 4.

Great Britain having, with the lavish aid of her colonies, driven France from Canada, needed them no more as allies in war. The problem was how to create a grand system of empire. James Otis of Boston would have had all kingdoms and all outlying possessions of the crown wrought into the flesh and

1 7 6 2-
1 7 6 5.

blood and membership of one organization; but this advice, which would have required home governments for every kingdom and for every colony, and, for general affairs, one imperial parliament representing the whole, found no favor.

In those days of aristocratic rule, the forming of a grand plan of union was assigned by the Bedford faction to George Grenville, a statesman bred to the law, the impersonation of idolatry of the protective system as the source of British prosperity, and of faith in the omnipotence of the British parliament as the groundwork of British liberty. He sought to unite the thirteen colonies in their home administration by the prerogative; in their home legislation by a royal veto of acts of their own legislatures; in the establishment of their general revenue and the regulation of their commerce by acts of the British parliament.

And now came into the view of the world the rare aptitude of the colonies for concert and organization. James Otis, in the general court of Massachusetts, spoke the word for an American congress, and in 1765 nine of the thirteen met at New York: the British parliament aimed at consolidating their administration without their own consent, and did but force them to unite in the denial of its power.

The tiniest and greatest Englishman of that century breasted the heaving wave and by his own force stayed it, but only for the moment. An aristocratic house of commons, piqued and vexed at its own concssion, imposed a tax on the colonies in the least hateful form that it could devise; and the sound of tea-chests, falling into Boston harbor, startled the nations with the news of a united and resistant America.

1774.

The British parliament thought proper to punish Boston and attempt coercion by arms; "delegates of the inhabitants" of twelve American colonies in a continental congress acted as one in a petition to the king.

1776. Jan. 8.

The petition was not received. Six months before the declaration of independence, Thomas Paine, in "Common Sense," had said: "Nothing but a continental form of government can keep the peace of the continent.[1] Let a CONTINENTAL CONFERENCE be held,[2] to frame a CONTINENTAL CHARTER, drawing the line of business and jurisdiction between members of congress and members of assembly, always remembering that our strength and happiness are continental, not provincial.[3] The bodies chosen conformably to said charter shall be the legislators and governors of this continent.[4] We have every opportunity and every encouragement to form the noblest, purest constitution on the face of the earth."[5] The continental convention which was to frame the constitution for the union was to represent both the colonies and the people of each colony; its members were to be chosen, two by congress from the delegation of each colony, two by the legislature of each colony out of its own body, and five directly by the people.[6]

---

[1] Common Sense: original edition of 8 Jan., 1776, p. 51
[2] Ibid., 55.
[3] Ibid., 56.
[4] Ibid., 56.
[5] Appendix, annexed to second edition of Common Sense, 14 Feb., 1776.
[6] Common Sense, original edition, 55.

Great Britain offered its transatlantic dominions no unity but under a parliament in which they were not represented; the people of thirteen colonies by special instructions to their delegates in congress declared themselves to be states, independent and united, and began the search for a fitting constitution.

In their first formative effort they missed the plain road of English and American experience. They had rightly been jealous of extending the supremacy of England, because it was a government outside of themselves; they now applied that jealousy to one another, forgetting that the general power would be in their own hands. Joseph Hawley of Massachusetts had, in November, 1775, advised annual parliaments of two houses; the committee for framing the confederation, misled partly by a rooted distrust for which the motive had ceased, and partly by erudition which studied Hellenic councils and leagues as well as later confederacies, took for its pattern the constitution of the United Provinces, with one house and no central power of final decision. These evils were nearly fatal to the United Provinces themselves, although every one of them could be reached by a messenger within a day's journey; and here was a continent of states which could not be consulted without the loss of many months, and would ever tend to anarchy from the want of agreement in their separate deliberations.

Hopeless of a good result from the deliberations of congress on a confederation, Edward Rutledge, in August, 1776, in a letter to Robert R. Livingston, avowed his readiness to "propose that the states should appoint a special congress, to be composed of new members, for this purpose."[1]

The necessities of the war called into being, north of the Potomac, successive conventions of a cluster of states. In August, 1780, a convention of the New England states at Boston declared for a more solid and permanent union with one supreme head, and "a congress competent for the government of all those common and national affairs which do not nor can come within the jurisdiction of the particular states." At the same time it issued an invitation for a convention of the New England states, New York, and "others that shall think proper to join them,"[2] to meet at Hartford.

The legislature of New York approved the measure.[3] "Our embarrassments in the prosecution of the war," such was the message of Governor George Clinton on the opening of the session in September, "are chiefly to be attributed to a defect of power in those who ought to exercise a supreme jurisdiction; for, while congress only recommends and the different states deliberate upon the propriety of the recommendation, we cannot expect a union of force or council." The senate answered in the words of Philip Schuyler: "We perceive the defects in the present system, and the necessity of a supreme and coercive power in the government of

[1] Rutledge to Livingston, Aug., 1778. MS.
[2] Hough's Convention of New England States at Boston, 50, 52.
[3] Duane to Washington; 19 Sept., 1780 Letters to Washington, iii. 92.

A RETROSPECT. MOVEMENTS TOWARD UNION. 13

these states; and are persuaded that, unless congress are authorized to direct uncontrollably the operations of war and enabled to enforce a compliance with their requisitions, the common force can never be properly united."[1]

Meantime, Alexander Hamilton in swiftness of thought outran all that was possible. Early in September, in a private letter to James Duane, then a member of congress, he took up the proposal, which, nearly five years before, Paine had made known, and advised that a convention of all the states should meet on the first of the following November, with full authority to conclude finally and set in motion a "vigorous" general confederation.[2] His ardor would have surprised the people into greater happiness without giving them an opportunity to view and reject his project.[3]

Before the end of the year the author of "Common Sense" himself, publishing in Philadelphia a tract asserting the right of the United States to the vacant western territory, closed his argument for the "Public Good" with these words: "I take the opportunity of renewing a hint which I formerly threw out in the pamphlet 'Common Sense,' and which the several states will, sooner or later, see the convenience, if not the necessity, of adopting; which is, that of electing a continental convention, for the purpose of forming a continental constitution, defining and describing the powers of congress. To have them marked out le-

---

[1] Hough's Convention, 63-65.
[2] Hamilton to Duane, 3 Sept., 1780. Hamilton, i. 157.
[3] Compare McHenry to Hamilton. Hamilton, i. 411.

14   THE CONFEDERATION.

CHAP.
I.
1780.

Nov.
11.

legally will give additional energy to the whole, and a new confidence to the several parts."[1]

"Call a convention of the states, and establish a congress upon a constitutional footing," wrote Greene, after taking command of the southern army, to a member of congress.[2]

On the eleventh of November able representatives from each of the four New England states and New York assembled at Hartford.[3] The lead in the convention was taken by the delegates from New York, John Sloss Hobart, a judge of its supreme court, and Egbert Benson, its attorney-general.[4] At their instance it was proposed, as a foundation for a safe system of finance, to provide by taxes or duties a certain and inalienable revenue, to discharge the interest on any funded part of the public debt, and on future loans. As it had proved impossible to at the valuation of lands, congress should be empowered to apportion taxes on the states according to their number of inhabitants, black as well as white. They then prepared a circular letter to all the states, in which they said: "Our embarrassments arise from a defect in the present government of the United States. All government supposes the power of coercion; this

---

[1] Thomas Paine's Public Good. Original edition, 38.

[2] Johnson's Life of Greene, ii. 446.

[3] The names of all the delegates are given in Papers of the Old Congress, xxxiii. 391, MS. John T. Gilman of New Hampshire, Thomas Gushing, Azor Orne, George Partridge of Massachusetts, William Bradford of Rhode Island, Eliphalet Dyer and William Williams of Connecticut, John Sloss Hobart and Egbert Benson of New York.

[4] That New York took the lead appears from comparison of the message of Clinton in September the circular letter of the convention; and from the public tribute of Hamilton to the New York delegates in the presence of Hobart. Hamilton, ii. 360.

power, however, never did exist in the general government of the continent, or has never been exercised. Under these circumstances, the resources and force of the country can never be properly united and drawn forth. The states individually considered, while they endeavor to retain too much of their independence, may finally lose the whole. By the expulsion of the enemy we may be emancipated from the tyranny of Great Britain; we shall, however, be without a solid hope of peace and freedom, unless we are properly cemented among ourselves."

The proceedings of this convention were sent to every state in the union, to Washington, and to congress.[1] They were read in congress on the twelfth of December, 1780; and were referred to a committee of five, on which were John Witherspoon and James Madison,[2] the master and his pupil. In the same days Pennsylvania instructed its delegates in congress that imposts on trade were absolutely necessary; and in order to prevent any state from taking advantage of a neighbor, congress should recommend to the several states in union a system of imposts.[3] Before the end of 1780 the legislative council and general assembly of New Jersey, while they insisted "that the rights of every state in the union should be strictly maintained," declared that "congress represent the federal republic."[4] Thus early was that

---

[1] Papers of the Old Congress, xxxiii. 391, containing copies of the credentials of the commissioners, the resolutions of the convention, and its letters to the several states, to congress, and to Washington. MS.

[2] Endorsement by Charles Thomson, secretary of congress. MS.

[3] Journals of Assembly, 564.

[4] Representation and Remonstrance, printed in Mulford's New Jersey, 469, 470.

16   THE CONFEDERATION.

CHAP.
I.

name applied to the United States. Both branches of the legislature of New York, which at that time was "as well disposed a state as any in the union,"1 approved the proceedings of the convention as promoting the interest of the continent.2

With the year 1781, when the ministry of Great Britain believed themselves in possession of the three southernmost states and were cheering Cornwallis to complete his glory by the conquest of Virginia; when congress was confessedly without the means to recover the city of New York; when a large contingent from France was at Newport, serious efforts for the creation of a federal republic began, and never ceased until it was established. The people of New York, from motives of the highest patriotism, had already ceded its claims to western lands.

Jan.
2.

The territory north-west of the Ohio, which Virginia had conquered, was on the second of January3 surrendered to the United States of America. For this renunciation one state and one state only had made delay. On the twenty-ninth, congress received the news so long anxiously waited for, that Maryland by a resolution of both branches of her legislature had acceded to the confederation, seven members only in the house voting in the negative. Duane, who had been taught by Washington that "greater powers to congress were indispensably necessary to the well-being and good government of public affairs,"4 instantly addressed him: "Let us devote

29.

---

[1] Washington to Jefferson, 1 Aug., 1786. Sparks, ix. 186.
[2] Journals of Assembly, 91, 93.
[3] Journal of Virginia House of Delegates, 79.
[4] Washington to James Duane, 26 Dec., 1780. MS.

this day to joy and congratulation, since by the accomplishment of our federal union we are become a nation. In a political view it is of more real importance than a victory over all our enemies. We shall not fail of taking advantage favorable temper of the states and recommending for ratification such additional articles as will give vigor and authority to government."[1] The enthusiasm of the moment could not hide the truth, that without amendments the new system would struggle vainly for life. Washington answered: "Our affairs will not put on a different aspect unless congress is vested with, or will assume, greater powers than they exert at present."[2]

To another member of congress, Washington wrote: "I never expect to see a happy termination of the war, nor great national concerns well conducted in peace, till there is something more than a recommendatory power in congress. The lastwords, therefore, of my letter and the first wish of my heart concur in favor of it."[3]

The legislature of Maryland swiftly transformed its resolution into an act. The delegates having full authority, in the presence of congress, on the first day of March, subscribed the articles of confederation, and its complete, formal, and final ratification by all the United States was announced to the public; to the executives of the several states; to the American ministers in Europe, and through them to

---

[1] James Duane to Washington, 29 Jan., 1781. MS.
[2] Washington to Duane, 19 Feb., 1781. MS.
[3] Washington to Sullivan, 4 Feb., 1781. Sparks, vii. 402.

18   THE CONFEDERATION.

CHAP.
I.

1881.

March 19.

the courts at which they resided; to the minister plenipotentiary of France in America; to the commander-in-chief and through him to the army.¹ Clinton communicated "the important event" to the legislature of New York, adding: "This great national compact establishes our union."² But the completion of the confederation was the instant revelation of its insufficiency, and the summons to the people of America to form a better constitution.

Washington rejoiced that Virginia had relinquished her claim to the laud south of the great lakes and north-west of the Ohio, which he said, "for fertility of soil, pleasantness of climate, and other natural advantages, is equal to any known tract of country of the same extent in the universe."³ He was pleased that Maryland had acceded to the confederation; but he saw no ground to rest satisfied.

On taking command of the army in Massachusetts in 1775, he at once discriminated between the proper functions of individual colonies and "that power and weight which ought of right to belong only to the whole;"⁴ and he applied to Richard Henry Lee, then in congress, for aid in establishing the distinction. In the following years he steadily counselled the formation of one continental army. As a faithful laborer in the cause, as a man injuring his private estate without the smallest personal advantage, as one who wished the prosperity of America most devoutly, he in the

---

[1] Journals of Congress, iii. 581, 582, 591.

[2] Journal of New York Assembly, for 19 March, 1781.

[3] Washington to Sullivan, 4 Feb., 1781. Sparks, vii. 400.

[4] Washington to Richard Henry Lee, 29 Aug., 1775. Sparks, iii. 68, 69.

A RETROSPECT. MOVEMENTS TOWARD UNION. 19

last days of 1778 had pleaded with the statesmen of Virginia for that which to him was more than life. He called on Benjamin Harrison, then speaker of the house of delegates, on Mason, Wythe, Jefferson, Nicholas, Pendleton, and Nelson, "not to be satisfied with places in their own state while the common interests of America were mouldering and sinking into irretrievable ruin, but to attend to the momentous concerns of an empire."[1] "Till the great national interest is fixed upon a solid basis," so he wrote in March, 1779, to George Mason, "I lament the fatal policy of the states of employing their ablest men at home. How useless to put in fine order the smallest parts of a clock, unless the great spring which is to set the whole in motion is well attended to! Let this voice call forth you, Jefferson, and others to save their country."[2] But now, with deeper emotion, he turns to his own state as he had done in the gloomy winter of 1778. He has no consolation but in the hope of a good federal government. His growing desire has the character of the forces of nature, which from the opening year increase in power till the earth is renewed.

A constant, close observer of what was done by Virginia, he held in mind that on the twenty-fourth day of December, 1779, on occasion of some unwise proceedings of congress, she had resolved "that the legislature of this commonwealth are greatly alarmed at the assumption of power lately exercised by congress. While the right of recommending measures to each state by congress is admitted, we contend for that

CHAP. I.

1778. Dec.

1779.

---

[1] Sparks, vi. 150.   [2] MS. letter to Geo. Mason.

of judging of their utility and expediency, and of course either to approve or reject. Making any state answerable for not agreeing to any of its recommenddations would establish a dangerous precedent against the authority of the legislature and the sovereignty of the separate states."[1]

This interposition of the Virginia legislature so haunted Washington's mind that he felt himself more particularly impelled to address with freedom men of whose abilities and judgments he wished to avail himself. He thoroughly understood the obstinacy and strength which he must encounter and overcome. His native state, reaching to the Mississippi and cutting off the mass of the south from the north, held, from its geographical place, its numbers, and the influence of its statesmen, a power of obstructing union such as belonged to no other state. He must persuade it to renounce some share of its individual sovereignty and forego "the liberty to reject or alter any act of congress which in a full representation of states has been solemnly debated and decided on,"[2] or there is no hope of consolidating the union. His position was one of extreme delicacy; for he was at the head of the army which could alone be employed to enforce the requisitions of congress. He therefore selected, as the Virginians to whom he could safely address himself, the three great civilians whom that commonwealth had appointed to codify its laws and adapt them to the new state of society consequent on independence, Jefferson, its governor, Pen-

[1] Journal of House of Delegates of Virginia, for 24 Dec., 1779, 108.
[2] Washington to James Duane, 26 Dec., 1780. MS.

dleton, the president of its court of appeals, and Wythe, its spotless chancellor.[1]

"The alliance of the states," he said, "is now complete. If the powers granted to the respective body of the states are inadequate, the defects should be considered and remedied. Danger may spring from delay; good will result from the timely application of a remedy. The present temper of the states is friendly to the establishment of a lasting union; the moment should be improved; if suffered to pass away it may never return, and, after gloriously and successfully contending against the usurpations of Britain, we may fall a prey to our own follies and disputes." He argued for the power of compelling the states to comply with the requisitions for men and money agreeably to their respective quotas; adding: "It would give me concern should it be thought of me that I am desirous of enlarging the powers of congress unnecessarily; I declare to God, my only aim is the general good." And he promised to make his views known to others besides the three.

His stepson, John Parke Custis, who was just entering into public life, he thus instructed: "The fear

[1] Washington to Jefferson, Pendleton, and Wythe, Madison Papers, 83, Gilpin's edition. The date of his letter is not given. It was written soon after the accession of Maryland to the confederation; probably in February, before the middle of the month, which was the time fixed for his departure from New Windsor for Newport. The dates of the letters of 1781, informing him of the accession of Maryland, were, from Duane, 29 Jan., MS.; from Sullivan, 29 Jan., MS.; from Matthews, 30 Jan. Letters to Washington, iii. 218. Washington's answer to Sullivan is 4 Feb., Sparks, vii. 402; to Matthews, 14 Feb. "The confederation being now closed will, I trust, enabled congress to speak decisively in their requisitions," etc. MS. On the evening of the fourteenth, Washington was preparing to leave for Newport; an unexpected letter from Rochambeau detained him in camp till the second of March. Sparks, vii. 446, note.

of giving sufficient powers to congress is futile. Under its present constitution, each assembly will be annihilated, and we must once more return to the government of Great Britain, and be made to kiss the rod preparing for our correction. A nominal head, which at present is but another name for congress, will no longer do. That honorable body, after hearing the interests and views of the several states fairly discussed and explained by their respective representatives, must dictate, and not merely recommend."[1]

To another Virginian, Joseph Jones of King George county, whom he regarded with sincere affection and perfect trust, he wrote: "Without a controlling power in congress it will be impossible to carry on the war; and we shall speedily be thirteen distinct states, each pursuing its local interests, till they are annihilated in a general crash. The fable of the bunch of sticks may well be applied to us."[2] In a like strain he addressed other trusty correspondents and friends.[3] His wants as commander-in-chief did not confine his attention to the progress of the war; he aimed at nothing less than an enduring government for all times of war and peace.

[1] Washington to John Parke Custis, 28 Feb., 1781. Sparks, vii. 440-444.

[2] Washington to Joseph Jones, 24 March, 1781. MS.

[3] Compare his letters to R. R. Livingston of New York, 31 Jan., 1781—Sparks, vii. 391; to John Sullivan of New Hampshire, 4 Feb., 1781—Sparks, vii. 401, 402; to John Matthews of South Carolina, 14 Feb., 1781, MS.; to James Duane of New York, 19 Feb., 1781, MS.; to Philip Schuyler of New York, 20 Feb., 1781, MS.; To John Parke Custis of Virginia, 28 Feb., 1781—Sparks, vii. 442; to William Gordon, in Massachuetts, 9 March, 1781—Sparks, vii. 448; to Joseph Jones of Virginia, 24 March, 1781, MS.; to John Armstrong of Pennsylvania, 26 March, 1781—Sparks vii. 403.

As soon as the new form of union was proclaimed, congress saw its want of real authority, and sought a way to remedy the defect. A report by Madison, from a committee,[1] was completed on the twelfth of March; and this was its reasoning: "The articles of confederation, which declare that every state shall abide by the determinations of congress, imply a general power vested in congress to enforce them and carry them into effect. The United States in congress assembled, being desirous as far as possible to cement and invigorate the federal union, recommend to the legislature of every state to give authority to employ the force of the United States as well by sea as by land to compel the states to fulfill their federal engagements."[2]

Madison enclosed to Jefferson a copy of his report, and, on account of the delicacy and importance of the subject, expressed a wish for his judgment on it before it should undergo the final decision of congress. No direct reply from him is preserved,[3] but Joseph Jones, who, after a visit to Richmond, was again in Philadelphia about the middle of May, gave to Madison a copy of the letter of Washington to Jefferson and his two associates.[4] There were no

CHAP. I.
1781.
March. 12.

---

[1] Reports of committees on increasing the powers of congress, p. 19. MS. This report is dated 12 March, and was read in congress 16 March.

[2] Madison Papers, Gilpin's Edition, 88—90. Reports of committees, 20, 22. MS. Madison was a member of the committee to which were referred the papers from the Hartford convention of November, 1780. That committee, on the sixteenth of February, 1781, made a report, which was referred back to it. Whether Madison's report of the twelfth of March proceeded from that committee, the imperfect record does not show.

[3] None of the letters of Jefferson to Madison of this year have been preserved,

[4] Madison Papers, Gilpin's Edition, 81.

24   THE CONFEDERATION.

CHAP. I.

1781.
May 2.

chances that the proposal of Madison would be approved by any one state, yet on the second of May it was referred to a grand committee; that is, to committee of one from each state.[1] On the eighteenth, the Chevalier de la Luzerne, then the French minister in America, sent this dispatch to Vergennes: "There is a feeling to reform the constitution of congress; but the articles of confederation, defective as they are, cost a year and a half of labor and of debates; a change will not encounter less difficulty, and it appears to me there is more room for desire than for hope."[2]

24.

Even while he was writing, the movement for reform received a new impulse. In a pamphlet dated the twenty-fourth, and dedicated to the congress of the United States of America and to the assembly of the state of Pennsylvania, William Barton insisted that congress should "not be left with the mere shadow of sovereign authority, without the right of exacting obedience to their ordinances, and destitute of the means of executing their resolves." To rem

---

[1] Reports of committees on increasing the powers of congress, 22. MS.

[2] Luzerne to Vergennes, 18 May, 1781. MS.

[3] Not by Pelatiah Webster, as stated by Madison. Introduction to debates, Madison Papers, Gilpin's Edition, 706; Elliot's stereotyped reprint, 117. First: at a later period, Webster collected his pamphlets in a volume, and this one is not among them; a disclaimer which, under the circumstances, is conclusive. Secondly: the style of this pamphlet of 1781 is totally unlike the style of those collected by Pelatiah Webster. My friend F. D. Stone of Philadelphia was good enough to communicate to me the bill for printing the pamphlet; it was made out against William Barton and paid by him. Further: Barton from time to time wrote pamphlets, of which, on a careful comparison, the style, language, and forms of expression are found to correspond to this pamphlet published in 1781. Without doubt it was written by William Barton.

edy this evil he did not look to congress itself, but "indicated the necessity of their calling a continental convention, for the express purpose of ascertaining, defining, enlarging, and limiting the duties and powers of their constitution."[1] This is the third time that the suggestion of a general constituent convention was brought before the country by the press of Philadelphia,

The grand committee of thirteen delayed their report till the twentieth of July, and then only expressed a wish to give congress power in time of war to layan embargo at least for sixty days, and to appoint receivers of the money of the United States as soon as collected by state officers. By their advice the business was then referred to a committee of three.[2]

Day seemed to break, when, on the twentieth of July, Edmund Randolph, who had just brought from Virginia the news of its disposition to strengthen the general government, Oliver Ellsworth of Connecticut, and James M. Varnum of Rhode Island, three of the ablest lawyers in their states, were selected to "prepare an exposition of the confederation, to devise a plan for its complete execution, and to present supplemental articles."[3]

In support of the proceedings of congress, Hamilton, during July and August, published a series of papers which he called "The Continentalist." "There is hardly a man," said he, "who will not acknowledge

---

[1] Observations on the Nature and Use of Paper Credit, etc., Philadelphia, 1781, 37. The preface of the pamphlet is dated 24 May, 1781.

[2] Report of the grand committee. MS.

[3] Report of the committee of three. MS.

26   THE CONFEDERATION.

CHAP.
I.
1781.

the confederation unequal to a vigorous prosecution of the war, or to the preservation of the union in peace. The federal government, too weak at first, will continually grow weaker."[1] "Already some of the states have evaded or refused the demands of congress; the currency is depreciated; public credit is at the lowest ebb; our army deficient in numbers and unprovoked with everything; the enemy making an alarming progress in the southern states; Cornwallis still formidable to Virginia.[2] As in explanation of our embarrassments nothing can be alleged to the disaffection of the people, we must have recourse to impolicy and mismanagement in their rulers.[3] We ought therefore not only to strain every nerve to render the present campaign as decisive as possible, but we ought without delay to enlarge the powers of congress. Every plan of which this is not the foundation will be illusory. The separate exertions of the states will never suffice. Nothing but a well-proportioned exertion of the resources for the whole, under the direction of a common council with power sufficient to give efficacy to their resolutions, can preserve us from being a conquered people now, or can make us a happy one hereafter."[4]

Aug. 22.

The committee of three, Randolph, Ellsworth, and Varnum, made their report on the twenty-second of August. They declined to prepare an exposition of the confederation, because such a comment would be voluminous if coextensive with the subject; and, in

---

[1] Continentalist. Reprinted in J. C. Hamilton's edition of the Federalist, cxl., cxli.
[2] Ibid., cxlv., cxlvi.
[3] Ibid., cxlvii.
[4] Ibid., cxlviii.

in the enumeration of powers, omissions would become an argument against their existence. With professional exactness they explained in twenty one cases the "manner" in which "the confederation required execution." As to delinquent states, they advised, "That— as America became a confederate republic to crush the present and future foes of her independence; as of this republic a general council is a necessary organ; and as, without the extension of its power, war may receive a fatal inclination and peace be exposed to daily convulsions—it be resolved to recommend to the several states to authorize the United States in congress assembled to lay embargoes and prescribe rules for impressing property in time of war; to appoint collectors of taxes required by congress; to admit new states with the consent of any dismembered state; to establish a consular system without reference to the states individually; to distrain the property of a state delinquent in its assigned proportion of men and money; and to vary the rules of suffrage in congress so as to decide the most important questions by the agreement of two thirds of the United States."[1]

It was further proposed to make a representation to the several states of the necessity for these supplemental powers, and of pursuing in their development one uniform plan.

At the time when this report was made, the country was rousing its energies for a final campaign. New England with its militia assisted to man the lines near New York; the commander-in-chief with

[1] Reports on increasing the powers of congress. MS.

his army had gone to meet Cornwallis in Virginia; and Greene was recovering the three southernmost states. Few persons in that moment of suspense cared to read the political essays of Hamilton, and he hastened to take part in the war under the command of Lafayette. The hurry of crowded hours left no opportunity for deliberation on the reform of the constitution. Moreover, the committee of three, while they recognised the duty of obedience on the part of the states to the requisitions of congress, knew no way to force men into the ranks of the army, or distrain the property of a state. There could be no coercion; for every state was a delinquent. Had it been otherwise, the coercion of a state by force of arms is civil war, and, from the weakness of the confederacy and the strength of organization of each separate state, would have been disunion.

Yet it was necessary for the public mind to pass through this process of reasoning. The conviction that the confederacy could propose no remedy for its weakness but the impracticable one of the coercion of sovereign states compelled the search for a really efficient and more humane form of government. Mean time the report of Randolph, Ellsworth, and Varnum, which was the result of the deliberations of nearly eight months, fell to the ground. We shall not have to wait long for a word from Washington; and, when he next speaks, he will propose "A NEW CONSTITUTION."

CHAPTER II.

THE STRUGGLE FOR REVENUE.

1781, 1782.

Schuyler had been led by his own experience to perceive the necessity for the states to surrender some part of their sovereignty, and "adopt another system of government." In the senate of New York, he moved to request eastern states to join in an early convention, which should form a perpetual league of incorporation, subservient, however, to the common interest of all the states; invite others to accede to it; erect Vermont into a state; devise a fund for the redemption of the common debts; substitute a permanent and uniform system for temporary expedients; and invest the confederacy with powers of coercion.[1]

"We stand ready on our part to confer adequate powers on congress," was the message of both houses to that body in a letter of the fifth of February,

---

[1] Philip Schuyler to Washington, 21 Jan., 1781. Letters to Washington, iii. 213.

written in the name of the state by their joint committee, on which were Schuyler and Benson.[1]

Washington had been taught by his earliest observation as general, and had often declared the indispensable necessity of more responsibility and permanency in the executive bodies.[2] The convention at Boston of August, 1780, had recommended "a permanent system for the several departments."[3] Hamilton "was among the first who were convinced that their administration by single men was essential to the proper management of affairs."[4] On the tenth of January, 1781, congress initiated a reform by estabishing a department of foreign affairs;[5] but more than eight months elapsed before it was filled by Robert R. Livingston.

There was the most pressing need of a minister of war. After tedious rivalries and delays, Benjamin Lincoln was elected;[6] but he did not enter upon the office till near the end of November, when the attempt of Great Britain to subjugate America had ceased.

For the treasury, John Sullivan suggested to Washington the name of Hamilton.[7] How far Hamilton had made a study of finance, Washington did not know; but he said: "Few of his age have a more

---

[1] Letter from the state of New York to congress, 5 Feb., 1781. Papers of Old Congress, lxvii. 344. MS. A copy of the letter was sent to Washington by Clinton, 14 Feb., 1781. Letters to Washington, xlvi. 172. MS.
[2] Washington to Duane, 26 Dec., 1780. MS.
[3] Hough's edition of Convention at Boston, 3-9 Aug., 1780, 51.
[4] Hamilton to Robert Morris, 30 April, 1781. Hamilton, i 223. Hamilton to Duane, 3 Sept., 1780. Ibid., i. 154.
[5] Journals of Congress, iii. 564.
[6] Ibid., 683.
[7] Sullivan to Washington, 29 Jan., 1781. MS.

THE STRUGGLE FOR REVENUE. 31

general knowledge, and no one is more firmly engaged in the cause, or exceeds him in probity and sterling virtue."[1] In February the choice fell on Robert Morris, and unanimously, except that Massachusetts abstained from the ballot,[2] Samuel Adams preferring the old system of committees.[3]

While Morris delayed his acceptance, Hamilton, who had been the first to present his name for the place, opened a correspondence with him. "A national debt," he wrote, "if it is not excessive, will be a national blessing, a powerful cement of union, a necessity for keeping up taxation, and a spur to industry."[4] He recommended a national bank, with a capital of ten or fifteen millions of dollars,[5] to be paid one third in hard money and the other two thirds in European funds or landed security.[6] It was to be erected into a legal corporation for thirty years, during which no other bank, public or private, was to be permitted.[7] Its capital and deposits were to be exempt from taxation,[8] and the United States, collectively and particularly, were to become conjointly responsible for all its transactions.[9] Its sources of profit were to be the sole right of issuing a currency for the United States equal in amount to the whole capital of the bank;[10] loans at a rate not exceeding eight per cent;[11] discount of bills of exchange;[12] con-

---

[1] Washington to Sullivan, 4 Feb., 1781. Sparks, vii. 399.
[2] Journals of Congress, iii. 580.
[3] Luzerne to Vergennes, 25 March, 1781. MS. Partly printed in Sparks, vii. 400.
[4] Hamilton, i. 257.
[5] Arts, i., ix. Ibid., 241, 245.
[6] Art. ii. Ibid., 241.
[7] Arts, iii., xvii., xviii. Ibid., 242, 252.
[8] Arts, i., xi. Ibid., 241, 246.
[9] Art. vi. Ibid., 243.
[10] Art. vii. Ibid., 243, 244.
[11] Art. viii., xiii., Ibid., 245, 247.
[12] Art. x. Ibid., 245.

32   THE CONFEDERATION.

CHAP.
II.

1781.

tracts with the French government for the supply of its fleets and armies in America, with the United States for the supply of their army;[1] dealings in real estates, especially,[2] with its large capital, buying at favorable opportunities the real estates of men who, having rendered themselves odious, would be obliged to leave the country.[3] Another source of immense gain, contingently even of one hundred per cent, was to be a contract with the United States for taking up all their paper emissions.[4] Incidentally, Hamilton expressed his "wish to see a convention of all the states, with full power to alter and amend, finally and irrevocably, the present futile and senseless confederation."

This communication led to the closest relations between Hamilton and Robert Morris; but, vehement as was the character of the older man, his schemes fell far short of the daring suggestions of his young counsellor. On the fourteenth of May, Morris was installed as the superintendent of finance, and three days later he laid before congress his plan for a national bank.[5] Its capital was to be four hundred thousand dollars in gold and silver, with power of increase at discretion; its notes were to form the currency of the country, and be receivable as specie for duties and taxes by every state and by the United States. Authority to constitute the company a legal body not being granted by the articles of confederation, Morris submitted that congress should apply to

May 14.

17.

[1] Art. xii. Ibid., 247.
[2] Art. x. Ibid., 245.
[3] Ibid., 245.
[4] Art. xiv. Ibid., 248.

[5] Journals of Congress, iii 624; Diplomatic Correspondence, vii. 444–440.

THE STRUGGLE FOR REVENUE.

the states for the power of incorporating a bank and prohibiting all other banks.¹

On the twenty-sixth, congress, without waiting to hear the voices of the states, resolved that the bank should be incorporated so soon as the subscription should be filled and officers chosen. This vote was carried by New Hampshire, New Jersey, and the five southernmost states, Massachusetts being in the negative, Pennsylvania divided, and Madison alone of the within the powers of the confederation.

From the want of a valuation of private lands and buildings, congress had not even the right to apportion requisitions. The five states which met at Hartford had suggested for the United States an impost as a source of revenue. New Jersey and North Carolina suffered from the legislation of the neighboring states, which were the natural channels of a part of their foreign trade; and now, on the third of February, Witherspoon and Burke, their representatives in congress, reviving an amendment to the articles of confederation proposed by New Jersey in 1778,² moved to vest in the United States the power of regulating commerce according to "the common interest," and, under restrictions calculated to soothe state jealousies, the exclusive right of laying duties upon imported articles. This motion, which was a memorable step toward union, failed of success"³ and on the same day congress contented itself with

---

¹ Robert Morris to congress, 17 May, 1781. Dip. Cor., xi. 364.
² Journals of Congress, ii. 604.
³ Ibid., iii. 573. The yeas and nays do not appear in the Journal.

asking of the states, as an "indispensable necessity," the power to levy a duty of five per cent ad valorem on all imports, with no permanent exemptions except of wool cards and cotton cards, and wire for making them. This first scheme of duties on foreign commerce sought to foster American industry by the free admission of materials necessary to the manufacturer.

The letter of the fifth of February from the state of New York was met on its way by the vote of congress of the third. In March, New York granted the duties, to "be collected in such manner and by such officers as congress should direct."[1] Connecticut had acted a month earlier at a special session called by Governor Trumbull, but had limited its grant to the end of the third year after the war.[2] New Hampshire followed in the first week of April.[3] Massachusetts delayed its consent till the next year, and then reserved to itself the appointment of the collectors.

Outside of the five states which met at Hartford, the first to agree to the new demand were Pennsylvania and New Jersey.[4] The general assembly of Virginia, which was to have met in Richmond on the seventh of May, was chased by the enemy to Charlottesville, where it elected Benjamin Harrison its speaker, and where John Taylor of Caroline,[5] accord-

---

[1] Papers of Old Congress, lxxv. MS.

[2] Journals of Congress, iii. 594, 600. Papers of Old Congress, lxxv. MS.

[3] Papers of Old Congress, lxxiv. 9. NS.

[4] Dallas' Laws of Pennsylvania, i. 890. The act was of 5 April, 1781. Journals of Congress, iii. 632. The act of New Jersey was passed 2 June, 1781. Wilson's Acts of New Jersey, 191.

[5] Journal of House of Delegates, 30 May, 1781.

THE STRUGGLE FOR REVENUE. 35

ing to order, presented a bill to enable the United States to levy the needed duty. Fleeing beyond the mountains, they completed the act at Staunton. The grant, of which Harrison had been the great promoter,¹ was restricted neither as to time nor as to form.² Early in September, North Carolina adopted the measure;³ Delaware in November;⁴ South Carolina in February, 1782;⁵ and Maryland in its following April session.⁶ The consent of Georgia was confidently expected.

After the surrender of Cornwallis, the legislature of New York once more declared the readiness of their state to comply with any measures to render the union of the United States more intimate, and to contribute their proportion of well-established funds.⁷ This alacrity Clinton, on the twenty-fourth of November, reported to congress as the highest "evidence of a sincere disposition in the state to promote the common interest."⁸

Meantime the subscriptions to the bank languished, and Morris thought fit to apply to John Jay for money from the court of Madrid for its benefit, saying: "I am determined that the bank shall be well supported until it can support itself, and then it will support us."⁹ But there was no ray of hope from that quarter. Though so late as October, 1781, the

CHAP. II.

1 7 8 1.

Nov.

---

¹ Harrison to Washington, 31 March, 1783. MS.
² Papers of Old Congress, ixxv. 359. MS. Hening's Statutes at Large, x. 409.
³ Papers of Old Congress, lxxvi. 91. MS. Journals of Congress, iii. 674.
⁴ Laws of Delaware, ii. 762.
⁵ Statutes at Large of South Carolina, iv. 512.
⁶ Laws of Maryland, chapter lxviii.
⁷ Papers of Old Congress, lxvii, 438. MS.
⁸ Ibid., 443.
⁹ Morris to Jay, 13 July, 1781. Dip. Cor., vii. 440.

subscription amounted to no more than seventy thousand dollars[1] he was yet able to prevail with congress, on the thirty-first day of December, to incorporate the bank "forever" by the name of the Bank of North America; but it was not to exercise powers in any one of the United States repugnant to the laws or constitution of that state.[2] Madison saw in the ordinance "a precedent of usurpation."[3]

The bank still wanted capital. During the autumn of 1781, a remittance in specie of nearly five hundred thousand dollars had been received from the king of France, and brought to Philadelphia. In January, 1782, Morris, with no clear warrant, subscribed all of this sum that remained in the treasury, being about two hundred and fifty-four thousand dollars to the stock of the bank,[4] which was thus nursed into life by the public moneys. In return, it did very little, and could do very little, for the United States. Its legal establishment was supported by a charter from the state of Massachusetts, in March, 1782; by an act of recognition from Pennsylvania in March, and a charter on the first of April; and ten days later by a charter from New York. The final proviso of the New York charter was, "that nothing in this act contained shall be construed to imply any right or power in the United States in congress assembled to create bodies politic, or grant letters of incorporation in any case whatsoever."[5] The acts of Pennsylvania were

---

[1] Life of Morris, 81.
[2] Ordinance to incorporate, etc. Journals of Congress, iii. 706, 707.
[3] Gilpin, 105.
[4] From the narrative of Robert Morris in Life of Morris, 90.
[5] Jones & Varick's edition of Laws of New York, 1789, 77.

THE STRUGGLE FOR REVENUE. 37

repealed in September, 1785. Delaware gave a charter in 1786.

Yet the confederacy promised itself a solid foundation for a system of finance from a duty on imports. Through the press, Hamilton now pleads for vesting congress with full power of regulating trade; and he contrasts the "prospect of a number of petty states, jarring, jealous, and perverse, fluctuating and unhappy at home, weak by their dissensions in the eyes of other nations," with the "noble and magnificent perspective of a great federal republic."

It is the glory of New York that its legislature was the first to impart the sanction of a state the great conception of a federal convention to frame a constitution for the United States. On the report of a committee of which Madison was the head, congress in May, 1782, took into consideration the desperate condition of the finances of the country, and divided between four of its members the office of explaining the common danger to every state.[1] At the request of the delegation which repaired to the north, Clinton convened an extra session of the senate and assembly of New York at Poughkeepsie, where, in July, they received from the committee of congress a full communication"[2] on the necessity of providing for a vigorous prosecution of the war."

The legislature had been in session for a week when Hamilton, who for a few months filled the office of United States receiver of revenue for his state, repaired to Poughkeepsie "to second the

CHAP. II.

1782.

July 4.

---

[1] Journals of Congress for 22 May and 15 and 18 July, 1782.
[2] Governor Clinton's message of 11 July, 1782.

views" of his superior. In obedience to instructions, he strongly represented "the necessity of solid arrangements of finance;" but he went to the work "without very sanguine expectations," for he believed that, "whatever momentary effort the legislature might make, very little would be done till the entire change of the present system;" and, before this could be effected, "mountains of prejudice and particular interest were to be levelled."[1]

On the nineteenth, three days after his arrival, on the motion of Schuyler, his father-in-law, who was ever constant in support of a national system, the senate resolved itself into a committee of the whole on the state of the nation." From its deliberations on two successive days a series of resolutions proceeded, which Hamilton probably drafted, and which, after they had been considered by paragraphs, were unanimously adopted by the senate. The house concurred in them without amendment and with equal unanimity. These resolutions as they went forth from the legislature find in the public experience "the strongest reason to apprehend from a continuance of the present constitution of the continental government a subversion of public credit," and a danger "to the safety and independence of the states." They repeat the words of the Hartford convention and of Clinton, that the radical source of the public embarrassments had been the want of sufficient power in congress, particularly the power of providing for itself a revenue, which could not be obtained by partial deliberations of the

[1] Hamilton, i. 286, 288.

THE STRUGGLE FOR REVENUE. 39

states separately. For these reasons the legislature of New York invite congress for the common welfare "to recommend and each state to adopt the measure of assembling a general convention of the states specially authorized to revise and amend the confederation, reserving a right to the respective legislatures to ratify their determinations."[1] These resolutions the governor of New York was requested to transmit to congress and to the executive of every state.

The legislature held a conference with Hamilton, as the receiver of revenue, but without permanent results; and it included him "pretty unanimously" in its appointment of delegates to congress for the ensuing year. The resolutions for a federal convention were communicated by Clinton[2] without a word of remark to the congress then in session. There, on the fifteenth of August, they were referred to a grand committee; but there is no evidence that that congress proceeded to its election.

In his distress for money, Morris solicited a new French loan of twenty millions of livres. The demand was excessive: the king, however, consented to a loan of six millions for the year 1783, and Franklin immediately received one fourth part of it. "You will take care," so Vergennes wrote to Luzerne, "not to leave them any hope that the king an make

CHAP. II.

1 7 8 2.

July.

August 4.

15.

---

[1] MS. Copy of the Journals of the Senate and Assembly of New York for the session of July, 1782. The grounds for believing Hamilton to have been the draughtsman of the resolutions are solely the circumstances above related, and that the language bears his impress.
[2] Clinton to president of congress, 4 Aug., 1782. MS.

40   THE CONFEDERATION.

CHAP. II.
1782.

them further advances or guarantee for them new loans from others;" and he complained that the United States did not give sufficient proofs of their readiness to create the means for meeting their debts.[1]

Dec. 24.

In December all of the French auxiliary forces in the United States, except one regiment which soon followed, embarked at Boston for the West Indies. The affections, the gratitude, the sympathy, the hopes of America followed the French officers as they left her shores. What boundless services they had rendered in the establishment of her independence! What creative ideas they were to carry home! How did they in later wars defy death in all climes, from San Domingo to Moscow and to the Nile, always ready to bleed for their beautiful land, often yielding up their lives for liberty! Rochambeau, who was received with special honor by Louis XVI., through a happy accident escaped the perils of the revolution, and lived to be more than fourscore years of age. Viomenil, his second in command, was mortally wounded while defending his king in the palace of the Tuileries. De Grasse died before a new war broke out. For more than fifty years, Lafayette,—in the states general, in convention, in legislative assemblies, at the head of armies, in exile, in cruel and illegal imprisonment, in retirement, in his renewed public life, the emancipator of slaves, the apostle of free labor, the dearest guest of America,—remained to his latest hour the true and the ever hopeful representative of loyalty to the cause of liberty. The Viscount de Noailles, who so gladly assisted to build in

[1] Vergennes to Luzerne, 21 Dec., 1782. MS.

America the home of human freedom for comers from all nations, was destined to make the motion which in one night swept from his own country feudal privilege and personal servitude. The young Count Henri de Saint-Simon,[1] who during his four campaigns in America mused on the never ending succession of sorrows for the many, devoted himself to the reform of society, government, and industry. Dumas survived long enough to take part in the revolution of July, 1830. Charles Lameth, in the states general and constituent assembly, proved one of the wisest and ablest of the popular party, truly loving liberty and hating all excesses in its name. Alexander Lameth, acting with the third estate in the states general, proposed the abolition of all privileges, the enfranchisement of every slave, and freedom of the press; he shared the captivity of Lafayette in Olmutz, and to the end of his life was a defender of constitutional rights. Custine of Metz, whose brilliant services in the United States had won for him very high promotion, represented in the states general the nobility of Lorraine, and insisted on a declaration of the rights of man. Of the Marquis de Chastellux Washington said: "I could not have bid a brother farewell with more regret; never have I parted with a man to whom my soul clave more sincerely."[2] His philanthropic zeal for "the greatest good of the greatest number"[3] was interrupted only by an early death.

---

[1] Lettres de H. Saint-Simon à un Americain, in "L'industrie, on discussions politiques, morales, etc.," par H. Simon. Paris, 1817. Tome ii., pp. 23-26, 33-35.

[2] Sparks, viii. 367.

[3] Cette unique fin de tout gouvernement ; le plus grand Bonheur du plus grand nombre d'individus. Chastellux, de la Félicité publique, tomeii., chap, iii., p. 70. Edition of 1822.

42   THE CONFEDERATION.

CHAP.
II.

1782.

Let it not be forgotten that Sécondat, a grandson[1] of the great Montesquieu, obtained promotion for good service in America. Nor may an American fail to name the young Prince de Broglie, though he arrived too late to take part in any battle. In the midday of life, just before lie was wantonly sent to the guillotine, he said to his child, then nine years old, afterward the self-sacrificing minister,[2] who kept faith with the United States at the cost of popularity and place: "My son, they may strive to draw you away from the side of liberty, by saying to you that it took the life of your father; never believe them, and remain true to its noble cause."

At the time when the strength which came from the presence of a wealthy and generous ally was departing, the ground was shaking beneath the feet of congress. Pennsylvania, the great central state, in two memorials offered to congress the dilemma, either to satisfy its creditors in that state, or to suffer them to be paid by the state itself out of its contributions to the general revenue. The first was impossible; the second would dissolve the union. Yet it was with extreme difficulty[3] that Rutledge, Madison, and Hamilton, a committee from congress, prevailed upon the assembly of Pennsylvania to desist for the time from appropriating funds raised for the confederation.[4]

Nov.

Dec.

The system for revenue by duties on importations

---

[1] Gilpin, 488.
[2] Saint-Simon. Les trios époqnes, In L'industrie, etc., tome ii., p. 291.
[3] I owe to him the opportunity of copying his father's journal while in America, in which is a beautiful tribute to Washington.
[4] Ibid.,of 199, 216, 224, 488; Journals of Congress, 4 Dec, 1782; Minutes of Assembly of Pennsylvania for 1782, pp. 663, 675, 733, where the memorials appear at large.

THE STRUGGLE FOR REVENUE. 43

seemed now to await only the assent of Rhode Island, That commonwealth in 1781 gave a wavering answer;[1] and then instructed its delegates in congress to uphold state sovereignty and independence.[2] On the first[3] of November, 1782, its assembly unanimously rejected the measure for three reasons: the impost would bear hardest on the most commercial states, particularly upon Rhode Island; officers unknown to the constitution would be introduced; a revenue for the expenditure of which congress is not to be accountable to the states would render that body independent of its constituents, and would be repugnant to the liberty of the United States.[4]

The necessity of the consent of every one of the thirteen states to any amendment of the confederacy gave to Rhode Island a terrible control over the destinies of America. Against its obstinacy the confederation was helpless. The reply to its communication, drafted by Hamilton, declared, first: that the duty would prove a charge not on the importing state, but on the consumer;—next, that no government can exist without a right of appointing officers for those purposes which proceed from and centre in itself, though the power may not be expressly known to the constitution;—lastly, the impost is a measure of necessity, "and, if not within the letter, is within the spirit of the confederation."[5]

CHAP. II.

1 7 8 2.
Nov. 1.

Dec. 16.

---

[1] GovernorWilliam Greene to Robert Morris, Oct., 1781, in Records of Rhode Island, ix. 487.
[2] Records of Rhode Island, ix 612
[3] Howell to the State of Rhode Island. Records of Rhode Island, ix. 682.
[4] Bradford, the speaker, to the President of congress, 30 Nov., 782. Records of Rhode Island, ix. 683, 684.
[5] Journals of Congress, iv. 200.

44   THE CONFEDERATION.

CHAP.
II.
1782.

Dec.
6, 7.

The growing discontent of the army, the clamor of public creditors, the enormous deficit in the revenue, were invincible arguments for a plan which promised relief. Congress having no resource except persuasion, three of its members would have borne its letter to Rhode Island but for intelligence from Virginia.[1]

In the legislature of that state, Richard Henry Lee, waiting till the business of the session was nearly over and the house very thin,[2] proposed to the assembly to withdraw its assent to the federal impost; and the repeal was carried in the house on the sixth, in the senate on the seventh of December,[3] without a negative. The reasons for the act, as recited in its preamble, were: "The permitting any power other than the general assembly of this commonwealth to levy duties or taxes upon the citizens of this state within the same is injurious to its sovereignty, may prove destructive of the rights and liberty of the people, and, so far as congress may exercise the same, is contravening the spirit of the confederation."[4]

Far-sighted members of congress prognosticated the most pernicious effects on the character, interests, and duration of the confederacy. The broad line of party division was clearly drawn. The contest was between the existing league of states and a republic of united states; between "state sovereignty"[5] and a "consolidated union;"[6] between "state

[1] Gilpin, 488, 238   Elliot, 17.
[2] Governor B. Harrison to Washington, 31 March, 1783. MS.
[3] In the Papers of old Congress, vol. lxv. MS. Journals of House of Delegates, 55-58.
[4] Hening, xi. 171.
[5] William Gordon to A. Lee. Lee's Life of Arthur Lee, ii. 291.
[6] Lafayette in Dip. Cor., x. 41.

THE STRUGGLE FOR REVENUE. 45

politics and continental politics;"[1] between the fear of "the centripetal" and the fear of "the centrifugal force" in the system.[2] Virginia made itself the battle-ground on which for the next six years the warring opinions were to meet. During all that time Washington and Madison led the striving for a more perfect union; Richard Henry Lee, at present sustained by the legislature of Virginia, was the persistent champion of separatism and the sovereignty of each state.

How beneficent was the authority of the union appeared at this time from a shining example. To quell the wild strife which had grown out of the claim of Connecticut to lands within the charter boundary of Pennsylvania, five commissioners appointed by congress opened their court at Trenton. "The case was well argued by learned counsel on both sides," and, after a session of more than six weeks, the court pronounced[3] their unanimous opinion, that the jurisdiction and pre-emption of the lands in controversy did of right belong to the state of Pennsylvania. The judgment was approved by congress; and the parties in the litigation gave the example of submission to this first settlement of a controversy between states by the decree of a court established by the United States.

---

[1] Hamilton, i. 356.
[2] Speech of Wilson, 28 Jan., 1783, in Gilpin, 290; Elliot, 34. The same figure was used by Hamilton, 24 March, 1783. Hamilton, i. 384.
[3] Journals of Congress, iv. 140, 30 Dec, 1782.

CHAPTER III.

AMIERICA AND GREAT BRITAIN.

1782, 1783.

CHAP. III.

1782. Dec.

The king of France heard from Vergennes, with surprise and resentment, that the American deputies had signed their treaty of peace;[1] Marie Antoinette was conciliated by the assurance that "they had obtained for their constituents the most advantageous conditions." "The English buy the peace rather than make it," wrote Vergennes to his subaltern in London; their "concessions as to boundaries, the fisheries, and the loyalists, exceed everything that I had thought possible."[2] "The treaty with America," answered Rayneval, "appears to me like a dream."[3] Kaunitz[4] and his emperor[5] mocked at its articles.

King George of England was mastered by a con-

---

[1] Count Mercy's report from Paris, 6 Dec, 1782. MS. From Vienna archives.

[2] Vergennes to Rayneval, 4 Dec., 1782. MS.

[3] Rayneval to Vergennes, 12 Dec., 1782 MS.

[4] Kaunitz' note of 22 Dec., 1782.

written on the emperor's copy of the speech of the king of England at the opening of parliament. MS.

[5] Autograph memorandum of Joseph. MS. Joseph II. und Leopold von Toscana. Ihr Briefwechsel von 1781 bis 1790, i. 146.

summing grief for the loss of America, and knew no ease of mind by day or by night. When, on the fifth of December, in his speech at the opening of parliament, he came to read that he had offered to declare the colonies of America free and independent states, his manner was constrained[1] and his voice fell. To wound him least, Shelburne in the house of lords, confining himself to the language of the speech from the throne, represented the offer of independence to America as contingent on peace with France. To a question from Fox on the following night in the other house, Pitt, with unfaltering courage, answered that the recognition was unqualified and irrevocable.

During the Christmas holidays the negotiations for a general peace were pursued with equal diligence and moderation by Vergennes and Shelburne; and France made sacrifices of its own to induce Spain to forego the recovery of Gibraltar and assent to terms which in all other respects were most generous. The Netherlands, though their definitive peace was delayed, agreed in the suspension of arms. Franklin shrewdly and truly observed that it would be better for the nations then possessing the West India islands to let them govern themselves as neutral powers, open to the commerce of all, the profits of the present monopolies being by no means equivalent to the expense of maintaining them;[2] but the old system was preserved. Conquests were restored, and England felt it to be no wound to her dignity to give back an unimportant island which she had

[1] Rayneval to Vergennes, 12. Dec., 1782. MS.   [2] Dip. Cor., iv. 69.

CHAP. III.

1 7 8 3.

wrested from the house of Bourbon in a former war. The East Indian allies of France, of whom the foremost was Tippoo Saib, the son and successor of Hyder Ali, were invited to join in the peace. France recovered St. Pierre and Miquelon and her old share in the fisheries of Newfoundland; Spain retained Minorca, and, what was of the greatest moment for the United States, both the Floridas, which she certainly would find a useless burden. Treaties of commerce between Great Britain and each of the two Bourbon kingdoms were to be made within two years.

Jan. 20.

When, on the twentieth of January, these preliminaries were signed by the respective plenipotentiaries, John Adams and Benjamin Franklin, on the summons of Vergennes, were present, and in the name of the United States acceded to the declaration of the cessation of hostilities. The provisional treaty between Great Britain and the United States was held to take effect from that day.

"At last," wrote Vergennes to Rayneval, as soon as the meeting was over, "we are about to breathe under the shadow of peace. Let us take care to make it a solid one; may the name of war be forgotten forever"[1] In a letter to Shelburne on that same day, he expressed the confident hope that all ancient distrust would be removed;[2] and Shelburne replied: "The liberal spirit and good faith which have governed our negotiations leave no room to fear for the future either distrust or jealousy."[3] King George

[1] Vergennes to Rayneval, 20 Jan., 1783. MS.
[2] Vergennes to Shelburne, 20 Jan., 1783. Lansdowne House MSS.
[3] Shelburne to Vergennes, 24 Jan., 1783. Lansdowne House MSS.

AMERICA AND GREAT BRITAIN. 49

dwelt with Rayneval on the the cordial understanding which lie desired to establish with Louis XVI. "I wish," said he, "never again to have a war with France; we have had a first division of Poland; there must not be a second."¹

So came the peace which recognised the right of a commonwealth of Europeans outside of Europe, occupying a continental territory within the temperate zone; remote from foreign interference; needing no standing armies; with every augury of a rapid growth; and sure of exercising the most quickening and widest influence on political ideas, "to assume an equal station among the powers of the earth."

The restoration of intercourse with America pressed for instant consideration. Burke was of opinion that the navigation act should be completely revised; Shelburne and his colleagues, aware that no paltry regulation would now succeed, were indefatigable in digesting a great and extensive system of trade, and sought, by the emancipation of commerce, to bring about with the Americans a family friendship more beneficial to England than their former dependence.² To promote this end, on the evening of the eleventh of February, William Pitt, with the permission of the king, repaired to Charles James Fox and invited him to join the ministry of Shelburne. The only good course for Fox was to take the hand which the young statesman offered; but he put aside the overture with coldness, if not with disdain choosing a desperate alliance with those whose conduct he had

---

¹ Rayneval to Vergennes, 24 and 28 Jan., 1783. MS.

² Price in Lee's Life of Arthur Lee, ii. 349.

pretended to detest, and whose principles it was in later years his redeeming glory to have opposed.

Pending the negotiations with France and Spain, Fox and Lord North remained quiet, from the desire to throw the undivided responsibility for the peace on Lord Shelburne; but when on the seventeenth of February, in a house of four hundred and fifty members, the treaties with the United States and with both branches of the Bourbons were laid before parliament, and an address of approval, promising a liberal revision of commercial law, was moved, the long-pent-up passions raged without restraint. No sooner had William Wilberforce, with grace and good feeling, seconded the motion and in the warmest language assured to the loyal refugees compensation for their losses, than Lord John Cavendish, the nearest friend of Fox, condemned the peace, though supporting its conditions. Lord North then pronounced against it a most elaborate, uncandid, and factious invective. He would have deprived the United States of access to the upper lakes; he would have retained for Canada the country north and north-west of the Ohio; and, bad as is a possession which gives no advantage but powers of annoyance, he would have kept East Florida as well as the Bahamas, so as to compel the ships of America, in passing through the Florida channel, to run the gauntlet between British posts. He would have had no peace without the reinstatement of the loyalists, nor without securing independence to the savage allies of Great Britain. He enumerated one by one the posts in the west which by the treaty fell to America, dwelt on the cost of their construction and on their importance of the fur-trade, and foreshadowed the policy of delaying their surrender. He not only censured the grant to the Americans of a right to fish on the coast of Nova Scotia, but spoke as if they derived from Great Britain the right to fish on the banks in the sea which are the exclusive property of no one. At the side of Lord North stood Edmund Burke, with hotter zeal as a partisan, though with better intentions toward America. Pitt answered every objection to the treaty; but, after a debate of twelve hours, the ministry on the division found themselves in a minority of sixteen.

On the same evening, to a larger number of peers than had met in their house since the accession of George III., Carlisle, the unsuccessful commissioner of 1778, Keppel, the inglorious admiral, and Stormont, the late headstrong ambassador at Paris, eager to become once more a secretary of state, Lord George Germain, now known as Lord Sackville, Wedderburn, now Lord Loughborough and coveting the office of lord chancellor, poured forth criminations of a treaty for which the necessity was due to their own incapacity. In perfect understanding with Fox and Lord North, they complained that the ministers had given up the banks of the Ohio, "the paradise of America," had surrendered the fur-trade, had broken faith with the Indians, had been false to the loyalists. Thurlow ably defended every article of the treaty that had been impeached, and then asked: "Is there any individual in this house who dares to avow that his wish is for war? "The interest of the debate centred in Shelburne, and the house gave him the closest attention as he spoke: "Noble lords who made a lavish use of these Indians have taken great pains to show their immense value, but those who abhorred their violence mil think the ministry have done wisely." Naming a British agent who had been detested for wanton cruelty, he continued: "The descendants of William Penn will manage them better than all the Stuarts, with all the trumpery and jobs that we could contrive.

"With regard to the loyalists, I have but one answer to give the house. It is the answer I gave my own bleeding heart. A part must be wounded that the whole empire may not perish. If better terms could have been had, think you, my lords, that I would not have embraced them? If it had been possible to put aside the bitter cup which the adverseties of this country presented to me, you know I would have done it.

"The fur-trade is not given up; it is only divided, and divided for our benefit. Its best resources lie to the northward. Monopolies, some way or other, are ever justly punished. They forbid rivalry, and rivalry is the very essence of the well-being of trade. This seems to be the era of protestantism in trade. All Europe appears enlightened and eager to throw off the vile shackles of oppressive, ignorant, unmanly monopoly. It is always unwise; but, if there is any nation under Heaven who ought to be the first to reject monopoly, it is the English. Situated as we are between the old world and the new, and between southern and northern Europe, all that we ought to covet equality and free-trade. With more Industry, with more enterprise, with more capital than any trading nation upon earth, it ought to be our constant cry, Let every market be open; let us meet our rivals fairly and ask no more, telling the Americans that we desire to live with them in communion of benefits and in sincerity of friendship."[1]

At near half past four in the morning, the majority for the ministry was only thirteen.

On the twenty-first, resolutions censuring them were offered in the house of commons. In the former debate, Fox had excused the change in his relations to Lord North by the plea that his friendships were perpetual, his enmities placable; keeping out of sight that political principles may not be sacrificed to personal reconciliations, he now proclaimed and justiied their coalition. "Their coalition," replied Pitt, "originated rather in an inclination to force the Earl of Shelburne from the treasury than in any real conviction that ministers deserve censure for the concessions they have made.[2] Whatever appears dishonorable or inadequate in the peace on your table is strictly chargeable to the noble lord in the blue ribbon," Lord North, "whose profusion of the public money, whose notorious temerity and obstinacy in prosecuting the war which originated in his pernicious and oppressive policy, and whose utter incapacity to fill the station he occupied, rendered peace of any description indispensable to the preservation of the state. The triumph of party shall never induce me to call

---

[1] Almon's Parliamentary Register. xxviii. 67, 68.

[2] Ibid., xxvvi. 347.

the abandonment of former principles a forgetting of ancient prejudices, or to pass an amnesty upon measures which have brought my country almost to the verge of ruin. I will never engage in political enmities without a public cause; I will never forego such enmities without the public approbation.[1] High situation and great influence I am solicitous to possess, whenever they can be acquired with dignity. I relinquish them the moment any duty to my country, my character, or my friends, renders such a sacrifice indispensable. I look to the independent part of the house and to the public at large for that acquittal from blame to which my innocence entitles me. My earliest impressions were in favor of the noblest and most disinterested modes of serving the public. These impressions I will cherish as a legacy infinitely more valuable than the greatest inheritance. You may take from me the privileges and emoluments of place, but you cannot, you shall not, take from me those habitual regards for the prosperity of Great Britain which constitute the honor, the happiness, the pride of my life. With this consolation, the loss of power and the loss of fortune, though I affect not to despise, I hope I shall soon be able to forget. I praise Fortune when constant; if she strikes her swift wing, I resign her gifts and seek upright, unportioned poverty."[2]

The eloquence of Pitt, his wise conduct, and the purity of his morals, gained him the confidence to which Fox vainly aspired.[3]

---

[1] Almon's Parliamentary Register, xxvi. 341 ; Life of Romilly, i. 205.
[2] Almon, xxvi. 352.
[3] Mousticrto Vergenues, 1 March, 1783. MS.

A majority of seventeen appearing against Shelburne, lie resigned on the twenty-fourth; and by his advice the king on the same day offered to Pitt, though not yet twenty-four years old, the treasury, with power to form an administration and with every assurance of support. But the young statesman, obeying alike the dictates of prudence and the custom of the British constitution, would not accept office without a majority in the house of commons; and on the twenty-seventh, finding that such a majority could not be obtained but by the aid, or at least the neutrality, of Lord North, he refused the splendid offer, unalterably firm alike against the entreaties and the reproaches of the king. This moderation in a young man, panting with ambition and conscious of his powers, added new lustre to his fame.[1]

While the imperfect agreement between the members of the coalition delayed the formation of a ministry, on the third of March, Pitt, as chancellor of the exchequer, presented a bill framed after the liberal principles of Shelburne.[2] Its preamble, which rightly described the Americans as aliens, declared "it highly expedient that the intercourse between Great Britain and the United States should be established on the most enlarged principles of reciprocal benefit; "and, as a consequence, not only were the ports of Great Britain to be opened to them on the same terms as to other sovereign states, but, alone of the foreign world, their ships and vessels laden with the produce or manufactures of their own country might

---

[1] Stanhope's Pitt, i. 110.
[2] Fox in Moustier to Vergennes, 11 April, 1783, MS.; Price in Life of A. Lee, ii. 349.

CHAP. III.

1783.
March 7.

as of old enter all British ports in America, paying other duties than those imposed on British vessels.

On the seventh, Eden objected, saying: "The bill will introduce a total revolution in our commercial system. Reciprocity with the United States is nearly impracticable, from their provincial constitutions. The plan is utterly improper, for it completely repeals the navigation act. The American states lie so contiguous to our West Indian islands, they will supply them with provisions to the ruin of the provision trade with Ireland. We shall lose the carrying trade, for the Americans are to be permitted under this bill to bring West Indian commodities to Europe. The Americans on their return from our ports may export our manufacturing tools, and, our artificers emigrating at the same time, we shall see our manufactures transplanted to America. Nothing more should be done than to repeal the prohibitory acts and vest the king in council with powers for six months to suspend such laws as stand in the way of an amicable intercourse."

Pitt agreed that "the bill was most complicated in its nature and most extensive in its consequences,"[1] and, giving it but faint support, he solicited the assistance and the information of every one present to mould it, so that it might prove most useful at home and most acceptable in America. "While there is an immense extent of unoccupied territory to attract the inhabitants to agriculture," said Edmund Burke, "they will not be able to rival us in manufactures. Do not treat them as aliens. Let all prohibitory acts be re-

[1] Alinon, xxvi. 439.

repealed, and leave the Americans in every respect as they were before in point of trade." The clause authorizing direct intercourse between the United States and the British West India islands was allowed to remain in the report to the house.[1]

Before the bill was discussed again, the coalition, after long delays caused by almost fatal dissensions among themselves, had been installed. In pursuit of an ascendency in the cabinet, Lord North plumed himself on having ever been a consistent whig; believing that "the appearance of power was all that a King of England could have;"[2] and insisting that during all his ministry "he had never attributed to the crown any other prerogative than it was acknowledged to possess by every sound whig and by all those authors who had written on the side of liberty."[3] But he betrayed his friends by contenting himself with a subordinate office in a cabinet in which there would always be a majority against him,[4] and, while Fox seized on the lead, the nominal chieftainship was left to the Duke of Portland, who had neither capacity for business, nor activity, nor power as a speaker, nor knowledge of liberal principles.

The necessity of accepting a ministry so composed drove the king to the verge of madness. He sorrowed over "the most profligate age;" "the most unnatural coalition;"[5] and he was heard to use "strong expressions of personal abhorrence of Lord North, whom he charged with treachery and ingratitude of the black-

---

[1] Almon, xxvi. 503.
[2] Lord John Russell's Memorials and Correspondence of Charles James Fox, ii. 38.
[3] Almon, xxvi. 355.
[4] Life of Romilly, i. 205.
[5] George Rex to Shelburne, 22 Feb., 1783. MS.

est nature."[1] "Wait till you see the end,"[2] said the king to the representative of France at the next levee; and Fox knew that the chances in the game were against him, as he called to mind that he had sought in vain the support of Pitt; had defied the king; and had joined himself to colleagues whom he had taught liberal Englishmen to despise, and whom he himself could not trust.

In the slowly advancing changes of the British constitution, the old whig party, as first conceived by Shaftesbury and Locke to resist the democratic revolution in England on the one side and the claim of arbitrary sovereignty by the Stuarts on the other, was near its end. The time was coming for the people to share in power. For the rest of his life, Fox battled for the reform of the house of commons, so that it became the rallying cry of the liberal party in England. A ministry divided within itself by irreconcilable opinions, detested by the king, confronted by a strong and watchful and cautious opposition, was forced to follow the line of precedents. The settlement of the commercial relations to be established with the United States had belonged to the treasury; it was at once brought by Fox within his department, although, from his ignorance of political economy, he could have neither firm convictions nor a consistent policy. He was not, indeed, without glimpses of the benefit of liberty in trade. To him it was a problem how far the act of navigation had ever been useful, and what ought to be its

---

[1] Memorials of Fox, ii 249.   [2] Moustier to Vergennes, 3 April, 1783. MS.

AMERICA AND GREAT BRITAIN. 59

fate;[1] but the bill in which the late ministry had begin to apply the principle of free trade to commerce with America he utterly condemned, "not," as he said, "from animosity toward Shelburne, but because great injury often came from reducing comercial theories to practice."[2] Moreover, the house of commons would insist on much deliberation and very much inquiry, before it would sacrifice the navigation act to the circumstances of the present crisis.[3]

In judging his conduct, it must be considered that the changes in the opinion of a people come from the slow evolution of thought in the public mind. One of the poets of England, in the flush of youth, had prophesied;[4]

"The time shall come when, free as seas or wind,
Unbounded Thames shall flow for all mankind,
Whole nations enter with each swelling tide,
And seas but join the regions they divide."

Three fourths of a century must pass away before the prophecy will come true by the efforts of statesmen, who, had they lived in the time of Fox, might have shared his indecision.

The coalition cabinet at its first meeting agreed to yield no part of the navigation act,[5] and, as a matter of policy, to put off the bill before parliament relating to commerce with America "till some progress should be made in a negotiation with the American commissioners at Paris." Thither Fox sent without delay,

---

[1] Moustier to Vergennes, 11 April, 1783. MS.
[2] Ibid.
[3] Fox to Hartley, 10 June, 1783. MS.
[4] Pope's Windsor Forest, 398.
[5] Fox to the king. Memorials of Fox, ii, 122.

as minister on the part of Great Britain, David Hartley, the friend of Franklin and a well-wisher to the United States.

The avowed liberal opinions of Hartley raising distrust, Lord Sheffield, a supporter of the ministry, and, on trade with America, the master authority of that day for parliament, immediately sounded an alarm. "Let the ministers know," said he on the fifteenth, in the house of lords, "the country is as tenacious of the principle of the navigation act as of the principle of Magna Charta. They must not allow America to take British colonial produce to ports in Europe. They must reserve to our remaining dominions the exclusive trade to the West India islands; otherwise, the only use of them will be lost. If we permit any state to trade with our islands or to carry into this country any produce but its own, we desert the navigation act and sacrifice the marine of England. The peace is in comparison a trifling object."[1] But there was no need of fear lest Fox should yield too much. In his instructions to Hartley, he was for taking the lion's share, as Vergennes truly said.[2] He proposed that the manufactures of the thirteen states should as a matter of course be excluded from Great Britain, but that British manufactures should be admitted everywhere in the United States. While America was dependent, parliament had taxed importations of its produce, but British ships and manufactures entered the colonies free of duty. "The true object t of the treaty in this business," so Fox enforced his plan, "is the

---

[1] Almon, xxvi. 615.   [2] Works of John Adams, iii. 380.

AMERICA AND GREAT BRITAIN. 61

mutual admission of ships and merchandise free from any new duty or imposition;"[1] that is, the Americans on their side should leave the British navigation act in full force and renounce all right to establish an act of navigation of their own; should continue to pay duties in the British ports on their own produce; and receive in their own ports British produce and manufactures duty free. One subject appealed successfully to the generous side of his nature. To the earnest wish of Jay that British ships should have no right under the convention to carry into the states any slaves from any part of the world, it being the intention of the United States entirely to prohibit their importation,[2] Fox answered promptly: "If that be their policy, it never can be competent to us to dispute with them their own regulations."[3] In like spirit, to formal complaints that Carleton, "in the face of the treaty, persisted in sending off negroes by hundreds," Fox made answer: "To restore negroes whom we invited, seduced if you will, under a promise of liberty, to the tyranny and possibly to the vengeance of their former masters, is such an act as scarce any orders from his employers (and no such orders exist) could have induced a man of honor to execute."[4]

The dignity and interests of the republic were safe, for they were confided to Adams, Franklin, and Jay. In America there existed as yet no system of restricttions; and congress had not power to protect shipping

---

[1] Fox to Hartley, 10 April, 1783. MS.
[2] June, 1783. Dip. Cor., x. 154.
[3] Fox to Hartley, 10 June, 1783. MS.
[4] Fox to Hartley, 9 August, 1783. MS.

or establish a custom-house. The states as dependencies had been so severely and so wantonly cramped by British navigation acts, and for more than a century had so steadily resisted them, that the desire of absolute freedom of commerce had become a part of their nature. The American commissioners were very much pleased with the trade-bill of Pitt, and with the principles expressed in its preamble; the debates upon it in parliament awakened their distrust. They were ready for any event, having but the one simple and invariable policy of reciprocity. Their choice and their offer was mutual unconditional free trade; but, however narrow might be the limits which England should impose, they were resolved to insist on like for like.[1] The British commissioner was himself in favor of the largest liberty for commerce, but he was reproved by Fox for transmitting a proposition not authorized by his instructions.

A debate in the house of lords on the sixth of May revealed the rapidity with which the conviction was spreading that America had no power to adopt measures of defensive legislation. There were many who considered the United States as having no government at all, and there were some who looked for the early dissolution of the governments even of the separate states. Lord Walsingham, accordingly, proposed that the law for admitting American ships should apply not merely to the ships of the United States, but to ships belonging to any one of the states and to any ship or vessel belonging to any of the inhabitants thereof. He was supported by Lord Thurlow, who

---

[1] Hartley to Fox, 20 May, 1783. MS.

said: "I have read an account which stated the government of America to be totally unsettled, and that each province seemed intent on establishing a distinct, independent, sovereign state. If this is really the case, the amendment will be highly necessary and proper."[1] The amendment was dropped; and the bill under discussion, in its final shape, repealed prohibitory acts made during the war, removed the formalities which attended the admission of ships from the colonies during their state of dependency, and left for a limited time the power of regulating commerce with America to the king in council.

Immediately the proclamation of an order in council of the second of July confined the trade between the American states and the British West India islands to British-built ships owned and navigated "by British subjects." "Undoubtedly," wrote the Mug, "the Americans cannot expect nor ever will receive any favor from me."[2] To an American, Fox said: "For myself, I have no objection to opening the West India trade to the Americans, but there are many parties to please."[3]

The blow fell heavily on America, and compelled a readjustment of its industry. Ships had been its great manufacture for exportation. For nicety of workmanship, the palm was awarded to Philadelphia, but nowhere could they be built so cheaply as at Boston. More than one third of the tonnage employed in British commerce before the war was of American construction. Britain renounced this re-

---

[1] Almon, xxviii. 180, 181.
[2] Correspondence of George III. With Lord North, ii. 442.
[3] Dip. Cor., ii. 513; Fox to Hartley, 10 June, 1783. MS.

CHAP.
III.

1783.
July.

source. The continent and West India islands had prospered by the convenient interchange of their produce; the trade between nearest and friendliest neighbors was forbidden, till England should find out that she was waging war against a higher power than the United States; that her adversary was nature itself. Her statesmen confounded the "navigation act" and "the marine of Britain;"[1] the one the offspring of selfishness, the other the sublime display of the creative power of a free people.

Such was the issue between the ancient nation which falsely and foolishly and mischievously believed that its superiority in commerce was due to artificial legislation, and a young people which solicited free trade. Yet thrice blessed was this assertion of monopoly by an ignorant parliament, for it went forth as a summons to the commercial and the manufacturing; interests of the American states and to the self-respect and patriotism of all their statesmen and citizens to speak an efficient government into being.

To Gouverneur Morris, Jay wrote: "The present ministry are duped by an opinion of our not having union and energy sufficient to retaliate their restricttions. No time is to be lost in raisins; and maintaining a national spirit in America. Power to govern the confederacy as to all general purposes should be granted and exercised. In a word, everything conducive to union and constitutional energy should be cultivated, cherished, and protected."[2] "The British ministers," answered Morris, "are deceived, for heir

[1] Sheffield's Commerce of the American States, preface, 10.
[2] Jay to Gouverneur Morris, 17 July, 1783. Sparks' Life of G. Morris, i. 258.

conduct itself will give congress a power to retaliate their restrictions.[1] This country has never yet been known in Europe, least of all to England, because they constantly view it through a medium of prejudice or of faction. True it is that the general government wants energy, and equally true it is that this want will eventually be supplied. Do not ask the British to take off their foolish restrictions; the present regulation does us more political good than commercial mischief."[2]

On the side of those in England who were willing to accept the doctrines of free trade, Josiah Tucker, the dean of Gloucester, remarked: "As to the future grandeur of America, and its being a rising empire, under one head, whether republican or monarchical, it is one of the idlest and most visionary notions that ever was conceived even by writers of romance. The mutual antipathies and clashing interests of the Americans, their difference of governments, habitudes, and manners, indicate that they will have no centre of union and no common interest. They never can be united into one compact empire under any species of government whatever; a disunited people till the end of time, suspicious and distrustful of each other, they will be divided and subdivided into little commonwealths or principalities according to natural boundaries, by great bays of the sea, and by vast rivers, lakes, and ridges of mountains."[3]

The principle of trade adopted by the coalition min-

---

[1] Gouverneur Morris to Jay, 24 Sept., 1783. Sparks' Life of G. Morris, i. 259.

[2] Gouverneur Morris to Jay 10 Jan., 1784. Ibid., 266, 267.

[3] Dean Tucker's Cui Bono, 1781, 117–119.

istry, Sheffield set forth with authority in a pamphlet, which was accepted as an oracle. "There should be no treaty with the American states because they will not place England on a better footing than France and Holland, and equal rights will be enjoyed of course without a treaty. The nominal subjects of congress in the distant and boundless regions of the valley of the Mississippi will speedily imitate and multiply the examples of independence. It will not be an easy matter to bring the American states to act as a nation; they are not to be feared as such by us. The confederation does not enable congress to form more than general treaties; when treaties become necessary, they must be made with the states separately. Each state has reserved every power relative to imposts, exports, prohibitions, duties, etc., to itself.[1] If the American states choose to send consuls, receive them and send a consul to each state. Each state will soon enter into all necessary regulations with the consul, and this is the whole that is necessary.[2] The American states will not have a very free trade in the Mediterranean, if the Barbary states know their interests. That the Barbary states are advantageous to the maritime powers is certain; if they were suppressed, little states would have much more of the carrying trade. The armed neutrality would be as hurtful to the great maritime powers as the Barbary states are useful."[3]

In London it was a maxim among the merchants

---

[1] Sheffield's Commerce of the American States, 183, 190, 191, 198–200.
[2] Ibid., 277.
[3] Ibid., 204, 205, note.

that, if there were no Algiers, it would be worth England's while to build one.¹

Already the navigation act was looked to as a protection to English commerce, because it would require at least three fourths of the crews of American ships to be Americans; and they pretended that during the war three fourths of the crews of the American privateers were Europeans.² The exclusion of European seamen from service in the American marine was made a part of British policy from the first establishment of the peace.

In August, Laurens, by the advice of his associates, came over to England to inquire whether a minister from the United States of America would be properly received. "Most undoubtedly," answered Fox, and Laurens left England in that belief.³ But the king, when his pleasure was taken, said: "I certainly can never express its being agreeable to me; and, indeed, I should think it wisest for both parties to have only agents who can settle any matters of commerce. That revolted state certainly for years cannot establish a stable government."⁴ The plan at court was to divide the United States, and for that end to receive only consuls from each one of the separate states and not a minister for the whole.⁵

British statesmen had begun to regret that any treaty whatever had been made with the United States collectively; they would have granted independence and peace, but without further stipulations

---

¹ Franklin in Dip. Cor., iv. 149.
² Sheffield's Commerce of the American States, 205, note.
³ Dip. Cor., ii. 510-515.
⁴ King to Fox, 7 Aug., 1783; Memorials of Fox, ii, 141.
⁵ Adhémar to Vergennes, 7 Aug., 1783. MS.

of any kind, so that all other questions might have been left at loose ends. Even Fox was disinclined to impart any new life to the provisional articles agreed upon by the ministry which he supplanted. He repeatedly avowed the opinion that "a definetive treaty with the United States was perfectly superfluous."[1] The American commissioners became uneasy; but Vergennes pledged himself not to proceed without them,[2] and Fox readily yielded. On the third of September, when the minister of France and the ambassadors of Great Britain and Spain concluded their conventions at Versailles, the American provisional articles, shaped into a definitive treaty, were signed by Hartley for Great Britain; by Adams, Franklin, and Jay for the United States of America.

The coalition ministry did not last long enough to exchange ratifications. To save the enormous expense of maintaining the British army in New York, Fox hastened its departure; but while "the speedy and complete evacuation of all the territories of the United States"[3] was authoritatively promised to the American commissioners at Paris, in the name of the king. Lord North, acting on the petition of merchants interested in the Canada trade,[4] withheld orders for the evacuation of the western and north-western interior posts, although by the treaty they were as much

---

[1] Fox to Duke of Manchester, 9 Aug., 1784. MS. Same to same, 4 Aug., 1783. MS. Same to Hartley, 4 Aug., 1783. MS.
[2] Hartley to Fox, 31 July, 1783. MS.
[3] Fox to Hartley, 10 June, 1783.
MS. Compare Fox to Hartley, 15 May, 1783. MS.
[4] Regulations proposed by the merchants interested in the trade to the province of Quebec, 1783. MS.

an integral part of the United States as Albany or Boston; and this policy, like that relating to commerce, was continued by the ministry that succeeded him.

We may not turn away from England without relating that Pitt for the second time proposed in the house of commons, though in vain, a more equal representation, by introducing one hundred new members from the counties and from the metropolis. Universal suffrage he condemned, and the privilege of the owners of rotten boroughs to name members of parliament had for him the sanctity of private property, to be taken away only after compensation. "Mankind," said Fox," are made for themselves, not for others. The best government is that in which the people have the greatest share. The present motion will not go far enough; but, as it is an amendment, I give it my hearty support."

An early and a most beneficent result of the American revolution was the reform of the British colonial system. Taxation of colonies by the parliament of Great Britain; treatment of them as worthless except as drudges for the enrichment of the ruling kingdom; plans of governing them on the maxims of a Hillsborough or a Thurlow,[1] came to an end. It grew to be the rule to give them content by the establishment of liberal constitutions.

[1] Sheffield's Commerce of the American States, 175–80.

CHAPTER IV.

AMERICA AND CONTINENTAL EUROPE.

1783.

The governments of continental Europe vied with each other in welcoming the new republic to its place among the powers of the world. In May, 1782, as soon as it was known at Stockholm that the negotiations for peace were begun, the adventurous king of Sweden sent messages of his desire, through Franklin above all others, to enter into a treaty with the United States. Franklin promptly accepted the invitation. The ambassador of Gustavus at Paris remarked:" I hope it will be remembered that Sweden was the first power in Europe which, without being solicited, offered its friendship to the United States."[1] Exactly five months before the definitive peace between the United States and Great Britain was signed, the treaty with Sweden was concluded. Each party was put on the footing of the most favored nations. Free ships were to make passengers free as well as goods. Liberty of commerce was to

---

[1] Franklin's Works, ix. 342.

extend to all kinds of merchandise. The number of contraband articles was carefully limited. In case of a maritime war in which both the contracting parties should remain neutral, their ships of war were to protect and assist each other's vessels. The treaty was ratified and proclaimed in the United States before The definitive treaty with Great Britain had arrived.[1]

The successful termination of the war aroused in Prussia hope for the new birth of Europe, that, by the teachings of America, despotism might be struck down, and the caste of hereditary nobility give place to republican equality. These aspirations were suffered to be printed at Berlin.[2]

The great Frederick had, late in 1782, declared to the British minister at his court, half in earnest and half cajoling, that "he was persuaded the American union could not long subsist under its present form. The great extent of country would alone be a sufficient obstacle, since a republican government had never been known to exist for any length of time where the territory was not limited and concentred. It would not be more absurd to propose the establishment of a democracy to govern the whole country from Brest to Riga. No inference could be drawn from the states of Venice, Holland, and Switzerland, of which the situation and circumstances were perfectly different from those of the colonies."[3] He did not know the power of the representative system, nor could he foresee that by the

---

[1] Journals of Congress, iv. 241.
[2] Die Freiheit Amerika's. Ode vom Herrn Pr. J. E. H. Berlinische Monatsschrift, April, 1783, 386.
See also J. Scherr's Kultur und Sittengeschichte, 508, 619.
[3] Sir John Stepney to secretary of state, 22 Oct., 1782. MS.

CHAP. IV.
1783.

wise use of it the fourth of his successors would evoke the German state from the eclipse of centuries, to shine with replenished light as the empire of a people. For the moment he kept close watch of the progress of the convention with Sweden, and, so soon as it was signed, directed his minister in France to make overtures to Franklin, which were most gladly received.[1]

Full seven months before the peace, a member of the government at Brussels intimated to William Lee, a former commissioner of congress at the court of Vienna, that Joseph II., who at that time harbored the hope of restoring to Belgian commerce its rights by opening the Scheldt[2] and so preparing the way for a direct trade with America, was disposed to enter into a treaty with the United States.[3] Soon after the preliminaries of peace between France and Great Britain had been signed, the emperor let it be insinuated to Franklin that he would be well received at Vienna as the minister of a sovereign power. In the following year an agent was sent from Belgium to the United States. The Belgians produced in unsurpassed excellence manufactures which America needed; but they were not enterprising enough to establish houses in America, or to grant its merchants the extended credits which were offered in England.[4] The subject gained less and less atten-

---

[1] Goltz to Frederick, 3 March, 28 April, 30 June, 1783 MSS.
[2] Hartley to Carmarthen, 9 Jan., 1785. MS.
[3] Dip. Cor., ii. 360, 31 March, 1783.
[4] Correspondence of the Austri- an accent. Baron de Beelen Bertholff, MS.; Wm. Lee to secretary of foreign affairs, 31 March, 1782, Dip. Cor., ii. 360; Gilpin, Elliot, 53, of 18 Feb., 1783; Letter to Franklin from Vienna, 8 April, 1783, Franklin's Works, ix., 501.

tion, for the emperor was compelled, in violation of natural rights, to suffer the Scheldt to be closed.

On the twenty-second of February, 1783, Rosencrone, minister of foreign affairs in Denmark, communicated to Franklin "the satisfaction with which the king's ministry had learned the glorious issue of the war for the United States of America," and their desire to form connections of friendship and commerce. "To overtures for a treaty like that between congress and the states general," he added, "we should eagerly and frankly reply." But a question of indemnity for violations of neutrality by Denmark during the war impeded the negotiation.

Before the end of March, the burgomaster and senate of the imperial free city of Hamburg, seeing "European powers courting in rivalry the friendship of" the new state, and impressed with "the illustrious event" of the acknowledged independence of America as "the wonder of that age and of remotest ages to come," deputed one of their citizens to bear to congress their letter, offering free trade between the two republics.

In midsummer, 1783, Portugal made overtures to treat with Franklin, but did not persist in them.

Russia was at that time too much engrossed by affairs in the East to take thought for opening new channels of commerce with the West; and the United States, recalling their minister, declined to make advances. But the two nations, without any mutual stipulations, had rendered each other the most precious services. Catherine had scornfully refused to lend troops to George III., rejected his entreaties for an alliance, and by the armed neutrality insulated his kingdom; the United States, by giving full employment to the maritime powers, had made for the empress the opportunity of annexing to her dominions the plains of Kuban and the Crimea.

Of the chief commercial nations of Europe, Holland entertained for America the most friendly sentiments, invited her trade, and readily granted to her congress all the credit which it had any right to expect.

The independence of the United States gave umbrage to the Spanish court. Galvez, the minister of the colonies, was fiercely and persistently hostile to the extent of the United States in the south-west. Florida Blanca himself wished for amicable rectifications of the boundary; but, on the remonstrances of Lafayette, he, in the presence of the ambassador of France, pledged his word of honor to accept the boundary as laid down in the Anglo-American treaty, and authorized Lafayette to bind him with congress to that pledge. The Spanish statesmen feared the loss of their own colonies, and the success of the American revolution excited new and never-ceasing alarm. They could have wished that North America might disappear from the face of the earth; but they tried to reconcile themselves to living in good harmony with the United States. The Mississippi was the great source of anxiety.

Spain thought it not for her interest that the American states should consolidate their union. She had dreaded the neighborhood of English colonies to her own; she dreaded still more to border all the way from the Atlantic to the fountains of the Mississippi on a republic whose colossal growth was distinctly foreseen. Besides this, the suppression of a rebellion in South America had just cost more than a hundred thousand lives; and the difficulty of governing distant and boundless regions was so great that de Aranda, the far-sighted statesman who had signed the treaty of peace, in his official dispatches to Florida Blanca, set forth the opinion that Portugal would be worth more to Spain than all the American mainland. Of the islands he never depreciated the value; but he clearly perceived how precarious was the hold of Spain on her continental possessions; and he left on record the advice which he may never have had an opportunity to offer personally to his king, that Spain should transform all the vice-royalties in America into secundo-genitures, retaining in direct dependence only Cuba and Porto Rico.[1]

Even Vergennes, while he believed that the attachment of America to the alliance would be safest if the confederation could keep itself alive, held it best for France that the United States should fail to attain the political consistency of which he saw that they were susceptible; and he remained a tranquil spectator of their efforts for a better constitution. Lafayette not only watched over the interests of America in Europe, but to the president of congress and to the secretary for foreign affairs he sent messages imploring American patriots to strengthen the federal union.

[1] Ferro del Rio, iii. 460, 407, note. Muriel, vi. 45-54. Revista Española de Ambos Mundos, for May, 1855, written by Ferro del Rio. In his letter on exchanging for Portugal the Spanish possessions in America, Aranda writes, "exceptuando las islas." The train of thought is the same.

CHAPTER V.

A PLAN TO FORCE A STRONGER GOVERNMENT.

JANUARY — MARCH, 1783.

Is the fall of 1782 the main army was moved for winter quarters to the wooded hills in the rear of Newburg. No part of the community had undergone equal hardships or borne them with equal fortitude. In the leisure of the camp they brooded over their wrongs and their chances of redress, and at the close of the year the officers sent to Philadelphia as their committee Major-General Macdougall and Colonels Ogden and Brooks, who, on the sixth of January, 1783, presented the following address.[1]

"To the United States in congress assembled: We, the officers of the army of the United States, in behalf of ourselves and our brethren the soldiers, beg leave freely to state to the supreme power, our head and sovereign, the distress under which we labor. Our embarrassments thicken so fast that many of us are unable to go further. Shadows have been offered to us, while the substance has been gleaned by others.

[1] Journals of Congress, iv. 206.

The citizens murmur at the greatness of their taxes, and no part reaches the army. We have borne all that men can bear. Our property is expended; our private resources are at an end. We therefore beg that a supply of money may be forwarded to the army as soon as possible.

"The uneasiness of the soldiers for want of pay is great and dangerous; further experiments on their patience may have fatal effects. There is a balance due upon the account for retained rations, forage, and arrearages on the score of clothing. Whenever there has been a want of means, defect in system, or neglect in execution, we have invariably been the sufferers by hunger and nakedness and languishing in a hospital. We beg leave to urge an immediate adjustment of all dues.

"We see with chagrin the odious point of view in which too many of the states endeavor to place the men entitled to half-pay. For the honor of human nature we hope that there are none so hardened in the sin of ingratitude as to deny the justice of the reward. To prevent altercations, we are willing to commute the half-pay pledged. And in this we pray that the disabled officers and soldiers, with the widows and orphans of those who have expended, or may expend, their lives in the service of their country, may be fully comprehended.

"General dissatisfaction is gaining ground in the army, from evils and injuries which, in the course of seven long years, have made their condition in many instances wretched. They therefore entreat that congress, to convince the army and the world that the

78   THE CONFEDERATION.

CHAP. V.

1783. Jan.

independence of America shall not be placed on the ruin of any particular class of her citizens, will point out a mode for immediate redress."

The grand committee to whom the memorial was referred held a conference with the superintendent of finance. He declared peremptorily that it was impossible, in the present state of the finances, to make any payment to the army, and that it would be imprudent to give assurances with regard to future pay until funds that could be relied upon should be established.[1] Not only had he no money in hand, but he had overdrawn his account in Europe to the amount of three and a half millions of livres.[2] He therefore asked a decision on the expediency of staking the public credit on further drafts to be met by the contingent proceeds of a loan from the Dutch and by the friendship of France. On the tenth of January,[3] congress, under an injunction of secrecy, authorized the superintendent to draw bills on the credit of applications for loans in Europe. Dyer of Connecticut alone opposed the measure as unwarranted and dishonorable, but allowed the resolution to be entered as unanimous.[4]

10.

13.

In an interview with the grand committee on the evening of the thirteenth,[5] the deputies from the army explained that, without an immediate payment of some part of the overdue pay, the discontent alike of officers and soldiers could not be soothed; that a mutiny might ensue; and that it would be hard to punish soldiers for a breach of engagements to the

---

[1] Gilpin, 248, 249; Elliot, 21.
[2] Gilpin, 251; Elliot, 21.
[3] Secret Journals of Congress, i. 253.
[4] Gilpin, 252; and compare Wilson, ibid., 299. Elliot, 22, 38.
[5] Gilpin, 256, 257; Elliot, 23.

A PLAN TO FORCE A STRONGER UNION. 79

public which the public itself had already flagrantly broken. "The army," said Macdougall," is verging to that state which, we are told, will make a wise man mad." It was a source of irritation that the members of the legislatures never adjourned till they had paid themselves fully, that all on the civil lists regularly received their salaries, and that all on the military lists were as regularly left unpaid.[1]

The deputies animadverted with surprise and even indignation on the repugnance of some of the states to establish a federal revenue for discharging federal engagements, while the affluence of the people indicated adequate resources. Speaking with peculiar emphasis and making a strong impression by his manner. General Macdougall declared "that the most intelligent part of the army were deeply touched by the debility of the federal government and the unwillingness of the states to invigorate it; in case of its dissolution, the benefits expected from the revolution would be greatly impaired; and the contests which might ensue among the states would be sure to embroil their respective officers."[2] As to the half-pay for life, they complained that men who had not received a shilling of emoluments were artfully called pensioners.

Hamilton had for himself renounced the half-pay."[3] The grand committee, in their report which he drafted, advised some payment to the army as soon as possible; for the rest, they were to have no priority

CHAP. V.

1783.
Jan. 13.

---

[1] Gilpin, 258; Elliot, 34; and compare Washington to Joseph Jones, 4 Dec, 1783, Sparks, viii. 370.

[2] Gilpin, 258, 259; Elliot, 24.
[3] Hamilton to Washington, 1 March, 1782. Hamilton, i. 274.

CHAP. V.
1783.
Jan.

over other creditors; all were to wait alike for the funding of the whole debt of the United States by general revenues. The officers were to have the option of preserving their claim to half-pay as it then stood, or accepting a commutation.[1]

"A great majority of the members of congress," avowed Robert Morris, "will not adopt the necessary measures because they are afraid of offending their states;"[2] and he undertook to drive them to decisive action.

24.

Accordingly, on the twenty-fourth, the day on which the report was taken up, he sent to them his resignation of office in these words:" The funding the public debts on solid revenues, I fear, will never be made. If before the end of May effectual measures to make permanent provision for the public debts of every kind are not taken, congress will be pleased to appoint some other man to be the superintendent of their finances: I will never be the minister of injustice."[3] The design of Robert Morris required the immediate publication of his letter, that, by uniting the army with all other creditors, congress and the states might be coerced into an efficient system; but congress reasoned that this authoritative statement of the financial ruin of the country would encourage the enemy, annihilate foreign and domestic credit, and provoke the army to mutiny. They therefore placed the communication under the injunction of secrecy.[4]

25.

Resuming the consideration of the report of their

[1] Gilpin, 276. 277; Elliot, 29, 30.
[2] Morris to Washington, 27 Feb., 1783. Dip. Cor., xii. 328.
[3] Morris to Washington, 27 Feb., 1783. Dip. Cor., xii. 326.
[4] Dip. Cor., xii. 325, 327, 338. Gilpin, 274, 275; Elliot, 29.

A PLAN TO FORCE A STRONGER UNION.

grand committee on the memorial from the army, they referred a present payment to the discretion of the superintendent of finance;[1] and, on the fifth of February, he issued a warrant, out of which the officers received one month's pay in notes and the private soldiers one month's pay in weekly instalments of half a dollar.[2]

The annual amount of the half-pay promised to the officers for life was nearly five hundred thousand dollars. The validity of the engagement was questioned. The grant was disliked by the common soldiers; it found no favor in the legislature of Massachusetts; the delegates of Connecticut and Rhode Island were instructed to oppose it altogether. To avoid defeat, this article was laid over till there should be a fuller representation.[3] Delegates from the states in which the domestic debt was chiefly held, hoped for efficient co-operation from the army.[4] Here came to light a great difference of interests. Pennsylvania was the largest creditor; Massachusetts ranked next; Georgia and South Carolina were the lowest; Virginia was but the ninth, holding less than New Hampshire and not half so much as Rhode Island. The zeal for the equal support of all classes of public creditors culminated in those states whose citizens originally owned nearly four times as much as those of all the six southern states, and by transfers were constantly acquiring more.[5]

---

[1] Journals of Congress, iv. 152.
[2] Report of the deputies in Sparks, viii. 553. The amount of this one month's pay was 253,232.86 dollars. Old account-books in Treasury dept. Waste-book D, Ledger B. MS.
[3] Gilpin, 281, 321 ; Elliot, 31, 45.
[4] Gilpin, 350 ; Elliot, 55.
[5] Gilpin, 364, note ; Elliot, 60.

Adopting unanimously a resolution which Hamilton had prepared, congress pledged itself to consider immediately the most likely mode of obtaining revenues adequate to the funding of the whole debt of the United States.[1] Encouraged by this seeming heartiness, Wilson of Pennsylvania, on the twenty-seventh, spoke for something more than a "form of words," and proposed "the establishment of general funds to be collected by congress."[2] To the dismay of the friends of a general revenue, Theodorick Bland of Virginia interposed and officially presented the act of his state repealing the grant of the impost, and a resolution of both its houses declaring its present inability to pay more than fifty thousand pounds Virginia currency toward the demands of congress for 1782.[3]

The debate, nevertheless, went on. Gorham of Massachusetts suggested polls and commerce as most proper objects of taxation. Hamilton, discussing the subject in a comprehensive manner, spoke for permanent sources of revenue which should extend uniformly throughout the United States, and be collected by the authority of congress. Dyer strongly disliked the appointment of collectors by congress; the states would never consent to it. Ramsay of South Carolina supported Gorham and Hamilton. Again Bland placed himself in the way, saying:" The states are so averse to a general revenue in the hands of congress that, even if it were proper, it is unattainable." He

---

[1] Gilpin, 277, 280; Elliot, 30, 31. Journal of the House of Delegates, pp. 80, 90.
[2] Gilpin, 282, 285; Elliot, 32.
[3] Resolution of 28 Dec., 1782, in

therefore advised congress to pursue the rule of the confederation and ground requisitions on an actual valuation of houses and lands in the several states.

At this stage of the discussion, an efficient reply could be made only by one who was of Virginia. To Randolph, then in Richmond, Madison had already written:" Virginia could never have cut off the impost at a more unlucky crisis than when she is protesting her inability to comply with the continental requisitions. Congress cannot abandon the plan as long as there is a spark of hope. Nay, other plans on a like principle must be added. Justice, gratitude, our reputation abroad and our tranquillity at home, require provision for a debt of not less than fifty millions of dollars; and this provision will not be adequately met by separate acts of the states. If there are not revenue laws which operate at the same time through all the states, and are exempt from the control of each, mutual jealousies will assuredly defraud both our foreign and domestic creditors of their just claims."[1]

Madison, on the twenty-eighth, presented a milder form of the resolution for a general revenue. Arthur Lee lost no time in confronting his colleague: "The states will never consent to a uniform tax, because it will be unequal; is repugnant to the articles of confederation; and, by placing the purse in the same hands with the sword, subverts the fundamental principles of liberty." Wilson explained: The articles of confederation have expressly provided

[1] Madison to Randolph, 22 Jan., 1783, in Gilpin, 111. The date is given as of 1782 by an obvious error.

CHAP. V.

1 7 8 3.
Jan. 28.

for amendments; there is more of a centrifugal than centripetal force in the states; the funding of a common debt would invigorate the union. Ellsworth despaired of a continental revenue; condemned periodical requisitions from congress as inadequate; and inclined to the trial of permanent state funds. In reply, Hamilton showed that state funds would meet with even greater obstacles than a general revenue; but he lost the sympathy of the house by adding that the influence of federal collectors would assist in giving energy to the federal government. Rutledge thought that the prejudices of the people were opposed to a general tax, and seemed disinclined to it himself. Williamson was of opinion that continental funds, though desirable, were unattainable.

"The idea," said Madison, "of erecting our national independence on the ruins of public faith and national honor must be horrid to every mind which retains either honesty or pride. Is a continental revenue indispensably necessary for doing complete justice to the public creditors? This is the question.

"A punctual compliance by thirteen independent governments with periodical demands of money from congress can never be reckoned upon with certainty. The articles of confederation authorize confess to borrow money. To borrow money, permanent and certain provision is necessary; and, as this cannot be made in any other way, a general revenue is within the spirit of the confederation. Congress are already invested by the states with constitutional authority over the purse as well as the sword. A general revenue would only give this authority a more certain and equal efficacy.

"The necessity and reasonableness of a general revenue have been gaining ground among the states. I am aware that one exception ought to be made. The state of Virginia, as appears by an act yesterday laid before congress, has withdrawn its assent once given to the scheme. This circumstance cannot but embarrass a representative of that state advocating it; one, too, whose principles are extremely unfavorable to a disregard of the sense of constituents. But, though the delegates who compose congress more immediately represent and are amenable to the states from which they come, yet they owe a fidelity to the collective interests of the whole. The part I take is the more fully justified to my own mind by my thorough persuasion that, with the same knowledge of public affairs which my station commands, the legislature of Virginia would not have repealed the law in favor of the impost, and would even now rescind the repeal."

On the following day, the proposition of Wilson and Madison, with slight amendments, passed the committee of the whole without opposition. On the twelfth of February, it was adopted in congress by seven states in the affirmative, and without the negative of any state.

For methods of revenue, the choice of Madison[1] was an impost, a poll-tax which should rate blacks somewhat lower than whites, and a moderate land-tax. To these, Wilson wished to add a duty on salt

[1] Gilpin, 300; Elliot, 38.

and an excise on wine, imported spirits, and coffee.[1] Hamilton, who held the attempt at a land-tax to be futile and impossible, suggested a house and window-tax.[2] Wolcott[3] of Connecticut thought requisitions should be in proportion to the population of each state; but was willing to include in the enumeration those only of the blacks who were within sixteen and sixty years of age.

The public mind was ripening for a transition from a confederation to a real government. Just at this time Pelatiah Webster, a graduate of Yale college, in a dissertation published at Philadelphia,[4] proposed for the legislature of the United States a congress of two houses which should have ample authority for making laws" of general necessity and utility," and enforcing them as well on individuals as on states. He further suggested not only heads of executive departments, but judges of law and chancery. The tract awakened so much attention that it was reprinted in Hartford, and called forth a reply.

These speculations offered only a remote solution of the difficulties under which the confederation was sinking. How the united demand of all public creditors could wrest immediately from congress and the states the grant of a general revenue and power for its collection employed the thoughts of Robert Morris and his friends. On Christmas eve, 1781, Gouverneur Morris, the assistant financier, had written to

---

[1] Gilpin, 304-306; Elliot, 39, 40.
[2] Gilpin, 300; Elliot, 38.
[3] Gilpin, 331; Elliot, 48.
[4] A Dissertation on the Political Union and Constitution of the thirteen United States of North America, written 16 Feb., 1783. In Pelatiah Webster's Political Essays, p. 228.

Greene: "I have no expectation that the government will acquire force; and no hope that our union can subsist, except in the form of an absolute monarchy, and this does not seem to consist with the taste and temper of the people."[1] To Jay, in January, 1783,[2] he wrote: "The army have swords in their hands. Good will arise from the situation to which we are hastening; much of convulsion will probably ensue, yet it must terminate in giving to government that power without which government is but a name."

Hamilton held it as certain that the army had secretly determined not to lay down their arms until due provision and a satisfactory prospect should be afforded on the subject of their pay; that the commander was already become extremely unpopular among all ranks from his known dislike to every unlawful proceeding; but, as from his virtue, his patriotism, and firmness, he would sooner suffer himself to be cut in pieces than yield to disloyal plans, Hamilton wished him to be the "conductor of the army in their plans for redress," to the exclusion of a leader like Horatio Gates.[3]

With these convictions and with exceeding; caution, he, on the seventh of February, addressed himself directly to Washington in a letter, of which Brooks, on his return to the camp, was the bearer. "Congress," so he wrote, "is a body not governed by reason or foresight, but by circumstances. Appearances afford too much ground for a prevailing opinion

---

[1] Gouveraeur Morris to General Greene, 24 Dec, 1781, Sparks' Life of G. Morris, i. 240.
[2] Gouverneur Morris to John Jay, Jan., 1783. Sparks' Life of Morris, i. 349.
[3] Gilpin, 350, 351 ; Elliot, 55.

in the army, that, if they once lay down their arms, they part with the means of obtaining justice. Their claims, urged with moderation but with firmness, may operate on those weak minds which are influenced by their apprehensions more than by their judgments, so as to produce a concurrence in the measures which the exigencies of affairs demand. To restore public credit is the object of all men of sense; in this the influence of the army, properly directed, may co-oper-ate." And he invited Washington to make use of General Knox,[1] to whom Gouverneur Morris wrote on the same day and by the same channel.

To ensure the concerted action of the southern army, Gouverneur Morris wrote privately to Greene: "The main army will not easily forego their expectations. Their murmurs, though not loud, are deep. If the army, in common with all other public creditors, insist on the grant of general, permanent funds for liquidating all the public debts, there can be little doubt that such revenues will be obtained, and will afford to every order of public creditors a solid security with the due exception of miracles, there is no probability that the states will ever make such grants unless the army be united and determined in the pursuit of it, and unless they be firmly supported by and as firmly support the other creditors. That this may happen must be the entire wish of every intelligently just man and of every real friend to our glorious revolution."[2]

[1] Hamilton to Washington, 7 Feb., 1783. Hamilton, i. 327.
[2] Gouverneur Morris to General Greene, 15 Feb., 1783. Sparks' Life of G. Morris, i. 250.

A PLAN TO FORCE A STRONGER UNION.

The letter of Gouverneur Morris to Knox, which was in reality designed to be a communication through Knox to Washington, cannot be found. It evidently expressed the opinion that the army might be made to co-operate in bringing about a closer union of the states and a stronger government. The answer of Knox expresses the advice of Washington: "The army are good patriots, and would forward everything that would tend to produce union and a permanent general constitution; but they are yet to be taught how their influence is to effect this matter. A 'hoop to the barrel' is their favorite toast. America will have fought and bled to little purpose, if the powers of government shall be insufficient to preserve the peace, and this must be the case without general funds. As the present constitution is so defective, why do not you great men call the people together and tell them so—that is, to have a convention of the states to form a better constitution? This appears to us, who have a superficial view only, to be the most efficacious remedy."[1]

CHAP. V.

1783. Feb.

21.

---

[1] Knox to G. Morris, 21 Feb., 1783, in Sparks' Life of G. Morris, i. 256. That the commander-in-chief and Knox consulted together, appears, among other reasons, from these :— they cherished the most affectionate relations to each other ; Hamilton on this occasion referred Washington to Knox : The words "America will have fought and bled to little purpose" are substantially words which Washington used to Hamilton, to Harrison the governor of Virginia, to Arthur Lee, to Gordon the historian, and to others ; Knox says, "the present constitution is so defective," Washington, "the great defect of our constitution." Knox writes to bid Morris address the people, and so does Washington to Hamilton ; Knox, as if announcing Washington's opinion, writes, "to us who have a superficial view only," and Washington complains to Hamilton of the want of information from Congress of the political and pecuniary state of affairs ; Knox stands at the side of Washington in all that follows at Newburg. Compare Washington to Bland, 4 April, 1783. MS.

On the thirteenth of February the speech of the king of Great Britain, at the opening of parliament in December, was received. His announcement of provisional articles of peace with the United States produced great joy; yet that joy was clouded by apprehensions from the impossibility of meeting the just claims of the army.[1]

Congress was brought no nearer to decisive action. Hamilton proposed that the doors of congress should be thrown wide open whenever the finances were under discussion, though the proposal, had it been accepted, would have filled the galleries with holders of certificates of the public debt.[2]

On the other side, Rutledge again and again moved that the proceeds of the impost should be appropriated exclusively to the army, but was supported only by his own state. Ruffled by his indifference to the civil creditors, Wilson had one day answered with warmth: "Pennsylvania will take her own measures without regard to those of congress, and she ought to do so. She is willing to sink or swim according to the common fate; but she will not suffer herself, with a millstone of six millions of the continental debt, to go to the bottom alone."[3] The weakness of the friends of a general revenue appeared from their consenting to leave to the several states the appointment of the collectors of taxes, and to limit the grant of the impost to twenty-five years.[4]

Once more, Mercer and Arthur Lee renewed their war upon Madison, who in reply made a convincing

---

[1] Gilpin, 336 ; Elliot, 50.
[2] Gilpin, 341 ; Elliot, 53.
[3] Gilpin, 314 ; Elliot, 43.
[4] Gilpin, 347, 348 ; Elliot, 54.

A PLAN TO FORCE A STRONGER UNION.

plea for the necessity of a permanent general revenue, "The purse," repeated Arthur Lee, "ought never to be put in the same hand with the sword. I will be explicit; I would rather see congress a rope of sand than a rod of iron. Virginia ought not to concur in granting to congress a permanent revenue." "If the federal compact is such as has been represented," said Mercer, "I will immediately withdraw from congress, and do everything in my power to destroy its existence." Chafed by these expressions, Gorham of Massachusetts cried out: "The sooner this is known the better, that some of the states may form other confederacies adequate to their safety."[1]

The assiduous labors of congress for two months had failed to devise the means for restoring public credit. In February some of its members thought the time had arrived when order and credit could come from the demands of the army supported by its strength. Robert Morris extorted from congress a removal of the injunction of secrecy on his letter of resignation, and forthwith sent a copy of it not only to Washington but to the public press, through which it immediately reached the army.

[1] Gilpin, 357, 511 ; Elliot, 57.

CHAPTER VI.

THE ARMY AND ITS CHIEF.

MARCH, 1783.

CHAP. VI.

1783. March.

The commander-in-chief would gladly have visited Mount Vernon during the winter, but suppressed the wish, for the army at Newburg was more unquiet than at any former period.[1] The Massachusetts line formed more than half of it, and so many of the remainder were from other eastern states that he could describe them all as New England men.[2] He had made the delicate state of affairs "the object of many contemplative hours," and he was aware of the prevailing sentiment that the prospect of compensation for past services would terminate with the war.[3]

4.

Now that peace was at hand, his first act was by a letter to Harrison, then governor of Virginia, to entreat his own state to enter upon the movement toward a real union. "From the observations have made

---

[1] Sparks, viii. 355, 369.
[2] Gorham in Gilpin, 315. Elliot, 43. Washington to Joseph Jones, 11 Feb., 1783. Sparks, viii. 383; and compare Sparks, viii. 456.
[3] Washington to Hamilton, 4 March, 1783. Sparks, viii. 389, 390.

in the course of this war—and my intercourse with the states in their united as well as separate capacities has afforded ample opportunities of judging—I am decided in my opinion," such were his words, "that, if the powers of congress are not enlarged and made competent to all general purposes, the blood which has been spilt, the expense that has been incurred, and the distresses which have been felt, will avail nothing; and that the band which holds us together, already too weak, will soon be broken; when anarchy and confusion will prevail.[1] I shall make no apology for the freedom of these sentiments; they proceed from an honest heart; they will at least prove the sincerity of my friendship, as they are altogether undisguised." The governor received this letter as a public appeal, and placed it among the archives of Virginia.

Before the officers had taken into consideration the cautious report of their committee to congress, Colonel Walter Stewart, an inspector of troops, coming back from Philadelphia, presented himself at the quarters of Gates as "a kind of agent from the friends of the army in congress;"[2] and rumors were immediately circulated through the camp that it was universally expected the army would not disband until they had obtained justice; that the public creditors looked up to them for aid, and, if necessary, would even join them in the field; that some members of congress wished the measure might take effect, in order to

---

[1] Washington to Harrison, 4 March, 1783. Maxwell's Virginia Historical Register, vi. 36, 37.
[2] Gates to Armstrong, 22 June, 1783. I follow a manuscript copy received from J. K. Armstrong. The letter has been printed in United States Magazine, i. 40.

compel the public, particularly the delinquent states, to do justice.¹

A plan of action was in the utmost secrecy devised by Gates and those around him. To touch "with ability the several chords of feeling which lay slumbering in the army, his aide-de-camp, Major John Armstrong, was selected to draft an address. This was copied, and Colonel Barber, the assistant adjutant-general of the division of Gates, taking care not to be tracked, put it in circulation through the line of every state,² with a notice for a meeting of the general and field officers on the next day, to consider what measures should be adopted to obtain that redress of grievances which they seemed to have solicited in vain.³

"My friends!" so ran the anonymous appeal, "after seven long years your suffering courage has conducted the United States of America through a doubtful and a bloody war; and peace returns to bless —whom? A country willing to redress your wrongs, cherish your worth, and reward your services? Or is it rather a country that tramples upon your rights, disdains your cries, and insults your distresses? Have you not lately, in the meek language of humble petitioners, begged from the justice of congress what you could no longer expect from their favor? How have you been answered? Let the letter which you are called to consider to-morrow make reply!

"If this be your treatment while the swords you wear are necessary for the defence of America, what

---

¹ Washington to Joseph Jones, 12 March, 1783. Sparks, viii. 393, 394. Washington to Hamilton, 12 March, 1783. Hamilton, i. 343.

² Gates to Armstrong, 22 June, 1783.

³ Journal of Congress, iv. 208.

have you to expect when those very swords, the instruments and companions of your glory, shall be taken from your sides, and no mark of military distinction left but your wants, infirmities, and scars? If you have sense enough to discover and spirit to oppose tyranny, whatever garb it may assume, awake to your situation. If the present moment be lost, your threats hereafter will be as empty as your entreaties now. Appeal from the justice to the fears of government; and suspect the man"—here Washington was pointed at—"who would advise to longer forbearance."[1]

A copy of the address reached Washington on Tuesday, the eleventh, and the meeting was to take place in the evening of that very day. Resolutions dictated by passion and tending to anarchy, if once adopted, could never be effaced, and might bring ruin on the army and the nation. There was need of instant action, "to arrest the feet that stood wavering on a precipice."[2] To change ill-considered menaces into a legal presentment of grievances, the commander, in general orders, disapproved the anonymous and irregular invitation to a meeting, and at the same time requested all the highest officers and a representtation of the rest to assemble at twelve o'clock on the next Saturday to hear the report of the committee which they had sent to congress. "After mature deliberation, they will devise what further measures ought to be adopted to attain the Just and important object in view. The senior officer in rank present

[1] Journal of Congress, iv. 308.   [2] Washington to Hamilton, 12 March, 1783. Hamilton, i. 344.

96   THE CONFEDERATION.

CHAP. VI.

1783.
March 11.

15.

will preside and report the result of their deliberations to the commander-in-chief." Gates quailed, and the gathering for that evening was given up; but under his eye Armstrong prepared a second anonymous address, which, while it professed to consider the general orders of Washington "as giving stability to their resolves," recommended "suspicion" as their "sentinel." During the week, Washington employed himself, with Knox and others whom he could trust, in preparing methods to avert every fatal consequence.

At noon on the fifteenth, the officers assembled, with Gates in the chair. They were surprised to find that the commander-in-chief was with them. Every eye was fixed on him; and all were mute, awaiting his words.[1]

After an apology to his "brother officers" for his presence, he read his analysis of the anonymous addresses. Their author he praised for his rhetorical skill, but denied the rectitude of his heart, and denounced his scheme as fit to proceed from no one but a British emissary. He thus continued:

"As I was among the first who embarked in the cause of our common country; as I have never left your side one moment, but when called from you on public duty; as I have been the constant companion and witness of your distresses, it can scarcely be supposed that I am indifferent to your interests." He proceeded to demonstrate that any attempt to compel an instant compliance with their demands would certainly remove to a still greater distance the attainment of their ends. They must place their reliance

[1] Shaw to Rev. John Eliot, 27 April, 1783.

on their plighted faith of their country and the purity of the intentions of congress to render them ample justice, though its deliberations, from the difficulty of reconciling different interests, might be slow.

"For myself," he said, "so far as consistent with the great duty I owe to my country and those powers we are bound to respect, you may command my services to the utmost extent of my abilities.

"While I give you these assurances, let me entreat you, gentlemen, on your part, not to take any measures which, in the calm light of reason, will lessen the dignity and sully the glory you have hitherto maintained. Let me conjure you in the name of our common country, as you value your own sacred honor, as you respect the rights of humanity, and as you regard the military and national character of America, to express your utmost horror and detestation of the man who wickedly attempts to open the floodgates of civil discord and deluge our rising empire in blood.

"By thus determining and thus acting, you will pursue the plain and direct road to the attainment of your wishes; you will give one more proof of unexampled patriotism and patient virtue, rising superior to the pressure of the most complicated sufferings; and you will afford occasion for posterity to say: 'Had this day been wanting, the world had never seen the last stage of perfection to which human nature is capable of attaining'"[1]

On concluding his address, the general, in further proof of the good disposition of congress, began to

---

[1] Journals of Congress, iv. 213.

read parts of a letter from a member of that body; but, after getting through a single paragraph, he paused, and asked leave of his audience to put on spectacles, which he had so lately received[1] that he had never yet worn them in public,[2] saying: "I have grown gray in your service, and now find myself growing blind." These unaffected words touched every heart. The letter, which was from Joseph Jones of Virginia, set forth the embarrassments of congress and their resolve that the army should at all events be justly dealt with. Washington then withdrew.

Officers, who a few hours before had yielded themselves to the anonymous addresses, veered about, and would now follow no counselor but their own commander. The assembly unanimously thanked him for his communications and assured him of their affection, "with the greatest sincerity of which the human heart is capable." Then, after a reference to Knox, Brooks, and Howard as their committee, they resolved unanimously: "At the commencement of the present war, the officers of the American army engaged in the service of their country from the purest love and attachment to the rights and liberties of human nature, which motives still exist in the highest degree; and no circumstances of distress or danger shall induce a conduct that may tend to sully the reputation and glory which they have acquired at the price of their blood and eight years' faithful

---

[1] From Rittenhouse. Washington to Rittenhouse, 16 Feb., 1783; Memoirs of Rittenhouse, 399, 300.

[2] "C'étoit la premiere fois qu'il Les prenoit en publique." Mazzei, Recherches, iv. 122.

services."[1] Making no demands and confining their expectations within the most reasonable limits, they declared their unshaken confidence in the justice of congress and their country, and they asked nothing of their chief but to urge congress to a speedy decision upon their late memorial.

CHAP. VI.

1783. March 15.

Another resolution declared, "that the officers of the American army view with abhorrence and reject with disdain the infamous propositions contained in a late anonymous address to them." Gates meekly put the question; and was obliged to report that it was carried unanimously.

No one ever ruled the hearts of his officers like Washington. The army of America had seen him calm and commanding in the rage of battle; patient and persistent under multiplied misfortunes; moderate in victory; but then he had been countenanced by his troops and his friends; here he stood alone, amidst injured men, of inflamed passions, with swords at their sides, persuaded that forbearance would be their ruin, and, for a fearful moment, looking upon him as their adversary. As he spoke, every cloud was scattered, and the full light of love of country broke forth. Happy for America that she had a patriot army; happy for America and for the world that that army had Washington for its chief!

The official narrative of these events was received in congress on the twenty-second; and, before the day came to an end, nine states concurred in a resolution[2] commuting the half-pay promised to the officers

22.

---

[1] Journals of Congress, iv. 215.   [2] Bland to Washington, 22 March, 1783. MS.

into a sum equal to five years, full pay, to be discharged by certificates, bearing interest at six per cent. Georgia and Rhode Island were not adequately represented; New Hampshire and New Jersey voted in the negative; all the other states irrevocably pledged the United States to redeem their promise made to the officers in the dark hours of their encampment at Valley Forge.

On the next day, a ship dispatched from Cadiz by d'Estaing, at the instance of Lafayette, brought authentic news that the American and British commissioners had signed definitively a provisional treaty, of which an official copy had been received eleven days before, and that peace with Great Britain had already taken effect. The American boundaries on the north-west exceeded alike the demands and the hopes of congress; and it was already believed that a later generation would make its way to the Pacific ocean.[1]

The glad tidings drew from Washington tears of joy in that "happiest moment of his life." "All the world is touched by his republican virtues," wrote Luzerne. "It will be in vain for him to wish to hide himself and live as a simple, private man; he will always be the first citizen of the United States."[2]

Upon official information from Franklin and Adams, congress on the eleventh of April made proclamation for the cessation of hostilities. In announcing the great event to the army, Washington did especial honor to the men who had enlisted for the war, and

---

[1] Luzerne to Vergennes, 19 March, 1783. MS.

[2] Luzerne to Vergennes, 29 March, 1783. MS.

added: "Happy, thrice happy shall they be pronounced hereafter who have contributed anything in erecting this stupendous fabric of freedom and empire; who have assisted in protecting the rights of human nature, and establishing an asylum for the poor and oppressed of all nations and religions."[1] The proclamation of congress that war was at an end was published to the army on the nineteenth, exactly eight years from the day when the embattled farmers of Concord "fired the shot heard round the world."

[1] Sparks, viii, 568.

CHAPTER VII.

DISBANDING THE ARMY.

MARCH — JULY, 1783.

Washington presented the rightful claims of the "patriot army"[1] with a warmth and energy which never but this once appear in his communications to congress; and his words gained intenser power from his disinterestedness. To a committee on which were Bland and Hamilton, he enforced, by every consideration of gratitude, justice, honor, and national pride, the "universal" expectations of the army, that, before their disbanding, they should receive pay for at least one month in hand, with an absolute assurance in a short time of pay for two months more. "The financier will take his own measures; but this sum must be procured. The soldier is willing to risk the hard-earned remainder due him for four, five, perhaps six years upon the same basis of security with the general mass of other public creditors."[2]

---

[1] Washington to congress, 18 March, 1783. parks, viii. 396–399.

[2] Washington to Bland, 4 April, 1783. MS.

DISBANDING THE ARMY. 103

"The expectations of the army," answered Hamilton, "are moderation itself."¹ But, after a week's reflection, Morris, who had already written to congress "our public credit is gone,"² replied to the committee that the amount of three months' pay was more than all the receipts from all the states since 1781; that there was no resource but the issue of paper notes in anticipation of revenue.³

A sharp admonition from Vergennes to the United States speedily to meet their engagements in France and Holland,⁴ and the representations of Washington, quickened the determination of congress. In preparing the plan for a revenue, Madison was assisted by Jefferson, who passed a large part of the winter in Philadelphia.

The national debt of Great Britain at the beginning of the war with America amounted to one hundred and thirty-six millions of pounds; at the close of it, including deficiencies that were still to be funded, it amounted to twice that sum. The debt of the United States did not much exceed forty-two millions of dollars; the annual interest on that debt was not far from two and a half millions, and to fund it successfully there was need of a yearly revenue of at least that sum. One million was hoped for from specific duties on enumerated imports, and a duty of five per cent, on the value of all others. A million and a half dollars more were to be raised by requisitions of congress, apportioned on the states

CHAP. VII.

1 7 8 3.
April.

---

¹ Hamilton to Washington, 11 April, 1783. Letters to Washington, iv. 17.
² Dip. Cor., xii. 342.
³ R. Morris to Hamilton, 14 April, 1783. Dip. Cor., xii, 346.
⁴ Luzerne to R. Morris, 15 March, 1783. Dip. Cor., xi. 157, 158.

according to population. This more convenient method had hitherto failed from conflicts on the rule for counting; slaves. The south had insisted on the ratio of two for one freeman. Williamson of North Carolina said: "I am principled against slavery. I think slaves an incumbrance to society instead of increasing its ability to pay taxes."[1] To effect an agreement, Madison, seconded by Rutledge, offered that slaves should be rated as five to three, and this compromise, which then affected taxation only and not representation, was accepted almost with unanimity.[2]

In the beginning of April, Hamilton had declared in congress that he wished to strengthen the federal constitution through a general convention, and should soon, in pursuance of instructions from his constituents, propose a plan for that purpose.[3] In the mean time, he remained inflexible in the opinion that an attempt to obtain revenue by an application to the several states would be futile, because an agreement could never be arrived at through partial deliberations. The vote on the report of the new financial measure, which he opposed as inadequate, was taken on the eighteenth of April. Georgia alone was absent; eleven states were fully represented; New Hampshire by a single delegate Higginson, of Massachusetts agreed with Hamilton; and for the most opposite reasons, they two and the two representatives of Rhode Island, answered no. New York being divided, nine states and a half against

---

[1] Gilpin, 423; Elliot, 79.
[2] Gilpin, 423, 424; Elliot, 79.
[3] Gilpin, 429, 430; Elliot, 81.

one, twenty-five delegates against four, gave their votes for the adoption of the report.

To the relentless exigencies of the moment the financial proposition of the eighteenth of April offered no relief, nor could it take effect until it should be accepted by every one of the thirteen states. To win this unanimous assent, congress, in the words of Madison, enforced the peculiar nature of their obligation to France, to members of the republic of Holland, and to the army. Moreover, "the citizens of the United States are responsible for the greatest trust ever confided to a political society. If justice, good faith, honor, gratitude, and all the other qualities which ennoble the character of a nation and fulfil the ends of government, be the fruits of our unadulterated forms of republican government, the cause of liberty will acquire a dignity and luster which it has never yet enjoyed; and an example will be set which cannot but have the most favorable influence on the rights of mankind." New York, North and South Carolina, and Massachusetts were following the example of Virginia, and repealing their revenue acts of former years; when the address went forth, accompanied by the letter of congress to the governor of Rhode Island which Hamilton had drafted, and by various papers showing the amount and the character of the debt of the United States.

Then, on the twenty-eighth, and so far as the records show never till then, congress appointed a committee on the New York resolutions of the preceding July in favor of a general convention. Its choice

CHAP.
VII.

1 7 8 3.

fell on Ellsworth, Carroll, Wilson, Gorham, Hamilton, Peters, McHenry, Izard, and Duane.¹

In October, 1780, congress provided for forming new states out of the north-western territory.² A most elaborate report, read in November, 1781, recommended that the lands for settlements "should be laid out into townships of about six miles square."³ Early in 1783 Rufus Putnam, and other officers and soldiers of the army in New England, engaged heartily in a plan to form a state westward of the Ohio, and Timothy Pickering proposed to them that "the total exclusion of slavery from the state should form an essential and irrevocable part of the constitution."⁴ To "unite the thirteen states in one great political interest," Bland, a man of culture, who had served with credit as a colonel of dragoons, and had been a member of congress from Virginia since 1780, now,

June 5.

on the fifth of June, 1783, brought forward an "ordinance" to accept conditionally the cession of Virginia, divide it into districts of two degrees of latitude by three degrees of longitude, and subdivide each district into townships of a fixed number of miles square; each district to be received into the union as a "sovereign" state, so soon as it could count twenty thousand inhabitants. In these em-

---

¹ Madison, on whom we depend for a report of the debates of congress of that period, was absent from Saturday, April the twenty-sixth, to Tuesday, May sixth So details are wanting. That Clinton's letter and the New York resolutions were committed on the twenty-eighth of April, we know from a MS. memorandum by Charles Thomson.

² Laws relating to Public Lands, 338 ; Journals of Congress, iii. 535.

³ Endorsement on the original report in the state department is: "Read in congress 3 Nov., 1781."

⁴ Pickering's Pickering, i. 546. He formed a complete plan for settling lands in Ohio.

bryo states, every one who had enlisted for the war or had served for three years was to receive the bounty lands promised him, and thirty acres more for each dollar due to him from the United States. One tenth part of the soil was to be reserved for "the payment of the civil list of the United States, the erecting of frontier posts, and the founding of seminaries of learning; the surplus to be appropriated to the building and equipping a navy, and to no other purpose whatever." This pioneer ordinance for colonizing the territory north-west of the Ohio was seconded by Hamilton, and referred to a grand committee.[1]

From the moment when it became officially known that a preliminary treaty of peace had been concluded, Robert Morris persistently demanded the immediate discharge of the army.[2] The city of New York and the interior posts being still in British hands, his importunity was resisted by Gorham and Hamilton, and disapproved by the secretary of foreign affairs; but the public penury overcame all scruples.

As the time drew near for the officers to pass from military service to civil life, they recalled the example of the Roman Cincinnatus, and, adopting his name, formed themselves into "one society of friends," to perpetuate "the spirit of brotherly kindness" and to help officers and their families in their times of need. An immutable attachment to the rights and

---

[1] Papers of Old Congress, xxxvi. MS. The ordinance is in the handwriting of Theodorick Bland, and indorsed by Charles Thomson: "Motion of Mr, Bland seconded by Mr. Hamilton. June 5, 1783. Referred to the grand committee of 30 May, 1783."

[2] Diary of Morris in Dip. Cor., xii. 367, note.

liberties of human nature was made the law of conduct for members, to whatever nation they might belong; and those who were Americans pledged to each other their "unalterable determination to promote and cherish union between the states."[1] By one grave error, which called forth from many sides in America and in Europe the severest censure, membership was made hereditary in their eldest male posterity. The commander-in-chief, who had no offspring, refused to separate himself from his faithful associates in the war; but by his influence the society at its first general meeting in May, 1784, proposed to its branches in the states to expunge from its constitution the clauses which had excited alarm and just complaint.

June 2.

The general order of the second day of June published the resolve of congress that the men engaged for the war, with a proper proportion of officers, were immediately to receive furloughs, on the reverse of which was their discharge, to take effect on the definitive treaty of peace. Washington felt the keenest sensibility at their distresses;[2] but he had exhausted all his influence. The army, for three months' pay, received only notes exactly "like other notes issued from the office of finance."[3] These were nominally due in six months to the bearer, with six per cent interest till paid. Their value in the market was two shillings or two and sixpence for twenty shil-

---

[1] Sparks, ix. 23, note.
[2] Washington to Heath, 6 June, 1783. Sparks, viii. 435.
[3] Washington to land, 4 April 1783, MS.; Journals of Congress, for July 9 and following days, iv. 237, 238; Morris to congress, 18 July, 1783, Dip. Cor., xii. 376, 380–386 and 387–389, and other letters.

DISBANDING THE ARMY.

shillings.¹ The veterans were enthusiasts for liberty, and therefore, with the consciousness of having done their duty to their native land and to mankind, they, in perfect good order, bearing with them their arms as memorials of their service, retired to their homes "without a settlement of their accounts, and without a farthing of money in their pockets."²

The events of the last four months called into full action the powers and emotions of Washington. "State politics," said he, "interfere too much with the more liberal and extensive plan of government which wisdom and foresight would dictate. The honor, power, and true interest of this country must be measured by a continental scale. To form a new constitution that will give consistency stability, and dignity to the union and sufficient powers to the great council of the nation for general purposes, is a duty incumbent upon every man who wishes well to his country."³

Lifted above himself, and borne on by the energy of his belief, he in June addressed the whole people through a last circular to the governor of every state,⁴ for he was persuaded that immediate and extreme danger overhung the life of the union. "With this conviction of the importance of the present crisis," such are his words, "silence in me would be a crime; I will therefore speak without disguise the language of freedom freedom and of sincerity. Those who

---

¹ Pelatiah Webster's Political Essays, 310; compare 272.
² Washington to Congress, 7 and 24 June, 1783. Sparks, viii. 438, 456.
³ Washington to Lafayette, 5 April, 1783. Sparks, viii. 412.
⁴ Sparks, viii. 439. The date of the circular varies with the time of its emission.

CHAP. VII.

1783.
June.

differ from me in political sentiment may remark that I am stepping out of the proper line of my duty; but the rectitude of my own heart, the part I have hitherto acted, experience acquired by long and close attention to the business of that country in whose service I have spent the prime of my life and whose happiness will always constitute my own, the ardent desire I feel of enjoying in private life, after all the toils of war, the benefits of a wise and liberal government, will sooner or later convince my countrymen that this address is the result of the purest intention."

Thoughtful for the defence of the republic, the retiring commander-in-chief recommended "a proper peace establishment," and an absolutely uniform organization of the "militia of the union" throughout "the continent." He leaded for complete justice to all classes of public creditors. He entreated the legislature of each state to pension its disabled non-commissioned officers and privates. He enforced the duty of the states, without "hesitating a single moment," to give their sanction to the act of congress establishing a revenue for the United States, for the only alternative was a national bankruptcy; and "honesty will be found on every experiment to be the best and only true policy. In what part of the continent shall we find any man or body of men who would not blush to propose measures purposely calculated to rob the soldier of his stipend, and the public creditor of his due?"

He then proceeded to pronounce solemn judgment, and to summon the people of America to fulfil their duty to Providence and to their fellow-men. "If a spirit of disunion, or obstinacy and perverseness, should in any of the states attempt to frustrate all the happy effects that might be expected to flow from the union, that state which puts itself in opposition to the aggregate wisdom of the continent will alone be responsible for all the consequences.[1]

"The citizens of America, the sole lords and proprietors of a vast tract of continent, are now acknowledged to be possessed of absolute freedom and independency. Here Heaven has crowned all its other blessings, by giving a fairer opportunity for political happiness than any other nation has ever been favored with. The rights of mankind are better understood and more clearly defined than at any former period. The collected wisdom acquired through a long succession of years is laid open for our use in the establishment of our forms of government. The free cultivation of letters, the unbounded extension of commerce, the progressive refinement of manners, the growing liberality of sentiment, and, above all, the pure and benign light of revelation, have had a meliorating influence on mankind. At this auspicious period, the United States came into existence as a nation.

"Happiness is ours, if we seize the occasion and make it our own. This is the moment to give such a tone to our federal government as will enable it to answer the ends of its institution. According to the system of policy the states shall adopt at this moment, it is to be decided whether the revolution must ultimately be considered as a blessing or a

[1] Sparks, viii. 446, 447.

curse; a blessing or accurse, not to the present age alone, for with our fate will the destiny of unborn millions be involved.

"Essential to the existence of the United States is the friendly disposition which will forget local prejudices and policies, make mutual concessions to the general prosperity, and, in some instances, sacrifice individual advantages to the interest of the community. Liberty is the basis of the glorious fabric of our independency and national character, and whoever would dare to sap the foundation, or overturn the structure, under whatever specious pretext he may attempt it, will merit the bitterest execration and the severest punishment which can be inflicted by his injured country.

"It is indispensable to the happiness of the individual states that there should be lodged somewhere a supreme power to regulate and govern the general concerns of the confederated republic, without which the union cannot be of long duration,[1] and everything must very rapidly tend to anarchy and confusion. Whatever measures have a tendency to dissolve the union, or to violate or lessen the sovereign authority, ought to be considered as hostile to the liberty and independence of America. It is only in our united character that we are known as an empire, that our independence is acknowledged, that our power can be regarded, or our credit supported among foreign nations. The treaties of the European powers with the United States of America will have no validity on a dissolution of the union. We shall be left nearly

[1] Sparks, viii. 444.

DISBANDING THE ARMY. 113

a state of nature; or we may find by our own unhappy experience that there is a natural and necessary progression from the extreme of anarchy to the extreme of tyranny, and that arbitrary power is most easily established on the ruins of liberty abused to licentiousness."

This circular letter of Washington the governors of each state, according to his request, communicated to their respective legislatures. In this way it was borne to every home in the United States, and he entreated the people to receive it as "his legacy" on his retirement to private life.

He avoided the appearance of dictating to congress how the constitution should be formed; but while he was careful to declare himself "no advocate for their having to do with the particular policy of any state further than it concerns the union at large," he had no reserve in avowing his" wish to see energy given to the federal constitution by a convention of the people."[1]

The newspapers of the day, as they carried the letter of Washington into every home, caught up the theme, and demanded a revision of the constitution, "not by congress, but by a continental convention, authorized for the purpose."[2]

---

[1] Washington to Dr. William Gordon, 8 July, 1783. MS.
[2] Among them: Philadelphia, 3 July, 1783; Maryland Gazette, 11 July; Virginia Gazette, 19 July.

BOOK II.

ON THE WAY TO A FEDERAL CONVENTION

1783–1787.

This Page Intentionally Left Blank

CHAPTER I.

HOW THE LAND RECEIVED THE LEGACY OF WASHINGTON.

JUNE—DECEMBER, 1783.

All movements conspired to form for the thirteen states a constitution, sooner than they dared to hope and "better than they knew." "The love of union and the resistance to the claims of Great Britain were the inseparable inmates of the same bosom. Brave men from different states, risking life and everything valuable in a common cause, believed by all to be most precious, were confirmed in the habit of considering America as their country and congress as their government."[1] Acting as one, they had attained independence. Moreover, it was their fixed belief that they had waged battle not for themselves alone, but for the hopes and the rights of mankind; and this faith overleapt the limits of states with the force of a religious conviction. For eighteen years the states had watched together over their liberties; for eight they had borne arms together to preserve them; for more than two they

---

[1] Marshall in Van Santvoord's Chief Justices of the U. S., 314, 315.

118 ON THE WAY TO A FEDERAL CONVENTION.

CHAP. I.
1 7 8 3.

had been confederates under a compact to remain united forever.

The federation excelled every one that had preceded it. Inter-citizenship and mutual equality of rights between all its members gave to it a new character and an enduring unity. The Hebrew commonwealth was intensely exclusive, both by descent and from religion; every Greek republic grew out of families and tribes; the word nation originally implied a common ancestry. All mediaeval republics, like the Roman municipalities, rested on privilege. The principle of inter-citizenship infused itself neither into the constitution of the old German empire, nor of Switzerland, nor of Holland. Even when the American people took up arms against Great Britain, congress defined only the membership[1] of each colony; the articles of confederation first brought in the rule that any one might at mil transfer his membership from one state to another. Of old a family, a sept, a clan, a tribe, a nation, a race, owed its unity to consanguinity. Inter-citizenship now took the place of consanguinity; the Americans became not only one people, but one nation. They had framed a union of several states in one confederacy, fortified and bound in with a further union of the inhabitants of every one of them by a mutual and reciprocally perfect naturalization.[2] This inter-citizenship, though only in its third year, has been so ratified by national affections, by the national acquisition of independence, by national treaties, by national interests, by

[1] Journals of Congress, i. 365.
[2] Bacon's speech for general naturalization, Spedding's Bacon's Letters and Life, iii. 319.

national history, that the people possessing it cannot but take one step more, and from an indwelling necessity form above the states a common constitution for the whole.

It was to a nation which had not as yet a self-existent government, and which needed and felt the need of one, that Washington's legacy went forth. The love which was everywhere cherished for him, in itself had become a bond of union. "They are compelled to await the result of his letter," reported Luzerne;[1] "they hope more from the weight of a single citizen than from the authority of the sovereign body." Jonathan Trumbull, the venerable governor of Connecticut, in his prompt reply extolled "this last address of Washington which exhibited the foundation principles" of "an indissoluble union of the states under one federal head."[2] When in the next autumn this faithful war governor, after more than fifty years of service, bade farewell to public life, imitating Washington, he set forth to the legislature of Connecticut, and through them to its people, that the grant to the federal constitution of powers clearly defined, ascertained, and understood, and sufficient for all the great purposes of union, could alone lead from the danger of anarchy to national happiness and glory.[3]

In June the general assembly of Delaware complied with all parts of the recommendation of congress, coupling the impost with the state's quota of

[1] Luzerne to Vergennes, 4 Aug., 1783. MS.
[2] Jonathan Trumbull to Washington, 10 June, 1783. MS.
[3] Stuart's Trumbull, 604-608.

120 ON THE WAY TO A FEDERAL CONVENTION.

CHAP. I.

1783. July.

the federal requisition[1] To Washington, Nicholas Van Dyke, the governor, on receiving the circular, reported this proof of their zeal for establishing the credit of the union, adding: "The state which declines a similar conduct must be blind to the united interest with which that of the individual states is inseparably connected." [2]

Pennsylvania, linking together the North and the South, never hesitated; then and ever after, it made the reasoning and the hopefulness of Washington its own. At a festival in Philadelphia, held near the middle of July, with Dickinson, the president of the state, in the chair, the leading toast was: "New strength to the union;" and, when "Honor and immortality to the principles in Washington's circular letter" was proposed, the company rose twice and manifested their approbation by nine huzzas.

Aug.

A month later, Dickinson and the council of Pennsylvania sent to the general assembly the valedictory of the commander-in-chief, quoting and enforcing his words, saying: "We most earnestly recommend that the confederation be strengthened and improved. To advance the dignity of the union is the best way to advance the interest of each state. A federal supremacy, with a competent national revenue, to govern firmly general and relative concerns," can alone "ensure the respect, tranquillity, and safety, that are naturally attached to an extensive and well-established empire. All the authorities before mentioned may be vested in a federal council, not only without

[1] Papers of Old Congress, lxxv. MS.
[2] Nicholas Van Dyke to Washington, 2 July, 1783. MS.

the least danger to liberty, but liberty will be thereby better secured."¹ The house on the twenty-fifth, joining together the impost and the quota of the state, unanimously ordered the grant of them both,² and at a later session thanked Washington specially for his final "circular letter, the inestimable legacy bequeathed to his country."

In March, during a session of the legislature of South Carolina, Greene, who had received the suggestions of Gouverneur Morris, addressed a letter to the state through Guerard, the governor, representing the sufferings and mutinous temper of the army, and the need of a revenue for congress, and saying: "Independence can only prove a blessing under congressional influence. More is to be dreaded from the members of congress exercising too little than too much power. The financier says his department is on the brink of ruin. To the northward, to the southward, the eyes of the army are turned upon the states, whose measures will determine their conduct. They will not be satisfied with general promises; nothing short of permanent and certain revenue will keep them subject to authority."

"No dictation by a Cromwell!" cried impatient members who could scarcely wait to hear the conclusion of the letter.³ To mark independence of congress and resistance to the requisitions of "its swordsmen," South Carolina revoked its grant to the United States of power to levy a five per cent duty on im-

[1] Colonial Records, xiii. 648, 649
[2] Papers of Old Congress, lxxv. MS.
[3] Johnson's Life of Greene, ii. 387, 388. MS.

ports.[1] Greene consoled himself with the thought that "he had done his duty and would await events;" was made wiser by the rebuff. While he perceived that without more effectual support the power of congress must expire, he saw that the movement of soldiers without civil authority is pregnant with danger, and would naturally fall under the "direction of the Clodiuses and Catilines in America."[2] The appeal of congress in April exercised little counteracting influence; but, when the circular of Washington arrived, the force and affection with which it was written produced an alteration of sentiment in more than one quarter of the members. "Washington was admired before; now he was little less than adored."[3] The continental impost act was adopted, though not without a clause reserving the collection of the duties to the officers of the state, and appropriating them to the payment of the federal quota of South Carolina.[4]

In October, Clinton, the governor of New York, responded to Washington: "Unless the powers of the national council are enlarged and that body better supported than at present, all its measures will discover such feebleness and want of energy as will stain us with disgrace and expose us to the worst of evils."[5] And in the following January, holding up to the legislature the last circular of the

---

[1] Johnson's Life of Greene, ii. 388.
[2] Greene to G. Morris, 3 April, 1783. Sparks' Life of G. Morris, i. 251, 252.
[3] Greene to Washington, 8 Aug., 1783. Letters to Washington, iv. 38.
[4] Statute No. 1190, passed 13 Aug., 1783, in Statutes at Large of South Carolina, iv. 570.
[5] Clinton to Washington, 14 Oct., 1783. Letters to Washington, iv. 48.

THE LEGACY OF WASHINGTON. 123

commander-in-chief, he charged them to "be attentive to every measure which has a tendency to cement the union and to give to the national councils that energy which may be necessary for the general welfare."[1]

The circular reached Massachusetts just when the legislature was complaining of the half-pay and of excessively large salaries to civil officers. The senate and the house despatched a most affectionate joint address to Washington, attributing to the guidance of an all-wise Providence his selection as commander-in-chief, adding: "While patriots shall not cease to applaud your' sacred attachment to the rights of citizens, your military virtue and achievements mil make the brightest pages in the history of mankind."[2] To congress the legislature gave assurances that "it could not without horror entertain the most distant idea of the dissolution of the union;" though "the extraordinary grants of congress to civil and military officers had produced in the commonwealth effects of a threatening aspect."[3] John Hancock, the popular governor, commending Washington's circular, looked to him as the statesman" of wisdom and experience," teaching them how to improve to the happiest purposes the advantages gained by arms.

As president of the senate, Samuel Adams officially signed the remonstrance of Massachusetts against half-pay; as a citizen, he frankly and boldly, in his state and in Connecticut, defended the advice of Washington: "In resisting encroachments

CHAP. I.

1783. June.

1783. Aug.

Sept. 25.

---

[1] Speech to the legislature, 21 Jan., 1784.
[2] Boston Gazette, 23 Aug., 1783.
[3] Journals of Congress, iv. 276.

on our rights, an army became necessary. Congress were and ought to be the sole judge of the means of supporting that army; they had an undoubted right in the very nature of their appointment to make the grant of half-pay; and, as it was made in behalf of the United States, each state is bound in justice to comply with it, even though it should seem to them to have been an ill-judged measure. States as well as individual persons are equally bound to fulfil their engagements, and it is one part of the description given to us in the sacred scriptures of an honest man, that, though 'he sweareth to his own hurt, he changeth not.' "[1]

In like spirit congress replied to the protest against half-pay. "The measure was the result of a deliberate judgment framed on a general view of the interests of the union, and pledged the national faith to carry it into effect. If a state every way so important as Massachusetts should withhold her solid support to constitutional measures of the confederacy, the result must be a dissolution of the union; and then she must hold herself as alone responsible for the anarchy and domestic confusion that may succeed."[2]

At the opening of the autumn session, Hancock, recalling the attention of the legislature to the words of Washington, said: "How to strengthen and im-

---

[1] Samuel Adams to a friend in Connecticut. Boston, 25 Sept., 1783. MS. Same to Noah Webster, 30 April, 1784. MS.

[2] Journals of Congress, iv. 277, 278. Congress, on which Washington was then in attendance, would surely have consulted him on the half-pay of which he was the author. The original papers prove that the congressional reply to Massachusetts was prepared after much consultation, and here and there show traces of is mind.

prove this union, so as to render it more completely adequate, demands the immediate attention of these states. Our very existence as a free nation is suspended upon it."[1]

On the ninth of October he cited to the general court extracts of letters from John Adams, confirming the sentiments of Washington. Near forty towns in the state had instructed their representatives against granting the impost recommended by congress. And yet it was carried in the house by seventy-two against sixty-five; a proviso that it should not be used to discharge half-pay or its commutation was rejected by a majority of ten; and the bill passed the senate almost unanimously,[2] Some of the towns still murmured, but Boston in town-meeting answered: "The commutation is wisely blended with the national debt. With respect to the impost, if we ever mean to be a nation, we must give power to Congress and funds too."

But Washington's letter achieved its greatest victory in his own state. Mercer had said in congress that, sooner than reinstate the impost, he would "crawl to Richmond on his bare knees."[3] The "legislature, which was in session when the communication from congress arrived, ordered a bill to grant the impost. Jefferson was hoping that Henry would speak for the grant; but he remained mute in his place.[4] Richard Henry Lee and Thruston spoke of congress

---

[1] Salem Gazette of 2 Oct., 1783.
[2] Samuel Cooper to Franklin, 16 Oct., 1783. Works of Franklin, x. 25. Salem Gazette, 30 Oct., 1783.
[3] Jefferson to Randolph, 18 Feb., 1783. Gilpin, 506.
[4] Jefferson to Madison, 7 May, 1 June, 17 June, 1783. MSS.

as "lusting for power." The extent of the implied powers which Hamilton Lad asserted in the letter of congress to Rhode Island was "reprobated as alarming and of dangerous tendency;"[1] and on the eleventh of June the proposition of congress was pronounced to be inadmissible, because the revenue-officers were not to be amenable to the commonwealth; because the power of collecting a revenue by penal laws could not be delegated without danger; and because the moneys to be raised from citizens of Virginia were to go into the general treasury. So the proposition of congress was left without any support. Virginia, to discharge her continental debt, preferred to establish a custom-house of her own, appropriating its income to congress for five-and-twenty years, and making good the deficiency by taxes on land, negroes, and polls. "The state," said Arthur Lee," is resolved not to suffer the exercise of any foreign power or influence within it."[2] But, when the words of Washington were read, the house gave leave to the advocates for a continental impost to provide for it by a bill which was to have its first reading at the opening of the next session.

These events did but render Richard Henry Lee more obdurate. Placing himself directly in the way of Washington and Madison, he wrote to a friend at the north: "The late address of congress to the states on the impost I think a too early and too strong attempt to overleap those fences established by the

---

[1] Joseph Jones to Madison, 14 June, 1783, MS.; in part in Rives' Madison, i. 436.

[2] Arthur Lee to Theodorick Bland, 13 June, 1783. Bland Papers, ii. 110.

confederation to secure the liberties of the respective states. Give the purse to an aristocratic assembly, the sword will follow, and liberty become an empty name. As for increasing the power of congress, I would answer as the discerning men of old, with the change of a word only: 'Nolumus leges confederationis mutari—we forbid change in the laws of the confederation.' "[1] But, in the time afforded for reflection, Washington's valedictory letter, which Jefferson describes as "deservedly applauded by the world,"[2] "gained more and more power; at the adjourned session, the legislature of Virginia, with absolute unanimity, reversed its decision and granted by law the continental impost.[3] "Everything will come right at last," said "Washington, as he heard the gladdening news."[4]

"Never," said George Mason, "have I heard one single man deny the necessity and propriety of the union. No object can be lost when the mind of every man in the country is strongly attached to it."[5] "I do not believe," witnesses Jefferson, "there has ever been a moment when a single whig in any one state would not have shuddered at the very idea of a separation of their' state from the confederacy."[6] A proposition had been made in June to revoke the release to the United States of the territory northwest of the river Ohio. Patrick Henry was for bounding the state reasonably enough, but, instead of ceding the parts lopped off, he was for forming

---

[1] R. H. Lee to William Whipple, 1 July, 1783. MS.
[2] Jefferson's Works, ix. 266.
[3] Henmg, xi. 313.
[4] Sparks, ix, 5.
[5] George Mason in the Virginia Convention, 11 June, 1788.
[6] Jefferson, ix. 251.

them into small republics¹ under the direction of Virginia. Nevertheless, the legislature, guided by the sincerity and perseverance of Joseph Jones of King George county, conformed to the wishes of congress, and on the nineteenth and twentieth of December cheerfully amended and confirmed their former cession.[2]

The last legislature to address Washington in his public character was Maryland, and they said: "By your letter you have taught us how to value, preserve, and improve that liberty which your services under the smiles of Providence have secured. If the powers given to congress by the confederation should be found incompetent to the purposes of the union, our constituents will readily consent to enlarge them."[3]

On the part of congress, its president, Elias Boudinot of New Jersey, transmitted to the ministers of America in Europe the circular letter of Washington as the most perfect evidence of "his inimitable character."[4]

Before the end of June, raw recruits of the Pennsylvania line, in the barracks at Philadelphia, many of them foreign born, joined by others from Lancaster,[5] "soldiers of a day who could have very few hardships to complain of,"[6] with some returning veterans whom they forced into their ranks,[7] encouraged by no officer of note,[8] surrounding congress[9] and the

---

[1] Jefferson to Madison, 17 June, 1783. MS.
[2] Journals of House of Delegates, 71, 79.
[3] Address of the Maryland legislature, 22 Dec, 1783. MS.
[4] Dip. Cor., i. 14.
[5] Ibid., i. 9.
[6] Sparks, viii. 455.
[7] Dip. Cor., i. 10, 22, 23; Hamilton, i. 387.
[8] Dip. Cor., ii. 514; i. 37, 50.
[9] Gilpin, 548; Colonial Records, xiii. 655.

THE LEGACY OF WASHINGTON. 129

council of Pennsylvania, mutinously presented to them demands for pay. Congress insisted with the state authorities that the militia should be called out to restore order, and, the request being refused,[1] it adjourned to Princeton. On the rumor that the commander-in-chief was sending troops to quell the mutiny, the insurgents, about three hundred in number, made their submission to the president of the state.[2]

The incident hastened the selection of a place for the permanent residence of congress. The articles of confederation left congress free to meet where it would. With the knowledge of the treaty of peace, the idea naturally arose of a federal town, and for its site there were many competitors. Of the thirteen states which at that time fringed the Atlantic, the central point was in Maryland or Virginia. In March, 1783, New York tendered Kingston; in May, Maryland urged the choice of Annapolis; in June, New Jersey offered a district below the falls of the Delaware. Virginia, having Georgetown for its object,[3] invited Maryland to join in a cession of equal portions of territory lying together on the Potomac; leaving congress to fix its residence on either side.[4]

During the summer, congress appointed a committee to consider what jurisdiction it should exercise in its abiding-place. Madison took counsel with Randolph, and especially with Jefferson;[5] and in September the committee of which he was a member reported that the state ceding the territory must

[1] Hamilton, ii. 276.
[2] Dip. Cor., i. 13.
[3] Madison to Randolph, 3 Oct., 1783. Gilpin, 578.
[3] Journals of the Virginia House of Delegates, June 28, 1783, p. 97.
[4] Gilpin, 573.

give up all jurisdiction over it; the inhabitants were to be assured of a government of laws made by representatives of their own election.[1] In October, congress took up the question of its permanent residence. Gerry struggled hard for the district on the Potomac; but, by the vote of Delaware and all the northern states, "a place on the Delaware near the falls" was selected. Within a few days the fear of an overpowering influence of the middle states led to what was called "the happy coalition;" on the seventeenth Gerry insisted that the alternate residence of congress in two places would secure the mutual confidence and affections of the states and preserve the federal balance of power. After a debate of several days, New England, with Maryland, Virginia, and the two Carolinas, decided that congress should reside for equal periods on the Delaware and near the lower falls of the Potomac. Till buildings for its use should be erected, it was to meet alternately in Annapolis and Trenton. To carry out the engagement, a committee, of which James Monroe was a member, made an excursion from Annapolis in the following May to view the country round Georgetown; and they reported in favor of the position on which the city of Washington now stands.[4]

The farewell circular letter of Washington addressed to all his countrymen had attracted the attention of congress, and in particular of Hamilton,

[1] Gilpin, 559, 571-576.
[2] Madison to Randolph, 13 Oct., 23 Oct., 1783. MS.
[3] Higginson to Bland, Jan., 1784 Bland Papers, ii. 113, 114. Compare Bondinot to R. R. Livingston, 23 Oct., 1783. MS.
[4] Monroe to Jefferson, May 20 and May 25, 1784. MSS.

THE LEGACY OF WASHINGTON. 131

who roused himself from his own desponding mood when he saw the great chieftain go forth alone to combat "the epidemic phrenzy"[1] of the supreme sovereignty of the separate states. During the time of disturbances in the army," could force have availed, he had almost wished to see it employed."[2] Knowing nothing beforehand of Washington's intention to address the people, he had favored some combined action of congress and the general to compel the states forthwith to choose between national anarchy and a consolidated union.[3] No sooner had confess established itself in Princeton[4] than the zeal of the youthful statesman bore him toward the same noble end, and by the same means as Washington. He drafted a most elaborate and comprehensive series of resolutions embodying in clear and definite language the defects in the confederation as a form of federal government; and closing with an earnest recommendation to the several states to appoint a convention to meet at a fixed time and place, with full powers to revise the confederation, and adopt and propose such alterations as to them should appear necessary; to be finally approved or rejected by the states respectively.[5]

But in the congress of that day he found little disposition to second an immediate effort for a new constitution. Of the committee elected on the twenty-eighth of April, which counted among its members the great names of Ellsworth, Wilson, and Ham-

---

[1] Hamilton, i. 402.
[2] Ibid., i. 352.
[3] Ibid., i. 402.
[4] Hamilton's endorsement on his own paper is: "Resolutions intended to be submitted to congress at Princeton in 1783, but abandoned for want of support." MS.
[5] Hamilton, i. 269-375.

ilton, Wilson and two others had gone home; Ellsworth followed in the first half of July, but not till he had announced to the governor of Connecticut: "It will soon be of very little consequence where congress go, if they are not made respectable as well as responsible; which can never be done without giving them a power to perform engagements as well as make them. There must be a revenue somehow established that can be relied on and applied for national purposes, independent of the will of a single state, or it will be impossible to support national faith, or national existence. The powers of congress must be adequate to the purposes of their constitution. It is possible there may be abuses and misapplications; still it is better to hazard something than to hazard all."[1] Nearly at the same moment Hamilton wrote to Greene: "There is so little disposition, either in or out of congress, to give solidity to our national system, that there is no motive to a man to lose his time in the public service who has no other view than to promote its welfare. Experience must convince us that our present establishments are Utopian before we shall be ready to part with them for better." To Jay his words were: "It is to be hoped that, when prejudice and folly have run themselves out of breath, we may return to reason and correct our errors."[2] Confirmed in "his ill forebodeings as to the future system of the country,"[3] "he abandoned his resolutions for the want of support."[4]

---

[1] Ellsworth, infra, 324.
[2] Johnson, i. 442. Jay's Jay, ii. 123.
[3] Hamilton, i. 352.
[4] Hamilton's memorandum. MS.

In congress, which he left near the end of July, three months before the period for which he was chosen expired, we know through his ardent friend that "his homilies were recollected with pleasure;" that his extreme zeal made impressions in favor of his integrity, honor, and republican principles; that he had displayed various knowledge, had been sometimes intemperate and sometimes, though rarely, visionary; that cautious statesmen thought, if he could pursue an object with as much cold perseverance as he could defend it with ardor and judgment, he would prove irresistible.[1] From the goodness of his heart, his pride, and his sense of duty, he gave up "future views of public life,"[2] to toil for the support of his wife and children in a profession of which to him the labors were alike engrossing and irksome.[3] In four successive years, with few to heed him, he had written and spoken for a constituent federal convention. His last official word to Clinton was: "Strengthen the confederation."[4]

On the second of September, more than a month after Hamilton had withdrawn, the remnant of the committee of the twenty-eighth of April, increased by Samuel Huntington, of Connecticut, reported that "until the effect of the resolution of congress, of April last, relating to revenue, should be known, it would be proper to postpone the further consideration of the concurrent resolutions of the senate and assem-

---

[1] McHenry to Hamilton, 22 Oct., 1783. Hamilton, i. 411.
[2] Hamilton to Clinton, 14 May, 1783. Hamilton, i. 368.
[3] That Hamilton disliked the labors of a lawyer, I received from Eliphalet Nott.
[4] Hamilton to Clinton, 3 Oct., 1783. Hamilton, i. 407.

bly of New York."¹ In this way the first proposition by a state for reforming the government through a federal convention was put to sleep.

All this while the British commander was preparing for the evacuation of New York. The malignant cruelty of royalists, especially in New York and South Carolina, who prompted and loved to execute the ruthless orders of Germain, aroused against them, as had been foretold, a just indignation, which unhappily extended to thousands of families in the United States who had taken no part in the excesses. Toward these Washington and Adams, Jay and Hamilton, and Jefferson, who was especially called "their protector and support,"² and many of the best counselled forbearance and forgiveness. Motives of policy urged their absorption into the population of the union now that the sovereign to whom they had continued their allegiance had given them their release. But a dread of their political influence prevailed, and before the end of 1783 more than twenty thousand loyalists, as many as the original planters of Massachusetts, and, like them, families of superior culture, were driven to seek homes in the wilds of Nova Scotia.³ In this way the United States out of their own children built up on their border a colony of rivals in navigation and the fishery whose loyalty to the British crown was sanctified by misfortunes. Nor did the British parliament hesitate for a moment to compensate all refugees for the confiscation of their

---

[1] Report of Peters, McHenry, Izard, Duane, and S. Huntingdon, of 3 Sept., 1783. MS.

[2] Luzerne to Rayneval, of 18 June, 1784. MS.

[3] Haliburton's Nova Scotia, i. 263.

THE LEGACY OF WASHINGTON. 135

property, and, when the amount was ascertained, it voted them from the British treasury as an indemnity very nearly fifteen and a half millions of dollars,[1]

The American army being nearly disbanded, Washington, on the eighteenth of July, with Governor Clinton as his companion, made an excursion into the interior, during which he personally examined the lines of water communication between branches of the Hudson and the Saint Lawrence, the lakes and the Susquehanna. By these observations, he comprehended more clearly "the immense extent and importance of the inland navigation of the United States. I shall not rest contented," said he, "till I have explored the western country and traversed great part of those lines which give bounds to a new empire."[2]

He wished at that time to visit the Niagara; but over the fort on the American side of that river the British flag still waved. Thrice Washington had invited the attention of congress to the western posts; and he was now instructed to demand them. He accordingly accredited Steuben to Haldimand, the British commander-in-chief in Canada, with power to receive them. At Sorel, on the eighth of August, Steuben explained his mission to Haldimand, who answered that he had not received any orders for making the least arrangements for the evacuation of a single post; and without positive orders he would not evacuate one inch of ground.[3] Nor would he

---

[1] Sabine's Loyalists, 111.
[2] Washington to Chastellux, 12 Oct., 1783. Sparks, viii. 489.
[3] Baron Steuben to Washington, 23 Aug., 1783. Letters to Washington, iv. 41, 42.

permit Steuben to communicate with the inhabitants of any occupied by the British.

On the seventh of August, Just as Washington had returned from his northern tour, congress, ten states being present, unanimously voted him a statue of bronze, to be executed by the best artist of Europe.[1] On the marble pedestal were to be represented, in low relief, the evacuation of Boston, the capture of Hessians at Trenton, the victory at Princeton, the action at Monmouth, and the surrender of Cornwallis at Yorktown. "The statue," wrote Luzerne, "is the only mark of public gratitude which Washington can accept, and the only one which the government in its poverty can offer."[2]

But a greater honor awaited him. At the request of congress, he removed his quarters to the neighborhood of Princeton; and on the twenty-sixth, in a public audience, Boudinot, the president, said to him: "In other nations many have deserved and received the thanks of the public; but to you, sir, peculiar praise is due; your services have been essential in acquiring and establishing the freedom and independence of your country. It still needs your services in forming arrangements for the time of peace." A committee was charged to receive his assistance in preparing and directing the necessary plans.[3]

The choice of Washington for a counsellor proved the sincerity of congress in favor of union, and a

---

[1] Journals of Congress, iv. 251. It still remains to give effect to the vote.

[2] Luzerne to ergennes, 25 Aug., 1783. MS.

[3] Journals of Congress, iv. 256.

series of national measures was inaugurated. For a peace establishment, he matured a system which was capable of a gradual development. He would have a regular and standing force of twenty-six hundred and thirty-one men, to be employed chiefly in garrisoning the frontier posts. Light troops he specially recommended as suited to the genius of the people. The people in all the states were to be organized and trained in arms as one grand national militia. He proposed a military academy like the Prussian schools, of which he had learned the character from Steuben. Vacancies in the class of officers were to be filled from its graduates; but promotions were not to depend on seniority alone. For the materials essential to war, there were to be not only national arsenals but national manufactories. The protection of foreign commerce would require a navy. All branches in the service were to look exclusively to congress for their orders and their pay. A penniless treasury, which congress knew not how to fill, made the scheme for the moment an ideal one.

To regulate intercourse with the tribes of Indians, Washington laid down the outlines of a system. Outside of the limits of the states no purchase of their lands was to be made, but by the United States as "the sovereign power." All traders with them were to be under strict control. He penetrated the sinister design of the British government to hold the western posts, and recommended friendly attention to the French and other settlers at Detroit and elsewhere in the western territory. Looking to "the formation of new states," he sketched the boundaries of Ohio and Michigan, and, on his advice,[1] congress in October resolved on appointing a committee to report a plan of a temporary government for the western territory whose inhabitants were one day to be received into the union under republican constitutions of their own choice. Here the greatness of the intention was not impaired by the public penury, for the work was to be executed by the emigrants themselves. In anticipation of an acceptable cession of the north-western lands by all the claimant states, officers and soldiers who had a right to bounty lands began to gain the west by way of the lakes or across the mountains.[2] This was the movement toward union which nothing could repress or weaken. Especially Maryland insisted that "the sovereignty over the western territory was vested in the United States as one undivided and independent nation."[3]

Among his latest official acts, Washington interceded with congress on behalf of Kosciuszko, pleading for him" his merit and services from the concurrent testimony of all who knew him; "and congress accordingly granted the Polish exile who was to become dear to many nations the brevet commission of brigadier-general.[4]

The last days of this congress were cheered by the arrival of Van Berckel, as envoy from the Dutch republic, the first minister accredited to America

---

[1] Washington to Duane, 7 Sept., 1783. Sparks, viii. 477. Secret Journals of Congress, i. 255–260.

[2] Journals of Congress, iv. 394-296.

[3] Journals of Congress, iv. 265. In the original MS., the word "one" is twice underscored.

[4] Washington to Congress, 2 Oct., 1783. Sparks, viii. 487.

THE LEGACY OF WASHINGTON. 139

since the peace.¹ An escort was sent out to meet him, and on the thirty-first of October, in a public audience, congress gave him a national welcome.

CHAP. I.

1783.

On the first of November the third congress under the confederation came together for the last time. It made persistent attempts to invigorate the union; declared the inviolable sanctity of the national debt; asked of the states a general revenue; prepared for planting new states in the continental domain; and extended diplomatic relations. Its demand of powers of government did not reach far enough, but it kept alive the desire of reform. It appointed a day of public thanksgiving that "all the people might assemble to give praise to their Supreme Benefactor for the freedom, sovereignty, and independence of the United States;" and, as the day came, the pulpit echoed the prayer: "May all the states be one."²

The principle of rotation drove Madison from the national councils. He was unmarried and above care; and, until he should again be eligible to congress, he devoted himself to the study of federal government and to public service in the legislature of his own state, where with strong convictions and unselfish patriotism he wrought with single-mindedness to bring about an efficient form of republican government. He was calm, wakeful, and cautious, pursuing with patience his one great object; never missing an opportunity to advance it; caring not over-

---

¹ Van Berckel to the states general, 3 Nov., 1783. MS.

² John Murray's thanksgiving sermon, Tyranny's grove destroyed, p. 71.

much for conspicuousness or fame; and ever ready to efface himself if he could but accomplish his design.

On Sunday, the second of November, the day before the discharge of all persons enlisted for the war, the commander-in-chief addressed the armies of the United States, however widely their member's might be dispersed. Mingling affectionate thanks with praise, he described their unparalleled perseverance for eight long years as little short of a standing miracle, and for their solace bade them call to recollection the astonishing events in which they had taken part, the enlarged prospects of happiness which they had assisted to open for the human race. He encouraged them as citizens to renew their old occupations; and, to those hardy soldiers who were fond of domestic enjoyment and personal independence, he pointed to the fertile regions beyond the Alleghanies as the most happy asylum. In the moment of parting, he held up as an example to the country the harmony which had prevailed in the camp, where men from different parts of the continent and of the most violent local prejudices instantly became but one patriotic band of brothers. "Although the general," these are the words of his last order, "has so frequently given it as his opinion in the most public and explicit manner, that, unless the principles of the federal government were properly supported, and the powers of the union increased, the honor, dignity, and justice of the nation would be lost forever, yet he cannot help leaving it as his last injunction to every officer and every soldier to add his best endeavors, toward effect-

THE LEGACY OF WASHINGTON. 141

ing these great purposes."[1] Washington sent forth every one of his fellow-soldiers as an apostle of union under a new constitution.

Almost all the Germans who had been prisoners preferred to abide in the United States, where they soon became useful citizens. The remnant of the British army had crossed to Staten Island and Long Island for embarkation, when, on the twenty-fifth of November, Washington and the governor and other officers of the state and city of New York were met at the Bowery by Knox and citizens, and in orderly procession made their glad progress into the heart of the town. Rejoicings followed. The emblem chosen to introduce the evening display of fireworks was a dove descending with the olive-branch.

For their farewell to Washington, the officers of the army, on the fourth of December, met at a public-house near the Battery, and were soon joined by their commander. The thoughts of the eight years which they had passed together, their common distresses, their victories, and now then parting from the public service, the future of themselves and of their country, came thronging to every mind. No relation of friendship is stronger or more tender than that between men who have shared together the perils of war in a noble and upright cause. The officers could attest that the courage which is the most perfect and the most rare, the courage which determines the man, without the least hesitation, to hold his life of less account than the success of the cause for which he

[1] Farewell address to the armies of the United States. Rocky Hill, near Princeton, 2 Nov., 1783. Sparks, viii. 493.

contends, was the habit of Washington. Pledging them in a glass of wine, he thus addressed them: "With an heart full of love and gratitude, I now take leave of you. May your latter days be as prosperous and happy as your former ones have been glorious. I shall be obliged to you if each of you will come and take me by the hand." With tears on his cheeks, he grasped the hand of Knox, who stood nearest, and embraced him. In the same manner he took leave of every officer. Followed by the company in a silent procession, he passed through a corps of light infantry to the ferry at Whitehall. Entering his barge, he waved his hat to them; with the same silence they returned that last voiceless farewell, and the boat pushed across the Hudson. A father parting from his children could not excite more regret nor draw more tears.[1]

On his way through New Jersey, the chief was received with the tenderest respect and affection by all classes of men. The roads were covered with people who came from all quarters to see him, to get near to him, to speak to him. Alone and ready to lay down in the hands of congress the command which had been confided to him, he appeared even greater than when he was at the head of the armies of the United States. The inhabitants of Philadelphia knew that he was drawing near, and, without other notice, an innumerable crowd placed themselves along the road where he was to pass. Women, aged men, left their houses to see him. Children passed among the horses to touch his garments. Acclamations of joy

---

[1] Luzerne to Vergennes, 13 Dec., 1783. MS.

and gratitude accompanied him in all the streets. Never was homage more spontaneous or more pure. The general enjoyed the scene, and owned himself by this moment repaid for eight years of toils and wants and tribulations.[1]

At Philadelphia, he put into the hands of the comptroller his accounts to the thirteenth of December, 1783, all written with minute exactness by his own hand, and accompanied by vouchers conveniently arranged. Every debit against him was credited; but, as he had not always made an entry of moneys of his own expended in the public service, he was, and chose to remain, a considerable loser. To the last he refused all compensation and all indemnity, though his resources had been greatly diminished by the war.

On the twenty-third of December, at noon, congress in Annapolis received the commander-in-chief. Its members, when seated, wore their hats, as a sign that they represented the sovereignty of the union. Places were assigned to the governor, council, and legislature of Maryland, to general officers, and to the representative of France. Spectators filled the gallery and crowded upon the floor. Hope gladdened all as they forecast the coming greatness of their land.

Rising with dignity, Washington spoke of the rectitude of the common cause; the support of congress; of his countrymen; of Providence; and he commended the interests of "our dearest country to the care of Almighty God." Then saying that he had

[1] Luzerne to Vergennes, 13 Dec., 1783. MS.

finished the work assigned him to do, he bade an affectionate farewell to the august body under whose orders he had so long acted, resigned with satisfaction the commission which he had accepted with diffidence, and took leave of public life. His emotion was so great that, as he advanced and delivered up his commission, he seemed unable to have uttered more.

The hand that wrote the declaration of independence prepared the words which, in the name of congress, its president, turning pale from excess of feeling, then addressed to Washington, who stood, filling and commanding every eye:

"Sir: The United States in congress assembled receive with emotions too affecting for utterance the solemn resignation of the authorities under which you have led their troops with success through a perilous and a doubtful war. Called upon by your country to defend its invaded rights, you accepted the sacred charge, before it had formed alliances, and whilst it was without funds or a government to support you. You have conducted the great military contest with wisdom and fortitude, invariably regarding the rights of the civil power through all disasters and changes. You have persevered, till these United States, aided by a magnanimous king and nation, have been enabled under a just Providence to close the war in freedom, safety, and independence. Having taught a lesson useful to those who inflict and to those who feel oppression, with the blessings of your fellow-citizens, you retire from the great theatre of action; but the glory of your virtues will continue to animate remotest ages. We join you in commending the interest of our dearest country to the protection of Almighty God, beseeching him to dispose the hearts and minds of its citizens to improve the opportunity afforded them of becoming a happy and respectable nation."

No more pleasing words could have reached Washington than those which pledged congress to the reform of the national government. The allusion to the alliance with France was right, for otherwise the achievement of independence would have been attributed to the United States alone. But France and England were now at peace; and after their reconciliation Washington, the happiest of warriors, as he unguided the sword, would not recall that they had been at war.

The business of the day being over, Washington set out for Mount Vernon, and on Christmas eve, after an absence of nearly nine years, he crossed the threshold of his own home; but not to find rest there, for the doom of greatness was upon him.

CHAPTER II.

VIRGINIA STATESMEN LEAD TOWARD A BETTER UNION.

1784.

CHAP. II.

1 7 8 3.

Of many causes promoting union, four above others exercised a steady and commanding influence. The new republic as one nation must have power to regulate its foreign commerce: to colonize its large domain; to provide an adequate revenue; and to establish justice in domestic trade by prohibiting the separate states from impairing the obligation of contracts. Each of these four causes was of vital importance; but the necessity for regulating commerce gave the immediate impulse to a more perfect constitution. Happily, the British order in council of the second of July, 1783, restricted to British subjects and ships the carrying of American produce from American ports to any British West India island, and the carrying of the produce of those islands to any port in America. "This proclamation," wrote John Adams to congress "is issued in full confidence that the United States cannot agree to act as one nation. They will soon see the necessity of measures to counteract their enemies. If there is not sufficient authority to draw together the minds, affections, and forces of the states in their common foreign concerns, we shall be the sport of transatlantic politicians, who hate liberty and every country that enjoys it."[1]

Letters of Adams and one of like tenor from Franklin having been fully considered, congress, on the twenty-ninth of September, 1783, agreed that the United States could become respectable only by more energy in government; but, as usual, they only referred "the important subject under consideration" to a special committee,[2] which, having Arthur Lee for one of its members, in due time reported that "as the several states are sovereign and independent, and possess the power of acting as may to them seem best, congress will not attempt to point out the path. The mode for joint efforts will suggest itself to the good sense of America."[3]

The states could not successfully defend themselves against the policy of Great Britain by separate legislation, because it was not the interest of any one of them to exclude British vessels from their harbors unless the like measure should be adopted by every other; and a union of thirteen distinct powers would encounter the very difficulty which had so often proved insuperable. But, while every increase of the power of congress in domestic affairs roused jealousies between the states, the selfish design of a

---

[1] Dip. Cor., vii. 81, 88, 100.
[2] Secret Journals of Congress, iii. 398–400.
[3] Reports of committees on increasinig the powers of congress, p. 95. MS.

CHAP. II.

1784.

Dec. 4.

9.

foreign government to repress their industry drew them together against a common adversary.

The complete cession of the north-west and the grant of the desired impost were the offerings of Virginia to the general welfare.[1] Simultaneously her legislature, in December, took cognizance of the aggression on equal commerce. The Virginians owned not much shipping, and had no special interest in the West India trade; but the British prohibitory policy offended their pride and their sense of honor, and, as in the war they had looked upon "union as the rock of their political salvation," so they again rang the bell to call the other states to council. They complained of "a disposition in Great Britain to gain partial advantages injurious to the rights of free commerce, and repugnant to the principles of reciprocal interest and convenience, which form the only permanent foundation of friendly intercourse;" and unanimously consented to empower congress to adopt the most effectual mode of counteracting restrictions on American navigation so long as they should be continued.[2] The governor, by direction, communicated the act to the executive authority of the other states, requesting their immediate adoption of similar measures;[3] and he sent to the delegates of his own state in congress a report of what had been done. This is the first in the series of measures through which Virginia marshalled the United States on their way to a better union.

[1] Joseph Jones to Jefferson, 21 and 29 Dec, 1783. MSS.
[2] Journal of House of Delegates, 50; Henmg, xi. 313.
[3] Journal of House of Delegates for 22 Dec., 1783. Governor Harrison to the governor of Massachusetts, 25 Dec, 1783. MS.

TOWARD A BETTER UNION. 149

In the fourth congress, Jefferson earned forward the work of Madison with alacrity. The two cherished for each other the closest and the most honorable friendship, agreeing in efforts to bind the states more closely in all that related to the common welfare. In their copious correspondence they opened their minds to each other with frankness and independence.

The delegates of Rhode Island insisted that the counteraction of the British navigation acts must be intrusted to each separate state; but they stood alone, Roger Sherman voting against them, and so dividing Connecticut. Then the proposal of the committee of which Jefferson was a member and of which all but Gerry were from the South, that congress, with the assent of nine states, might exercise prohibitory powers over foreign commerce for the term of fifteen years, was adopted without opposition.[1]

Keeping in mind that, while the articles of confederation did not directly confer on congress the regulation of commerce by enactments, they granted the amplest authority to frame commercial treaties, Jefferson prepared a plan for intercourse with powers of Europe, from Britain to the Ottoman Porte, and with the Barbary states. His draft of instructions[2] described "the United States as one nation upon the principles of the federal constitution."[3] In a document of the preceding congress, mention had been made of "the federal government," and Rhode Island

---

[1] Journals of Congress, iv. 393, 398. 30 March, 1826 G. Jefferson, vii. 436.
[2] Jefferson to John Q. Adams. [3] Secret Journals of Congress, iii. 453.

had forthwith moved to substitute the word union, conceding that there was a union of the states, but not a government; but the motion had been supported by no other state, and by no individuals outside of Rhode Island except Holten and Arthur Lee. This time Sherman and his colleague, James Wadsworth, placed Connecticut by the side of Rhode Island. They were joined only by Arthur Lee, and congress, adopting the words of Jefferson, by the vote of eight states to two, of nineteen individuals to five, decided that in treaties and in all cases arising under them the United States form "one nation."[1]

On the principles according to which commercial treaties should be framed America was unanimous. In October, 1783, congress had proposed the most perfect equality and reciprocity.[2] Jefferson, while he would accept a system of reciprocity, reported as the choice of America that there should be no navigation laws; no distinction between metropolitan and colonial ports; an equal right for each party to carry its own products in its own ships into all ports of the other and to take away its products, freely if possible, if not, paying no other duties than are paid by the most favored nation. In time of war there should be an abandonment of privateering; the least possible interference with industry on land; the inviolability of fishermen; the strictest limitation of contraband; free commerce between neutrals and belligerents in articles not contraband; no paper blockades; in short, free trade and a humane inter-

---

[1] Secret Journals of Congress for 26 March, 1784, iii. 452-454.

[2] Secret Journals of Congress, iii. 413, 413.

national code. These instructions congress accepted, and, to give them effect, Adams, Franklin, and Jefferson were commissioned for two years, with the consent of any two of them, to negotiate treaties of ten or fifteen years' duration.[1]

The foreign commercial system of the nation was to be blended with the domestic intercourse of the states. Highways by water and land from Virginia to the west would advance its welfare and strengthen the union. Jefferson opened the subject to Madison,[2] who, in reply, explained the necessity of a mutual appointment of commissioners by Maryland and Virginia for regulating; the navigation of the Potomac. "The good humor into which the cession of the back lands must have put Maryland forms an apt crisis for negotiations."[3]

Jefferson cautiously introduced the subject to Washington,[4] and then wrote more urgently: "Your future time and wishes are sacred in my eye; but, if the superintendence of this work would be only a dignified amusement to you, what a monument of your retirement would follow that of your public life!"[5]

Washington "was very happy that a man of discernment and liberality like Jefferson thought as he did." More than ten years before he had been a principal mover of a bill for the extension of navigation from tide-water to Will's creek. "To get the business in

---

[1] Secret Journals of Congress, iii. 484, 485, and 491-499.
[2] Jefferson to Madison, Annapolis, 20 Feb., 1784. MS.
[3] Madison to Jefferson, 16 March, 1784. Madison, i. 74.
[4] Jefferson to Washington, 6 March, 1784. MS.
[5] Jefferson to Washington, 15 March, 1784. Letters to W., iv. 62-66.

motion," he writes, "I was obliged to comprehend James river. The plan was in a tolerably good train when I set out for Cambridge in 1775, and would have been in an excellent way, had it not met with difficulties in the Maryland assembly. Not a moment ought to be lost in recommencing this business."[1]

He too, like Madison, advised concert with the men of Maryland. Conforming to their advice, Jefferson conferred with Thomas Stone, then one of the Maryland delegates in congress, and undertook by letters to originate the subject in the legislature of Virginia[2]

Before the end of June the two houses unanimously requested the executive to procure a statue of Washington, to be of the finest marble and best workmanship, with this inscription on its pedestal:

"The general assembly of the commonwealth of Virginia have caused this statue to be erected as a monument of affection and gratitude to George Washington, who, to the endowments of the hero uniting the virtues of the patriot, and exerting both in establishing the liberties of his country, has rendered his name dear to his fellow-citizens, and given the world an immortal example of true glory.[3]

The vote, emanating from the affections of the people of Virginia, marks his mastery over the heart of his native state. That mastery he always used to promote the formation of a national Constitution.

[1] Washington to Jefferson, 29 March, 1784. MS. Partly printed in parks, ix. 31, 32. Rives, i. 550.
[2] Jefferson to Madison, 25 April, 1784. [3] Hening, xi. 552.

He had hardly reached home from the war, when he poured out his inmost thoughts to Harrison, the doubting governor of his commonwealth:

"The prospect before us is fair; I believe all things will come right at last; but the disinclination of the states to yield competent powers to congress for the federal government will, if there is not a change in the system, be our downfall as a nation. This is as clear to me as A, B, C. We have arrived at peace and independency to very little purpose, if we cannot conquer our own prejudices. The powers of Europe begin to see this, and our newly acquired friends, the British, are already and professedly acting upon this ground; and wisely too, if we are determined to persevere in our folly. They know that individual opposition to their measures is futile, and boast that we are not sufficiently united as a nation to give a general one. Is not the indignity of this declaration, in the very act of peace-making and conciliation, sufficient to stimulate us to vest adequate powers in the sovereign of these United States?

"An extension of federal powers would make us one of the most wealthy, happy, respectable, and powerful nations that ever inhabited the terrestrial globe. Without them, we shall soon be everything which is the direct reverse. I predict the worst consequences from a half-starved, limping government, always moving upon crutches and tottering at every step."[1]

The immensity of the ungranted public domain which had passed from the English crown to the

---

[1] Washington to Harrison, 18 Jan., 1784. Sparks, ix. 11.

American people invited them to establish a continental empire of republics. Lines of communication with the western country implied its colonization. In the war, Jefferson, as a member of the legislature, had promoted the expedition by which Virginia conquered the region north-west of the Ohio; as governor he had taken part in its cession to the United States. The cession had included the demand of a guarantee to Virginia of the remainder of its territory. This the United States had refused, and Virginia receded from the demand. On the first day of March, 1784, Jefferson, in congress, with his colleagues, Hardy, Arthur Lee, and James Monroe, in conformity with full powers from their commonwealth, signed, sealed, and delivered a deed by which, with some reservation of land, they ceded to the United States all claim to the territory northwest of the Ohio. On that same day, before the deed could be recorded and enrolled among the acts of the United States, Jefferson, as chairman of a committee, presented a plan for the temporary government of the western territory from the southern boundary of the United States in the latitude of thirty-one degrees to the Lake of the Woods. It is still preserved in the national archives in his own handwriting, and is as completely his own work as the declaration of independence.

He pressed upon Virginia to establish the meridian of the mouth of the Kanawha as its western boundary, and to cede all beyond to the United States. To Madison he wrote: "For God's sake, push this at the next session of assembly. We hope North

Carolina will cede all beyond the same meridian,"[1] his object being to obtain cessions to the United States of all southern territory west of the meridian of the Kanawha.

In dividing all the country north-west of the Ohio into ten states, Jefferson was controlled by an act of congress of 1780 which was incorporated into the cession of Virginia; No land was to be taken up till it should have been purchased from the Indian proprietors and offered for sale by the United States. In each incipient state no property qualification was required either of the electors or the elected; it was enough for them to be free men, resident, and of full age. Under the authority of congress, and following the precedent of any one of the states, the settlers were to establish a temporary government; when they should have increased to twenty thousand, they might institute a permanent government, with a member in congress, having a right to debate but not to vote; and, when they should be equal in number to the inhabitants of the least populous state, their delegates, with the consent of nine states, as required by the confederation, were to be admitted into the congress of the United States on an equal footing.

The ordinance contained five other articles: The new states shall remain forever a part of the United States of America; they shall bear the same relation to the confederation as the original states; they shall pay their apportionment of the federal debts; they shall in their governments uphold republican

[1] Jefferson to Madison, 20 Feb., 1784. MS.

forms; and after the year 1800 of the Christian era there shall be neither slavery nor involuntary servitude in any of them.

At that time slavery prevailed throughout much more than half the lands of Europe. Jefferson, following an impulse from his own mind, designed by his ordinance to establish from end to end of the whole country a north and south line, at which the westward extension of slavery should be stayed by an impassable bound. Of the men held in bondage beyond that line, he did not propose the instant emancipation; but slavery was to be rung out with the departing century, so that in all the western territory, whether held in 1784 by Georgia, North Carolina, Virginia, or the United States, the sun of the new century might dawn on no slave.

To make the decree irrevocable, he further proposed that all the articles should form a charter of compact, to be executed in congress under the seal of the United States, to be promulgated, and to stand as fundamental constitutions between the thirteen original states and the new states to be erected under the ordinance.

The design of Jefferson marks an era in the history of universal freedom. For the moment more was attempted than could be accomplished. North Carolina, in the following June, made a cession of all her western lands, but soon revoked it; and Virginia did not release Kentucky till it became a state of the union. Moreover, the sixteen years during which slavery was to have a respite might nurse it into such strength that at the end of them it would be able to defy or reverse the ordinance.

Exactly on the ninth anniversary of the fight at Concord and Lexington, Richard Dobbs Spaight of North Carolina, seconded by Jacob Read of South Carolina, moved "to strike out" the fifth article. The presiding officer, following the rule of the time, put the question: "Shall the words stand?" Seven states, and seven only, were needed to carry the affirmative. Let Jefferson, who did not refrain from describing Spaight as "a young fool," relate what followed. "The clause was lost by an individual vote only. Ten states were present. The four eastern states, New York, and Pennsylvania were for the clause; Jersey would have been for it, but there were but two members, one of whom was sick in his chambers. South Carolina, Maryland, and !Virginia! voted against it. North Carolina was divided, as would have been Virginia, had not one of its delegates been sick in bed."[1] The absent Virginian was Monroe, who for himself has left no evidence of such an intention, and who was again absent when in the following year the question was revived. For North Carolina, the vote of Spaight was neutralized by Williamson.

Six states against three, sixteen men against seven, proscribed slavery. Jefferson bore witness against it all his life long. "Wythe and himself, as commissioners to codify the laws of Virginia, had provided for gradual emancipation. When, in 1785, the legislature refused to consider the proposal, Jefferson

[1] Jefferson to Madison, 25 April, 1784. MS.

wrote: "We must hope that an overruling Providence is preparing the deliverance of these our suffering brethren."[1] In 1786, narrating the loss of the clause against slavery in the ordinance of 1784, he said: "The voice of a single individual would have prevented this abominable crime; heaven will not always be silent; the friends to the rights of human nature will in the end prevail."[2]

To friends who visited him in the last period of his life, he delighted to renew these aspirations of his earlier years.[3] In a letter written just forty-five days before his death, he refers to the ordinance of 1784, saying: "My sentiments have been forty years before the public; although I shall not live to see them consummated, they will not die with me; but, living or dying, they will ever be in my most fervent prayer."[4]

The ordinance for the government of the northwestern territory, shorn of its proscription of slavery, was adopted, and remained in force for three years. Later in the session, Jefferson reported an ordinance for ascertaining the mode of locating and disposing of the public lands. The continental domain, when purchased of the Indians, was to be divided by the surveyors into townships of ten geographical miles square, the townships into hundreds of one mile square, and with such precautions that the wilderness could be mapped out into ranges of lots so exactly as to preclude uncertainty of title. As to inheritance, the words of the ordinance were: "The

---

[1] Jefferson, ix. 279.
[2] Ibid., 276.
[3] Oral communication from William Campbell Preston of South Carolina.
[4] Jefferson to James Heaton, 20 May, 1826.

lands therein shall pass in descent and dower according to the customs known in the common law by the name of gavelkind." [1] Upon this ordinance of Jefferson, most thoughtfully prepared and written wholly by his own hand, no final vote was taken.

Congress had already decided to establish a mint. For the American coinage, Robert and Gouverneur Morris proposed the decimal system of computation, with silver as the only metallic money, and the fourteen hundred and fortieth part of a Spanish piece of eight reals, or, as the Americans called it, the dollar, as the unit of the currency. Jefferson chose the dollar, which circulated freely in every part of the American continent, as the money unit for computation; and the subdivision of the dollar into a tenth, a hundredth, and a thousandth part. For coinage, he proposed a gold coin of ten dollars; silver coins of one dollar and of one tenth of a dollar: and copper coins of one hundredth part of a dollar.[2] This system steadily grew in favor; and, in 1786, was established by congress without a negative vote.[3]

The total cost of the war, from the first blood shed at Lexington to the general orders of Washington in April, 1783, proclaiming peace, was reckoned by Jefferson[4] at one hundred and forty millions of dollars. Congress, before the formation of the confederacy, had emitted paper money to the amount of two hundred millions of dollars, which at the time of its emis-

---

[1] Papers of Old Congress, xxx. 59. MS.
[2] Jefferson, i. 54. Notes on the Establishment of a money unit and of a coinage for the United States. Ibid., 162-174.
[3] Journals of Congress, iv, 376, for 8 Aug., 1786.
[4] Jefferson, ix. 360.

sion might, as he thought, have had the value of thirty-six millions of silver dollars; the value of the masses of paper emitted by the several states at various stages of the war he estimated at thirty-six millions more. This estimate of the values of the paper money rests in part upon conjecture, and the materials for correcting it with accuracy, especially as it regards the issues of the states, are wanting. The remaining cost of the war, or sixty-eight millions of dollars, with the exception of about one and a half million paid on requisition by the several states, existed on the first of January, 1784, in the form of debts in Europe to the amount of nearly eight millions of dollars; of debts due to the several classes of domestic creditors; and of debts due to states for advances on the common account. The value of the paper money issued by congress had perished as it passed from hand to hand, and its circulation had ceased.

In preparing the appropriations for the coming year, congress was met at the threshold by an unforeseen difficulty. Bills of Morris on Holland, that were protested for non-acceptance, would amount, with damages on protest for non-acceptance, to six hundred and thirty-six thousand dollars. To save the honor of the country, this sum was demanded of the separate states in a circular letter drawn by Jefferson. But, meantime, John Adams, in Amsterdam, manfully struggled to meet the drafts, and, by combining the allurement of a lottery with that of a very profitable loan, he succeeded.

The court of France, with delicacy and generosity, of its own motion released the United States from

TOWARD A BETTER UNION. 161

the payment of interest on their obligations during the war and for the first period of peace; and they on their part by formal treaty bound themselves to the payment of interest as it should accrue from the beginning of the year 1784.

For that year, the sum required for the several branches of the public service was estimated at about four hundred and fifty thousand dollars; for the interest on the foreign debt, nearly four hundred thousand dollars; the balance of interest and the interest on the domestic debt, about six hundred and eighty thousand dollars; the deficit of the last two years, one million; other arrears connected with the debt, nearly one million three hundred thousand dollars: in all, about four millions. This was a greater sum than could be asked for. Instead of making new requisitions, Jefferson credited all federal payments of the states to the requisition of eight millions of dollars in the first year of the confederacy. One half of that requisition was remitted; of the other, three states had paid nothing, the rest had paid less than a million and a half; a balance would remain of nearly two millions seven hundred thousand dollars; and of this balance a requisition was made on each of the states for its just proportion. Could the apportionment be collected within the year, it would defray the expenses of all the departments of the general government and the interest on the foreign and domestic loans, leaving only some part of domestic arrears to be provided for at a later day. Could this system be carried into effect, the credit of the government would be established.

162   ON THE WAY TO A FEDERAL CONVENTION.

CHAP.
II.

1784.

Madison had acceded to the wishes of his county, that he should be one of its representatives in the legislature, believing: that he might there best awaken Virginia to the glory of taking the lead in the rescue of the union and the blessings staked on union from an impending catastrophe.[1] Jefferson had kept him thoroughly informed of the movement for bringing order into the public finances. At the instigation of Madison, Philip Mazzei, an Italian, then in quest of a consular appointment in Europe,[2] paid a visit to Patrick Henry, "the great leader who had been violently opposed to every idea of increasing the power of congress."[3] On his return, Mazzei reported that the present politics of Henry comprehended very friendly views toward the confederacy, and a support of the payment of British debts.[4]

May. 14.

At Richmond, in May, before the assembly proceeded to active business, Henry sought a conference with Madison and Jones, and declared to them that "a bold example set by Virginia would have influence on the other states;" "he saw ruin inevitable unless something was done to give congress a compulsory process on delinquent states." This conviction, he said, was his only inducement for coming into the present assembly. It was agreed that Jones and Madison should sketch some plan for giving greater power to the federal government, and Henry promised to sustain it on the floor. A majority of the assembly were new members, composed

[1] Gilpin, 693, 694; Elliot, 113.
[2] Jefferson to Madison, 16 March, 1784. MS.
[3] Edward Bancroft to William Frazer, 28 May, 1784. MS.
[4] Madison to Jefferson, 5 April, 1784. Madison, i. 77.

of young men and officers of the late army, so that new measures were expected. Great hopes were formed of Madison, and those who knew him best were sure that he would not disappoint the most sanguine expectations.[1]

Virginia passed an act empowering congress, for any term not exceeding fifteen years, to prohibit the importation or exportation of goods to or from that state in vessels belonging to subjects of powers with whom the United States had no commercial treaty[2] They further consented that the contributions of the state to the general treasury should be in proportion to the population, counting three fifths of the slaves. All apprehension of danger from conceding a revenue to the confederacy seemed to have passed away; and it was agreed that, pending the acceptance of the amendment to the constitution, any apportionment of the requisitions directed by congress for the purpose of discharging the national debt and the expenses of the national government ought to be complied with. It was further resolved that the accounts subsisting between the United States and individual states should be settled, and that then the balance due ought to be enforced, if necessary, by distress on the property of defaulting states or of their citizens. And these resolutions passed the legislature without a division.[3] It remained only to see what effect the measures of Virginia

---

[1] William Short to T. Jefferson, 14 May.,1784, MS. ; Madison to Jefferson. 15 May, 1784, Madison, I 80 ; Edward Bancroft to William Frazer, 28 May, 1784, MS. In the letter of Short to Jefferson, the date is probably an error for May 15. See Madison, i. 80, "last evening."

[2] Hening, xi. 388.

[3] Journal of the Committee of the States, p. 7.

164   ON THE WAY TO A FEDERAL CONVENTION.

CHAP. II.

1 7 8 4.

July. 8.

June. 4.

would have on the other twelve states and on herself.

Experience had proved the impossibility of keeping together a sufficient representation of the states in congress. It began to be thought better to hold but a short and active annual session of the national congress with compulsory attendance of its members, and appoint commissioners of the states to conduct executive business for the rest of the year. This proposition was one of the last which Jefferson assisted to carry through. He had wished to visit Washington before his voyage; but, armed with at least one-and-twenty commissions for himself and his two associates to negotiate treaties with foreign powers, he was obliged to repair to Boston, where, after "experiencing in the highest degree its hospitality and civilities,"[1] he embarked for France, full of hope that the attempt to negotiate a treaty of commerce with Great Britain would meet with success.[2] Before leaving the country, he wrote to Madison: "The best effects are produced by sending our young statesmen to congress. Here they see the affairs of the confederacy from a high ground; they learn the importance of the union, and befriend federal measures when they return."[3]

The committee of states came together on the fourth of June. Four states never attended; and, as the assent of nine was required to carry any proposition except adjournment, the absence or the negative

---

[1] Jefferson to Gerry, 2 July, 1784. Austin's Life of Gerry, i. 55.

[2] Information from Edward Bancroft, 26 Aug., 1784. MS.

[3] Jefferson to Madison, 25 April, 1784. MS.

TOWARD A BETTER UNION. 165

of one state stopped all proceedings. A difference occurring on the eleventh of August, the members from three New England states went home; the remaining six states met irregularly till the nineteenth of that month; and then, from inability to do any manner of business, they withdrew. The United States of America were left without any visible representation whatever. The chief benefit from the experiment was to establish in the minds of Americans the necessity of vesting the executive power, not in a body of men, but, as Jefferson phrased it, in a single arbiter.

This was the state of the government when, on the first of November, Robert Morris retired from his office as superintendent of the finances of the United States. He had conciliated the support of the moneyed men at home.[1] His bank of North America, necessarily of little advantage to the United States, proved highly remunerative to its stockholders;[2] the bankruptcy of the nation could have been prevented only by the nation itself. Congress passed an act that for the future no person, appointed a commissioner of the treasury of the United States, should be permitted to be engaged, either directly or indirectly, in any trade or commerce whatsoever.[3] Before retiring, Morris announced to the representative of France in America that he could not pay the

CHAP. II.

1 7 8 4.
Aug.
19.

Nov.
1.

---

[1] Hamilton, i. 316, 317.
[2] The dividend for the first half year of the bank was four and a half per cent; for the second, four and one fourth; for the third, six and one half; for the fourth, eight; for the fifth, a little more than nine and a half per cent. Official report in Pennsylvania Packet for 6 July, 1782; 7 Jan., 1783; 8 July, 1783; 6 Jan., 1784; 8 July, 1784.
[3] Journals of Congress for 28 May, 1784.

interest on the Dutch loan of ten million livres for which France was the guarantee;[1] a default which deeply injured the reputation of the United States in Paris.[2] He could still less provide for paying the interest for 1784 on the direct debt to France.

The members of the fifth congress arrived so slowly at Trenton, that Marbois, who was charged with French affairs, on the twentieth of November reported what at the moment was true: "There is in America no general government, neither congress, nor president, nor head of any one administrative department."[3] Six days later, while there was still no quorum in congress, Richard Henry Lee, a delegate from Virginia, wrote to Madison: "It is by many here suggested, as a very necessary step for congress to take, the calling on the states to form a convention for the sole purpose of revising the confederation, so far as to enable congress to execute with more energy, effect, and vigor the powers assigned to it than it appears by experience that they can do under the present state of things." In a letter of the same date Mercer said: "There will be a motion made early in the ensuing congress for such a convention."[4] Madison, who knew the heart of his correspondents, answered Lee firmly and yet warily: "The union of the states is essential to their safety against foreign danger and internal contention; the perpetuity and efficacy of the present

---

[1] Robert Morris to Marbois, 17 Aug., 1784. Dip. Cor., xii. 494.

[2] Edward Bancroft to Lord Carmarthen, Paris, 8 Dec, 1784. MS.

[3] Marbois to Rayneval, 20 Nov., 1784. MS.

[4] J. F. Mercer to Madison, 26 Nov., 1784. MS.

system cannot be confided in; the question, therefore, is, in what mode and at what moment the experiment for supplying the defects ought to be made."¹

"The American confederation," so thought the French minister at Versailles, "has a strong tendency to dissolution; it is well that on this point we have neither obligations to fulfil nor any interest to cherish."²

¹ Madison Papers, 707, 708. ² To Marbois, Versailles, 14 Dec, 1784. MS.

CHAPTER III.

THE WEST.

1784, 1785.

The desire to hold and to people the great western domain mingled with every effort for imparting greater energy to the union. In that happy region each state saw the means of granting lands to its soldiers of the revolution and a possession of inestimable promise. Washington took up the office of securing the national allegiance of the transmontane woodsmen by improving the channels of communication with the states on the Atlantic. For that purpose, more than to look after lands of his own, he, on the first day of September, began a tour to the westward to make an examination of the portages between the nearest navigable branches of the Potomac and James river on the one side and of the Ohio and the Kanawha on the other. Wherever he came, he sought and closely questioned the men famed for personal observation of the streams and paths on each side of the Alleghanies.

From Fort Cumberland he took the usual road

over the mountains to the valley of the Yohogany,[1] and studied closely the branches of that stream. The country between the Little Kanawha and the branches of the James river being at that moment infested with hostile Indians, he returned through the houseless solitude between affluents of the Cheat river and of the Potomac. As he traced the way for commerce over that wild region he was compelled to pass a night on a rough mountain-side in a pouring rain, "with no companion but a servant and no protection but his cloak; one day he was without food; sometimes he could find no path except the track of buffaloes; and in unceasing showers his ride through the close bushes seemed to him little better than the swimming of rivulets.[2]

Reaching home after an absence of thirty-three days, he declared himself pleased with the results of his tour. Combining his observations with the reminiscences of his youthful mission to the French in the heart of Ohio, he sketched in his mind a system of internal communication of the Potomac with the Ohio; of an affluent of the Ohio with the Cuyahoga; and so from the site of Cleveland to Detroit, and onward to the Lake of the Woods.

Six days after his return he sent a most able report to Harrison, then governor of Virginia. "We should do our part toward opening the communication for the fur and peltry trade of the lakes," such were his

---

[1] Yohogany is the "phonetical" Mode of spelling for yOugHlOgany, as the English wrote the Indian name; the French, discarding the gutturals, wrote Ohio. So at the north-east, in Passamaquoddy, the French dropped the first two syllables and made of the last three Acadie. The name, Belle Riviere, is a translation of Allegh-any.
[2] Washington's Journal. MS.

words, "and for the produce of the country, which will be settled faster than any other ever was, or any one would imagine. But there is a political consideration for so doing which is of still greater importance.

"I need not remark to you, sir, that the flanks and rear of the United States are possessed by other powers, and formidable ones too; nor how necessary it is to apply interest to bind all parts of the union together by indissoluble bonds. The western states, I speak now from my own observation, stand as it were upon a pivot; the touch of a feather would turn them any way. They have looked down the Mississippi until the Spaniards threw difficulties in their way. The untoward disposition of the Spaniards on the one hand and the policy of Great Britain on the other to retain as long as possible the posts of Detroit, Niagara, and Oswego, may be improved to the greatest advantage by this state if she would open the avenues to the trade of that country."[1]

Harrison heartily approved the views of Washington, and laid his letter before the assembly of Virginia, whose members gladly accepted its large views and stood ready to give them legislative support.[2]

Mean time Lafayette, who was making a tour through the United States and receiving everywhere a grateful and joyous welcome, was expected in Virginia. For the occasion, Washington repaired to Richmond; and there the assembly, to mark their reverence and affection, sent Patrick Henry, Madison, and others to

---

[1] Washington to Harrison, 10 Oct., 1784. Sparks, ix. 58.

[2] Harrison to Washington, 13 Nov., 1784. Sparks, ix. 68.

assure him that they retained the most lasting impressions of the transcendent services rendered in his late public character, and had proofs that no change of situation could turn his thoughts from the welfare of his country.

Three days later the house, by the same committee, addressed Lafayette, recalling "his cool intrepidity and wise conduct during his command in the campaign of 1781, and, as the wish most suitable to his character, desired that those who might emulate his glory would equally pursue the interests of humanity."

From Richmond Lafayette accompanied Washington to Mount Vernon and after a short visit was attended by his host as far as Annapolis, where he received the congratulations of Maryland. Near the middle of December, congress, in a public session, took leave of him with every mark of honor. In his answer he repeated the great injunctions of Washington's farewell letter, and, having travelled widely in the country, bore witness to "the prevailing disposition of the people to strengthen the confederation." In his love for America, his three "hobbies," as he called them, were the closer federal union, the alliance with France, and the abolition of slavery. He embarked for his native land "fraught with affecttion to America, and disposed to render it every possible service."[1]   To Washington he announced from Europe that he was about to attempt the relief of the protestants in France.[2]

[1] Jefferson to Madison, 18 March 785. MS.

[2] Lafayette to Washington, 11 May, 1785.

The conversation of Washington during his stay in Richmond had still further impressed members of the legislature with the magnitude of his designs. Shortly after his departure a joint memorial from inhabitants of Maryland and of Virginia, representing the advantages which would flow from establishing under the authority of the two states a company for improving the navigation of the Potomac, was presented to the general assembly of each of them. But the proposed plan had defects, and moreover previous communication between the two states could alone secure uniformity of action. It was decided to consult with Maryland, and the negotiation was committed to Washington himself. Leaving; Mount Vernon at a few hours' notice, the general hastened to Annapolis. Amendments of the plan were thoughtfully digested, rapidly carried through both houses, and despatched to Richmond. There a law of the same tenor was immediately passed[1] without opposition, "to the mutual satisfaction of both states," and, as Washington hoped, "to the advantage of the union."[2]

At the same time the two governments made appropriations for opening a road from the highest practicable navigation of the Potomac to that of the river Cheat or Monongahela, and they concurred in an application to Pennsylvania for permission to open another road from Fort Cumberland to the Yohogany. Like measures were initiated by Virginia for connecting James river with some affluent of the Great Kanawha. Moreover, the executive was authorized to

---

[1] Hening, x. 510.   [2] Madison, i. 123, 124. Sparks, ix. 82.

appoint commissioners to examine the most convenient course for a canal between Elizabeth river and the waters of the Roanoke, and contingently to make application to the legislature of North Carolina for its concurrence.[1]

Early in 1785 the legislature of Virginia, repeating, in words written by Madison, "their sense of the unexampled merits of George Washington toward his country," vested in him shares in both the companies alike of the Potomac and of James river.[2] But, animated by a pure zeal for the general good and conscious of the weight of his counsels, he was resolved never to suffer his influence to be impaired by any suspicion of interested motives, and, not able to undo an act of the legislature, held the shares, but only as a trustee for the public.

Another question between Maryland and Virginia remained for solution. The charter to Lord Baltimore, which Virginia had resisted as a severance of her territory, bounded his jurisdiction by the "further bank" of the Potomac. When both states assumed independence, Virginia welcomed her northern neighbor to the common war for liberty by releasing every claim to its territory, but she reserved the navigation of the border stream. To define with exactness their respective rights on its waters, the Virginia legislature in June, 1784, led the way by naming George Mason, Edmund Randolph, Madison, and Alexander Henderson, as their commissioners to frame, "in concert with commissioners of Maryland, liberal, liberal, equit-

---

[1] Washington to R. H. Lee, 8 Feb., 1785. Sparks, ix. 91.   [2] Hening, xi. 525, 526.

174 ON THE WAY TO A FEDERAL CONVENTION.

CHAP. III.

1 7 8 3.

Nov. 30.

able and mutually advantageous regulations touching the jurisdiction and navigation of the river."[1] Maryland gladly accepted the invitation, and in the following March the Joint commission was to meet at Alexandria, hard by Mount Vernon. In this manner, through the acts and appropriations of the legislature of Virginia, Washington connected the interests and hopes of her people with the largest and noblest conceptions, and to the states alike on her southern and her northern border and to the rising empire in the west, where she would surely meet New York and New England, she gave the weightiest pledges of inviolable attachment to the union. To carry forward these designs, the next step must be taken by congress, which should have met at Trenton on the first day of November, but, from the tardy arrival of its members, was not organized until the thirtieth. It was the rule of congress that its president should be chosen in succession from each one of the different states. In eight years, beginning with Virginia, it had proceeded by rotation through them all except New Hampshire, Rhode Island, North Carolina and Georgia. But now the rule, which in itself was a bad one, was broken,[2] and Richard Henry Lee was elected president. The rule of rotation was never again followed; but this want of fidelity to a custom that had long been respected tended to increase the jealousy of the small states. Before Christmas and before finishing any important business, congress, not finding sufficient accommodations

[1] Journals of House of Delegates for 28 June, 1784.

[2] Madison, i. 117. Compare Otto to Vergenues, 15 June, 1786. MS.

in Trenton, adjourned to the eleventh of January, 1785, and to New York as its abode.

Congress had put at its head the most determined and the most restlessly indefatigable opponent of any change whatever in the articles of confederation. Lee renewed intimate relations with Gerry, the leading member of congress from Massachusetts. He sought to revive his earlier influence in Boston through Samuel Adams. The venerable patriot shared his jealousy of conferring too great powers on a body far removed from its constituents, but had always supported a strict enforcement of the just authority of government, and he replied: "It would have been better to have fallen in the struggle than now to become a contemptible nation."[1]

The harbor at the mouth of the Hudson was at that time the most convenient port of entry for New Jersey and Connecticut, and the state of New York, through its custom-house, levied on their inhabitants as well as on its own an ever increasing revenue by imposts. The collector was a stubborn partisan. The last legislature had elected to the fifth congress Jay, Robert K. Livingston, Egbert Benson, and Lansing, of whom, even after Jay became the minister for foreign affairs, a majority favored the founding of a nation. But the opinions of the president of congress, who was respected as one of the most illustrious statesmen of Virginia, assisted to bring about a revolution in the politics of New York.[2] On the

---

[1] S. Adams to R. H. Lee, 23 Dec., 1784. MS.

[2] Jay to Washington, 27 June, 1786. Letters to Washington, iv. 136.

176 ON THE WAY TO A FEDERAL CONVENTION.

CHAP. III.

1785.
March.
19.

nineteenth of March its legislature appointed three "additional delegates" to congress, of whom Haring and Melaneton Smith, like Lansing, opposed federal measures; and for the next four years the state of New York obstinately resisted a thorough revision of the constitution. Of the city of New York, the aspirations for a national union could not be repressed.

1784.
Dec.
14.

Immediately on the organization of congress, Washington, with a careful discrimination between the office of that body and the functions of the states, urged through its president that congress should have the western waters well explored, their capacities for navigation ascertained as far as the communications between Lake Erie and the Wabash, and between Lake Michigan and the Mississippi, and a complete and perfect map made of the country at least as far west as the Miamis, which run into the Ohio and Lake Erie. And he pointed out the Miami village as the place for a very important post for the union. The expense attending such an undertaking could not be great; the advantages would be unbounded. "Nature," he said," has made such a display of her bounty in those regions that the more the country is explored the more it will rise in estimation. The spirit of emigration is great; people have got impatient; and, though you cannot stop the road, it is yet in your power to mark the way. A little while and you will not be able to do either."[1]

In the same week in which the legislature of New York reversed its position on national policy, Wash-

---

[1] Washington to R. H. Lee, 14 Dec, 1784. Sparks, ix. 80, 81.

ington renewed his admonitions to Lee on planting the western territory. "The mission of congress will now be to fix a medium price on these lands and to point out the most advantageous mode of seating them, so that law and good government may be administered, and the union strengthened and supported. Progressive seating is the only means by which this can be effected;" and, resisting the politicians who might wish to balance northern states by; southern, he insisted that to mark out but one new state would better advance the public welfare than to mark out ten.[1]

On the eleventh of March William Grayson took his seat for the first time as a member of congress. He had been educated in England at Oxford and had resided at the Temple in London. His short career furnishes only glimpses of his character. In 1776 he had been an aide-de-camp to Washington, with whom he kept up affectionate relations; in 1777 he commanded a Virginia regiment and gained honors at Monmouth. His private life appears to have been faultless; his public acts show independence, courage, and a humane and noble nature. In the state legislature of the previous winter he was chairman of the committee to which Washington's report on the negotiations with Maryland had been referred.[2] The first evidence of his arrival in New York is a letter of the tenth of March, 1785, to his former chief, announcing that Jefferson's ordinance for disposing of western lands, which had had its first read-

11.

[1] Washington to R. H. Lee, 15 March, 1785. MS.
[2] Journals Virginia House of Delegates, 99

178 ON THE WAY TO A FEDERAL CONVENTION.

CHAP. III.

1785. March. 8.

ing in May, 1784, had been brought once more before congress.

Not Washington alone had reminded congress of its duties to the West. Informed by Gerry of the course of public business, Timothy Pickering, from Philadelphia, addressed most earnest letters to Rufus King. He complained that no reservation of land was made for the support of ministers of the gospel, nor even for schools and academies, and he further wrote: "Congress once made this important declaration, 'that all men are created equal; that they are endowed by their Creator with certain unalienable rights; that among these are life, liberty, and the pursuit of happiness'; and these truths were held to be self-evident. To suffer the continuance of slaves till they can gradually be emancipated, in states already overrun with them, may be pardonable, because unavoidable without hazarding greater evils; but to introduce them into countries where none now exist can never be forgiven. For God's sake, then, let one more effort be made to prevent so terrible a calamity! The fundamental constitutions for those states are yet liable to alterations, and this is probably the only time when the evil can certainly be prevented." Nor would Pickering harbor the thought of delay in the exclusion of slavery. "It will be infinitely easier," he said," to prevent the evil at first than to eradicate it or check it in any future time."[1]

16.

The sixteenth of March was fixed for the discussion of the affairs of the West. The report that was

[1] Pickering to King, 8 March, 1785. Pickering's Pickering, i. 509, 510.

before congress was Jefferson's scheme for "locating and disposing of land in the western territory;" and it was readily referred to a committee of one from each state, Grayson being the member from Virginia and King from Massachusetts. King, seconded by Ellery of Rhode Island, proposed that a part of the rejected anti-slavery clause in Jefferson's ordinance for the government of the western territory should be referred to a committee; all that related to the western territory of the three southern states was omitted; and so too was the clause postponing the prohibition of slavery.

On the question for committing this proposition, the four New England states, New York, New Jersey, and Pennsylvania, voted unanimously in the affirmative; Maryland by a majority, McHenry going with the South, John Henry and William Hindman with the North. For Virginia, Grayson voted aye, but was overpowered by Hardy and Richard Henry Lee. The two Carolinas were unanimous for the negative. So the vote stood, eight states against three; eighteen members against eight;[2] and the motion was forthwith committed to King, Howell, and Ellery.[3]

On the sixth of April, King from his committee reported his resolution, which is entirely in his own handwriting[4] and which consists of two clauses: it

CHAP. III.

1784. March. 16.

April. 6.

---

[1] The original motion of Rufus King for the reference, in his handwriting, Is preserved in Papers of Old Congress, xxxi. MS.

[2] Journals of Congress, iv. 481, 482.

[3] It is endorsed in the handwriting of Charles Thomson: "Motion for preventing slavery in new states, March 16, 1785. Referred to Mr. King, Mr. Howell, Mr. Ellery."

[4] It is to be found in Papers of Old Congress, xxxi. 329, and

180 ON THE WAY TO A FEDERAL CONVENTION.

CHAP. III.

1785. April. 6.

allowed slavery in the North-west until the first day of the year 1801, but no longer; and it "provided that always, upon the escape of any person into any of the states described in the resolve of congress of the twenty-third day of April, 1784, from whom labor or service is lawfully claimed in any one of the thirteen original states, such fugitive might be lawfully reclaimed and carried back to the person claiming his labor or service, this resolve notwithstanding;"[1] King reserved his resolution to be brought forward as a separate measure, after the land ordinance should be passed. "I expect," wrote Grayson to Madison, "seven states may be found liberal enough to adopt it;"[2] but there is no evidence that it was ever again called up in that congress.

12.

On the twelfth of April[3] the committee for framing an ordinance for the disposal of the western lands made their report. It was written by Grayson,[4] who formed it out of a conflict of opinions, and took the chief part in conducting it through the house. As an inducement for neighborhoods of the same re-

is endorsed in the handwriting of Rufus King: "Report on Mr. King's motion for the exclusion of slavery in the new states. "And it is further endorsed in the handwriting of Charles Thomson: "Mr. King, Mr. Howell, Mr. Ellery. Entered 6 April, 1785, read. Thursday, April 14, assigned for consideration."

[1] The printed copy of this report of King is to be found in Papers of Old Congress, xxxi. 331, and is endorsed in the handwriting of Charles Thomson: "To prevent slavery in the new states. Included in substance in the ordinance for a temporary government passed the 13 July, 1787."

[2] Grayson to Madison, 1 May, 1785. MS. The ordinance for the sale of lands required the consent of nine states; the regulative ordinance, of but seven.

[3] Grayson to Washington, 15 April, 1785. MS.

[3] The original report in the handwriting of Grayson is preserved in the apers of Old Congress, lvi. 451.

ligious sentiments to confederate for the purpose of purchasing and settling together, it was a land law for a people going forth to take possession of a seemingly endless domain. Its division was to be into townships, with a perpetual reservation of one mile square in every township for the support of religion, and another for education. The house refused its assent to the reservation for the support of religion, as connecting the church with the state; but the reservation for the support of schools received a general welcome. Jefferson had proposed townships of ten miles square; the committee, of seven; but the motion of Grayson, that they should be of six miles square,[1] was finally accepted. The South, accustomed to the mode of indiscriminate locations and settlements, insisted on the rule which would give the most free scope to the roving emigrant; and, as the bill required the vote of nine states for adoption, and during the debates on the subject more than ten were never present, the eastern people, though "amazingly attached to their own custom of planting by townships," yielded to the compromise that every other township should be sold by sections.[2] The surveys were to be confined to one state and to five ranges, extending from the Ohio to Lake Erie, and were to be made under the direction of the geographer of the United States. The bounds of every parcel that was sold were fixed beyond a question; the mode of registry was simple, convenient, and almost without cost; the form of conveyance most concise

[1] Journals of Congress, iv. 513. [2] Grayson to Madison, 1 May, 1785. MS.

and clear. Never was land offered to a poor man at less cost or with a safer title. For one bad provision, which, however, was three years after repealed, the consent of congress was for the moment extorted; the lands, as surveyed, were to be drawn for by lot by the several states in proportion to the requisitions made upon them, and were to be sold publicly within the states. But it was carefully provided that they should be paid for in the obligations of the United States, at the rate of a dollar an acre. To secure the promises made to Virginia, chiefly on behalf of the officers and soldiers who took part in conquering the North-west from British authority, it was agreed, after a discussion of four days,[1] to reserve the district between the Little Miami and the Scioto.

The land ordinance of Jefferson, as amended from 1784 to 1788, definitively settled the character of the national land laws, which are still treasured up as one of the most precious heritages from the founders of the republic.

The frontier settlements at the west needed the protection of a military force. In 1784, soon after the exchange of the ratifications of peace, Gerry at Annapolis protested against the right of Congress on its own authority to raise standing armies or even a few armed men in time of peace. His conduct was approved by his state, whose delegation was instructed to oppose and protest on all occasions against the exercise of the power. From that time congress had done no more than recommend the states to raise

---

[1] Grayson to Madison, 1 May, 1785. MS.

troops. It was now thought necessary to raise seven hundred men to protect the West. The recommenddation should have been proportioned among all the states; but congress ventured to call only on Connecticut, New York, New Jersey and Pennsylvania as the states most conveniently situated to furnish troops who were to be formed into one regiment and for three years guard the north-western frontiers and the public stores.

CHAPTER IV.

THE REGULATION OF COMMERCE. THE FIFTH CONGRESS.

1784, 1785.

CHAP. IV.

1782.

The legislature of Connecticut in 1783, angry at the grant of half pay to the officers of the army, insisted that the requisitions of Congress had no validity until they received the approval of the state. But the vote was only "a fire among the brambles;" and the people at the next election chose a legislature which accepted the general impost on commerce, even though it should be assented to by no more than twelve states.[1] The Virginia assembly of that year discountenanced the deviation from the rule of unanimity as a dangerous precedent;[2] but it was adopted by Maryland.[3]

1784.

In the following winter Noah Webster, of Hartford, busied himself in the search for a form of a continental government which should act as efficaciously on its members as a local government. "So long as

---

[1] Monroe to Madison, 14 Dec., 1784. MS.
[2] Madison to Monroe, 24 Dec., 1784, Madison, 1. 114, 115.
[3] Act of Maryland. Session of 1784, 1785. In Penn. Packet of 8 Feb., 1785.

any individual state has power to defeat the measures of the other twelve, our pretended union," so he expressed the opinion which began to prevail, "is but a name, and our confederation a cobweb. The sovereignty of each state ought not to be abridged in any article relating to its own government; in a matter that equally respects all the states, a majority of the states must decide. We cannot and ought not to divest ourselves of provincial attachments, but we should subordinate them to the general interest of the continent; as a citizen of the American empire, every individual has a national interest far superior to all others."[1]

The outlays in America of the British in the last year of their occupation of New York, and the previous expenditures for the French army, had supplied the Northern states with specie; so that purchasers were found for the bills of Robert Morris on Europe, which were sold at a discount of twenty or even forty per cent.[2] The prospect of enormous gains tempted American merchants to import in one year more than their exports could pay for in three;[3] while factors of English houses, bringing over British goods on British account, jostled the American merchants in their own streets. Fires which still burn were then lighted. He that will trace the American policy of that day to its cause must look to British restrictions and British protective duties suddenly applied to Americans as aliens.

[1] Sketches of American Policy by Noah Webster, pp. 32-38.
[2] Pelatiah Webster's Essays, Ed. 1791, 266, 267, note.
[3] E. Bancroft to W. Frazer, 8 Nov., 1783. MS.

CHAP. IV.

1784.

The people had looked for peace and prosperity to come hand in hand, and, when hostilities ceased, they ran into debt for English goods, never doubting that their wonted industries would yield them the means of payment as of old. But excessive importations at low prices crushed domestic manufactures; trade with the British West Indies was obstructed; neither rice, tobacco, pitch, turpentine, nor ships could be remitted as heretofore. The whale fishery of Massachusetts had brought to its mariners in a year more than eight hundred thousand dollars in specie, the clear gain of perilous labor. The export of their oil was now obstructed by a duty in England of ninety dollars the ton. Importations from England must be paid for chiefly by cash and bills of exchange. The Americans had chosen to be aliens to England; they could not complain of being taxed like aliens, but they awoke to demand powers of retaliation.

1785.

The country began to be in earnest as it summoned congress to change its barren discussions for efficient remedies. The ever increasing voice of complaint broke out from the impatient commercial towns of the northern and central states. On the eleventh of January, 1785, the day on which congress established itself in New York, the artificers, tradesmen, and mechanics of that city, as they gave it a welcome, added these brave words:" We hope our representatives will coincide with the other states in augmenting your power to every exigency of the union."[1] The New York chamber of commerce in like manner entreated it to make the commerce of

---

[1] MS. vol. of Remonstrances and Addresses, 343.

the United States one of the first objects of its care, and to counteract the injurious restrictions of foreign nations.¹ The New York legislature, then in session, imposed a double duty on all goods imported in British bottoms.²

On the twenty-second of March, 1785, a bill to "protect the manufactures" of Pennsylvania by specific or ad valorem duties on more than seventy articles, among them on manufactures of iron and steel, was read in its assembly for the second time, debated by paragraphs, and then ordered to be printed for public consideration.³ The citizens of Philadelphia, recalling the usages of the revolution, on the second of June held a town meeting; and, after the deliberations of their committee for eighteen days, they declared that relief from the oppressions under which the American trade and manufactures languished could spring only from the grant to congress of full constitutional powers over the commerce of the United States; that foreign manufactures interfering with domestic industry ought to be discouraged by prohibitions or protective duties. They raised a committee to lay their resolutions in the form of a petition before their own assembly, and to correspond with committees appointed elsewhere for similar purposes. On the twentieth of September, after the bill of the Pennsylvania legislature had been nearly six months under consideration by the people, and after it had been amended by an increase of duties, especially on manufactures of iron, and by

---

[1] MS. vol. of Remonstrances and Addresses, 351.
[2] Chief Justice Smith's extract of letters from New York. MS.
[3] Penn. Packet, 13 May, 1785.

188 ON THE WAY TO A FEDERAL CONVENTION.

CHAP.
IV.
1785.

a discriminating tonnage duty on ships of nations having no treaty of commerce with congress, it became a law[1] with general acclamation.

Pennsylvania had been cheered on its way by voices from Boston. On the eighteenth of April the merchants and tradesmen of that town, meeting in Faneuil Hall, established a committee of correspondence with merchants of other towns, bound themselves not to buy British goods of resident British factors, and prayed Congress for the needed immediate relief.[2] Their petition was reserved by congress for consideration when the report of its committee on commerce should be taken up. The movement in Boston penetrated every class of its citizens; its artisans and mechanics joined the merchants and tradesmen in condemning; the ruinous excess of British importations. To these proceedings Grayson directed the attention of Madison.[3]

On the tenth of May the town of Boston elected its representatives to the general court, among them Hancock, whose health had not permitted him to be a candidate for the place of governor. Two years before, Boston, in its mandate to the men of its choice, had, in extreme language, vindicated the absolute sovereignty of the state; the town, no longer wedded to the pride of independence, instructed its representatives in this wise: Peace has not brought back prosperity; foreigners monopolize our commerce; the American carrying trade and the American finances

[1] The Act appears in full in Pa. Packet of 22 Sept., 1785. Van Berckel's report to the States General, 4 Oct., 1785. MS.

[2] Journals of Congress, iv. 516, 517.

[3] Grayson to Madison, 1 May, 1785. MS.

are threatened with annihilation; the government should encourage agriculture, protect manufactures, and establish a public revenue; the confederacy is inadequate to its purposes; congress should be invested with power competent to the wants of the country; the legislature of Massachusetts should request the executive to open a correspondence with the governors of all the states; from national unanimity and national exertion we have derived our freedom; the joint action of the several parts of the union can alone restore happiness and security.[1]

No candidate for the office of governor of Massachusetts having for that year received a majority of the votes of the people, the general court, in May, 1785, made choice of James Bowdoin, a veteran statesman who thirty years before had distinguished himself in the legislature by a speech in favor of the union of the colonies. He had led one branch of the government in its resistance to British usurpations; and, when hostilities broke out, he served his native state as president of its supreme executive council till the British were driven from the commonwealth. His long years of public service had established his fame for moderation, courage, consistency, and uprightness. A republican at heart, he had had an important share in framing the constitution of Massachusetts. In his inaugural address he scorned to complain of the restrictive policy of England, saying rather: Britain and other nations have an undoubted right to regulate their trade with us; and the United States have an equal right to regulate ours with them. Congress

[1] Boston Town Records. MS.

should be vested with all the powers necessary to preserve the union; manage its general concerns; and promote the common interest. For the commercial intercourse with foreign nations the confederation does not sufficiently provide. "This matter," these were his words, "merits your particular attention; if you think that congress should be vested with ampler powers, and that special delegates should be convened to settle and define them, you will take measures for such a convention, whose agreement, when confirmed by the states, would ascertain those powers."

In reply, the two branches of the legislature jointly pledged "their most earnest endeavor" to establish "the federal government on a firm basis, and to perfect the union;" and on the first day of July the general court united in the following resolve: "The present powers of the congress of the United States, as contained in the articles of confederation, are not fully adequate to the great purposes they were originally designed to effect."[1]

That the want of adequate powers in the federal government might find a remedy as soon as possible, they sent to the president of congress, through their own delegation, the resolution which they had adopted, with a circular letter to be forwarded by him to the supreme executive of each state; and they further "directed the delegates of the state to take the earliest opportunity of laying them before congress, and making every exertion to carry the object of them into effect."[2]

---

[1] Mass. Resolve, lxxvi. in Resolves, July, 1785, 38, 39.

[2] Mass. Resolve, lxxix.

REGULATION OF COMMERCE. FIFTH CONGRESS. 191

In concert with New Hampshire, and followed by Rhode Island, they passed a navigation act forbidding exports from their harbors in British bottoms, and establishing a discriminating tonnage duty on foreign vessels;[1] but only as "a temporary expedient, until a well-guarded power to regulate trade shall be entrusted to congress."[2] Domestic manufactures were protected by more than a fourfold increase of duties;[3] and "congress was requested to recommend a convention of delegates from all the states to revise the confederation, and report how far it may be necessary to alter or enlarge the same, in order to secure and perpetuate the primary objects of the union."[4]

In August, the council of Pennsylvania and Dickinson, its president, in a message to the general assembly, renewed the recommendation adopted in that state two years before, saying: "We again declare that further authorities ought to be vested in the federal council; may the present dispositions lead to as perfect an establishment as can be devised."[5]

To his friend Bowdoin John Adams wrote: "The Massachusetts has often been wise and able; but she never took a deeper measure than her late navigation act. I hope she mil persist in it even though she should be alone."[6]

The nation looked to congress for relief. In 1776 James Monroe left the college of William and Mary

---

[1] Annual Register xxvii. 356. Penn. Packet of 18 July, 1785, has the Massachusetts act, and of 20 July that of New Hampshire.

[2] Bowdoin's circular of 28 July enclosing the act. MS.

[3] Bradford's Massachusetts, ii. 244; Pa. Packet, 19 July, 1785.

[4] Massachusetts Resolves, lxxvi. July, 1785. Resolves of the General Court. p. 38.

[5] Minutes of Pa. Council, 25 Aug., 1785. Colonial Records, xiv. 523.

[6] Adams to Governor Bowdoin, 2 Sept., 1785. MS.

to enter the army; when but nineteen he gained an honorable wound and promotion; and rapidly rose to the rank of colonel. Jefferson in 1781 described him as a Virginian "of abilities, merit, and fortune," and as "his own particular friend."[1] In 1782 he was of the assembly of Virginia; and was chosen at three-and-twenty a member of the executive council. In 1783 he was elected to the fourth congress, and at Annapolis saw Washington resign his commission. When Jefferson embarked for France, he remained, not the ablest, but the most conspicuous representative of Virginia on the floor of congress. He sought the friendship of nearly every leading statesman of his commonwealth; and every one seemed glad to call him a friend. It was hard to say whether he was addressed with most affection by Jefferson or by John Marshall. His ambition made him jealous of Randolph; the precedence of Madison he acknowledged, yet not so but that he might consent to become his rival. To Richard Henry Lee he turned as to one from whose zeal for liberty he might seek the confirmation of his own.

Everybody in Virginia resented the restrictive policy of England. Monroe, elected to the fifth congress, embarked on the tide of the rising popular feeling. He was willing to invest the confederation with a perpetual grant of power to regulate commerce; but on condition that it should not be exercised without the consent of nine states. He favored a revenue to be derived from imports, provided that the revenue should be collected under the authority

---

[1] Jefferson to Franklin, 5 Oct., 1781. MS.

REGULATION OF COMMERCE. FIFTH CONGRESS. 193

and pass into the treasury of the state in which it should accrue.[1]

He from the first applauded the good temper and propriety of the new congress, the comprehensiveness of mind with which they attended to the public interests, and their inclination to the most general and liberal principles, which seemed to him, "really to promise great good to the union." They showed the like good-will for him. On bringing forward the all-important motion on commerce, they readily referred it to himself as the chief of the committee, with four associates, of whom Spaight, from North Carolina, and Houston, from Georgia, represented the South; King, of Massachusetts, and Johnson, of Connecticut, the North.

The complaisant committee lent their names to the proposal of Monroe, whose report was read in congress on the twenty-eighth of March.[2] It was accompanied by a letter to be addressed to the legislatures of the several states explaining and recommending it; and the fifth day of April was assigned for its consideration.

But it was no part of Monroe's plan to press the matter for a decision. "It will be best," so he wrote to

CHAP. IV.

1785.

---

[1] Monroe to Jefferson, 14 Dec., 1784. MS.
[2] Sparks, ix. 503, gives the report in its first form; his date, however, is erroneous, from a misunderstanding of a letter of Grayson, in Letters of Washington, iv. 102, 103. The day on which the report was made is not certain; the day on which it was read was certainly the 28th of March. The report of the committee is in the volume, "Reports of Committees on Increasing the Powers of Congress," p. 125, with a copy in print. The few corrections that have been made in the copy are in the handwriting of Monroe. The State Dept. "MS. Copy is endorsed: Report of Mr. Monroe, Mr. Straight, Mr. Houston, Mr. Johnson, Mr. King. See 11 March — to grant congress power of regulating trade Entered — read 28 March, 1785. Tuesday, April 5, assigned."

Jefferson, "to postpone this for the present; its adoption must depend on the several legislatures. It hath been brought so far without a prejudice against it. If earned farther here, I fear prejudices will take place. It proposes a radical change in the whole system of our government. It can be carried only by thorough investigation and a conviction of every citizen that it is right. The slower it moves on, therefore, in my opinion, the better."[1]

Jefferson, as he was passing through Boston on his way to France, had shown pleasure at finding "the conviction growing strongly that nothing could preserve the confederacy unless the bond of union, their common council, should be strengthened."[2]

He now made answer to the urgent inquiries of Monroe: "The interests of the states ought to be made joint in every possible instance, in order to cultivate the idea of our being one nation, and to multiply the instances in which the people shall look up to congress as their head." He approved Monroe's report without reservation; but wished it adopted at once, "before the admission of Western states."[3]

Months passed away, but still the subject was not called up in congress; and the mind of Monroe as a southern statesman became shaken. The confederation seemed to him at present but little more than an offensive and defensive alliance, and if the right to raise troops at pleasure was denied, merely a defen-

---

[1] Monroe to Jefferson, New York, 12 April, 1785. MS.
[2] Jefferson to Madison, Boston, 1 July, 1784. MS.
[3] Jefferson to Monroe, Paris, 17 June, 1785. Jefferson, i. 347.

sive one. His report would put the commercial economy of every state entirely and permanently into the hands of the union; which might then protect the carrying trade, and encourage domestic industry by a tax on foreign industry. He asked himself if the carrying trade would increase the wealth of the South; and he cited "a Mr. Smith on the Wealth of Nations," as having written "that the doctrine of the balance of trade is a chimera."[1]

The southernmost states began to reason that Maryland had a great commercial port, and, like Delaware, excelled in naval architecture; and these, joining the seven northern states, might vote to themselves the monopoly of the transport of southern products. Besides, Virginia, more than any other state in the union, was opposed to the slave trade; and Virginia and all north of her might join in its absolute prohibition. The three more southern states were, therefore, unwilling to trust a navigation act to the voice even of ten; and in his report Monroe substituted eleven states for his first proposal of nine.[2]

At last, on the thirteenth and fourteenth of July, the report was considered in a committee of the whole. It was held that the regulation of trade by the union was desirable, because it would open a way to encourage domestic industry by imposing a tax upon foreign manufactures; because it was needed in order to secure reciprocity in commercial intercourse with foreign nations; because it would counteract

[1] Monroe to Jefferson, 6 June, 1785. MS.
[2] Monroe to Madison, 26 July, 1785. MS.

external commercial influence by establishing a commercial interest at home; and because it would prepare way for a navy. These ends could never be obtained unless the states should act in concert, for their regulations would impede and defeat each other.

The opponents of the measure left their cause in the hands of Richard Henry Lee, as their only spokesman; and his mature age, courteous manner, skill as an orator and debater, and his rank as president of congress, gave him great authority. He insisted that the new grant of power would endanger public liberty; that it would be made subservient to further attempts to enlarge the authority of the government; that the concentration of the control of commerce would put the country more in the power of other nations; that the interests of the North were different from the interests of the South; that the regulation of trade which suited the one would not suit the other; that eight states were interested in the carrying trade, and would combine together to shackle and fetter the five Southern states, which, without having shipping of their own, raised the chief staples for exportation; and, finally, that any attempt whatever at a change in the articles of confederation had a tendency to weaken the union.

In these objections Lee was consistent. He pressed upon Madison, with earnest frankness, that power in congress to legislate over the trade of the union would expose the five staple states, from their want of ships and seamen, to a most pernicious and destructive monopoly; that even the purchase, as well as the carrying, of their produce, might be at the mercy of the East and the North; and that the spirit of commerce throughout the world is a spirit of avarice.[1] His views were shared by Grayson; and even King and Gerry, of Massachusetts, refused to invest congress with power over foreign intercourse,[2] unless the grant should be restricted to a short period of years.

A plan of a navigation act originated with McHenry, of Maryland; but it came before congress only as a subject of conversation. Nothing was done with the report of Monroe, who said of it: "The longer it is delayed, the more certain is its passage through the several states ultimately;"[3] and his committee only asked leave to sit again. "We have nothing pleasing in prospect," wrote Jacob Read to Madison; "and, if in a short time the states do not enable congress to act with vigor and put the power of compulsion into the hand of the union, I think it almost time to give over the form of what I cannot consider as an efficient government. We want, greatly want, the assistance of your abilities and experience in congress; one cannot help drawing comparisons between the language of 1783 and 1785."[4]

From the delegation of Virginia no hope could spring; but the state which exceeded all others in the number of its freemen, and in age was second only to the Old Dominion, had directed its delegates

---

[1] R. H. Lee to Madison, 11 Aug., 1785. Rives, ii. 31, 32.
[2] Monroe to Madison, 26 July, 1785. MS.
[3] Monroe to Jefferson, 15 Aug., 1785. MS.
[4] Jacob Read, of South Carolina, to Madison, 29 Aug., 1785. MS.

to present to congress to the and through congress to the states, an invitation to meet in a convention and revise the confederation. And now Gerry, Holten, and Rufus King saw fit to disobey their instructions, and suppressed the acts and resolves of Massachusetts, writing: "Any alteration of the confederation is premature; the grant of commercial power should be temporary, like the proposed treaties with European powers; and for its adoption should depend on an experience of its beneficial results. Power over commerce, once delegated to the confederation, can never be revoked but by the unanimous consent of the states. To seek a reform through a convention is a violation of the rights of congress, and, as a manifestation of a want of confidence in them, must meet their disapprobation. A further question arises whether the convention should revise the constitution generally or only for express purposes. Each of the states in forming its own, as well as the federal constitution, has adopted republican principles; yet plans have been laid which would have changed our republican government into baleful aristocracies. The same spirit remains in their abettors. The institution of the Cincinnati will have the same tendency. The rotation of members is the best check to corrupttion. The requirement of the unanimous consent of the legislatures of the states for altering the confederation effectually prevents innovations by intrigue or surprise. The cry for more power in congress comes especially from those whose views are extended to an aristocracy that will afford lucrative employments, civil and military, and require a standing army, pensioners, and placemen. The present confederation is preferable to the risk of general dissensions and animosities."[1]

Bowdoin replied: "If in the union discordant principles make it hazardous to intrust congress with powers necessary to its well-being, the union cannot long subsist."[2] Gerry and King rejoined: "The best and surest mode of obtaining an addition to the powers of congress is to make the powers temporary in the first instance. If a convention of the states is necessary, its members should be confined to the revision of such parts of the confederation as are supposed defective; and not intrusted with a general revision of the articles and the right to report a plan of federal government essentially different from the republican form now administered."[3]

These letters of Gerry and King met with the concurrence of Samuel Adams,[4] and had so much weight with the general court as to stay its further action. Nor did the evil end there. All the arguments and insinuations against a new constitution as sure to supersede republican government by a corrupt and wasteful aristocracy, were carried into every village in Massachusetts, as the persistent judgment of their representatives in congress with the assent of the home legislature.

It remained to see if anything could come from

---

[1] This paper, and a letter which preceded it of Aug. 18, 1785, I found only as copied into the Letter Book in the office of the Secretary of State of Massachusetts, Letter Book, viii. 204, 205, 210-213.

[2] Bowdoin to Massachusetts delegates in Congress, 24 Oct., 1785.

[3] Gerry and King to Governor Bowdoin, 3 Nov., 1785. MS.

[4] Adams to Gerry, 19 Sept., 1785, in reply to a letter from Gerry of 5 Sept. MS.

negotiations in Europe. A treaty with England was in importance paramount to all others. In 1783 Adams with Jay had crossed the channel to England, but had been received with coldness. The assent of the United States to the definitive treaty of peace was long delayed by the difficulty of assembling in congress nine states for its confirmation. At length, on the twelfth of May, 1784, the exchange of ratifications took place at Paris. The way being thus opened, the three American commissioners for negotiating treaties,—Franklin, John Adams, and Jefferson,—informed the Duke of Dorset, then British ambassador at Paris, that they had full powers to negotiate a commercial treaty with Great Britain, and for that end were ready to repair to London. The British government consulted the English merchants trading with North America; and near the end of March of the following year the duke answered: "I have been instructed to learn from you, gentlemen, what is the real nature of the powers with which you are invested; whether you are merely commissioned by congress, or have received separate powers from the separate states. The apparent determination of the respective states to regulate their own separate interests renders it absolutely necessary, toward forming a permanent system of commerce, that my court should be informed how far the commissioners can be duly authorized to enter into any engagements with Great Britain, which it may not be in the power of any one of the states to render totally fruitless and ineffectual."

When Franklin, taking with him the love of

France.[1] prepared to sail for America, congress, breaking up their triumviral commission in Europe, appointed Jefferson to be minister to France, John Adams to Great Britain. Adams gave the heartiest welcome to his "old friend and coadjutor," in whom he found undiminished" industry, intelligence, and talents," and, full of courage if not of hope, hastened to London. On the first day of June Lord Carmarthen, the secretary of state, presented him to the king. Delivering his credentials, he in perfect sincerity declared: "I shall esteem myself the happiest of men if I can be instrumental in recommending my country more and more to your Majesty's royal benevolence, and of restoring the old good nature, and the old good humor, between people who, though separated by an ocean and under different governments, have the same language, a similar religion, and kindred blood."

The king answered with more tremor than the bold republican had shown: "I wish it understood in America that I have done nothing in the late contest but what I thought myself indispensably bound to do by the duty which I owed to my people. I will be very frank with you. I was the last to consent to the separation; but, the separation having been made, I have always said, as I say now, that I would be the first to meet the friendship of the United States as an independent power. The moment I see such sentiments and language as yours prevail, and a disposetion to give to this country the preference, that moment I shall say, let the circumstances of language,

---

[1] Rayneval to Franklin, 8 May, 1785. Dip. Cor., ii. 47.

religion, and blood have their natural and full effect."[1]

The suggestion of a preference was out of place. The English had it without a treaty by their skill, the reciprocal confidence of the merchants of the two nations, and the habits of the Americans who were accustomed only to the consumption of British goods. But a change had come over the spirit of England. Before three years of peace, all respect and regard for America were changed into bitter discontent at its independence, and a disbelief in its capacity to establish a firm government. The national judgment and popular voice, as expressed in pamphlets, newspapers, coffee-houses, the streets, and in both houses of parliament, had grown into an unchangeable determination to maintain against them the navigation acts and protective duties, and neither the administration nor the opposition had a thought of relaxing them. Great Britain was sure of its power of attracting American commerce, and believed that the American states were not, and never could be, united. All this had been so often affirmed by the refugees, and Englishmen had so often repeated them to one another, that to argue against it was like breathing against a trade-wind. "I may reason till I die to no purpose,"[2] wrote Adams; "it is unanimity in America which will produce a fair treaty of commerce." Yet he presented to Carmarthen a draft of one, though without hope of success. It rested on principles of freedom and reciprocity, and the

---

[1] Dip. Cor., iv. 200, 201. [2] Adams to Jay, 26 June, 1785. Works, viii. 273.

principles of the armed neutrality with regard to neutral vessels.

Like Franklin, like Jefferson, like Madison, he was at heart for free trade. "I should be sorry," said he to his friend Jefferson, "to adopt a monopoly, but, driven to the necessity of it, I would not do things by halves."[1] "If monopolies and exclusions are the only arms of defence against monopolies and exclusions, I would venture upon them without fear of offending Dean Tucker or the ghost of Doctor Quesnay." "But means of preserving ourselves can never be secured until congress shall be made supreme in foreign commerce."[2]

In August, when the adjournment of parliament brought comparative leisure, Adams, then fifty years of age, met the youthful prime minister of Britain. Pitt, as any one may see in his portrait at Kensington, had in his nature far more of his mother than of the great Englishman who was his father. He had pride, but suffered from a feebleness of will which left him the prey of inferior men. His own chosen measures were noble ones—peace, commercial relations with France, the improvement of the public finances, the payment of the national debt. The policy to be adopted with America he left to others, who took counsel of bitter refugees and the traders to North America. At the instance of Shelburne, he once brought in a bill to promote commerce with America by modifying the navigation act, but meeting with opposition he readily abandoned the hopeless attempt.

---

[1] Adams to Jefferson, 7 Aug., 1785. Works, viii. 273.   [2] Same to John Jay, 10 Aug., ibid., 299, 300.

Reverting to the treaty of commerce which Adams had proposed, Pitt asked: "What are the lowest terms which will content America?" Adams replied that the project he had communicated would secure the friendship of the United States and all the best part of their trade; the public mind of America is balancing between free trade and a navigation act; and the question will be decided now by England; but if the Americans are driven to a navigation act, they will become attached to the system. "The United States," answered Pitt, "are forever become a foreign nation; our navigation act would not answer its end if we should dispense with it toward you." "The end of the navigation act," replied Adams, "was to confine the commerce of the colonies to the mother country; if carried into execution against us, now that we are become independent, instead of confining our trade to Great Britain, it will drive it to other countries." "You allow we have a right to impose on you our navigation act," said Pitt. "Certainly," answered Adams, "and you will allow we have a corresponding right." "You cannot blame Englishmen," said Pitt, "for being attached to their ships and seamen." "Indeed, I do not," answered Adams; "nor can you blame Americans for being attached to theirs." Pitt then asked plainly: "Can you grant by treaty to England advantages which would not become immediately the right of France?" "We cannot," answered Adams; "to the advantage granted to England without a compensation France would be entitled without a compensation; if an equivalent is stipulated for, France, to claim it, must allow us the same equivalent." Pitt then put the question: "What do you think that Great Britain ought to do?" And Adams answered: "This country ought to prescribe to herself no other rule than to receive from America everything she can send as a remittance; in which case America will take as much of British productions as she can pay for."

There were mutual complaints of failure in observing the conditions of the peace between the two nations. Pitt frankly declared "the carrying off of negroes to be so clearly against the treaty that England must satisfy that demand;" but he never took a step toward satisfying it. The British government, yielding to the importunity of British merchants who grasped at a continued monopoly of the fur trade, kept possession of the American posts at the west. This was a continuance of war; but Pitt excused it on the ground that, in Virginia and at least two other states, hindrances still remained in the way of the British creditor. In perfect good faith Congress was untiring in its requisitions on the States to grant to British creditors unimpeded resort to their courts for the recovery of debts contracted before the war; but it wanted power to enforce the requisition. Moreover, the Virginia legislature, not without a ground of equity, delayed judgment against the Virginia debtors, yet only until an offset could be made of the indemnity which the British minister owned to be due to them. The holding of the western posts, which was a continuance of war, had no connection with this debt and no proportion to it; for the profits of the fur trade, thus secured to Great Britain, in each single year very far exceeded the whole debt of which the collection was postponed.

The end of the interview was, that Pitt enforced the navigation acts of England without mitigation against America. For the western posts, Haldimand, as his last act, had strengthened the garrison at Oswego, and charged his successor to exclude the Americans from the increasing and enormously remunerative commerce in furs by restricting transportation on the lakes to British vessels alone;[1] and the secretary of state announced that the posts could be retained till justice should be done to British creditors.[2]

"They mean," wrote Adams, "that Americans should have no ships, nor sailors, to annoy their trade." "Patience will do no good; nothing but reciprocal prohibitions and imposts mil have any effect." He counselled the United States as their only resource to confine their exports to their own ships and encourage their own manufactures, though he foresaw that these measures would so annoy England as in a few years to bring on the danger of war.[3]

The French government could not be induced to change its commercial system for the sake of pleasing the United States; it granted free ports; but the Americans wanted not places of deposit for their staples, but an open market. On one point only did

---

[1] Haldimand to St. Leger, Nov., 1784; Sidney to St. Leger, 30 April, 1775, and other letters of the like tenor.

[2] Carmarthen to Adams, 28 Feb., 1786.

[3] Adams to Jay, 30 Aug. and 15 Oct., 1785. Works, viii. 313 and 321.

Vergennes bestow anxious attention. He feared the United States might grant favors to England; and, at the request of France, congress, when preparing to treat with the nations of Europe, gave a formal assurance that it would "place no people on more advantageous ground than the subjects of his most christian Majesty." To give the most binding force to the pledge, Vergennes answered: "This declaration, founded on the treaty of the sixth of February, 1778, very agreeable to the king; and you can assure congress that the United States shall constantly experience a perfect reciprocity in France."[1]

Jefferson, as minister, obtained permission for American fishermen to ship cured fish to the French West Indies, though under the burden of a heavy duty,[2] and a great reduction of the duty on American oil manufactured from fish;[3] but he was compelled to hear thrice over complaints that the trade of the United States had not learned the way to France; and thrice over that the French government could not depend on engagements taken with the United States. Complaints, too, were made of the navigation acts of Massachusetts and New Hampshire, not without hints at retaliation.

While some of the states of Europe forgot their early zeal to form commercial relations with the United States, the convention for ten years with Frederick of Prussia, to whose despatch, intelligence, and decision Adams bore witness, was completed in May, 1785, and in the following May was unani-

[1] Dip. Cor., ii. 33, 34, 36.
[2] Ibid., ii. 490.
[3] Ibid., ii. . 491, .492.

mously ratified by congress. Free vessels made free goods. Arms, ammunition, and military stores were taken out of the class of contraband. In case of war between the two parties, merchant vessels were still to pass unmolested. Privateering was pronounced a form of piracy. Citizens of the one country domiciled in the other were to enjoy freedom of conscience and worship; and, in case of war between the two parties, they might still continue their respective employments.

Spain had anxieties with respect to its future relations with America, and thought proper to accredit an agent to congress; but neither with Spain, nor with France, nor with England was there the least hope of forming liberal commercial relations. American diplomacy had failed; the attempt of the fifth congress to take charge of commerce had failed; the movement for a federal convention, which was desired by the mercantile class throughout the union, had failed; but encouragement came from South Carolina. There William Moultrie, its governor, gave support to Bowdoin, of Massachusetts, saying: "The existence of this state with every other as a nation depends on the strength of the union. Cemented together in one common interest, they are invincible; divided, they must fall a sacrifice to internal dissensions and foreign usurpations."[1]

The confederation, before it expired, framed a treaty with the emperor of Morocco; it was not rich enough to buy from the corsair powers of Barbary immunity for its ships in the Mediterranean.

[1] Moultrie to Bowdoin, 18 Oct. 1785. MS.

Through congress no hope for the regeneration of the union could be cherished. Before we look for the light that may rise outside of that body, it will be well to narrate what real or seeming; obstacles to union were removed or quieted, and what motives compelling the forming of a new constitution sprung from the impairment of the obligation of contracts by the states.

CHAPTER V.

OBSTACLES TO UNION REMOVED OR QUIETED.

1783 — 1787.

The early confederacy of New England though all its colonies were non-conformists, refused fellowship to Rhode Island on account of its variance in dissent. Virginia and Maryland were settled in connection with the church of England, which at the period of the revolution was still the established church of them both. In the constitution of the Carolinas the philosopher Locke introduced a clause for the disfranchisement of the atheist, not considering that the power in the magistrate to inflict a penalty on atheism implied the power which doomed Socrates to drink poison and filled the catacombs of Rome with the graves of martyrs. On the other hand, the Baptists, nurslings of adversity, driven by persecution to find resources within their own souls, when they came to found a state in America, rested it on the truth that the spirit and the mind are not subordinate to the temporal power. For the great central state, the people called Quakers in like manner affirmed the right to spiritual and intellectual liberty, and denied to the magistrate all control over the support of religion. To form a perfect political union, it was necessary, in all that relates to religion, that state should not be in conflict with state, and that every citizen, in the exercise of his rights of intercitizenship, should be at his ease in any state in which he might sojourn or abide. In a republican country of wide extent, ideas rule legislation; and the history of reform is the history of thought, gaining strength as it passes from mind to mind, till it finds a place in a statute. We have now to see how it came to pass that the oldest state in the union, first in territory and in numbers, and, from its origin, the upholder of an established church, disestablished its church, renounced the support of religious worship by law, and established the largest liberty of conscience.

The legislature of Virginia, within a half year after the declaration of independence, while it presented for public consideration the idea of a general assessment for the support of the Christian religion,[1] exempted dissenters from contributions to the established church. In 1779 this exemption was extended to churchmen, so that the church was disestablished. But the law for religious freedom, which Jefferson prepared as a part of the revised code, was submitted to the deliberate reflection of the people before the vote should be taken for its adoption.

The Massachusetts constitution of 1780 compelled every member of its legislature on taking his seat to

[1] Hening, ix. 165. Jefferson's Autobiography.

subscribe a declaration that he believed the Christian religion. This regulation, Joseph Hawley, who had been elected to the first senate of Massachusetts, in a letter to that body, sternly condemned. A member of the Congregational church of Northampton, severe in his morality and of unquestioned orthodoxy, he called to mind that the founders of Massachusetts, while church membership was their condition for granting the privilege of an elector, never suffered a profession of the Christian religion to be made before a temporal court. Moreover, he held the new requirement to be against common right and the natural franchises of every member of the commonwealth.[1] In this way, from the heart of rigid Calvinism a protest was heard against any right in the temporal power to demand or to receive a profession of faith in the Christian religion. The church member was subject to no supervision but of those with whom he had entered into covenant. The temporal power might punish the evil deed, but not punish or even search after the thought of the mind.

The inherent perverseness of a religious establishment, of which a king residing in another part of the world and enforcing hostile political interests was the head, showed itself in Virginia. The majority of the legislators were still churchmen; but gradually a decided majority of the people had become dissenters, of whom the foremost were Baptists and Presbyterians. When the struggle for independence was ended, of ninety-one clergymen of the Anglican church in Virginia, twenty-eight only

---

[1] Joseph Hawley to Massachusetts Senate, 28 Oct., 1780.

OBSTICLES TO UNION REMOVED OR QUIETED. 213

remained. One fourth of the parishes had become extinct.

Churchmen began to fear the enfeeblement of religion from its want of compulsory support and from the excesses of fanaticism among dissenters. These last had made their way, not only without aid from the state, but under the burden of supporting a church which was not their own. The church which had leaned on the state was alone in a decline. The system of an impartial support by the state of all branches of Christians was revived by members of "the Protestant Episcopal church," as it now began to be called. Their petitions, favored by Patrick Henry, Harrison, then governor, Pendleton, the chancellor, Richard Henry Lee, and many others of the foremost men, alleged a decay of public morals; and the remedy asked for was a general assessment, analogous to the clause in the constitution of Massachusetts which enjoined upon its towns "the maintenance of public Protestant teachers of piety, religion, and morality."[1]

The Presbyterians at first were divided. Their clergy even while they held that human legislation should concern human affairs alone, that conscience and religious worship lie beyond its reach, accepted the measure, provided it should respect every human belief, even "of the Mussulman and the Gentoo." The Presbyterian laity, accustomed to support their own ministry, chose rather to continue to do so. Of the Baptists, alike ministers and people rejected any alliance with the state.

[1] Massachusetts Declaration of Rights, Article III. of 1780.

Early in the autumnal session of the legislature Patrick Henry proposed a resolution for a legal provision for the teachers of the Christian religion. In the absence of Jefferson, the opponents of the measure were led by Madison, whom Witherspoon had imbued with theological lore. The assessment bill, he said, exceeds the functions of civil authority. The question has been stated as if it were, is religion necessary? The true question is, are establishments necessary for religion? And the answer is, they corrupt religion. The difficulty of providing for the support of religion is the result of the war, to be remedied by voluntary association for religious purposes In the event of a statute for the support of the Christian religion, are the courts of law to decide what is Christianity? and, as a consequence, to decide what is orthodoxy and what is heresy? The enforced support of the Christian religion dishonors Christianity. Yet, in spite of all the opposition that could be mustered, leave to bring in the bill was granted by forty-seven votes against thirty-two.[1] The bill when reported prescribed a general assessment on all taxable property for the support of teachers of the Christian religion. Each person as he paid his tax was to say to which society he dedicated it; in case he refused to do so, his payment was to be applied toward the maintenance of a county school. On the third reading the bill received a check, and was ordered by a small majority to be printed and distributed for the consideration of the people. Thus the people of Virginia had before them for their choice the bill of the

---

[1] Madison to Jefferson, 9 Jan., 1785. Madison, i. 129, 131.

revised code for establishing religious freedom, and the plan of desponding churchmen for supporting religion by a general assessment.

All the state, from the sea to the mountains and beyond them, was alive with the discussion. Madison, in a remonstrance addressed to the legislature, embodied all that could be said against the compulsory maintenance of Christianity and in behalf of religious freedom as a natural right, the glory of Christianity itself, the surest method of supporting religion, and the only way to produce moderation and harmony among its several sects. George Mason, who was an enthusiast for entire freedom, asked of Washington his opinion, and received for answer that "no man's sentiments were more opposed to any kind of restraint upon religious principles." While he was not among those who were so much alarmed at the thought of making people of the denominations of Christians pay toward the support of that denomination which they professed, provided Jews, Mahometans, and others who were not Christians, might obtain proper relief, his advice was given in these words: "As the matter now stands, I wish an assessment had never been agitated; and, as it has gone so far, that the bill could die an easy death."[1]

The general committee of the Baptists unanimously appointed a delegate to remonstrate with the general assembly against the assessment; and they resolved that no human laws ought to be established for that purpose; that every free person ought to be free in

---

[1] Madison to Jefferson, 9 Jan., 1785. Madison, i. 129, 131.

matters of religion.[1] The general convention of the Presbyterian church prayed the legislature expressly that the bill concerning religious freedom might be passed into a law as the best safeguard then attainable for their religious rights.[2]

When the legislature of Virginia assembled, no one was willing to bring forward the assessment bill; and it was never heard of more. Out of one hundred and seventeen articles of the revised code which were then reported, Madison selected for immediate consideration the one which related to religious freedom. The people of Virginia had held it under deliberation for six years; in December, 1785, it passed the house by a vote of nearly four to one. Attempts in the senate for amendment produced only insignificant changes in the preamble, and on the sixteenth of January, 1786, Virginia placed among its statutes the very words of the original draft by Jefferson with the hope that they would endure forever: "No man shall be compelled to frequent or support any religious worship, place, or ministry whatsoever, nor shall suffer on account of his religious opinions or belief; opinion in matters of religion shall in no wise diminish, enlarge, or affect civil capacities. The rights hereby asserted are of the natural rights of mankind."[3]

"Thus," says Madison, "in Virginia was extinguished forever the ambitious hope of making laws for the human mind." The principle on which religious liberty was settled in Virginia prevailed at once in Maryland. In every other American state

---

[1] Semple, 71; Foote's ketches of Virginia, 344.
[2] Madison, i. 213.
[3] Hening, xii. 86.

OBSTICLES TO UNION REMOVED OR QUIETED. 217

oppressive statutes concerning religion fell into disuse, and were gradually repealed. Survivals may still be found, but it is only as in our day we meet with survivals of an earlier geological period. It had been foreseen that "the happy consequences of the grand experiment on the advantages which accompany tolerance and liberty would not be limited to America."[1] The statute of Virginia, translated into French and into Italian, was widely circulated through Europe. A part of the work of "the noble army of martyrs" was done.

During the colonial period the Anglican establishment was feared, because its head was an external temporal power engaged in the suppression of colonial liberties, and was favored by the officers of that power even to the disregard of Justice. National independence and religious freedom dispelled the last remnant of Jealousy. The American branch at first thought it possible to perfect their organization by themselves; but they soon preferred as their starting point a final fraternal act of the church of England. No part of the country, no sect, no person showed a disposition to thwart them in their purpose; and no one complained of the unofficial agency of Jay, the American minister of foreign affairs at home, and of John Adams, the American minister in London, in aid of their desire, which required the consent of the British parliament and a consecration by the Anglican hierarchy. Their wish having been fulfilled in the form to which all of them gave assent and which many of them regarded as indispensable, the

CHAP. V.

1786.

---

[1] Luzerne to Rayneval, 6 Nov., 1784. MS.

CHAP. V.

1786.

Protestant Episcopal church of the United States moved onward with a life of its own to the position which it could never have gained but by independence. For America no bishop was to be chosen at the dictation of a temporal power to electors under the penalty of high treason for disobedience; no advowson of church livings could be tolerated; no room was left for simony; no tenure of a ministry as a life estate was endured where a sufficient reason required a change; the laity was not represented by the highest officer of state and the legislature, but stood for itself; no alteration of prayer, or creed, or government could be introduced by the temporal chief, or by that chief and the legislature. The rule of the church proceeded from its own living power representing all its members. The Protestant Episcopal congregations in the several United States of America, including the clergy of Connecticut who at first went a way of their own, soon fell into the custom of meeting in convention as one church, and gave a new bond to union. Since the year 1785, they have never asked of any American government a share in any general assessment, and have grown into greatness by self-reliance.

1783.

The acknowledged independence of the United States called suddenly into a like independence a new and self-created rival Episcopal church, destined to spread its branches far and wide over the land with astonishing rapidity. Out of a society of devout and studious scholars in the University of Oxford, within less than sixty years grew the society of Methodists. As some of the little republics of ancient time select-

OBSTICLES TO UNION REMOVED OR QUIETED. 219

ed one man as their law-giver, as all men on board a ship trust implicitly to one commander during the period of the voyage, so the Methodist connection in its beginning left to John Wesley to rule them as he would. Its oldest society in the states was at New York, and of the year 1766. In 1782 Wesley appointed, as his "general assistant" in America,[1] Francis Asbury, a missionary from England, a man from the people, who had "much wisdom and meekness; and under all this, though hardly to be perceived, much command and authority."[2]

Wesley never yielded to the temptation to found a separate church within British dominions, and during the war of American independence used his influence to keep the societies which he governed from renouncing their old allegiance. But no sooner had the people of the United States been recognised as a nation by the king of England himself, and the movement to found an American episcopacy had begun, than he burst the bonds that in England held him from schism, and resolved to get the start of the English hierarchy. In October, 1783, in a general epistle, he peremptorily directed his American brethren to receive "Francis Asbury as the general assistant."[3]

For nearly forty years Wesley had been persuaded that the apostolical succession is a "fable"; that "bishops and presbyters are the same order, and have the same right to ordain." He looked upon himself to be as much a bishop "as any man in Europe," though he never allowed any one to call him by that

---

[1] Asbury's Journal, 10 Oct., 1773.
[2] Coke's Journal, 16.
[3] Wesley to the brethren in America, 3 Oct., 1783.

name. In his service for the Methodists he substituted the word elders for priests, and superintendents for bishops. He, therefore, did not scruple, on the second day of September, 1784, himself, in his own private room at Bristol, in England, assisted by Coke and another English presbyter, to ordain two persons as ministers, and then he, with the assistance of other ministers ordained by himself, equal at least in number to the requisition of the canon, did, "by the imposition of his hands and prayer, set apart Thomas Coke, presbyter of the church of England, as a superintendent, and, under his hand and seal, recommended him to whom it might concern as a fit person to preside over the flock of Christ," It is Coke himself who writes of Wesley: "He did, indeed, solemnly invest me, as far as he had a right so to do, with episcopal authority."[1] Eight days later, in a general epistle, he thus addressed Thomas Coke, Francis Asbury, and the brethren in North America: "By a very uncommon train of providences, provinces in North America are erected into independent states. The English government has no authority over them, either civil or ecclesiastical. Bishops and presbyters are the same order, and consequently of the same right to ordain. In America there are no bishops who have a legal jurisdiction. Here, therefore, my scruples are at an end. I have accordingly appointed Dr. Coke and Mr. Francis Asbury to be joint superintendents over our brethren in North America. I cannot see a more rational and scriptural way of feeding and guiding those poor sheep in the wilderness. As

[1] Coke to Bishop White, 34 April, 1791, in White's Memoirs, 424.

OBSTICLES TO UNION REMOVED OR QUIETED. 221

our American brethren are now totally disentangled both from the state and from the English hierarchy, we dare not entangle them again either with the one or the other. They are now at full liberty simply to follow the Scriptures and the primitive church, and we judge it best that they should stand fast in that liberty wherewith God has so strangely made them free."

Nor did Wesley neglect to frame from the Anglican Book of Common Prayer a revised liturgy for the new church, and a creed from which the article on predestination was left out.

About two months before the nonjuring bishops of Scotland consecrated a bishop for Connecticut, Coke, the first Methodist "superintendent" for America, was on the water, emulous of the glory of Francis Xavier. "Oh, for a soul like his!" he cried. "I seem to want the wings of an eagle or the voice of a trumpet, that I may proclaim the gospel through the east and the west, and the north and the south."[1] Arriving in New York, he explained to the preacher stationed at that place the new regulation, and received for answer: "Mr. Wesley has determined the point; and therefore it is not to be investigated, but complied with."[2]

Coke journeyed at once toward Baltimore, where Asbury had his station. At Dover, in Delaware, "he met with Freeborn Garretson, an excellent young man, all meekness and love, and yet all activity." On Sunday, the fourteenth of November, the day on which a bishop for Connecticut was consecrated at

---
[1] Coke's First Journal, 7.   [2] Ibid., 13.

Aberdeen, he preached in a chapel in the midst of a forest to a noble congregation. After the service, a plain, robust man came up to him in the pulpit and kissed him. He was not deceived when he thought it could be no other than Francis Asbury, who had collected there a considerable number of preachers in council. The plan of Wesley pleased them all. At the instance of Asbury, it was resolved to hold a general conference; and "they sent off Freeborn Garretson like an arrow from north to south, directing him to dispatch messengers right and left and gather all the preachers together at Baltimore on Christmas eve."[1]

Thence Coke moved onward, baptizing adults and infants, preaching sometimes in a church, though it would not hold half the persons who washed to hear; sometimes at the door of a cottage when the church door was locked against him.[2]

On Christmas eve, at Baltimore, began the great conference which organized the Methodists of America as a separate fold in the one "flock of Christ." Of the eighty-one American preachers, nearly sixty were present, most of them young. Here Coke took his seat as superintendent; and here, joining to himself two elders, he set apart Francis Asbury as a deacon and on the next day as an elder. Here eleven or more persons were elected elders, and all of them who were present were consecrated; here Asbury, who refused to receive the office of superintendent at the will of Wesley alone, was unanimously "elected bishop or superintendent by the suffrages of the whole body

---

[1] Coke's First Journal, 16.   [2] Ibid., 27.

of Methodist ministers through the continent, assembled in general conference;" and here Coke, obeying the directions of Wesley, took to himself at least the canonical number of presbyters, and ordained him, Francis Asbury, as "a superintendent of the Methodist Episcopal Church in America."[1] In the ordination sermon delivered on that day and published at the time, Coke asserts his own "right to exercise the episcopal office," and defines the title of superintendent as the equivalent of "bishop,"[2]

In April, 1785, Coke began to exhort the Methodist societies in Virginia to emancipate their slaves, and bore public testimony against slavery and against slave-holding. It provoked the unawakened to combine against him; but one of the brethren gave liberty to his eight slaves. In North Carolina, where the laws of the state forbade any to emancipate their negroes, the Methodist conference drew up a petition to the assembly, entreating them to authorize those who were so disposed to set them free. Asbury visited the governor and gained him over.[3] At the Virginia conference in May they formed a petition, of which a copy was given to every preacher, inviting the general assembly of Virginia to pass a law for the immediate or gradual emancipation of all slaves. For this they sought the signature of freeholders. And yet in June the conference thought it prudent to suspend the minute concerning slavery on account of the great opposition given it, "our work," they said, "being in too infantile a state to push things to extremity."

---

[1] Coke's certificate, 27 Dec, 784.
[2] Coke in Tyerman's Life and Times of John Wesley, iii. 437.
[3] Coke's first Journal, 37.

224 ON THE WAY TO A FEDERAL CONVENTION.

CHAP. V.

1785-1789.

The Methodist itinerant ministers learned to love more and more "a romantic way of life," the preaching to large congregations in the midst of great forests with scores of horses tied to the trees." They had delight in the beauties of Nature, and knew how to extract "from them all the sweetness they are capable of yielding." The Methodists did not come to rend an empire in twain, nor to begin a long series of wars which should shatter the civil and the religious hierarchies of former centuries, nor to tumble down ancient orders by some new aristocracy of the elect. Avoiding metaphysical controversy and wars of revolution, they came in an age of tranquillity when the feeling for that which is his/her than man had grown dull; and they claimed it as their mission to awaken conscience, to revive religion, to substitute glowing affections for the calm of indifference. They stood in the mountain forests of the Alleghanies and in the plains beyond them, ready to kindle in emigrants, who might come without hymn-book or bible, their own vivid sense of religion; and their leaders received from all parts, especially from Kentucky, most cheering letters concerning the progress of the cause in the "new western world." They were at peace with the institutions of the country in which they prospered, and the ready friends to union.

America was most thoroughly a Protestant country. The whole number of Catholics within the thirteen states, as reported by themselves, about the year 1784, was thirty-two thousand five hundred. Twenty thousand, of whom eight thousand were slaves, dwelt in Maryland. The four southernmost states had but

OBSTICLES TO UNION REMOVED OR QUIETED. 225

two thousand five hundred; New England but six hundred; New York and New Jersey, collectively, only seventeen hundred. Pennsylvania and Delaware, lands of tolerance, had seven thousand seven hundred. The French Catholics settled between the western boundary of the states and the Mississippi were estimated at twelve thousand more.[1]

CHAP. V.

1784-1789.

The rancor of the Jesuits against the house of Bourbon for exiling them from France and Spain was relentless. The Roman Catholic clergy in the insurgent British colonies had been superintended by a person who resided in London; and during the war they were directed by Jesuits who favored the British. The influences which in South America led to most disastrous results for Spain were of little consequence in the United States. It was Franklin's desire to do away with this influence unfriendly to France. The Roman see proceeded with caution; and a letter from its nuncio at Paris, on the appointment of a bishop in the United States, was communicated to congress. In May, 1786, they, in reply, expressed a readiness to testify respect to the sovereign and the state represented by the nuncio, but, disavowing jurisdiction over a purely spiritual subject, referred him to the several states individually."[2]

The British crown, and, at a later period, British legislation, had arbitrarily changed the grants of territory held under the several colonial charters. Nearly three years before the preliminary treaty of peace, New York, to facilitate union among the United

---

[1] Marbois to Vergennes, 27 March, 1785. MS.
[2] Franklin's Works, ix. 548. Dip. Cor., i. 158, 159. Secret Journals of Congress, iii. 493.

VOL. I. 15

CHAP.
V.
1780.

States of America, led the way of relinquishing pretensions to any part of the lands acquired by the treaty of peace. Virginia, which had a better claim to western territory, resigned it for the like purpose, reserving only a tract between the Scioto and the Miami as an indemnity for the expenses of its conquest. Massachusetts persisted in no claim except to the ownership of lands in New York. The charter of Connecticut carried its line all the way to the Pacific ocean; with great wariness Roger Sherman, so Grayson relates, connected the cession of the claims of his state with the reserve of a district in the northeast of Ohio. The right of Connecticut to a reservetion was denied by Grayson, and, in Sherman's absence from Congress, stoutly and successfully defended by Johnson. A small piece of land between the line of New York and the eastern line of the Connecticut reserve remained to the United States. Pennsylvania purchased the land and obtained of congress a willing cession of the jurisdiction, thus gaining access to the lake and the harbor of Erie. South Carolina had certain undefined rights to territory in the West; she ceded them without qualification to the United States. The rights of Virginia, North Carolina, and Georgia to extend to the Mississippi, like the right of Massachusetts to the lands in Maine, were unquestioned. In this manner the public domain, instead of exciting animosities and conflicting claims between rival states or between individual states and the general interest, served only to bind the members of the confederacy more closely together by securing one vast territory in the West extending from the Ohio to the Lake of the Woods, to be filled, under the laws of the United States, alike by emigrants from them all.

A more serious matter was that of the customs. New York had yielded to the temptation to establish a custom-house for the sole benefit of its own treasury. Richard Henry Lee taught the authors of the measure that they were defending the rights of the states, and preserving congress from the corrupting influence of an independent revenue. Comforted by these opinions of an eminent statesman whom congress had raised to its presidency. New York persisted in treating the revenue levied on the commerce of its port as its own; and here was a real impediment to union.

Sadder was the institution of slavery; for the conlicting opinions and interests involved in its permanence could never be reconciled.

CHAPTER VI.

STATE LAWS IMPAIRING THE OBLIGATION OF CONTRACTS PROVE THE NEED OF AN OVERRULING UNION.

BEFORE MAY, 1787.

CHAP. VI.

1606-1700.

A BRILLIANT artist has painted Fortune as a beautiful woman enthroned on a globe, which for the moment is at rest, but is ready to roll at the slightest touch. A country whose people are marked by inventive genius, industry, and skill, whose immense domain is exuberantly fertile, whose abounding products the rest of the world cannot dispense with, may hold her fast, and seat her immovably on a pedestal of four square sides.

The thirteen American states had a larger experience of the baleful consequences of paper money than all the world besides. As each of them had a legislation of its own, the laws were as variant as they were inconvenient and unjust. The shilling had differing rates from its sterling value to an eighth of a dollar. The confusion in computing the worth of the currency of one state in that of another was hopelessly increased by the laws, which discriminated between different kinds of paper issued by the same state; so that a volume could hardly hold the tables of the reciprocal rates of exchange. Moreover, any man loaning money or making a contract, in his own state or in another, was liable at any time to loss by some fitful act of separate legislation. The necessity of providing more effectually for the security of private rights and the steady dispensation of justice, more, perhaps, than anything else, brought about the new constitution.[1]

No sooner had the cry of the martyrs of Lexington reached Connecticut than its legislature put forth paper money for war expenses, and continued to do so till October, 1777. There were no other issues till 1780, and these were not made legal tender in private transactions.[2]

In October of that year the legislature of the state, once for all, interposed itself between the creditor and debtor. It discriminated between contracts that were rightly to be paid in gold and silver and contracts understood to be made in paper currency, whether of the continent or of the state. A paytable for settling the progressive rate of depreciation was constructed; and, to avoid the injustice which might come from a strict application of the laws, it gave to the court authority through referees, or, if either party refused a reference, by itself, to take all circumstances into consideration, and to determine the case according to the rules of equity.[3]

In this wise the relations between debtor and cred-

---

[1] Gilpin, 804 ; Elliot, 163.
[2] Bronson's Connecticut Currency, 137.
[3] Laws of Connecticut, ed. 1786, 49, 50.

230 ON THE WAY TO A FEDERAL CONVENTION.

itor in Connecticut were settled summarily and finally, and no room left for rankling discontent. The first of the New England states to issue paper money on the sudden call to arms was the first to return to the use of coin. The wide-spread movements of 1786 for the issue of paper money never prevailed within its borders. Its people, as they were frugal, Industrious, and honest, dwelt together in peace, while other states were rent by faction.

Massachusetts, after the downfall of the continental paper, returned to the sole use of gold and silver in contracts; but its statesmen had before them a most difficult task, for the people had been tempted by the low prices of foreign goods to run into debt, and their resources, from the interruption of their sale of ships and fish-oil in England, of fish and lumber in the British West Indies, and from the ruin of home manufacturers by the cheapness of foreign goods, were exhausted. While it established its scale of depreciation, it did not, like Connecticut, order an impartial and definitive settlement between the creditor and debtor, but dallied with danger. In July, 1782, it allowed, for one year, judgments to be satisfied by the tender of neat cattle or other enumerated articles at an appraisement; but the creditor had only to wait till the year should expire. Repeated temporary stay-laws gave no real relief; they flattered and deceived the hope of the debtor, exasperating alike him and his creditor.[1] But when, in May, 1786, a petition was presented from towns in Bristol county for an emission of paper money, out of one hundred and

---

[1] Minot's Insurrection of Massachusetts, 14.

eighteen members in the house of representatives, it received only nineteen votes, and only thirty-five out of one hundred and twenty-four supported the plan of making real and personal estate tender on an appraisement in discharge of an execution.

In like manner New Hampshire, after the peace, shunned the emission of paper money. Its people suffered less than Massachusetts, because they were far less in debt.

Alone of the New England states, Rhode Island, after the peace, resumed the attempt to legislate value into paper. The question had divided the electors of the state into political parties; the farmers in the villages were arrayed against the merchants and traders of the larger towns; and in May, 1786, after a hard contest, the party in favor of paper money, with John Collins for governor, came into power.

In all haste the legislature authorized the issue of one hundred thousand pounds to be loaned out to any man of Rhode Island at four per cent for seven years, after which one seventh was to be repaid annually. These bills were made a legal tender except for debts due to charitable corporations. A large part of the debt of the state was paid in them.

To escape the very heavy fine for refusing to sell goods for paper as the full equivalent of specie,[1] the merchants of Newport closed their shops. The act speedily provoked litigation. In September a complaint was made against a butcher for refusing to receive paper at par in payment for meat. The case was tried before a full bench of the five judges.

[1] Compare Otto to Vergennes, 6 Aug., 1786.

Varnum in an elaborate argument set forth the unconstitutionality of the law and its danger as a precedent. Goodwin answered that it conflicted with nothing in the charter, which was the fundamental law of Rhode Island. Judge Howell the next morning, delivering the unanimous opinion of the court, declared the acts unconstitutional and void, and dismissed the case as not within the jurisdiction of the court. At the decision, one universal shout of joy rang through the court-house. The assembly of Rhode Island summoned the judges to assign the reasons for their judgment. Three of the five obeyed the summons. At the next session of the legislature Howell, with two associates, defended the opinion of the bench and denied the accountability of the supreme judiciary to the general assembly. The assembly resolved that no satisfactory reasons had been rendered by the bench for its judgment, and discharged them from further attendance.

New York successfully extricated itself from the confusion of continental and state paper money; but in April of the fatal year 1786 its legislature, after long debates, made remarkable by the remonstrances of Duer, voted to emit two hundred thousand pounds in bills of credit. The money so emitted was receivable for duties, and was made a legal tender in all suits.[1]

In the council of revision strong but not successful objections were raised. Livingston,[2] the chancellor, set forth that a scarcity of money can be remedied

---

[1] Jones and Varick's New York Laws, ed. 1789, 283.

[2] Street's Council of Revision of the State of New York, 409.

NEED OF AN OVERRULING UNION. 233

only by industry and economy, not by laws that foster idleness and dissipation; that the bill, under the appearance of relief, would add to the distress of the debtor; that it at the same instant solicited and destroyed credit; that it would cause the taxes and debts of the state to the United States to be paid in paper. Hobart, one of the justices, reported that it would prove an unwarrantable interference in private contracts,[1] and to this objection Livingston[2] gave his adhesion. Morris, the chief justice, objected to receiving the bills in the custom-house treasury as money, and held that the enactment would be working iniquity by the aid of law;[3] but a veto was not agreed upon.

Livingston, the governor of New Jersey, communicating to its legislature in May, 1783, the tidings of peace, said: "Let us show ourselves worthy of freedom by an inflexible attachment to public faith and national honor; let us establish our character as a sovereign state[4] on the only durable basis of impartial and universal justice." The legislature responded to his words by authorizing the United States to levy the duty on commerce which had been required, and by making a provision for raising ninety thousand pounds by taxation for the exigencies of the year. In settling debts it was made lawful for the court and jury to decide the case to the best of their knowledge, agreeably to equity and good conscience.[5] But in the following December it returned to paper

---

[1] Street's Council of Revision of the State of New York, 412
[2] Ibid., 415.
[3] Ibid.
[4] Mulford's New Jersey, 473.
[5] Act of June, 1783. Paterson's Laws of New Jersey, ed. 1800, 50.

234 ON THE WAY TO A FEDERAL CONVENTION.

CHAP. VI.

1783.

money, and authorized the issue of more than thirty-one thousand pounds[1] to supply its quota of the state for the year.

1786.

Once launched again into the issue of paper money, it yielded to the impulse of the times.

In the conflict, the arguments against paper money were stated so fully and so strongly that later writers on political economy have added nothing to the practical wisdom of the thoughtful men of that day; and yet in 1786 a bill for the emission of one hundred thousand pounds marched in triumph through its assembly, sitting with closed doors. In the council it was lost by eight voices to five[2] In consequence of this check, the effigy of Livingston, the aged governor, was drawn up to the stake near Elizabethtown, but not consigned to the flames from reverence for the first magistrate of the commonwealth; that of a member of the council was burned. In May the governor and council thought proper to yield, and the bill for paper money became a law. A law for paying debts in lands or chattels was repealed within eight months of its enactment.

The opulent state of Pennsylvania by a series of laws emerged from the paper currency of the war.

1784.

But in December, 1784, debts contracted before 1777 were made payable in three annual instalments.[3] In

1785.

1785 one hundred and fifty thousand pounds were issued in bills of credit, to be received as gold and

---

[1] Wilson's Laws of New Jersey, ed. 1784, 363.
[2] Grayson to Madison, 23 March, 1786. MS. Otto to Vergennes, 17 March, 1786. MS.
[3] Dallas's Laws of Pennsylvania, ii. 236.

silver in payments to the state;[1] and fifty thousand pounds were emitted in bills of credit on loan.[2] The bank of the United States refusing to receive these bills as of equal value with its own, its act of incorporation by the state was repealed.

In February, 1785, Delaware called in all its outstanding bills of credit, whether emitted before or since the declaration of independence, with orders for redeeming them at the rate of one pound for seventy-five. After six months they would cease to be redeemable.[3]

Maryland, in its June session of 1780, emitted thirty thousand pounds sterling to be a legal tender for all debts and contracts. In the same session it was enacted that all contracts expressed in writing to be in specie were to be paid in specie. In 1782 it enacted a stay-law extending to January, 1784, and during that time the debtor might make a tender of slaves, or land, or almost anything that land produced; but the great attempt in 1786 to renew paper money, though pursued with the utmost violence and passion, and carried in the assembly, was successfully held in check by the senate.

Georgia, in August, 1782, stayed execution for two years from and after the passing of the act. In February, 1785, its bills of credit were ordered to be redeemed in specie certificates, at the rate of one thousand for one. This having been done, in August of the next year fifty thousand pounds were emitted in bills of credit, which were secured "by the guaran-

---

[1] Dallas's Laws of Pennsylvania, ii. 257.
[2] Ibid., 394.
[3] Laws of Delaware, ed. 1797, 801.

236 ON THE WAY TO A FEDERAL CONVENTION.

teed honor and faith" of the state, and by a mortgage on a vast and most fertile tract of public land.[1]

South Carolina attracted more attention. In February, 1782, that state repealed its laws making paper money a legal tender. Twenty days later the commencement of suits was suspended till ten days after the sitting of the next general assembly.[2] The new legislature, in March, 1783, established, as in other states, a table of depreciation, so that debts might be discharged according to their real value at the time of the original contract.[2] On the twenty-sixth day of March, 1784, came the great ordinance for the payment of debts in four annual instalments, beginning on the first day of January, 1786;[3] but before the arrival of the first epoch a law of October, 1785, which soon became known as the "barren land law," authorized the debtor to tender to the plaintiff such part of his property, real or personal, as he should think proper, even though it were the very poorest of his estate, and the creditor must accept it at three fourths of its appraised value. Simultaneously with this act South Carolina issued one hundred thousand pounds in bills of credit, to be loaned at seven per cent. The period for the instalments was renewed and prolonged.[3]

During the war, North Carolina made lavish use of paper money. In April, 1783, after the return of peace, it still, under various pretences, put into circulation one hundred thousand pounds—the pound in

---

[1] Watkins's Digest of the Laws of Georjria, 314, 315.
[2] Statutes at Large of South Carolina, iv. 513.
[3] Ibid., 563.
[4] Ibid., 640, 641.
[5] Ibid., 710-12.

that state being equal to two and one half Spanish milled dollars; and in the same session, but after much debate, suits were suspended for twelve months.¹ The town of Edenton, using the words of James Iredell, instructed their representatives and senator in these words: "We earnestly entreat, for the sake of our officers and soldiers, as well as our own and that of the public at large, that no more paper money under any circumstances may be made, and that, as far as possible, the present emission may be redeemed and burned."² But the protest availed nothing. In November, 1785, one hundred thousand pounds paper currency were again ordered to be emitted, and to be a lawful tender in all payments whatever. So, while the confederation was gasping for life, the finances of North Carolina, both public and private, were threatened with ruin by an irredeemable currency.

The redemption of the country from the blight of paper money depended largely on Virginia. The greatest state in the union, resisting its governor and British forces at the outbreak of the revolution, conquering the North-west, supplying almost the chief force of Greene at the South, then again the seat of the war in its last active year, it far exceeded any other state in its emission of millions in paper money. After the victory at Yorktown, Virginia ceased to vote new paper money. The old was declared to be no longer receivable, except for the taxes of the year, and it was made redeemable in loan office certificates at the rate of one thousand for one.³ In retaliation

---

¹ Life of Iredell, ii. 63.
² Ibid, 68.
³ Heniog, x. 456.

238 ON THE WAY TO A FEDERAL CONVENTION.

CHAP. VI.

1 7 8 2.

1 7 8 5.

1 7 8 6.

for the most wanton destruction of property, British debts were not recoverable in the courts. For others it constructed a scale of depreciation in the settlement of contracts made in the six years following the first of January, 1777. It had stay-laws. For a short time it allowed executions to be satisfied by the tender of tobacco, flour, and hemp at a price to be settled every month by county courts.[1] For a year or two lands and negroes might be tendered on judgments, but every contract made since the first of January, 1782,[2] was to be discharged in the manner specified by the contract. So Virginia returned to the use of coin. But in 1785 rumors went abroad that the assembly was resolved to issue a paper currency. George Mason, then in private life, scoffed at solemnly pledging the public credit which had so often been disregarded, and declared that, though they might pass a law to issue paper money, twenty laws would not make the people receive it.[3] At the end of the session Madison could write to Jefferson[4] that, though the desire of paper money had discovered itself, "no overt attempt was made!"

It became known that Meriwether Smith and others, aided by an unfavorable balance of trade and the burden of heavy taxation, would at the next session move for a paper medium. Aware of the danger, Washington insisted that George Mason should be a candidate for the assembly; and his election proved a counterpoise to the popular cry. Again, quoting from his own circular of June, 1783, that "honesty

[1] Hening, xi. 75, 76.
[2] Ibid., 176-180.
[3] George Mason to Washington, 9 Nov., 1785. MS.
[4] Works of Madison, i. 218.

will be found, on every experiment, the best policy," he encouraged Bland to firmness. The subject of paper money was introduced in October, 1786, by petitions from two counties, was faintly supported by "a few obscure patrons," was resisted as an encouragement to "fraud in states against each other," and "as a disgrace to republican governments in the eyes of mankind;" then, by eighty-five against seventeen, it was voted to be "unjust, impolitic, destructive of public and private confidence, and of that virtue which is the basis of republican government." The words show the mind and hand of Madison.

There was need of a new bill on the district courts, but it was clogged with the proposal for the payment of private debts in three annual instalments. Madison held that "no legislative principle could vindicate such, an interposition of the law in private contracts," and the bill was lost, though but by one vote.[1] The taxes of the year were allowed to be paid in tobacco as "a commutable." "These and such like things," such was the unbending criticism of Washington, "are extremeely hurtful, and may be reckoned among the principal sources of the evils and the corruption of the present day; and this, too, without accomplishing the object in view, for, if we mean to be honest, debts and taxes must be paid with the substance and not the shadow."[2]

Excusing the legislature, Madison answered: "The original object was paper money; petitions for graduated certificates succeeded; next came instalments, and lastly a project for making property a tender for

---

[1] Madison, i. 239, 252, 253, 255, 260, 365, 266.

[2] Washington to Madison. MS.

debts at four fifths of its value; all these have been happily got rid of by very large majorities."[1]

The mind of the country bent itself with all its energy to root out the evils of paper money and establish among the states one common rule by which the obligation of contracts might be preserved unimpaired. No remedy would avail that did not reach them all. They found that for the security of money there were but two remedies: frugality to diminish the need of it, and increased industry to produce more of it. They found that paper money drives specie away; that every new issue hastens its disappearance, destroying credit and creating a famine of money; that every penalty for the refusal to accept paper money at par lowers its worth, and that the heavier the penalty the more sure is the decline. They saw the death-blow that is given to credit when confidence, which must be voluntary, is commanded by force. They saw that the use of paper money robs industry, frugality, and honesty of their natural rights in behalf of spendthrifts and adventurers.[2] Grayson held that paper money with a tender annexed to it was in conflict with that degree of security to property which was fundamental in every state in the union.[3] He further thought that "congress should have the power of preventing states from cheating one another, as well as their own citizens, by means of paper money."[4]

[1] Madison, i. 267, 268.
[2] Compare the writings and opinions of William Paterson, R. R. Livingston, R. H. Lee, Madison, and others, written or uttered in the years immediately preceding 1787.
[3] Grayson to Madison, 23 March, 1784. MS.
[4] Ibid., 28 May, 1786. MS.

NEED OF AN OVERRULING UNION.   241

Madison classified the evils to be remedied under the four heads of depreciated paper as a legal tender, of property substituted for money in payment of debts, of laws for paying debts by instalments, and "of the occlusion of the courts of Justice;" to root out the dishonest system effectually, he held it necessary to give the general government not only the right to regulate coin as in the confederation, but to prevent interference with state, inter-state, and foreign contracts by separate legislation of any state. The evil was everywhere the subject of reprobation; the citizens of Massachusetts, as we learn from one of its historians,[1] complained of "retrospective laws;" Pelatiah Webster, of Philadelphia, set forth that "these acts alter the value of contracts,"[2] and William Paterson, of New Jersey, one of the best writers of that day on the subject, pointed out that "the legislature should leave the parties to the law under which they contracted."

For resisting; reform, Rhode Island and North Carolina were likely to be the foremost; for demanding it, and for persisting in the demand, Connecticut had the most hopeful record. Among the statesmen to whom the country might look in the emergency, no one had been more conspicuous or more efficient than Madison; but Roger Sherman had all the while been a member of the superior court of his own state, and so by near observation under great responsibility had thoroughly studied every aspect of the obligation of contracts.

CHAP. VI.

1787.

[2] Minot's Insurrection, 15.   [3] Webster's Essays, 129, 138.

CHAPTER VII.

CONGRESS CONFESSES ITS HELPLESSNESS.

"At length," so wrote Washington to La Fayette in 1783, "I am become a private citizen on the banks of the Potomac, solacing myself with tranquil enjoyments, retiring within myself, able to tread the paths of private life with heartfelt satisfaction, envious of none, determined to be pleased with all; and, this being the order for my march, I will move gently down the stream of life till I sleep "with my fathers." The French minister, Luzerne, who visited Washington a few weeks after his return to private life, "found him attuned in a plain gray suit like a Virginia farmer." "To secure the happiness of those around him appeared to be his chief occupation."[1] His country with one voice acknowledged that but for him its war of revolution must have failed. His glory pervaded the world, and the proofs of it followed him to his retirement.

Houdon, the great French sculptor of his day, moved more by enthusiasm for him than by the expected compensation for making his statue, came over

---

[1] Luzerne to Rayneval, 12 April, 1784.

with his assistants to Mount Vernon to take a mould of his person, to study his countenance, to watch his step as he walked over his fields, his attitude as he paused; and so he has preserved for posterity the features and the form of Washington.

Marie Antoinette added words of her own to those of the King of France, who invited him to visit them. Luzerne pressed the invitation as the heartfelt desire of the French people. "Come to France," wrote Rochambeau, speaking the wish of all the French officers who had served in America; "come, and, in a country which honors you, be assured of a reception without example, after a revolution which has not its like in history." But his presence was needed at home to retrieve his affairs from the confusion consequent on his long service in the war; during which he not only refused all pay, but subscribed what he could to the public loans. Of these the amount of the principal had been reduced, and the interest, proportionately reduced, was paid in paper almost worthless. Moreover, persons indebted to him had seized their opportunity to pay him in depreciated continental bills.

His estate, than which "no one in United America" seemed to him "more pleasantly situated," consisted of over nine thousand acres, for the most part of a grayish clay soil, lying on the south bank of the Potomac, and having, on the east and west, rivulets which rose and fell with the tides, and which, like the main stream, abounded in fish. He would gladly have found a tenant for two thirds of it at an annual rent of three thousand dollars; but was obliged to retain the management of the whole.

His unpretending mansion, with rooms of low ceilings, and neither many nor large, was well placed on a high bank of the river. For beautifying the grounds around it, he would ride in the fine season into the forests and select great numbers of well-shaped trees and shrubs, elms and live-oaks, the pines and the hemlock, holly-trees and magnolias, the red-bud, the thorn, and many others, and would transplant them in the proper season. His orchard he filled with the best cherries and pears and apples.

At the end of a year and a half he had not been able "to rescue his private concerns from the disorder into which they had been thrown by the war," though success in the effort "was become absolutely necessary for his support."[1] After he had been at home for two seasons, his inventory showed of horses one hundred and thirty, of cattle three hundred and thirty-six, of sheep two hundred and eighty-three; the hogs were untold, but on one winter's day a hundred and twenty-eight were killed, weighing more than seventeen thousand pounds. His "negroes," in February, 1786, numbered two hundred and sixteen.[2] No one of them was willing to leave him for another master. As it was his fixed rule never either to buy or to sell a slave, they had the institution of marriage and secure relations of family. The sick were provided with the best medical attendance; children, the infirm, and the aged were well cared for. Washington was but the director of his community of black people in their labor, mainly for their own subsistence. For the

[1] Washington to Humphreys. Sparks, ix. 113.   [2] From entries in Washington's unpublished Diary.

market they produced scarcely anything but "a little wheat:" and after a season of drought even their own support had to be eked out from other resources; so that, with all his method and good judgment, he, like Madison of a later day, and in accord with common experience in Virginia, found that where negroes continued on the same land, and they and all their increase were maintained upon it, their owner would gradually become more and more embarrassed or impoverished. As to bounty lands received for service in the seven years' war, and his other domains beyond the Alleghany, he "found distant property in lands more pregnant of perplexities than profit." His income, uncertain in its amount, was not sufficient to meet his unavoidable expenses, and he became more straitened for money than he had ever been since his boyhood; so that he was even obliged to delay paying the annual bill of his physician, to put off the tax-gatherer once and again, and, what was harder, to defer his charities; for, while it was his habit to conceal his gifts, he loved to give, and to give liberally.

Toward the runaway slave Washington was severe. He wished that the Northern states would permit men of the South to travel in them with their attendants, though they might be slaves; and he earnestly disapproved of the interposition of the philanthropist between the slave and his holder; but, while expressing these opinions, he at the same time took care to write, most emphatically, that no one more desired universal emancipation than himself. He pressed his conviction upon the leading politicians in Virginia that the gradual abolition of slavery "certainly might, and assuredly ought to, be effected; and that too, by legislative authority."[1] When Coke and Asbury, the first superintendents of the Methodists, asked him to aid their petition to the Virginia legislature for an act of universal emancipation, he told them frankly that "he was of their sentiments, and should this petition be taken into consideration he would signify it to the assembly in a letter."[2] Finding that the legislature of the state would not entertain a motion to do away with slavery, he sought to devise practicable plans for emancipating his negroes and providing for himself and them; not succeeding, he secured their enfranchisement by his will.[3]

The hardships of the camp had worn upon his constitution, and he was persuaded that he would not live to great age."[4] The price of health to him from day to day was to pass much of the time in the open air, especially on horseback. Receiving from Europe gifts of the best fox-hounds, he would join in the chase, sometimes came in first, but delighted most in a good run when every one was present at the death.

It was his earliest care at Mount Vernon to arrange his papers relating to the war for the use of the historian. Being asked to write his commentaries, he answered: "If I had talents for it, the consciousness

---

[1] Sparks, ix. 163, 164.
[2] Coke's First Journal, 45.
[3] Washington could emancipate his own slaves, but not those of his wife's estate; and the two classes were linked together by marriage and family ties. To this difficulty in the way of emancipating his own negroes, Madison directed my attention. The idea has prevailed that Washington married a woman of fortune. Her first husband dying, left his affairs in an embarrassed condition, and they certainly remained so in the hands of his executor or agent for early thirty years, and probably longer.
[4] Sparks, ix. 78.

of a defective education, and a certainty of a want of time, unfit me for such an undertaking."[1]

Every one agreed that Washington's "character was perfectly amiable." In his retirement he so practiced all the virtues of private life that the synod of the Presbyterians held him up to the world as the example of purity. To use the words of one who knew him well, "The breath of slander never breathed upon him in his life nor upon his ashes." He was generous to the extent of his means and beyond them. Young persons who came under his control or his guardianship he taught method in their expenses, and above all he inculcated on them the duty of husbanding their means so as to be always able and ready to give.

Washington was from his heart truly and deeply religious. His convictions became more intense from the influence of the great events of his life on his character. As he looked back upon the thick-set dangers through which he had steered, we know from himself, that he could not but feel that he had been sustained by "the all-powerful guide and dispenser of human things."[2] Of the Protestant Episcopal Church, he belonged decidedly to the party of moderation, and "had no desire to open a correspondence with the newly ordained bishop" of Connecticut.[3] Not a metaphysician nor an analyzer of creeds, his religious faith came from his experience in action. No man more thoroughly believed in the overruling Providence of a just and almighty power;

[1] Sparks, ix. 113.
[2] Ibid., 21, 22.
[3] Diary for Monday, 10 Oct., 1785. MS.

and as a chemist knows that the leaf for its greenness and beauty and health needs the help of an effluence from beyond this planet, so Washington beheld in the movements of nations a marshalling intelligence which is above them all, and which gives order and unity to the universe.

Like almost every great warrior, he hated war, and wished to see that plague to mankind banished from the earth.[1] "I never expect to draw my sword again," he said in 1785 to one of the French officers who had served in America. "I can scarcely conceive the cause that would induce me to do it. My first wish is to see the whole world in peace, and its inhabitants one band of brothers striving; who should contribute most to the happiness of mankind."[2] "As a citizen of the great republic of humanity," such are his words, "I indulge the idea that the period is not remote when the benefits of free commerce will succeed the devastations and horrors of war."[3] He loved to contemplate human nature in the state of progressive amelioration.[4] His faith in Providence led him to found that hope on the belief that justice has a strength of its own which will by degrees command respect as the rule for all nations.

He wished success to every people that were struggling for better days. Afflicted by the abject penury of the mass of the Irish,[5] he gave them his sympathies. A hope dawned of renewed national life for the Greeks. He could scarcely conceive that the Turks would be permitted to hold any of their possessions in Europe.[6]

---

[1] Sparks, ix. 112, 113.
[2] Ibid., 138, 139.
[3] Ibid., 193, 194.
[4] Ibid., 306.
[5] Ibid., 398.
[6] Ibid., 860.

CONGRESS CONFESSES ITS HELPLESSNESS. 249

He welcomed with enthusiasm the approach of the French revolution, and at an early day pointed out the danger that menaced the king and his only avenue of safety; saying: "His Most Christian Majesty speaks and acts in a style not very pleasing to republican ears or to republican forms, nor to the temper of his own subjects at this day. Liberty, when it begins to take root, is a plant of rapid growth; the checks he endeavors to give it by armies and the nobility will kindle a flame, which may be smothered for a while but not extinguished! When people are oppressed with taxes, and have cause to believe that there has been a misapplication of the money, they ill brook the language of despotism."[1]

To Lafayette, whose desire to signalize himself he well understood, he said: "Great moderation should be used on both sides; I caution you against running into extremes and prejudicing your cause."[2]

In foreign affairs Washington inclined neither to France nor to England; his system of politics was impartially American. At home he was devoted to no state, to no party. His mind, though he was of Virginia, was free from any bias, northern or southern, the allegiance of his heart being given to United America.

At Mount Vernon, on the twenty-eighth of March, 1785, the joint commissioners of the two states divided by the Potomac, George Mason and Alexander Henderson, of Virginia; Daniel of St, Thomas Jenifer, Thomas Stone, and Samuel Chase, of Maryland, met under the auspices of Washington. As his near

---

[1] Sparks, ix. 332.   [2] Ibid., 381.

250 ON THE WAY TO A FEDERAL CONVENTION.

CHAP. VII.

1785.

neighbor, intimate friend, and old political associate, Mason felt his influence and entered with zeal and a strong sense of duty into the movements that led to union.

The commissioners prepared the terms of a compact between the two states for the jurisdiction over the waters of the Chesapeake bay and the rivers that were common to both states; and, conforming to the wishes of Washington, they requested Pennsylvania to grant the free use of the branches of the Ohio within its limits, for establishing the connection between that river and the Potomac.[1]

The primary object of their commission being fulfilled, they took up matters of general policy, and recommended to the two states a uniformity of duties on imports, a uniformity of commercial regulations, and a uniformity of currency.[2] George Mason was charged with the report of their doings to the legislature of his state.

Nov.

When the assembly of Virginia came together, congress and the country were rent by the question of investing congress with an adequate power over trade. The Eastern and Middle states were zealous for the measure; the Southern were divided; Pennsylvania had established duties of its own, with the avowed object of encouraging domestic manufactures; South Carolina was deliberating on the distresses of her commerce. In the assembly of Virginia, in which there was a great conflict of opinion, Madison[3] spoke for the grant of power as fraught with no danger to

[1] Pennsylvania Archives, 511.
[2] Rives' Madison, ii. 58.
[3] Notes of Madison's speech in Madison, i. 201, 303.

CONGRESS CONFESSES ITS HELPLESSNESS. 251

the liberties of the states, and as needful in order to conduct the foreign relations, to arrest contention between the states, to prevent enactments of one state to the injury of another, to establish a system intelligible to foreigners trading with the United States, to counteract the evident design of Great Britain to weaken the confederacy, and to preserve the federal constitution, which, like all other institutions, could not remain long after it should cease to be useful. The dissolution of the union would be the signal for standing armies in the several states, burdensome and perpetual taxes, clashing systems of foreign politics, and an appeal to the sword in every petty squabble. Washington being invited to offer suggestions,[1] answered: "The proposition is self-evident. We are either a united people or we are not so. If the former, let us in all matters of national concern act as a nation which has a national character to support."[2] "If the states individually attempt to regulate commerce, an abortion or a many-headed monster would be the issue. If we consider ourselves or wish to be considered by others as a united people, why not adopt the measures which are characteristic of it, and support the honor and dignity of one? If we are afraid to trust one another under qualified powers, there is an end of the union."[3]

The house was disposed to confide to congress a power over trade; but, by the stratagem of the adversaries of the resolutions, the duration of the grant was limited to thirteen years. This limitation, which

---

[1] David Stuart to Washington, 16 Nov., 1785. MS.
[2] Sparks, ix. 145, 146.
[3] Washington to Stuart, 30 Nov., 1785.

252 ON THE WAY TO A FEDERAL CONVENTION.

CHAP. VII.

1785.

was reported on the last day of November, took from the movement all its value. It is better," so wrote Madison to Washington, "to trust to further experience, and even to distress, for an adequate remedy than to try a temporary measure which may stand in the way of a permanent one. The difficulty now found in obtaining a unanimous concurrence of the states in any measure must increase with every increase of their numbers."[1]

Dec.

All was at a stand, when suddenly a ray of light was thrown upon the assembly by Maryland. On the fifth of December the adhesion of that state to the compact relating to the jurisdiction of the waters of Chesapeake bay and the Potomac was laid before Virginia, which without delay enacted a corresponding law of equal liberality and precision.[2] The desire of Maryland was likewise announced to invite the concurrence of Delaware and Pennsylvania in a plan for a canal between the Chesapeake and the Delaware; "and if that is done," said Madison, "Delaware and Pennsylvania will wish the same compliment paid to their neighbors." But the immediate measure of Maryland was communicated in a letter from its legislature to the legislature of Virginia, proposing that commissioners from all the states should be invited to meet and regulate the restrictions on commerce for the whole.[3] Madison instantly saw the advantage of "a politico-commercial commission" for the continent.

[1] In Elliot, i. 114, the resolutions as reported on the 30th November are published as Madison's; but they found in Madison their strongest opponent. Madison, i. 205, 206, and compare 203.
[2] Hening, xii. 50, 55.
[3] Stuart to Washington, 18 Dec., 1785. MS.

CONGRESS CONFESSES ITS HELPLESSNESS. 253

Tyler, late speaker of the house, who "whished congress to have the" entire "regulation of trade," acting in concert with him, a resolution was drafted for the appointment of commissioners from Virginia and all the other states to digest a report with requisite argumentation of the powers of congress over trade, their report to be of no force until it should be unanimously, ratified by the several states.[1] Madison kept in reserve. Tyler, who having never served in the federal council was free from every suspicion of inclining to grant it too much power, presented the resolution. It was suffered to lie on the table till the last day in the session; then, on the twenty-first of January, 1786, it went through both branches of the legislature by a large majority. Among the commissioners who were chosen, Madison was the first selection on the part of the house. The commissioners named the first Monday of September for the day of their meeting, and Annapolis as the place, on account of its remoteness from the influences of congress and the centres of trade. The invitations to the states were made through the executive of Virginia.

On the twenty-second Madison wrote to Monroe: "The expedient is better than nothing; and, as the recommendation of additional powers to congress is within the purview of the commission, it may possibly lead to better consequences than at first occur:"[2]

The sixth congress could not be organized until the twenty-third of November, 1785, when, seven states being present, David Ramsay of Carolina, was elected chairman. For the half of December not

---

[1] Rives, ii. 60.   [2] Madison, i. 222.

states enough were present to do business. So soon as there was a permanent quorum, it was agreed that the confederation had its vices, and the question of policy was: Shall these vices be corrected gradually through congress, or at once and completely through a convention? Just seventeen days after Virginia had invited the states to a common consultation at Annapolis, Charles Pinckney, of South Carolina, in a motion of very great length, ascribed the extension of the commerce and the security of the liberties of the states to the joint efforts of the whole: "They have, therefore," he insisted "wisely determined to make the welfare of the union their first object, reflecting that in all federal regulations something: must be yielded to aid the whole, and that those who expect support must be ready to afford it."[1] The motion, after being under discussion for two days, was referred to a committee of five. On the fifteenth, King, Pinckney, Kean, Monroe, and Pettit, representatives of South Carolina and the three great states, reported: "The requisitions of congress, for eight years past, have been so irregular in their operation, so uncertain in their collection, and so evidently unproductive, that a reliance on them in future as a source from whence moneys are to be drawn to discharge the engagements of the confederacy would be not less Dishonorable to the understandings of those who entertain such confidence than dangerous to the welfare and peace of the union. The committee are, therefore, seriously impressed with the indispensable obligation that congress are under of representing to

[1] Journals of Congress, iv. 617.

CONGRESS CONFESSES ITS HELPLESSNESS. 255

the immediate and impartial consideration of the several states the utter impossibility of maintaining and preserving the faith of the federal government by temporary requisitions on the states, and the consequent necessity of an early and complete accession of all the states to the revenue system of the eighteenth of April, 1783."[1] "After the most solemn deliberation, and under the fullest conviction that the public embarrassments are such as above represented, and that they are daily increasing, the committee are of opinion that it has become the duty of congress to declare most explicitly that the crisis has arrived when the people of these United States, by whose will and for whose benefit the federal government was instituted, must decide whether they will support their rank as a nation by maintaining the public faith at home and abroad; or whether, for want of a timely exertion in establishing a general revenue and thereby giving strength to the confederacy, they will hazard not only the existence of the union, but of those great and invaluable privileges for which they have so arduously and so honorably contended."[2]

Thus congress put itself on trial before the country, and the result of the year was to on their competency to be the guardians of the union and the upholders of its good faith. They must either exercise negation of self and invite the states to call a general convention, or they must themselves present to the country for its approval an mended constitution, or they must find out how to make their own powers under the confederation work efficiently.

---

[1] Journals of Congress, iv. 619. [2] Ibid., 620.

Should they fail in all the three, they will have given an irreversible verdict against themselves. The course of events relating to the welfare of the whole was watched by the country more carefully than ever before. Far and wide a general convention was become the subject of thought; and "a plan for it was forming, though it was as yet immature."[1]

New Jersey, which had all along vainly sought the protection of the general government against the taxation of her people by a local duty levied on all their importations from abroad for their own consumption through the port of New York, at last, kindled with a sense of her wrongs, and in a resentful mood, voted by a very large majority that she would pay no part of the last requisition of congress until all the states should have accepted the measure of an impost for the benefit of the general treasury. Alarmed at this movement, congress deputed Charles Pinckney, Gorham, and Grayson to represent to the legislature of New Jersey the fatal consequences that must inevitably result to that state and to the union from their refusal to comply with the requisition of the last congress. Grayson looked upon their vote as little else than a declaration of independence. Again Pinckney of South Carolina took the lead, and, in an address to the New Jersey legislature of the thirteenth of March, this was part of his language: "When these states united, convinced of the inability of each to support a separate system and that their protection and existence depended on their union, policy as well as prudence dictated the necessity of forming one general and

---

[1] Jay to Washington, 16 March, 1786.

efficient government, which, while it protected and secured the whole, left to the several states those rights of internal sovereignty which it was not necessary to delegate and which could be exercised without injury to the federal authority. If New Jersey conceives herself oppressed under the present confederation, let her, through her delegates in congress, state to them the oppression she complains of, and urge the calling of a general convention of the states for the purpose of increasing the powers of the federal government and rendering it more adequate for the ends for which it was instituted; in this constitutional mode of application there can be no doubt of her meeting with all the support and attention she can wish. I have long been of opinion that it is the only true and radical remedy for our public defects, and shall with pleasure assent to and support any measure of that kind which may be introduced while I continue a member of that body."[1]

Pleased with the idea of a general convention, New Jersey recalled its vote, accepted within a week the invitation of Virginia to a convention at Annapolis, elected its commissioners, and empowered them "to consider how far a uniform system in their commercial regulations and OTHER, IMPORTANT MATTERS might be necessary to the common interest and permanent harmony of the several states; and to report such an act on the subject as, when ratified by them, would enable the United States in congress assembled effectually to provide for the exigencies of the union."[2]

---

[1] Carey's Museum, ii. 155. Otto to Vergennes, 17 March, 1786. Report of Bertholff, the Austrian agent.
[2] Elliot, i. 117, 118.

258 ON THE WAY TO A FEDERAL CONVENTION.

CHAP. VII.

1786.

"If it should be determined that the reform of the confederation is to be made by a convention," so wrote Monroe at this time to Madison, "the powers of the Virginia commissioners who are to go to Annapolis are inadequate."[1] explaining why more extended powers had not been given, Madison answered: "The assembly would have revolted against a plenipotentiary commission to their deputies for the convention; the option lay between doing what was done and doing nothing."[2]

March. 22.

"There have been serious thoughts in the minds of members of congress," wrote Grayson to Madison, "to recommend to the states the meeting of a general convention to consider of an alteration of the confederation, and there is a motion to that effect under consideration. I have not made up my mind whether it would not be 'better to bear the ills we have than fly to those we know not of. I am, however, in no doubt about the weakness of the federal government. If it remains much longer in its present state of imbecility, we shall be one of the most contemptible nations on the face of the earth."[3]

The subject lingered in congress till the third of May. Then South Carolina for a third time raised her voice, and Charles Pinckney moved that a grand committee be appointed on the affairs of the nation. "It is necessary," he said, "to inform the states of our condition. Congress must be invested with

---

[1] This letter from Monroe, of a date previous to 19 March, 1786, is missing. Its contents are known only from the citation of it by Madison.

[2] Madison to Monroe, 19 March, 1786. Madison, i. 228, 229.

[3] Grayson to Madison, 23 March, 1786. MS.

CONGRESS CONFESSES ITS HELPLESSNESS. 259

greater powers, or the federal government must fall. It is, therefore, necessary for congress either to appoint a convention for that purpose, or by requisition to call on the states for such powers as are necessary to enable it to administer the federal government." Among some of the defects in the confederation which he enumerated were, the want of powers for regulating commerce, for raising troops, and for executing those powers that were given. Monroe replied: "Congress has full power to raise troops, and has a right to compel compliance with every requisition which does not go beyond the powers with which it is invested by the confederation. All the states but New York have invested congress with commercial powers, and New York is at this time framing an act on the subject. I, therefore, see no occasion for a convention." The discussion was continued at great length, and the matter referred to a committee of the whole.[1] But the discussion brought confess no nearer to the recommenddation of a general convention; its self-love refused to surrender any of its functions, least of all on the ground of its own incapacity to discharge them.

Should congress then of itself lay a revision of the articles of confederation before the states for their acceptance? Here Grayson, surveying his colleagues with a discerning eye, at once convinced himself that congress could never agree on amendments, even among themselves[2] For himself, he held it essential that the general government should have power to

[1] Thomas Rodney's Journal. MS. [2] Grayson to Madison, 28 May, 1786. MS.

regulate commerce; to prohibit the states from issuing paper money; to prohibit the slave trade; to fix the site of the government in the centre of the union, that is to say, near Georgetown; and to change the method of voting by states to a vote according to population. Of effecting these reforms he had no hope. He was sure if the question of commerce should be settled, Massachusetts would be satisfied and refuse to go further. "Pinckney, the champion of powers over commerce," he said, "will be astounded when he meets with a proposition to prevent the states from importing any more of the seed of Cain." New York and Pennsylvania would feel themselves aggrieved if, by a national compact, the sessions of congress should always be held in the centre of the empire. Neither Maryland, nor Rhode Island, nor New Jersey, would like to surrender its equal vote for one proportioned to its real importance in the Union. Grayson, therefore, did not "think it would be for the advantage of the union that the convention at Annapolis should produce anything decisive," since it was restricted in its scope to commerce, and the question which he proposed to Madison was: "The state of Virginia having gone thus far, had she not better go further and propose to the other states to augment the powers of the delegates so as to comprehend all the grievances of the union?"[1]

But Pinckney, of South Carolina, was not daunted. Failing to secure the vote of congress for a general convention, he next obtained the appointment of a grand committee "to report such amendments to the

[1] Grayson to Madison, 28 May 1786. MS.

confederation as it may be necessary to recommend to the several states for the purpose of obtaining from them such powers as will render the federal government adequate to the ends for which it was instituted." Congress, in a committee of the whole, devoted seven days of July and six of August to the solution of the great question, and before the end of August the report, which was made by a sub-committee consisting of Pinckney, Dane, and Johnson, and accepted by a grand committee, received its final amended form.[1]

To the original thirteen articles of confederation seven new ones were added.

The United States were to regulate foreign and domestic trade and collect duties on imports, but without violating the constitutions of the states. The revenue collected was to be paid to the state in which it should accrue.

Congress, on making requisitions on the states, was to fix "the proper periods when the states shall pass legislative acts giving full and complete effect to the same." In case of neglect, the state was to be charged at the rate of ten per cent, per annum on its quota in money, and twelve per cent, on the ascertained average expenses on its quota of land forces.

If a state should, for ten months, neglect to pass laws in compliance with the requisition, and if a majority of the states should have passed such laws, then, but not till then, the revenue required by con-

---

[1] From MS. reports of the committee. These amended resolutions may well be taken as representing the intentions of Charles Pinckney at that time. A copy of them, very greatly abridged, is preserved in the French archives.

gress was to be apportioned on towns or counties and collected by tie collectors of the last state tax. Should they refuse to act, congress might appoint others with similar rights and powers, and with full power and authority to enforce the collections. Should a state, or citizens without the disapproval of the state, offer opposition, the conduct of the state was to be considered "as an open violation of the federal compact."

Interest was to be allowed on advances by states and charged on arrears.

A new system of revenue could be established by eleven states out of the thirteen; and so in proportion as the number of states might increase.

The United States were to have the sole and exclusive power to define and punish treason against them, misprision of treason, piracy or felonies on the high seas, and to institute, by appointments from the different parts of the union, a federal court of seven judges, of whom four would constitute a quorum, to hear appeals from the state courts on matters concerning treaties with foreign powers, or the law of nations, or commerce, or the federal revenues, or important questions wherein the United States should be a party.

To enforce the attendance of members of congress, a state might punish its faulty delegate by a disqualification to hold office under the United States or any state.

These resolutions, though most earnestly discussed in congress, were left to repose among its countless reports. They did not offer one effective remedy for

CONGRESS CONFESSES ITS HELPLESSNESS. 263

existing evils; they never could gain a majority in congress; no one fancied that they could obtain the unanimous assent of the states; and, could they have gained it, the articles of confederation would have remained as feeble as before. Still less was it possible for congress to raise an annual revenue. The country was in arrears for the interest on its funded debt, and in the last two years had received not more than half a million dollars in specie from all the states—a sum not sufficient for the annual ordinary charges of the federal government. Pennsylvania had complied with the late requisitions almost with exactitude; Maryland and Virginia had furnished liberal supplies; New York exerted herself, and successfully, by the aid of her custom-house; but Massachusetts and all the other New England states were in arrears, and the three southernmost states had paid little money since the conclusion of the late war. Congress confessed that it could not raise a revenue unless measures were adopted for funding the foreign and domestic debts, and they went back to the system framed by Madison in April, 1783; but the success of that measure depended on a unanimous grant of new power to the general government. All the states except New York had assented to the principle of deriving a federal revenue from imports, though the assenting acts of a majority of them still required modifications. Congress saw fit to assume that nothing remained but to obtain the consent of that one state.

In March a meeting of inhabitants of the city of New York unanimously petitioned the legislature to consent to the system which could alone give energy to the union or prosperity to commerce. On the other hand, it was contended that the confederation and the constitution of each state are the foundations which neither congress nor the legislatures of the states can alter, and on which it is the duty of both to build; that the surrender to congress of an independent authority to levy duties would be the surrender of an authority that inheres necessarily in the respective legislatures of each state: that deviation from the fundamental principles of the American constitutions would be ruinous, first, to the liberty of the states, and then to their existence; that congress, already holding: in one hand the sword, would hold in the other the purse, and concentrate in itself the sovereignty of the thirteen states; that it is the division of the great republic into different republics of a middling; size and confederated laws which save it from despotism.[1]

The legislature of New York conformed to these opinions, and, while on the fourth of May it imposed the duty of five per cent., it reserved to itself the revenue with the sole right of its collection. Nor was it long before Pennsylvania, which held a large part of the public debt, suspended its adhesion to the revenue plan of congress unless it should include supplementary funds. In August, King and Monroe were despatched by congress to confer with its legislature. It is on record that the speech of King was adapted to insure applause even from an Attic audience;[2] but the subject was referred to the next assembly.

[1] Report of the Austrian agent Bertholff, 1 April, 1786. MS.
[2] Henry Hill to Washington, 1 Oct., 1786. MS.

Congress joined battle more earnestly with, New York. They recommended the executive to convene its legislature immediately for the purpose of granting the impost. The governor made reply: "I have not power to convene the legislature except on extraordinary occasions, and, as the present business has repeatedly been laid before them, and has so recently received their determination, it cannot come within that description." Congress repeated its demand, and it only served to call from Clinton a firm renewal of his refusal. The strife had degenerated into an altercation which only established before the country that congress, which would not call a convention and could not of itself frame fit amendments to the confederation, could not raise an annual revenue for the merest wants of the government, and could not rescue the honor of the nation from default in payments of interest on moneys borrowed to secure their independence.

The case was the same in everything that congress undertook. Every treaty introduced a foreign power; but, still, congress had no other means of fulfilling its treaty obligations than through the good-will and concurrence of each one of its states; though it was the theory of the articles of confederation that the United States presented themselves to foreign powers as one nation.

The difficulty which caused all these perpetual failures was inherent and incurable. Congress, a deliberative body, undertook to enact requisitions, and then direct the legislatures of thirteen independent states, which were equally deliberative bodies, to pass laws to give them effect, itself remaining helpless till they should do so. A deliberative body ordering another independent deliberative body what laws to make is an anomaly; and, in the case of congress, the hopelessness of harmony was heightened by the immense extent of the United States, by the differences of time when the legislatures of the several states convened, and by a conflict of the interests, passions, hesitancies, and wills of thirteen legislatures independent of each other, and uncontrolled by a common head. No ray of hope remained but from the convention which Virginia had invited to assemble on the first Monday in September at Annapolis.

CHAPTER VIII.

VIRGINIA INVITES DEPUTIES OF THE SEVERAL LEGISLATURES OF THE STATES TO MEET IN CONVENTION.

Congress having confessedly failed to find ways and means for carrying on the government, the convention which had been called to Annapolis became the ground of hope for the nation. The house of delegates of Maryland promptly accepted the invitation of Virginia, but the senate, in its zeal to strengthen the appeal which congress was then addressing to the states for a revenue, refused its concurrence. Neither Connecticut, nor South Carolina, nor Georgia sent delegates to the meeting. In Massachusetts two sets of nominees, among whom appears the name of George Cabot, declined the service; the third were, like the Rhode Island delegates, arrested on the way by tidings that the convention was over.

Every one of the commissioners chosen for New York, among whom were Egbert Benson and Hamilton, was engrossed by pressing duties. Egbert Benson, the guiding statesman in the Hartford convention of 1780, was engaged as attorney-general in the courts at Albany. With Schloss Hobart, the upright judge, he agreed that the present opportunity for obtaining a revision of the system of general government ought not to be neglected. He, therefore, consigned his public business to a friend, reported the conversation with Schloss Hobart to Hamilton in New York, and repaired with him to Annapolis, There, on the eleventh of September, they found Madison with the commissioners of Virginia aiming at a plenipotentiary general convention, and commisioners from New Jersey instructed by their legislature to be content with nothing less than a new federal government. No state north of New York was represented, and no one south of Delaware save Virginia. It was a meeting of central states. One thought animated the assembly. Dickinson, a principal author of the articles of confederation, was unanimously elected chairman; and, with the same unanimity, a committee was raised to prepare a report. Hamilton, though not of the committee, made a draft; this the convention employed two days in considering and amending, when the resulting form was unanimously adopted. In clear and passionless language they expressed their' conviction that it would advance the interests of the union if the states which they represented would agree, and use their endeavors to procure the concurrence of the other states to agree, "to meet at Philadelphia on the second Monday of the next May to consider the situation of the United States, and devise such further provisions as should appear necessary to render the constitution of the federal government adequate to the exigencies of the union; and to report to con-

VIRGINIA'S INVITATION TO A CONVENTION. 269

gress such an act as, when agreed to by them and confirmed by the legislatures of every state, would effectually provide for the same."¹ The proposition was explicit; the place for meeting wisely chosen; and the time within which congress and the thirteen states must decide and the convention meet for its work was limited to less than eight months.

In a few days the report, signed by the venerated name of Dickinson, was received by congress; but the delegation from Massachusetts, led by King, prevented the recommendation of the measure which the deputations at Annapolis had asked for.² The governor of New York was of opinion that the confederation as it stood was equal to the purposes of the union, or, with little alteration, could be made so; and that the commissioners from New York should have confined themselves to the purposes of their errand.³

On the tenth of October Rufus King appeared before the house of representatives of Massachusetts, and, in the presence of an audience which crowded the galleries, insisted that the confederation was the act of the people; that no part could be altered but on the initiation of congress and the confirmation of all the several legislatures; if the work should be done by a convention, no legislature could have a right to confirm it; congress, and congress only, was the proper body to propose alterations. In these views he was, a few days later, supported by Nathan Dane. This house of representatives

---

[1] Elliot, i. 117-120.
[2] Carrington to Madison, 18 Dec., 1786. MS.
[3] Hamilton, vi. 605.

conforming to this advice, refused to adopt the suggestions that came from Annapolis; and there was not to be another session before the time proposed for the general convention at Philadelphia.[1]

From this state of despair the country was lifted by Madison and Virginia. The recommendation of a plenipotentiary convention was well received by the assembly of Virginia. The utter failure of congress alike in administration and in reform, the rapid advances of the confederation toward ruin, at length proselyted the most obstinate adversaries to a political renovation. On the motion of Madison, the assembly, showing the revolution of sentiment which the experience of one year had effected, gave its unanimous sanction to the recommendation from Annapolis.[2] We come now upon the week glorious for Virginia beyond any event in its annals, or in the history of any republic that had ever before existed. Madison had been calm and prudent and indefatigable, always acting with moderation, and always persistent of purpose. The hour was come for frank and bold words, and decisive action. Madison, giving effect to his own long-cherished wishes and the still earlier wishes of Washington, addressing as it were the whole country and marshalling all the states, recorded the motives to the action of his own commonwealth in these words:

"The commissioners who assembled at Annapolis, on the fourteenth day of September last, for the purpose of devising and reporting the means of enabling

[1] Carrington to Madison, 18 Dec., 1786. MS.   [2] Madison, i. 259.

congress to provide effectually for the commercial interests of the United States, have represented the necessity of extending the revision of the federal system to all its defects, and have recommended that deputies for that purpose be appointed by the several legislatures, to meet in convention in the city of Philadelphia on the second day of May next—a provision preferable to a discussion of the subject in congress, where it might be too much interrupted by ordinary business, and where it would, besides, be deprived of the counsels of individuals who are restrained from a seat in that assembly. The general assembly of this commonwealth, taking into view the situation of the confederacy, as well as reflecting on the alarming representations made from time to time by the United States in congress, particularly in their act of the fifteenth day of February last, can no longer doubt that the crisis is arrived at which the people of America are to decide the solemn question whether they will, by wise and magnanimous efforts, reap the fruits of independence and of union; or whether, by giving way to unmanly jealousies and prejudices, or to partial and transitory interests, they will renounce the blessings prepared for them by the revolution. The same noble and extended policy, and the same fraternal and affectionate sentiments which originally determined the citizens of this commonwealth to unite with their brethren of the other states in establishing a federal government, cannot but be felt with equal force now as motives to lay aside every inferior consideration, and to concur in such further concessions and provisions as may be necessary to

272   ON THE WAY TO A FEDERAL CONVENTION.

CHAP. VIII.

1786. Nov.

secure the objects for which that government was instituted, and render the United States as happy in peace as they have been glorious in war."

This is the preamble adopted without a dissenting voice by the general assembly of the commonwealth of Virginia, as they acceded to the proposal from Annapolis with this one variation, that the new federal constitution, after it should be agreed to by congress, was to be established, not by the legislatures of the states, but by the states themselves, thus opening the way for special conventions of the several states.

In selecting her own delegates, Virginia placed "Washington at their head, surrounded by Madison, Randolph, and Mason. Randolph, the newly elected governor of the state, adopting words of Washington, sent the act of his state to congress, and to the executive of each one of the states in the union, asking their concurrence.

23.

Dec.

1787. Jan. Feb.

Hardly had the tardy post of that day brought the gladdening news to New Jersey, when that state, first of the twelve, on the twenty-third of November, took its place at the side of Virginia. Pennsylvania did not let the year go by without joining them. North Carolina acceded in January, and Delaware in February of the following year.

The solemn words of Virginia, the example of the three central states, the inspiring influence of Hamilton, the return to congress of Madison, who was preparing himself for the convention, and professed great expectations of good effects from the measure, caused the scales to fall from the eyes of King. The year was but six weeks old when he wrote to Gerry,

VIRGINIA'S INVITATION TO A CONVENTION. 273

who had thus far been his ally: "Although my sentiments are the same as to the legality of the measure, I think we ought not to oppose, but to coincide with this project. Events are hurrying us to a crisis. Prudent and sagacious men should be ready to seize the most favorable circumstances to establish a more perfect and vigorous government."[1]

A grand committee of the seventh congress reported in February, by a bare majority of one, that, "entirely coinciding with the proceedings of the commissioners, they did strongly recommend to the different legislatures to send forward delegates to the proposed convention at Philadelphia;" but they never ventured to ask for a vote upon their report. Meantime, the legislature of New York, in an instruction to their delegates in congress, taking no notice of the meeting at Annapolis, recommended a general convention to be initiated by congress itself. The proposition, as brought forward by the New York delegates, named no place or time for the convention, and knew nothing of any acts which had not proceeded from congress. It failed by a large majority. King, of Massachusetts, seizing the opportunity to reconcile his present coalition with Madison and Hamilton with his old opinion that congress alone could initiate a reform of the constitution, substituted a motion which carefully ignored the act of the meeting at Annapolis, and made a recommendation of a convention as an original measure, but identical in time and place. This motion, which was so framed as not to invalidate any elections already made, was accepted without op-

[1] Austin's Gerry, ii. 3, 4, 7, and 8.

CHAP.
VIII.
1787.

position.[1] In this way the self-love of congress was appeased, and its authority arrayed in favor of a general convention.

All parties in the legislature of New York then took up the subject of representation in the convention. Yates, in the senate, proposed that "the new provisions in the articles of confederation should not be repugnant to or inconsistent with the constitution of the state." The motion was rejected by the casting vote of the president. The house would have appointed five delegates to the convention, but the inflexible senate limited the number to three, and named Yates, Lansing, and Hamilton, who were elected in both branches without opposition.

1786.

Meantime, the sufferings of the debtors in Massachusetts, especially in its central and western counties, embittered by the devices of attorneys to increase their own emoluments, and aggrieved by the barbarous laws of that day which doomed the debtor, however innocent, to imprisonment at the caprice of his creditor, had driven them to interrupt the courts in Worcester. In the three western counties measures were taken to close the courts; and once, for a moment, the national armory at Springfield was menaced. The movement assumed the aspect of an insurrection, almost of a rebellion, which received support even from husbandmen otherwise firm supporters of the law. The measures of Bowdoin, in which he was throughout supported by Samuel Adams, were marked by decision, celerity, and lenity. The real cause of the distress was, in part, the failure

[1] Journals, iv. 723. Gilpin, 587, 619, 620. Elliot, v. 96, 106.

VIRGINIA'S INVITATION TO A CONVENTION. 275

of the state of Massachusetts itself to meet its obligations; and, still more, the bankruptcy of the general government, which owed large sums of money to inhabitants of almost every town for service in achieving the independence of their country. Wherever the insurgents gathered in numbers, Bowdoin sent a larger force than they could muster. In this way he gave authority to every branch of the government and peace to every town. He maintained the majesty of the law by opening the courts for the conviction of the worst offenders; but, interposing with his prerogative of mercy, he did not suffer the life of any one of them to be taken. For the restoration of the public and private finances, he called together the legislature of the commonwealth, which applauded his conduct, and fulfilled the long desire of his heart. On the twenty-second of February, six days in advance of New York, and as yet in ignorance of what had been done in congress, they acceded to the invitation from Annapolis. Before its delegates were chosen, the recommendation of a convention by that body was known; and Bowdoin, in their commissions, wisely made use of the words of congress.

The two Southern states chose their delegates to the convention in April. Connecticut waited for its April day of election in May. Then Elizur Goodrich, the preacher of the election sermon, proved from one of the prophets of Israel the duty of strengthening the national union and restoring the national honor, or they would be obliged themselves to repeat the lamentation that "from the daughter of Zion all her beauty was departed." "Gentlemen," he broke out to those to whom he was preaching, "Heaven unite the wisdom and patriotism of America in the proposed convention of the states in some equal system of federal subordination and sovereignty of the states." On the twelfth, Samuel Huntington, the governor, addressing the legislature, recommended a superintending power that should secure peace and justice between the states, and between all the states and foreign nations. "I am," he said, "an advocate for an efficient general government, and for a revenue adequate to its nature and its exigencies. Should the imposts be carried to excess, it will promote the growth of manufacture among yourselves of the articles affected by them, and proportionally increase our wealth and independence. Manufactures more than any other employment will increase our numbers, in which consists the strength and glory of a people."[1] The assembly then chose to the convention three men who were all closely united, and so able that scarce any delegation stood before them.

New Hampshire, from the poverty of her treasury, delayed its choice till June. Maryland, rent by a faction eager for the issue of paper money, did not elect delegates till near the end of May. Rhode Island alone, under the sway of a party spirit which was fast ebbing, refused to be represented in the convention.

The people of the United States watched the result of the convention with trembling hope. "Shall we have a king?" asked Jay, and himself answered: "Not, in my opinion, while other expedients remain untried."[2] It was foreseen that a failure would be

---

[1] Carey's Museum, ii. 396.   [2] Sparks, ix. 510.

followed by the establishment of three separate confederacies.¹ The ministry of England harbored the thought of a constitutional monarchy, with a son of George III. as king; and they were not without alarm lest gratitude to France should place on an American throne a prince of the house of Bourbon.²

The task of preparing the outlines of a constitution as the basis for the deliberations of the convention was undertaken by Madison. His experience and his studies fitted him for the office. He had been a member of the convention which formed the first constitution for Virginia; of its first legislature as a state; of its executive council when Patrick Henry and Jefferson were governors; for three years a delegate in congress; then a member of the Virginia legislature; a commissioner at Annapolis; and, so soon as the rule of rotation permitted, once more a member of congress. From the declaration of independence he had devoted himself to the study of republican and of federal government. On the failure at Annapolis, Jefferson cheered him on to a broader reformation; to make the states one nation as to foreign concerns, and keep them distinct in domestic ones; to organize "the federal head into legislative, executive, and judiciary;" to control the interference of states in general affairs by an appeal to a federal court. With Edmund Randolph, Madison insisted that from him, as governor of Virginia, the convention would expect some leading proposition, and dwelt on the necessity of his bending his thoughts seriously to the great work of preparation; but Ran-

---

[1] Madison, i. 280.   [2] Temple, infra; Adams, viii. 420.

dolph declined, pleading his want of the necessary leisure. Madison proceeded without dismay. He held as a fixed principle that the new system should be ratified by the people of the several states, so that it might be clearly paramount to their individual legislative authority. He would make no material sacrifices to local or transient prejudices. To him the independence of each separate state was utterly irreconcilable with the idea of an aggregate sovereignty, while a consolidation of the states into one simple republic was neither expedient nor attainable.[1] In the endeavor to reconcile the due supremeacy of the nation with the preservation of the local authorities in their subordinate usefulness, he did not escape mistakes; but he saw clearly that a widely extended territory was the true sphere for a republic, and in advance of the federal convention he sketched for his own use[2] and that of his friends,[3] and ultimately of the convention, thoroughly comprehensive constitutional government for the union.

Washington at Mount Vernon was equally studious. He made himself familiar with the reasonings of Montesquieu; and he obtained the opinions, not of Madison only, but of Knox and of Jay. From their letters and his own experience, he drew three separate outlines of a new constitution, differing in manifold ways, and yet each of the three designed to restore and consolidate the union.[4]

[1] Madison, i. 287.
[2] Notes on the confederacy, Madison. i. 320-328.
[3] Madison to Jefferson, 17 March,
Madison, 1, 284 to Randolph, Gilpin, 631; Elliot, 107; to Washington, Sparks, ix. 516.
[4] N. American Review, xxv, 263.

LETTERS AND PAPERS

ILLUSTRATING THE FORMATION OF THE FEDERAL

CONSTITUTION.

This Page Intentionally Left Blank

APPENDIX.

George Washington to George Mason, Middlebrook, 27 March, 1779. Ex.

I view things very differently, I fear, from what the people in general do, who seem to think the contest is at an end, and to make money and get place the only things now remaining to do. I have seen, without desponding even for a moment, the hours which America has styled her gloomy ones, but I have beheld no day since the commencement of hostilities that I have thought her liberties in such eminent danger as at present. Friends and foes seem now to combine to pull down the goodly fabric we have hitherto been raising at the expense of so much time, blood, and treasure; and, unless the bodies politic will exert themselves to bring things back to first principles, correct abuses, and punish our internal foes, inevitable ruin must follow. Indeed, we seem to be verging so fast to destruction that I am filled with sensetions to which I have been a stranger till within these three months. Our enemies behold with exultation and joy how effectually we labor for their benefit; and from being in a state of absolute despair, and on the point of evacuating America, are now on tiptoe. Nothing, therefore, in my judgment, can save us but a total reformation in our own conduct or some decisive turn to affairs in Europe. The former, alas! to our shame be it spoken, is less likely to happen than the latter, as it is not consistent with the views of the speculators, various tribes of money-makers, and stock-jobbers of all denominations to continue the war for their own private emolument, without considering that their avarice and thirst for gain must plunge everything, including themselves, in one common ruin.

Were I to indulge my personal feelings, and give a loose to that freedom of expression which my unreserved friendship for you would prompt me to, I should say a great deal on this subject. But letters are liable to so many accidents, and the sentiments of men in office sought after by the enemy with so much avidity, and, besides conveying useful knowledge (if they get into their hands) for the superstructure of their plans, are so often perverted to the worst of purposes, that I shall be somewhat reserved, notwithstanding this letter goes by a private hand to Mount Vernon. I cannot refrain lamenting, however, in the most poignant terms, the fatal policy too prevalent in most of the states of employing their ablest men at home in posts of honor or profit till the great national interest is fixed upon a solid basis. To me it appears no unjust simile to compare the affairs of this great continent to the mechanism of a clock, each state representing some one or other of the smaller parts of it which they are endeavoring to put in fine order, without considering how useless and unavailing their labor is unless the great wheel or spring which is to set the whole in motion is also well attended to and kept in good order. I allude to no particular state, nor do I mean to cast reflections upon any one of them, nor ought I, it may be said, to do so upon their representatives; but as it is a fact, too notorious to be concealed, that congress is rent by party, that much business of a trifling nature and personal concernment withdraws their attention from matters of great national moment at this critical period, when it is also known that idleness and dissipation take the place of close attention and application, no man who wishes well to the liberties of his country and desires to see its rights established can avoid crying out, Where are our men of abilities? Why do they not come forth to save their country? Let this voice, my dear sir, call upon you, Jefferson, and others. Do not, from a mistaken opinion that we are about to sit down under our own vine and our own fig-tree, let our hitherto noble struggle end in ignominy. Believe me when I tell you there is danger of it. I have pretty good reasons for thinking that administration a little while ago had resolved to give the matter up, and negotiate a peace with us upon almost any terms; but I shall be much mistaken if they do not now, from the present state of our currency, dissensions, and other circumstances, push matters to the utmost extremity. Nothing, I am sure, will prevent it but the interposition of Spain and their disappointed hope from Russia.

I thank you most cordially for your kind offer of rendering me services. I shall, without reserve, as heretofore, call upon you whenever instances occur that may require it; being with the sincerest regard, dear sir, your most obedient and affectionate servant,

Washington to James Duane, New Windsor, 20 Dec., 1780. Ex.

There are two things, as I have often declared, which, in my opinion, are indispensably necessary to the well-being and good government of our public affairs. These are, greater powers to congress, and more responsibility and permanency in the executive bodies. If individual states conceive themselves at liberty to reject or alter any act of congress, which in a full representation of them has been solemnly debated and decided on, it will be madness in us to think of prosecuting the war. And, if congress suppose that boards composed of their body and always fluctuating are competent to the great business of war (which requires not only close application, but a constant and uniform train of thinking and acting), they will most assuredly deceive themselves. Many, many instances might be deduced in proof of this, but to a mind as observant as yours there is no need to enumerate them.

James Duane to Washington, Philadelphia, 29 Jan., 1781. Ex.

There are some political regulations of great importance, which I have exceedingly at heart, and which are drawn near to a conclusion. The principal measures to which I allude are the establishment of executives or ministers in the departments of finances, war, the marine, and foreign affairs; the accomplishment of the confederation; the procuring to congress an augmentation of power and permanent revenues for carrying on the war.

The day is at length arrived when dangers and distresses have opened the eyes of the people, and they perceive the want of a common head to draw forth in some just proportion the resources of the several branches of the federal union. They perceive that the deliberative power exercised by states individually over the acts of congress must terminate in the common ruin; and the legislatures, however reluctantly, must resign a portion of their authority in the national representative or cease to be legislatures.

You will be pleased to hear that our worthy friend, Mr. Jones, of Virginia, has resumed his seat in congress. That state has relinquished, for the common benefit, all her claim to the westward of the Ohio; and Maryland has acceded to the confederation; at least, I have read the act or resolution of their house of delegates to that purpose, only seven members being in the negative; and Mr. Jones was assured, from good authority, that the senate had concurred. These are events of infinite importance, and will put a new face on our affairs at home, but much more so abroad.

Let us devote this day to joy and congratulation, since by the accomplishment of our federal union we are become a nation. In a political view it is of more real importance than a victory over all our enemies. We shall not fail of taking advantage of the favorable temper of the states, and recommending for ratification such additional articles as will give vigor and authority to government.

Mr. Jones and Mr. Madison entreat you to accept their respectful compliments.

Washington to James Duane, New Windsor, 19 Feb., 1781. Ex.

DEAR SIR: The receipt of your letter of the 29th ultimo, and of a former by the Marquis De la Fayette, I have the honor to acknowledge, and to return you my thanks for them.

The contents of that of the 29th are very important. It presents a fair field, capable of yielding an abundant harvest, if it is well improved. Skilful laborers are all that are wanting, and much depends upon a judicious choice of them. Men of abilities at the head of the respective departments will soon introduce system, order, and economy. Our affairs, consequently, will put on a different aspect; but not unless congress is vested with, or will assume, greater powers than they exert at present, and will dispense them freely, upon general principles, to the ministers of state.

But for the assurance you give me of being soon at head-quarters, I would go more into detail on the several important points of your letter. I will, under the expectation of it, defer the pleasure of a further converse on these matters till I see you.

I cannot close my letter, however, without expressing the joy I feel at the completion of the federal union, and that Virginia has relinquished her claim to the lands west of Ohio. The first, I trust, will enable congress to speak with decision. The other will heal differences and contribute to our funds, as there is no finer country in the known world than is encircled by the Ohio, Mississippi, and great lakes. A few days ago I was on the eve of a journey to Rhode Island; some important matters delayed it, and now the time of my setting off is precarious.

Mrs. Washington and the rest of the family salute you cordially,

Washington to Joseph Jones, New Windsor, 24 March, 1781. Ex.

I was much pleased to hear that Virginia had given up her claim to the land west of Ohio, that the confederation was completed, and that the states seemed disposed to grant more competent powers to congress. Without a controlling power in that body for all the purposes of war, it will be impossible to carry on the war. The reasons are many and conclusive; but the want of room will not allow me to enumerate them at this time. The most important are obvious: the noncompliance with the recommendations of congress in some states, the unseasonable compliance in time and manner by others, the heavy expense accumulated thereby to no purpose, the injury to some and the jealousy of all the states proceeding from these causes, with the consequent dissatisfaction in people of every class from the prolongation of the war, are alone sufficient to prove the necessity of a controlling power. Without it, and speedily, we shall be thirteen distinct states; each pursuing its local interests till they are annihilated in a general crash of them. The fable of the bunch of rods or sticks may well be applied to us I am, sincerely and affectionately, yours.

Tench Tilghman to Robert Morris, Head-quarters, New Windsor, 24. June, 1781.

DEAR SIR: I have received your favor of the 11th instant, accompanied by a delegation from Messrs. Clymer and Nixon, to take in subscriptions to the bank. I am afraid I shall be a very unprofitable agent, for I believe it may, with truth, be said that there is not an officer in the army, from the commander-in-chief downward, who is at this time able to pay in a single subscription. You know they have received no real money from the public for a long time past, and, consequently, have been forced to spend all they could possibly raise for their own support. I am, however, happy to inform you that there is no scheme of economy which you can propose that the army will not cheerfully comply with, and they will do what is in fact subscribing:

they will be content with very little of their pay until the state of our finances can enable you to furnish it regularly. The general desires me to inform you candidly that, desirous as he is to patronize and support the scheme, he has it not in his power to set his name to the subscription just now. He assures me that so far has the income of his estate for several years back fallen short of his family expenses and taxes, that he has lately been obliged to sell part of his real estate to pay his taxes.

Paper money of all kinds has so far become useless that I must beg the favor of you to send me twenty or thirty dollars in specie, by Doctor Craik, who accompanies Mrs. Washington as far as Philadelphia.

We are all very anxious to see you at the army. You will find us in the field, somewhere between Peekskill and Kingsbridge. I am, with very sincere respect and affection.

Report of Mr. Randolph, Mr. Ellsworth, Mr. Varnum, committee to Prepare an exposition of the confederation, a plan for its complete execution, and supplemental articles, delivered 22 Aug., 1781.

The committee appointed to prepare an exposition of the confederation, a plan for its complete execution and supplemental articles, report: That they ought to be discharged from the exposition of the confederation because such a comment would be voluminous if co-extensive with the subject. The omission to enumerate any congressional powers would become an argument against their existence, and it will be early enough to insist upon them when they shall be exercised and disputed.

They farther report that the confederation requires execution in the following manner :

1. By adjusting the mode and proportions of the militia aid to be furnished to a sister state laboring under invasion.

2. By describing the privileges and immunities to which the citizens of one state are entitled in another.

3. By setting forth the conditions upon which a criminal is to be delivered up by one state upon the demand of the executive of another.

4. By declaring the method of exemplifying records and the operation of the acts and judicial proceedings of the courts of one state, contravening those of the states in which they are asserted.

5. By a form to be observed in the notification of the appointment or suspension of delegates.

6. By an oath to be taken by every delegate against secret trusts of salaries.

7. By specifying the privileges of delegates from arrests, imprisonent, questioning for free speech and debates in congress, saving as well their amenability to their constituents as protesting against the authority of individual legislatures to absolve them from obligations to secrecy.

8. By instituting an oath to be taken by the officers of the United States or any of them against presents, emoluments, office or title of any kind from a king, prince, or foreign state.

9. By one universal plan of equipping, training, and governing the militia.

10. By a scheme for estimating the value of all land within each state granted to or surveyed for any person or persons, together with the buildings and improvements thereon: and the appointment of certain periods at which payment shall be made.

11. By establishing rules for captures on land and the distribution of the sales.

12. By ascertaining the jurisdiction of congress in territorial questions.

13. By erecting a mint.

14. By fixing a standard of weights and measures throughout the United States.

15. By appointing a committee for Indian affairs.

16. By regulating the post-office.

17. By establishing a census of white inhabitants in each state.

18. By publishing the Journal of Congress monthly.

19. By registering seamen.

20. By liquidation of old accounts against the United States; and

21. By providing means of animadverting on delinquent states.

Resolved, That of the preceding articles, the 9th be referred to the Board of War, the 13th, 14th, and 16th. to the Superintendent of Finance, and the others to a committee in order that the subject matter thereof may be extended in detail for the consideration of congress.

And your committee further report, That as America became a confederate republic to crush the present and future foes of her independence;

As of this republic a general council is a necessary organ;

And without the extension of its power in the cases hereinafter enumerated war may receive a fatal inclination and peace be exposed to daily convulsions:

It be resolved to recommend to the several states to authorize your the United States in Congress assembled—

1. To lay embargoes in time of war without any limitation.

2. To prescribe rules for impressing property into the service of the United States during the present war.

3. To appoint the collectors of and direct the mode of accounting for taxes imposed according to the requisitions of congress.

4. To recognise the independence of and admit into the federal union any part of one or more of the United States with the consent of the dismembered state.

5. To stipulate in treaties with foreign nations for the establishment of consular power, without reference to the states individually.

6. To distrain the property of a state delinquent in its assigned proportion of men and money.

7. To vary the rules of suffrage in congress, taking care that in questions for waging war, granting letters of marque and reprisal in time of peace, concluding or giving instructions for any alliance, coining money, regulating the value of coin, determining the total number of land and sea forces, and allotting to each state its quota of men or money, emit-ting bills of credit, borrowing money, fixing the number and force of vessels of war, and appointing a commander-in-chief of the army and navy—at least two thirds of the United States shall agree therein.

Resolved, that a committee be appointed to prepare a representation to the several states of the necessity of these supplemental powers, and of pursuing, in the modification thereof, one uniform plan.

Thomas Jefferson to Benjamin Franklin, Virginia, 5 Oct., 1781. Ex.

DEAR SIR: The bearer hereof. Colonel James Monroe, who served some time as an officer in the American army, and as such distinguished himself in the affair of Princeton as well as on other occasions, having resumed his studies, comes to Europe to complete them. Being a citizen of this state, of abilities, merit, and fortune, and my particular friend, I take the liberty of making him known to you, that should any circumstances render your patronage and protection as necessary as they would be always agreeable to him, you may be assured they are bestowed on one fully worthy of them.[1]

---

[1] Monroe did not visit Europe at that time.

He will be able to give you a particular detail of American affairs, and especially of the prospect we have, through the aid of our father of France, of making captives of Lord Cornwallis and his army, of the recovery of Georgia and South Carolina, and the possibility that Charlestown itself will be opened to us.

Secretary George Germain to General Haldimand, Governor of Quebec, Whitehall, 2 Jan., 1782. Ex.

I was well pleased to find that your negotiation with the Vermont leaders was in so fair a train as to afford good ground to expect that country would speedily be restored to the king's obedience. I therefore must repeat to you my recommendations to make the recovery of Vermont to the king's obedience the primary object of your attention, and I can assure you that whatever expense you may incur in effecting it will not be repined at.

Count de Montmorin to Vergennes, Madrid, 11 Jan., 1782. Ex. Translation.

I have communicated to Count Florida Blanca what you did me the honor to write me, sir, respecting the inhabitants of Jamaica, who would appear to wish to follow the example of the United States of America. He asked of me a note on the subject, that he might send it to Mr. de Galvez. I have given it to him. He agreed with me that it would in fact be desirable that the inhabitants of that island, seduced by the hope of being able to secure themselves an independent government, should leave exclusively to the British troops the care of defending their island. He sent in consequence an instruction to Don Bernardo de Galvez; but I have no need to tell you, sir, how much the forming of a republic in these regions would displease Spain, and in fact I believe that that would neither suit her interests nor ours. In fine, I have put aside everything which could give the idea that that was our intention, and in giving to Mr. Florida Blanca the copy of this part of your despatch, I took care to make him observe that it was not proposed to satisfy the wishes of the inhabitants of Jamaica, but only not to destroy the hope that they might have conceived. For the rest I think, sir, if the Spaniards unite with us for the conquest of Jamaica, we must expect more resistance on the part of the inhabitants than if we were alone. You know, sir, how much Spanish rule is dreaded throughout all America, and in truth it is so with reason.

There reigns in almost all the possessions of that power in America a discontent of which I think the consequences are to be feared. I had hoped to be able to give you some details on this matter, but the papers which contained them could not be confided to me, and I could only read them rapidly. From these letters, and from original relations which I have seen, there is no room to doubt that there exists a very serious fermentation in the province of Buenos Ayres and in Peru. The Indians are furious, and they are powerful. In a word, a frightful spirit of revolt appears to reign in all that part.

If these troubles in the Spanish colonies obtain for us from Spain some facilities in the progress of the campaign, they increase the aversion of her ministry to any connection with the United States of America. The deputies of congress, who are obliged to render an account to their constituents of the difficulties of every kind which they have experienced in attempting to begin any sort of negotiation, have lately received in reply instructions which prove the discontent with congress. Mr. Jay has given me to understand that the resolutions which had been adopted relative to the navigation of the Mississippi would be revoked, and that he was constantly expecting orders to quit Spain. I should be very much vexed on account of the bad effect which would result from it every way, and especially because a division between Spain and the United States of America would keep a door always open for the intrigues of England at this court.

But that which I believe indispensable is to lose no occasion of inculcating on Spain that we cannot consent to peace without the establishment of the independence of the United States. There will lie the great difficulty when the time shall come for serious negotiations, and I have no doubt that Spain will see with chagrin their independence established.

Montmorin to Vergennes, 25 Jan., 1782.   Ex. Tr.

The troubles of Spanish America are by no means a trifle; and I much fear, if the war lasts some time longer, that the evil will make great progress. It is certain that, if the English have knowledge of what is passing, as I have no doubt they have, and that they are in a condition to send any or the least succor to the rebels, a conflagration will be kindled of which it will be difficult to foresee the consequences.

If the English, understanding their interest better, would accord without restriction the independence of their colonies, and would throw themselves with all their strength upon the Spanish colonies, I have no doubt but they would very soon be able to make there a revolution which would amply compensate them for all that their commerce would suffer by the conflict in North America.

Montmorin to Vergennes, Madrid, 30 March, 1782. Ex. Tr.

We afterward spoke of the Americans, and Mr. Florida Blanca said to me, with a sort of heat, and more than once, that the Americans would always be English at heart; that we should be convinced of it as soon as their lot should be decided. The deputies of the Americans were on the point of bankruptcy, on account of bills for forty or fifty thousand dollars, which had fallen due and which they had accepted; but the protest has not the less been made, and with all possible publicity. I have thought, sir, I ought to report this incident to you, inviting you to observe the epoch, so that you might perfectly understand the absolute indifference, or even the repugnance, of Spain to the establishment of American independence. If she is so decided now, how will it be if Spain should get possession of Gibraltar? Then the war would leave no other object than this very independence, which she looks upon with so much indifference, and, perhaps, with terror. Mr. Florida Blanca has never been willing to declare himself openly for the United States, and at this very moment he seems to draw back from them more than ever.

Montmorin to Vergennes, Aranjuez, 5 May, 1782. Ex.

Mr. de Florida Blanca said to me: "If they will not cede to us Gibraltar, they have only to give us Jamaica." I answered him that I thought this sacrifice still more hard than that of Gibraltar. At last he ended our consultation by saying to me that if this war does not restore Gibraltar to Spain he would go turn monk; "and that," he added, "seems to me the most contemptible part a man of sense can take." I have thought it, Mons. le Compte, my duty to report to you these details, which will prove to you how much they are possessed with the purpose to take Gibraltar from the hands of England. If they do not succeed in gaining possession of this rock, it will become as deadly to our negotiation for peace as it has been to our combinations for a plan of war.

I see generally a little disquiet ever since England has appeared pretty much determined to acknowledge the independence of the

United States, and, above all, since she addresses us from choice to open a negotiation.

I think that you will soon see Mr. Jay at Paris; at least, Mr. Franklin urges it upon him. For the rest, if he has to treat with Mr. de Aranda, I don't know how they will come to an understanding, for assuredly neither the one nor the other of them is conciliatory.

Montmorin to Vergennes, Madrid, 8 June, 1782. Ex. Tr.

There is no doubt whatever that the restitution of Gibraltar will be insisted upon, and that Spain, unless she shall be crushed, will never consent to peace without having obtained it. On the other side, it is not probable that England will be resigned to this sacrifice unless it is torn from her by main strength. I therefore think that the whole negotiation will go forward very slowly, until the enterprise against that place is terminated. The projects against Gibraltar, and the hope to see them succeed, absorb at this moment all ideas.

George the King to the Earl of Shelburne, Windsor, 10 Nov., 1782, 6:55 p. m. Ex.

I cannot conclude without mentioning how sensibly I feel the dismemberment of America from this empire, and that I should be miserable indeed if I did not feel that no blame on that account can be laid at my door, and did I not also know that knavery seems to be so much the striking feature of its inhabitants that it may not in the end be an evil that they will become aliens to this kingdom.   G. R.

George the King to the Earl of Shelburne, Windsor, 8 Dec., 1782, 2:10 a. m.

By Lord Shelburne's account, it very clearly appears that Mr. Pitt, on Friday, stated the Article of Independence as irrevocable, though the treaty should prove abortive; this undoubtedly was a mistake, for the independence is alone granted for peace. I have always thought it best and wisest if a mistake is made openly to avow it; and therefore Mr. Pitt ought, if his words have been understood to bear so strong a meaning, to say it is no wonder that so young a man should have made a slip. This would do him honor. I think at all events it highly material that Lord Shelburne should not, by any language in the House of Lords, appear to change his conduct, let the blame fall where it may. I do not wish he should appear but in that dignified light which his station in my service requires, and which can only be maintained by his conduct in the whole negotiation of peace having been neat, which would not be the case if Mr. Fox could prove that independence was granted otherwise than as the price of peace; besides, Mr. Vaughan's letter shows further demands are to come from Franklin, which must the more make us stiff on this article. G. R.

Vergennes to Luzerne, 21 Dee, 1782. Ex. Tr.

You are informed of the demands of congress on the king for pecuniary succors; they amount to not less than to a loan of twenty millions of our livres. This sum too much exceeds all proportions to admit the consideration for it; but his majesty, wishing to make to the United States a new proof of his friendship and of the interest he takes in their welfare, accords to them for the year 1783 a loan of six millions of our livres, of which we are going to advance immediately to Mr. Franklin six hundred thousand livres, that he may ship them by the Washington to Mr. Morris. I shall not dissimulate to you, sir, that this effort is oppressive, after five years of a war of which the expenses have been and are still enormous, and of which we are not assured of soon seeing the end. You will take care to make congress sensible of this new mark of interest; but you will at the same time not leave any hope that the king can be disposed to give to it a larger extent, be it by new advances, be it in lending his guarantee. The United States do not seem enough inclined to create for themselves the means of meeting their debts, to dispose any one to think of acquiring their obligations. This will certainly be the last.

Sir Guy Carleton to Secretary Townshend, New York, 18 Jan., 1783. Ex.

SIR: I transmit copies of letters, though of an old date, written to the president of congress by Mr. Morris, financier, from which his opinion at that time of the state of American finance, and some other matters, may be known. He proceeds upon the ground that certain taxes may be permanently raised, and that the confederation may be constantly upheld. The first supposition has already been found erroneous; the latter seems wholly improbable.

Luzerne to Vergennes, 6 Feb., 1783. Ex. Tr.

The appearances of an approaching peace have given occasion to examine questions of a great importance for the United States; and so many persons of weight and experience have spoken to me about them that I cannot doubt that they are actually at this moment one of the principal objects of the attention of men charged in this continent with the management of public affairs. Can the federal assembly subsist when it shall cease to rest on a common peril and a common interest? And what would be the consequences of a dissolution of congress? The United States, they have said to me, present a vast country divided into thirteen republics, and susceptible of being divided into still more states, in proportion as population and culture make progress. These states, if their union is close and permanent, will be of consideration and respect; if division is introduced among them, they will be contemptible abroad and miserable at home. Congress up to this day has been the common centre of union; it has maintained itself by extraordinary means, by the general danger, by the assistance in men and money received from France, by the prestige of a money which cost nothing for its creation but an act of sovereign will. If all these means were to fail at once, nothing would be more easy than to break the bonds of union.

There will remain no other resource to congress but that of the influence which it can exercise over the people and the respect that its conduct may be able to inspire them. But these are weak means to govern so vast a confederation, and to make people, so jealous of their liberty, obey. The confederation is evidently imperfect and faulty. Congress will need a sufficient authority to direct affairs relative to commerce, peace, and war, independently of every other power, and to regulate the differences which may arise between the states. As to the objects of a general utility, but which do not essentially belong to congress, it is for the influence of this body to obtain them from the different states, without force and without coercion. This influence will be established, if congress can fund the public debt on a permanent revenue; then a numerous class of citizens will be interested in the preservation of the federal union; but facts demonstrate that the constitution of congress is insufficient for the establishment of a public revenue. Let it be attempted in the present condition of affairs to make the people pay the burden of the present war, and the interest on debts already contracted, and they will refuse to do it. If it is wished to force them to do it, instead of a simple refusal, their resistance is to be expected. The insufficiency of the powers of congress being demonstrated, a proposition, perhaps, will be made to extend them; but this would only show an imperfect knowledge of the dispositions of the people. Jealousies and disquietude will be excited, a long and complicated by a discussion will be begun, and the proposition will finally be rejected by a majority of the states, if not by all the states without exception. Are they then to limit themselves to simple requisitions? The legislatures then will consent as to the form, but they will not obtain any great amount; in fact, the people, doubting of the extent of their resources, will make little effort, even with the best disposition; and this disposition, if it exists, is always affected by the doubt in which each state is of the intentions and efforts that the other states will make. The legislatures do not grant the subsidies but for one year; at the expiration of the term those who make the least delay regret their efforts, seeing the little that their neighbors have done; and they recover themselves the next year by reducing their effective contingent. If it should prove possible to establish a permanent revenue, it would probably be used to fund the public debt and fulfil the engagements of the United States to the army. These are the objects best suited to draw contributions from the people, because these demands are founded in justice, and because they will be supported by the numerous creditors of the United States. It is not probable that the efforts of the people in regard to taxes and impositions will be very considerable after the peace. In this state of things the question is asked. What ought to be the conduct of France? England will, without doubt, endeavor to deprive France of its new ally or make it useless. To the well-known causes of a reconciliation between that power and its ancient colonies there may be opposed perhaps jealousy, resulting from neighborhood, and even the interest of the United States; but these last considerations will have weight only in congress. It is in that body that the attachment to France will be preserved, while the inclination of habits, language, and customs will incline the people to England. The present union, feeble as it is, results from the most urgent necessity; after the peace the most trifling causes may dissolve it. It is agreed that the seat of attachment to the alliance is in congress; it is then essential for France and for the United States to preserve to this body its influence and its authority.

Thomas Jefferson to James Madison, Baltimore, H Feb., 1783. Ex.

I shall write to E. Randolph on the subject of his going into the legislature, and use my interest to promote it. I hope you will be there too, when you can no longer be in any more important place.

Jefferson to Madison, Baltimore, 14 Feb., 1783. Ex.

The newspapers must be wrong when they say that Mr. Adams has taken up his abode with Dr. Franklin, I am really at a loss to judge how he will act in the negotiation. He has Franklin, he has Jay, he has the French, he has the English: to whom will he adhere? His vanity is a lineament in his character which had entirely escaped me; his want of taste I had observed. Notwithstanding all this, he has a sound head on substantial points, and I think he has integrity. I am glad, therefore, that he is of the commission, and expect he will be use-ful in it. His dislike of all parties and all men, by balancing his pre-judices, may give the same fair play to his reason as would a general benevolence of temper. At any rate, honesty may be extracted from poisonous weeds.

Jefferson to Madison, 15 Feb., 1783. Ex.

I wish no supposed inclination of mine to stand in the way of a free change of measure, if congress should think the public interest required it. The argument of economy is much strengthened by the impossibility (now certain) of going but in an express vessel. The principal matters confided to me were : 1. The new instruction; which perhaps may have been sent by Count Rochambeau, or may yet be sent. 2. The details of the financier's department, which Mr. Morris, not choosing to trust to paper, had communicated verbally. These in the event of peace or truce may safely go in paper. 3. The topics which support our right to the fisheries, to the western country, and the navigation of the Mississippi. The first of these is probably settled. The two latter should only come into discussion in the Spanish negotiation, and therefore would only have been the subject of private conversation with Mr. Jay, whose good sense and knowledge of the subject will hardly need any suggestions.

Letters from Philadelphia, 18 Feb., 1783, in Sir Guy Carleton's despatch of 15 March, 1783. Ex.

A number of officers are just come to town from the army, who appear to be as much alarmed with the idea of peace as any other class of people; they have adopted an opinion that, if a peace is now obtained, congress will no longer be at a loss to pay them their arrears; but that they will immediately disband the army in order to expunge the debt. Both officers and soldiers, I am told, swear most solemnly that they will not lay down their arms until they are paid. Congress is now become so very contemptible a body that, whether it is peace or war, I think the army is ripe for annihilating them. *20 Feb.*—The limited powers of congress are now become the subject of general conversation. It is agreed on by men of the most extensive knowledge that congress have not the power of concluding a peace; that the union must either be dissolved or the powers of congress enlarged.

Vergennes to Luzerne, 27 Feb., 1783. Ex. Tr.

Peace establishes a new order of things in America. The Americans, acknowledged henceforth by all the powers of Europe, will without doubt employ themselves in fixing the principles to serve as the basis of political and commercial relations which they will seek to establish everywhere, and principally with their former mother country. You will feel yourself, sir, that it is important for the king to be informed on this subject with the greatest promptitude, because his future conduct ought to be traced on the system that the United States will develop; although we do not count in any degree on the gratitude of the Americans, we nevertheless look upon our alliance with them as unalterable.

As to commerce, we never claimed exclusive advantages; but we flatter ourselves that no other nation will obtain them to our prejudice. Such, sir, in a few words, are our principles and our expectation with regard to the United States. We have informed you, sir, that the king has consented to advance them for this year a sum of six millions. You may inform Mr. Morris that it will be paid with exactness; but you will take from this superintendent every hope of obtaining the slightest augmentation for this year, or any assistance for the next. The state of our finances will not permit it. Besides, a whole year's enjoyment of peace after an inactive campaign will put Mr. Morris in a condition to meet the expenses with which he is charged.

Information from Philadelphia, in Sir Guy Carleton's No. 60, of 15 March, 1783. Ex.

I have explored the designs and feelings of the army, of congress, and the country in general, and I must say that the enclosed extract of a letter from a gentleman in Philadelphia speaks the truth; you may lay the more weight to it as it is the undisguised language of a firm Whig, who has been long conversant with all these matters.

Extract of a letter from a person in Philadelphia to his friend in the New England Provinces, in Sir Guy Carleton's No. 60, of 15 March, 1783.

Being at present at the court of America, you have a right to expect some account of the prevailing political subjects and sentiments: though I am happily removed from the control of congress, yet a long habit of attending to their affairs makes me still a kind of spy upon their movements, and observer of passing things; and I wish it was in my power to entertain you better in this way.

In some lucubration's which I sent my friend from Hudson's river, I offered in opinion the frail nature of our general government, and the certainty of an approaching convulsion of that general government in which the particular governments must be involved. I can venture to offer it as my opinion that a dissolution of the Federal government (the beginning of those evils which I then apprehended) is now at hand; the symptoms of it will be seen by every one in the course of the winter; perhaps the dissolution itself may be effected in that time. What the change or changes will be (for I cannot flatter myself with the prospect of an easy transition from a weak unstrung government to a strong fixed one) no wisdom short of omnipotence can foresee. The reasons why a revolution has not been wrought before appear to me to be these: the avarice and total inattention to public matters which have so strongly marked the conduct of the people of this country for several years past among those in office; the designs of some who expect to profit by public commotions; the timidity of others who have supposed it would look like treason to propose an alteration in government; and, lastly, the ignorance of a very great part who wanted a system marked out for them to conduct themselves by: in all cases of this kind it is necessary some supervening circumstance should be ready to speak before words. It is from this I imagine it is so common for people to say that such or such an event was owing to accident alone. This necessary harbinger to a revolution is arrived. The army, who have been so long groaning under accumulated evils and grievances, have at last come to make a serious prospective and retrospective view of their case. They have sent a committee to congress, which may be called commissioners, to settle a peace between congress and the army. The amount of their memorial which I have

[1] The letter must be of February; its author only lately in office in Philadelphia and now on a visit there. These conditions are fulfilled by Gouverneur Morris.

seen is this: they demand, in the first place, an immediate supply of money; a settlement of all their accounts of arrearages; a compliance with all the resolutions of congress respecting the army, and a mode pointed out by which they may see a certainty of having all their accounts and promises finally adjusted and settled. They look to congress, and to congress only, as their lawful sovereign for a fulfilment of those things, knowing at the same time that it is as impossible for them to do it as to make bread of stones; but it would not become the army to suppose anything impossible to be done which their lawful sovereigns have promised to do; so that, in the way of a kind of ironical modesty, they point out to congress their weakness and danger, and are determined to go no farther blindfolded. With such a case as this to back him, even a member of congress himself, and in congress, may venture to propose a change of government to their federal head; a change that must create a strict accountability from each to that head; a change that must disunite the legislative from the executive authority in that federal head (which if they had any power at all would be mischievous, but in their state of imbecility is harmless); and of this monstrous compound, they must draw out two distinct and well-organized bodies: legislative and executive; whose powers and capacities shall be equal to the task of managing the unruly affairs of America. To effect this, I am sure you will judge with me, that at the head of the last branch there must be a great and fearful executive officer to do anything; the power of that officer must be greater than that which is hereditary in the house of Orange, and as nearly like the head of that power we are contending with as can well be imagined, the name only excepted. In short, it will require the most vigorous government to keep the country in the form of an empire, and keep her from splitting into innumerable divisions, and becoming the wretched prey of ravenous and designing harpies, a change so essential as will meet great opposition from the east of Connecticut river more especially, and the attempt to produce it may bring upon us all those evils which the design of it may be intended to prevent. A state of suspense is undesirable; I wish to see the issue, therefore; I acknowledge I wish to see it begin. The country has a better chance if this change happens before the war is closed; the enemy and their own army to fear will be necessary to check a wanton and riotous spirit. You will say wretched must be that government which is formed and established under the influence of an army; to this I must oppose one of my maxims, that the worst government is better than the want of government; you will say, doubly wretched is that country which has no government at all.

Letter from Philadelphia, 7 March, 1783, in Sir Guy Carleton's No. 60, of 15 March, 1783. Ex.

If accounts of a peace do not soon arrive, we shall be in a state ten times worse than anything we have yet experienced. A most violent political storm is gathering; it is yet too new to form any opinion with respect to its progress; but whether dependence or independence, whether peace or war, sure I am that it must and will produce an overthrow of our republican constitution. The resignation of Mr. Morris has a surprising effect upon the minds of the people; and when you compare this with our poverty, the internal broils which subsist at present, and the uneasiness of the army, I think you will not be surprised that I have adopted this opinion. I had a long conversation yesterday with an important member of congress upon this subject, who very candidly declared to me that it was not in the power of congress to satisfy the public creditors; that their powers were unequal to the business; that the people must delegate more power to them, or create some other power quite new.

Alleyne Fitz Herbert to Secretary Grantham, Paris, 13 March, 1783.

I took the earliest opportunity of communicating to the American commissioners the printed bill contained in your lordship's letter No. 32. They all of them expressed to me, in very warm terms, the satisfaction they felt from its contents, and from the liberal spirit that prevails in every part of it; saying further that it could not fail of proving a most powerful means of restoring not only the commercial intercourse, but the harmony and good-will which formerly subsisted between the two countries. They have likewise authorized me to acquaint your lordship that they conceive themselves to be empowered and are ready to secure reciprocally to the commerce of Great Britain the same advantages which are granted by this bill to the commerce of America, and they will take this step forthwith, in the shape either of a declaration from themselves to the proposed effect, or of a separate and additional article in the definitive treaty. They, however, rather prefer the latter of these forms, principally from the idea that by that means a commercial intercourse with Ireland (which kingdom is not comprehended in the aforesaid bill) may possibly be secured to them likewise; but, as this is a most delicate point, I could not venture to speak to it without special instructions.

As this matter seems to press for a speedy conclusion, it may not be amiss to repeat to your lordship that, in case Mr. Oswald should not be able to return forthwith, the American commissioners would make no difficulty of signing such an article as that I have mentioned above jointly with myself, upon the strength of the general expressions used in the several full powers I am intrusted with.

Luzerne to Vergennes, 29 March, 1783. Ex. Tr.

General Washington conducts himself with his usual wisdom. It conciliates to him more and more the respect and affection of the people. After a war of eight years, during which he has scarcely ever left his army, and has never taken any repose, he has received the news of the peace with the greatest joy. It made him shed tears, and he said it was the happiest hour of his life. It will be in vain for him to wish to conceal himself and to live as a private man. He will always be the first citizen of the United States; and, although military men are not agreed as to his military talents, all the world is agreed touching his republican virtues, and agreed that there is no character more eminent among those who have taken part in this grand revolution.

Benjamin Harrison, Governor of Virginia, to George Washington, 31 March, 1783. Ex.

You ask me, in your favor of the 6th instant, what induced our assembly to repeal the duty law, which is as difficult a question to answer as you could well have put to me, no one reason of force having ever occurred, though I have a thousand on the other side of the question. Indeed, the bill was a work of my own when I was in the house of delegates. I have been told it was done by R. H, and A. Lee, and that their arguments were such as you have seen from Rhode Island. The act was certainly brought in by them in the latter part of the session, when the house was very thin, and hurried through without due consideration. They were so very quick that the mischief was done before I knew they had the subject under consideration, or they would probably have missed their aim; for, from conversation I had with many of the member's on the subject afterward, I am fully of opinion they would have re-enacted the law if they had time; but whether they will do it, now a peace is concluded, admits of a doubt.

I observe, by a clause in the articles, we are to have our negroes again. I have thirty missing, many of which I understand are dead; but there are still some that are very valuable. If it is not too much to ask, I shall ever be under the greatest obligation if you will fall on some method to secure them. There will no doubt be vessels coming immediately from New York to this country that will probably take them in. Their passage I will pay, with thanks. You have a list of a few of them that I know are in the town, and may easily be come at.

"A conversation at Paris relative to America, in April, 1783." Ex.

I have seen Mr. Jay, who expressed his astonishment at what passed in parliament on the American trade bill. He says they are ready to do anything England wishes in that matter, and go beyond her; that America does not desire to interfere with your chartered companies at all; that opening the trade between the two countries was the first article of the rough draft of the preliminaries; that it was upon the most liberal footing on the part of America, opening the lakes and rivers to the English. "Good God!" he says," we have gone beyond you in everything, and you will not follow us."

Washington to Theodorick Bland, Head-quarters, 4 April, 1783.

SIR: The subject of your private letter is so important, and involves so many considerations, that I could not hazard my own opinion only for a reply. I have, therefore, communicated its contents to some of the most intelligent, well informed, and confidential officers whose judgment I have consulted, and endeavored to collect from them what is the general sense and expectation of the army at large respecting the points you mention. And as this is meant to be equally private and confidential as yours, I shall communicate my sentiments to you without reserve and with the most entire freedom.

The idea of the officers in keeping the army together until settlement of their accounts is effected, and funds established for their security, is, perhaps, not so extensive as the words of their resolution seem to intimate. "When that idea was first expressed, our prospects of peace were distant, and it was supposed that settlement and funds might both be effected before a dissolution of the army would probably take place; they wished, therefore, to have both at once. But since the expectation of peace is brought so near, however desirable it would be to the officers to have their balances secured to them upon sufficient funds, as well as their settlement ascertained, yet it is not in idea that the army should be held together for the sole purpose of enforcing either; nor do they suppose that, by such means, they could operate on the fears of the civil power, or of the people at large. The impracticability as well as ill policy, of such a mode of conduct is easily discoverable by every sensible intelligent officer. The thought is reprobated as ridiculous and inadmissible.

Though these are their ideas on the particular point you have mentioned, yet they have their expectations; and they are of a very serious nature, and will require all the attention and consideration of congress to gratify them. These I will endeavor to explain with freedom and candor.

In the first place, I fix it as an indispensable measure that, previous to the disbanding the army, all their accounts should be completely liquidated and settled; and that every person shall be ascertained of the balance due to him. And it is equally essential, in my opinion, that this settlement should be effected with the army in its collected body, without any dispersion of the different lines to their respective states. For this way, the accounts will be drawn into one view, properly digested upon one general system, and compared with a variety of circumstances which will require references upon a much easier plan than to be diffused over all the states. The settlements will be effected with greater ease, in less time, and with much more economy in this than in a scattered situation; at the same time, jealousies will be removed, the minds of the army will be impressed with greater ease and quiet, and they better prepared with good opinions and proper dispositions to fall back into the great mass of citizens.

But, after settlement is formed, there remains another circumstance of more importance still, and without which it will be of little consequence to have the sums due them ascertained; that is, the payment of some part of the balance. The distresses of officers and soldiers are now driven to the extreme, and, without this provision, will not be lessened by the prospect of dissolution. It is, therefore, universally expected that three months' pay at least must be given them before they are disbanded. This sum it is confidently imagined may be procured, and it is absolutely indispensable. They are the rather confirmed in the belief of the practicability of obtaining it, as the pay of the army has formed great part of the sum in the estimates which have been made for the expenses of the war, and although this has been obliged to give way to more necessary claims, yet when these demands cease, as many will upon the disbanding the army, the pay will then come into view, and have its equal claim to notice. They will not, however, be unreasonable in this expectation. If the whole cannot be obtained before they are dispersed, the receipt of one month in hand, with an absolute assurance of having the other two months in a short time, will be satisfactory. Should Mr. Morris not be able to assure them the two last months from the treasury, it is suggested that it may be obtained in the' states by drafts from him upon their several continental receivers, to be collected by the individual officers and soldiers out of the last year's arrears due from the several states apportionments, and for which taxes have long since been assessed by the legislatures. This mode, though troublesome to the officer, and perhaps inconvenient for the financier, yet from the necessity of circumstances may be adopted, and might be a means of collecting more taxes from the people than would in any other way be done. This is only hinted as an expedient. The financier will take his own measures. But, I repeat it as an indispensable point, that this sum at least must by some means be procured. Without this provision, it will be absolutely impossible for many to get from camp, or to return to their friends, and, driven to such necessities, it is impossible to foresee what may be the consequences of their not obtaining it, but the worst is to be apprehended. A credit built by their funds, and such others as have been good enough to supply their wants upon the expectation of being refunded at the close of the war, out of the large sums which by their toils in the course of many years' hard service have become due to them from the public, has supported the greatest number of them to the present time, and that debt now remains upon them. But to be disbanded at last without this little pittance (which is necessary to quit quarters), like a set of beggars, needles, distressed and without prospect, will not only blast the expectations of their creditors, and expose the officers to the utmost indignity and the worst of consequences, but will drive every man of honor and sensibility to the extremest horrors of despair. On the other hand, to give them this sum, however small in comparison of their dues, yet by fulfilling their expectations will sweeten their tempers, cheer their hopes of the future, enable them to subsist themselves till they can cast about for some future means of business. It will gratify their pressing creditors, and will throw the officer back with ease and confidence into the bosom of this country, and enable him to mix with cordiality and affection among the mass of useful, happy, and contented citizens. An object of the most desirable importance.

I cannot, at this point of distance, know the arrangements of the financier, what have been his anticipations or what his prospects. But the necessity of fulfilling this expectation of the army affects me so exceeding forcibly that I cannot help dwelling upon it; nor is there in my present apprehension a point of greater consequence, or that requires more serious attention. Under this impression I have thought, if a spirited, pointed, and well-adopted address was framed by congress and sent to the states on this occasion, that gratitude, justice, honor, national pride, and every consideration, would operate upon them to strain every nerve, and exert every endeavor, to throw into the public treasury a sum equal to this requisition. It cannot be denied, especially when they reflect, how small the expectation is compared with the large sum of arrears which is due; and though I know that distinctions are commonly odious, and are looked upon with a jealous and envious eye, yet it is impossible that in this case it can have this operation. For whatever the feelings of individuals at large may be in contemplating on their own demands, yet upon a candid comparison every man, even the most interested, will be forced to yield to the superior merit and sufferings of the soldier, who, for a course of years, has contributed his services in the field, not only at the expense of his fortune and former employment, but at the risk of ease, domestic happiness, comfort, and even life. After all these considerations, how must he be struck with the mediocrity of his demand, when, instead of the pay due him for four, five, perhaps six years' hard-earned toil and distress, he is content for the present with receiving three months' only, and is willing to risk the remainder upon the same basis of security with the general mass of other public creditors.

Another expectation seems to have possessed the minds of the officers; that, as the objects above mentioned are not the only ones which must occupy the attention of congress in connection with the army, it may probably be thought advisable that congress should send to the army a respectable, well chosen, and well instructed committee of their own body, with liberal powers, to confer with the army, to know their sentiments, their expectations, their distresses, their necessities, and the impossibility of their falling back from the soldier to citizenship without some gratification to their most reasonable demands. This would be considered as a compliment; and to add still greater satisfaction and advantage, it is thought very advisable that the secretary at war and the financier should be of this delegation. Previous to a dissolution of the army, many arrangements will doubtless be thought necessary in both those departments to procure a happy and honorable close to the war, and to introduce peace with a prospect of national glory, stability, and benefit. It is not for me to dictate, but I should suppose that some peace establishment will be necessary. Some posts will be kept up and garrisoned, arsenals for the deposit of ordnance and military stores will be determined on, and the stores collected and deposited. Arrangements will be necessary for the discharge of the army, at what periods and under what circumstances? The terms of the soldiers' service are on different grounds; those for the war will suppose, and they have a right to do so, their periods of service to expire at the close of the war and proclamation of peace. What period shall be fixed for these? The levy-men may be retained while the British force remain in our country, if it shall be judged advisable. If I am not consulted in these matters, it will be necessary for me to have an early knowledge of the intentions of congress on these and many other points. But I can think of no mode so effectual as the one suggested of a committee accompanied by the financier and secretary at war. Plans, which to us may appear feasible and practicable, may be attended with insurmountable difficulties. On the other hand, measures may be adopted at Philadelphia which cannot be carried into execution; but here, in the manner proposed, something might be hit upon which would accommodate itself to the ideas of both, with greater ease and satisfaction than may now be expected, and which could not be effected by writing quires of paper and spending a length of time.

Upon the whole, you will be able to collect from the foregoing sentiments what are the expectations of the army, that they will involve complete settlement and partial payment, previous to any dispersion. (This they suppose may be done within the time that they must necessarily remain together.) Upon the fulfilment of these two, they will readily retire in full assurance that ample security, at the earliest period and on the best ground it can be had, will be obtained for the remainder of their balances.

If the idea of a committee to visit the army should not be adopted, and you find it necessary to pass any further resolutions, you will easily collect from the foregoing sentiments what will be satisfactory without my troubling you any further.

I pray you to communicate the contents of this letter to Colonel Hamilton, from whom I received a request similar to yours. I have the honor to be, etc.

John Jay to Washington, Paris, 6 April, 1783. Ex.

I think the motto of *si recte facies* on one of the continental bills may be changed for *recte fecisti*. You have saved your country, and lived to "see her blessed with liberty and peace. As an American I present you my thanks, and as a friend my congratulations.

Notwithstanding the favorable aspect of our affairs, I doubt the propriety of disbanding the army until all the foreign forces in our country shall be removed from it. The experience of ages recommends caution on this head.

It is very evident to me that the increasing power of America is a serious object of jealousy to France and Spain as well as Britain.[1] I verily believe they will secretly endeavor to foment divisions among us, and I think it highly expedient that Ave should proceed to settle the boundaries of such of the states as have disputes about them, and endeavor to secure the continuance of harmony and union by carefully removing such causes of dissension as may from time to time arise. I write thus freely from a persuasion that this letter will go safe. Mr. Mason, of Virginia, will be the bearer of it.

Mrs. Jay speaks often of your happiness, and rejoices in it. We both request the favor of you to make our compliments and congratulations to Mrs. Washington.

There are many here who expect to see you in Europe, but I think they don't know you.

General Edward Hand to General Irvine, Orderly Office, Newburgh, 19 April, 1783. Ex.

DEAR IRVINE: Enclosed you will receive a letter from head-quarters and a copy of our resolutions of the 15th of March. A letter from the South, read by his excellency, turned all right about. Some grumbling from old Pennsylvania, but the vote, *nem. con.* Do present my respects to Colonel Gibson, and all my acquaintance on the Ohio.

[1] Mr. Sparks has written on the margin in pencil, "Mr. J. is a man of suspicions."

John Armstrong to Washington, Carlisle, 22 April, 1783. Ex.

The highest matter of national concern, in my opinion, is the preservation and regular settlement of the western country. That country, in a certain ratio, is equally the property of every state in the union; and, if properly guarded from avaricious claimants and vagrants, may, at a very moderate price, in process of time, be sold out to a large amount indeed. It is also, under proper government, a solid fund for the security or discharge of national debt, and good titles there must induce the emigration of men of character and wealth from foreign parts. A proper republican plan for this great purpose is not very easily laid, but neither the plan nor the execution of it, I hope, will be thought impracticable. If that country is settled or taken up in an irregular and loose manner, these states will sustain an unknown loss, and the regular establishment of government will be greatly impeded, or, perhaps, something worse. I cannot consider that country in the same light we used to do other back lands clearly belonging to individual states; it is the price of united blood and treasure, and ought neither to be partially engrossed, neglected, nor lavished away. Should these thoughts happen to concur with yours, an early hint to congress may call this matter into contemplation.

Washington to Tench Tilghman, Newburgh, 24 April, 1783.

DEAR SIR: I received with much pleasure the kind congratulations contained in your letter of the 25th ult. from Philadelphia, on the honorable termination of the war. No man, indeed, can relish the approaching peace with more heartfelt and grateful satisfaction than myself. A mind always upon the stretch, and tortured with a diversity of perplexing circumstances, needed a respite; and I anticipate the pleasure of a little repose. It has been happy for me always to have gentlemen about me willing to share my troubles and help me out of difficulties. To none of these can I attribute a greater share of merit than to you.

I can scarce form an idea at this moment when I shall be able to leave this place. The distresses of the army for want of money, the embarrassments of congress and the consequent delays and disappointments on all sides, encompass me with difficulties, and produce every day some fresh source of uneasiness. But, as I now see the port opening to which I have been steering, I shall persevere till I have gained the entrance of it. I will then leave the states to improve their present constitution so as to make that peace and independency, which we have fought for and obtained, a blessing to the millions, yet unborn. But, to do this, liberality must supply the place of prejudice, and unreasonable jealousies must yield to that confidence which ought to be placed in the sovereign power of these states. In a word, the constitution of congress must be competent to the general purposes of government, and of such a nature as to bind us together. Otherwise we shall be like a rope of sand, and as easily broken; and may in a short time become the sport of European politics, even if we should be disposed to peace among ourselves.

From the intimation in your letter, and what I have heard from others, I presume this letter will find you in a state of wedlock. On this happy event, I pray you and your lady to accept of my best wishes and sincerest congratulations, in which Mrs. Washington joins hers most cordially. With the most affectionate esteem and regard, etc.

Washington to Governor Harrison, Newburgh, SO April, 1783.

MY DEAR SIR: I thank you very sincerely for your kind congratulations on the close of the war, and the glorious peace which is held out to us, but not yet made definitive. I return them with great cordiality and heartfelt pleasure, and only wish that the business was so far wound up as that I might return to the walks of private life, and in retirement enjoy that relaxation and repose which is absolutely necessary for me.

My first wish now is that the states may be wise; that they may improve the advantages which they have obtained; that they may consider themselves individually as parts of the great whole, and not by unreasonable jealousies and ill founded prejudices destroy the goodly fabric we have been eight years laboring to erect. But without more liberality of sentiment and action I expect but little.

Immediately on the receipt of your letter of the 31st ultimo I transmitted the list of your slaves to a gentleman—a worthy, active man of my acquaintance in New York—and requested him to use his endeavors to obtain and forward them to you. All that can be done I am sure he will do, but I have but little expectation that many will be recovered. Several of my own are with the enemy, but I scarce ever bestowed a thought on them. They have so many doors through which they can escape from New York that scarce anything but an inclination to return, or voluntarily surrendering themselves, will restore many to their former masters, even supposing every disposition on the part of the enemy to deliver them.

Jefferson to Madison, Tuckahoe, 7 May, 1783. Ex.

DEAR SIR: I received your favor of April 22d, and am not a little concerned at the alteration which took place in the report on the impost, etc., after I left you. The article which bound the whole together was, I fear, essential to get the whole passed, as that which proposed the conversion of state into federal debts was one palatable ingredient, at least, in the pill we were to swallow. This proposition being then hopeful, I never consulted you whether the payment of our western expenditures, annexed as a condition to our passing the articles recommended, would not be acceded to by congress; more especially when one of those articles is the cession of that very territory for the acquisition and defence of which these expenditures have been incurred. If I recollect rightly, congress offered this in their first proposition for a cession. I beg your sentiments, however, on this subject by return of the first post. Notwithstanding the unpromising form of these articles, I have waited a fortnight in the neighborhood of Richmond, that I might see some of the members. I passed yesterday in associating and conversing with as many of them as I could. The attorney has cooperated in this work.

This is the view I form, at present, of the leaders. Dr. Lee, R. H. Lee, M. Page, Taylor, will be against them. So will Thurston and White, if elected. And even an A. Campbell is thought worthy of being named with those as having some influence in the southwestern quarter. In their favor will probably be Tyler, Tazewell, General Nelson, W. Nelson, Nicholas, and a Mr. Stewart, a young man of good talents, from the westward. Henry, as usual, is involved in mystery. Should the popular tide run strongly in either direction, he will fall in with it. Should it not, he will have a struggle between his enmity to the Lees and his enmity to everything which may give influence to congress. T. Mason is a meteor whose path cannot be calculated. All the powers of his mind seem at present to be concentrated in one single object—the producing a convention to new-model the state constitution. This is a subject much agitated, and seems the only one they will have to amuse themselves with till they shall receive your propositions. These should be hastened, as I think the session will be short. I have seen Mr. Wythe; he has none of his amendments or notes on the confederation.

Washington to Elisha Boudinot, Newburgh, 10 May, 1783. Ex.

The accomplishment of the great object we had in view, in so short a time, and under such propitious circumstances, must, I am confident, fill every bosom with the purest joy; and, for my own part, I will not strive to conceal the pleasure I already anticipate from my approaching retirement to the placid walks of domestic life. Having no rewards to ask for myself, if I have been so happy as to obtain the approbation of my countrymen, I shall be satisfied. But it still rests with them to complete my wishes by adopting [such] a system of policy as will ensure the future reputation, tranquillity, happiness, and glory of this extensive empire; to which desirable object, I am well assured, nothing can contribute so much as an inviolable adherence to the principles of the union, and a fixed resolution of building the national faith on the basis of public justice, without which all that has been done and suffered is in vain; to effect which, therefore, the abilities of every true patriot ought to be exerted with the greatest zeal and assiduity.

Jefferson to Madison, Monticello, 1 June, 1783. Ex.

Mr. Henry has declared in favor of the impost. This will ensure it. How he is as to the other questions of importance, I do not know.

Washington to Robert Morris, Newburgh, 3 June, 1783.

DEAR SIR: Your favor of the 29th ultimo has been duly received. We are now preparing to carry into execution the resolution of congress of the 26th of May, and I am making out the furloughs accordingly; but I am extremely apprehensive that insuperable difficulties and the worst of consequences may be expected unless the notes you mention shall be paid to the officers and men before their departure from this cantonment. It is for the sole purpose of bringing them forward to the paymaster, with the greatest expedition, that I send the messenger who is the bearer of this; pray do not delay him a single instant; but, if all the notes should not be ready, forward the remainder by the earliest opportunity, and be so good as to inform me when they may be expected.

I write in haste and with earnestness, because some circumstances which have just come to my knowledge make it necessary not a moment's time should be lost.

Though it is much to be lamented that at least a month's pay could not have been given to the troops in money before they left this place, yet I am in hopes your notes will in some measure remedy the evils which might have been expected from their disappointment. Nothing else can now avert the most alarming consequences or distresses of the most cruel nature, particularly to the officers.

Before I retire from public life I shall, with the greatest freedom, give my sentiments to the states on several political subjects; among those will be comprehended the particular objects you recommend to my attention.

Motion of Mr. Bland, seconded by Mr. Hamilton, 5 June, 1783. Referred to Grand Committee of 30 May, 1783. In the handwriting of Theodorick Bland.

Whereas, It has pleased the Almighty Disposer of human affairs to put a period to a long and bloody war, which has terminated in the establishment of independence to these United States, and whereas it is the duty as well as the wish of congress to remove as speedily as possible every cause which might disturb the tranquillity and harmony of these states, so happily united in one great political interest, as well as to reward the brave and virtuous who have by their valor and perseverance established that independence and strengthened that union, and to provide for the future government and prosperity of these states—

Resolved, Therefore, that congress will and do hereby accept the cession of territory made to the United States by the act of the assembly of Virginia, having date the day   of   , 178 , on the terms therein stipulated; except so far as relates to a specific guarantee of the remaining territory reserved by the said state.

Resolved, That, if the aforesaid acceptance shall be agreeable to the said state, and they shall be willing to withdraw the said stipulation, and if the consent and approbation of the army of the United States shall be signified to the following act of the United States in congress assembled, then and in that case the following ordinance shall begin to take effect and be in full force for all and every the purposes therein mentioned, viz.:

It is hereby ordained by the United States in congress assembled, that, in lieu of the commutation for the half pay of the army, and in lieu of the arrearages due to the officers and soldiers of the armies of the United States, and of all other debts due to the said officers and soldiers who now constitute the said army, or who have served therein for a term not less than three years during the war, and for the representatives of such officers and soldiers who shall have died in the service, that there shall be assigned and set apart a tract of unlocated or vacant territory laying within the boundaries of the United States, as ceded by the preliminary articles between Great Britain and America, and bounded as follows, viz.: (here insert the boundaries); that the said territory shall be laid off in districts not exceeding two degrees of latitude and three degrees of longitude each, and each district in townships not exceeding   miles square; that the lines of the said districts shall be run at the expense of the United States by surveyors appointed by the United States in congress assembled, and amenable to congress for their conduct; that each of the said districts shall, when it contains 20,000 male inhabitants, become and ever after be and constitute a separate, independent, free and sovereign state, and be admitted into the union as such with all the privileges and immunities of those states which now compose the union; that each officer and soldier now in the army of the United States shall be entitled to and shall have a grant for thirty acres of the said land for every dollar which shall appear to be due to such officer or soldier from the United States for his services in the army, over and above the bounty promised by an act of congress of the   day of,   , 1776. And, moreover, that every officer and soldier who shall make it appear that he has served three years in the army of the United States, shall be entitled to receive a grant of the said lands equal to the bounties promised to officers and soldiers serving during the war, in lieu of all debts due for their services, half pay, etc. Where the said debts have been liquidated, they shall be entitled to receive a grant of thirty acres for every dollar ascertained to be due to them in like manner as the officers and soldiers whose commutation and arrearages have been liquidated. And be it further ordained, that out of every hundred thousand acres so granted there shall be reserved as a domain for the use of the United States ten thousand acres, each of which ten thousand acres shall remain forever a common property of the United States, unalienable but by the consent of the United States in congress assembled; the rents, shares, profits, and produce of which lands, when any such shall arise, to be appropriated to the payment of the civil list of the United States, the erecting frontier forts, the founding of seminaries of learning, and the surplus after such purposes (if any) to be appropriated to the building and equipping a navy, and to no other use or purpose whatever. And be it further ordained, that the said lands so granted to the officers and soldiers shall be free of all taxes and quit-rents for the space of seven years from the passing this ordinance.

[Endorsement in handwriting of Chas. Thomson. Motion of Mr. land, seconded by Mr. Hamilton, 5 June, 1783. Referred to the Grand Committee of 30 May, 1783.] B

Jonathan Trumbull to Washington, Lebanon, 10 June, 1783. Ex.

Permit me to address your Excellency on the pathetic manner you take leave of myself and the state over which I have the honor to preside; to assure you how great pleasure and satisfaction we have enjoyed in the patriotic virtue displayed in this last address, which exhibits the foundation principles so necessary to be freely and fully inculcated, and appear to be the interest of all to agree in and pursue, to maintain and support an indissoluble union of the states under one federal head.

Lord North to Sir Guy Carleton, Whitehall, 15 June, 1783. Ex.

P. S.—With respect to the person recommended to fill the office of Bishop of Nova Scotia, his Majesty is so well acquainted with the character, merit, and loyalty of Dr. Chandler, and of the very respectable persons who have recommended him, that there will be no difficulty in the choice of the first bishop as soon as a decisive resolution has been taken upon the proposed institution.

Petition to Congress, 16 June, 1783.

To his Excellency the President and Honorable Delegates of the United States of America in Congress assembled: The petition of the subscribers, officers in the continental line of the army, humbly sheweth that, by a resolution of the honorable congress, passed 20 September, 1770, and other subsequent resolves, the officers (and soldiers engaged for the war) of the American army who shall continue in service till the establishment of peace, or in case of their dying in service, their heirs are entitled to receive certain grants of lands according to their several grades, to be procured for them at the expense of the United States.

That your petitioners are informed that that tract of country bounded north on Lake Erie, east on the Pennsylvania, southeast and south on the river Ohio, west on a line beginning at that part of the Ohio which lies twenty-four miles west of the river Scioto, thence running north on a meridian line till it intersects the river Miami, which falls into Lake Erie, thence down the middle of that river to the lake, is a tract of country not claimed as the property of or within the jurisdiction of any particular state in the union.

That this country is of sufficient extent, the land of such quality, and situation such as may induce congress to assign and mark it out as a tract or territory suitable to form a distinct government (or colony of the United States), in time to be admitted one of the confederate states of America.

Wherefore your petitioners pray that, whenever the honorable congress should be pleased to procure the aforesaid lands of the natives, they will make provision for the location and survey of the lands to which we are entitled within the aforesaid district, and also for all officers and soldiers who wish to take up their lands in that quarter.

That provision may also be made for a further grant of lands to such of the army as wish to become adventurers in the new government, in such quantities and on such conditions of settlement and purchases as congress shall judge most for the interest of the intended government, and rendering it of lasting consequence to the American empire.

And your petitioners as in duty bound shall ever pray.

[Signed by two hundred and eighty-six officers of the Massachusetts, Connecticut, New Hampshire, New Jersey, and Maryland lines.]

Washington to the President of Congress, Head-quarters, Newburgh, 17 June, 1783.

SIR: I have the honor of transmitting to your Excellency for the consideration of congress a petition from a large number of officers of the army in behalf of themselves, and such other officers and soldiers of the continental army as »are entitled to rewards in lands, and may choose to avail themselves of any privileges and grants which shall be obtained in consequence of the present solicitation. I enclose also the copy of a letter from Brigadier-General Putnam, in which the sentiments and expectations of the petitioners are more fully explained; and in which the ideas of occupying the posts in the western country will be found to correspond very nearly with those I have some time since communicated to a committee of congress in treating of the subject of a peace establishment. I will beg leave to make a few more observations on the general benefits of the location and settlement now proposed; and then submit the justice and policy of the measure to the wisdom of congress.

Although I pretend not myself to determine how far the district of unsettled country which is described in the petition is free from the claim of every state, or how far this disposal of it may interfere with the views of congress, yet it appears to me this is the tract which, from its local position and peculiar advantages, ought to be first settled in preference to any other whatever, and I am perfectly convinced that it cannot be so advantageously settled by any other class of men as by the disbanded officers and soldiers of the army, to whom the faith of government hath long since been pledged, that lands should be granted at the expiration of the war in certain proportions agreeably to their respective grades.

I am induced to give my sentiments thus freely on the advantages to be expected from this plan of colonization, because it would connect our governments with the frontiers, extend our settlements progressively, and plant a brave, a hardy and respectable race of people as our advanced post, who would be always ready and willing (in case of hostility) to combat the savages and check their incursions. A settlement formed by such men would give security to our frontiers; the very name of it would awe the Indians, and more than probably prevent the murder of many innocent families, which frequently in the usual mode of extending our settlements and encroachments on the hunting grounds of the natives fall the hapless victims to savage barbarity. Besides the emoluments which might be derived from the paltry trade at our factories, if such should be established, the appearance of so formidable a settlement in the vicinity of their towns (to say nothing of the barrier it would form against our other neighbors) would be the most likely means to enable us to purchase, upon equitable terms, of the aborigines their right of preoccupancy; and to induce them to relinquish our territories and to remove into the illimitable regions of the West.

Much more might be said of the public utility of such a location as well as of the private felicity it would afford to the individuals concerned in it. I will venture to say it is the most rational and practicable scheme which can be adopted by a great proportion of the officers and soldiers of our army, and promises them more happiness than they can expect in any other way. The settlers being in the prime of life, inured to hardship, and taught by experience to accommodate themselves to every situation, going in a considerable body, and under the patronage of government, would enjoy in the first instance advantages in procuring subsistence and all the necessaries for a comfortable beginning superior to any common class of emigrants, and quite unknown to those who have heretofore extended themselves beyond the Appalachian mountains. They may expect, after a little perseverance, competence and independence for themselves, a pleasant retreat in old age, and the fairest prospects for their children.

Jefferson to Madison, Monticello, 17 June, 1783. Ex.

My hopes of the success of the congressional proposition here have lessened exceedingly. Mr. Henry had declared in favor of the impost, but when the question came on he was utterly silent. I understand it will certainly be lost, if it be not already; instead of ceding more lands to the United States, a proposition is made to revoke the former cession. Mr. Henry is for bounding our state reasonably enough, but, instead of ceding the parts lopped off, he is for laying them off into small republics. What further his plan is, I do not hear; however, you get the parliamentary news so much more directly from Richmond that it is idle for me to give it to you from hence.

A convention for the amendment of our constitution having been much the topic of conversation for some time, I have turned my thoughts to the amendments necessary. The result I enclose to you. You will have opportunities during your stay in Philadelphia of inquiring into the success of some of the parts of it which, though new to us, have been tried in other states. I shall only except against your communicating it to any one of my own country, as I have found prejudices frequently produced against propositions handed to the world without explanation or support. I trust that you will either now, or in some future situation, turn your attention to this subject in time to give your aid when it shall be finally discussed. The paper enclosed may serve as a basis for your amendment, or may suggest amendments to a better groundwork. I further learn that the assembly are excluding members of congress from among them. Whether the information they may derive from their presence, or their being marked by the confidence of the people, is the cause of this exclusion, I cannot tell.

318 APPENDIX.

Sir Guy Carleton to Lord North, New York, 17 June, 1783.   Ex.

The mode of reducing the army near West Point, as mentioned in my letter No. 76, has been altered by congress. All who were enlisted to serve during the war have received furloughs until the definitive treaty shall be announced; on the reverse of the furlough is a discharge, to take place from that event. In the mean time they are engaged to return to head-quarters should it be necessary. That army is thereby reduced considerably below four thousand. It was not found convenient to lay down the three months' pay formerly voted, but a credit was given at the magazines for supplying the troops with necessaries to nearly that amount. The high prices these were rated at occasioned much discontent.

Horatio Gates to John Armstrong, Jr., 22 June, 1783.   Ex.

Gordon has been very importunate to know what he calls the secret history of the anonymous letters, etc., and has an impression that they were connected with some great financial arrangements. As he is an old friend and an honest man, I have answered frankly: That Stewart[1] was a kind of agent from our friends in congress and in the administration, with no object, however, beyond that of getting the army to co-operate with the civil creditors, as the way most likely for both to obtain justice; and that the letters were written in my quarters by you,[2] copied by Richmond, and circulated by Barber,[3] and were intended to produce a strong remonstrance to congress in favor of the object prayed for in a former one; and that the conjecture that it was meant to offer the crown to Caesar, was without any foundation; referring him to his townsman or neighbor, Dr. Eustis, for further information, as well as for the correctness of this.

Richard Henry Lee to William Whipple, Chantilly in Virginia, 1 July, 1783.   Ex.

What think you of the late address of congress to the states on the subject of the five per cent impost? To me it seems, and I am sorry to be compelled to think so, a too early and too strong attempt

---

[1] Washington alludes to tewart in a letter to Jones, 12 March, 1783. Sparks, viii. 393. Note by G. B. My copy of this letter from Gates I received from General Armstrong's son, Kosciuszko.

[2] John Armstrong, aide-de-camp to Gates. G. B.

[3] Colonel William Barber, assistant adjutant-general of Gates division, brother of Colonel F. Barber, who died about that time. G. B.

to overleap those fences established by the confederation to secure the liberties of the respective states. Where the possession of power creates, as it too frequently does, a thirst for more, plausible arguments are seldom wanting to persuade acquiescence. Thus the excellent plan of the confederation, which leaves the apportioned sum to be "laid and levied by the authority and direction of the legislature of the several states," &c., is to be gradually sapped, and the all-important power of the purse vested (under arguments, some only of which are plausible) in an aristocratic assembly. For give the purse, and the sword will follow, and with these the wheel of rotation, so much relied on, will presently be trashed, to use the phrase of Mr. Harrington, and that liberty which we love and now deserve will become an empty name. Let us be cautious how we introduce such radical defects into our system as may furnish the most distant pretext for foreign troops to interpose in favor of government against the people, as hath lately happened in Geneva. So far as the question shall be for increasing the power of congress, I would answer, with the change of a word only, as the discerning men of old did when the imperial law was proposed to be introduced upon the ruins of the common law, "nolumus leges confederationis mutari."

The general assembly of this state adjourned the other day without adopting the plan of congress proposed in the address. But in their law for appropriating the public revenue, they have appropriated from the land and slave taxes $400,000 annually for the treasury of the United States, which is the sum demanded of us by the address. These two funds are our most certain and most productive ones, amounting to £212,000 lawful money annually—that is, dollars at 6s.

Governor Nicholas van Dyke of Delaware to Washington, 2 July, 1783. Ex.

The general assembly of this state, in their late sessions, have fully adopted the views of congress for establishing the credit of the union, and rendering justice to creditors both in the civil and military line, and the state which declines a similar conduct, in my opinion, must be blind to the united interest, in which that of the individual states are inseparably connected.

Nothing can be plainer than that by a proper union these states are strong and respectable; the contrary condition will render them worse, if possible, than weak and despicable.

Washington to Dr. William Gordon, Head-quarters, Newburgh, 8 July, 1783.

DEAR SIR: Your favor of the 19th of June came to my hands on Sunday last by the southern mail. From this circumstance and the date of it, I conclude it has been to Philadelphia, a mistake not very unusual for the postmaster at Fishkill to commit.

I delayed not a moment to forward the letters which came to me under your cover of the 26th of February to New York. I did not answer the letter which accompanied them in due season, not so much from the hurry of the business as because my sentiments on the essential part of it had been communicated to you before, and because the annunciation of peace, which came close upon the heels of it, put an end to all speculative opinions with respect to the time and terms of it.

I now thank you for your kind congratulations on this event. I feel sensibly the flattering expressions and fervent wishes with which you have accompanied them, and make a tender of mine, with much cordiality, in return. It now rests with the confederated powers, by the line of conduct they mean to adopt, to make this country great, happy, and respectable, or to sink it into littleness; worse, perhaps, into anarchy and confusion; for certain I am that, unless adequate powers are given to congress for the general purposes of the federal union, we shall soon moulder into dust, and become contemptible in the eyes of Europe, if we are not made the sport of their polities. To suppose that the general concerns of this country can be directed by thirteen heads, or one head without competent powers, is a solecism, the bad effects of which every man, who has had the practical knowledge to judge from that I have, is fully convinced of, though none perhaps has felt them in so forcible and distressing a degree.

The people at large and at a distance from the theatre of action, who only know that the machine was kept in motion, and that they are at last arrived at the first object of their wishes, are satisfied with the event without investigating the causes of the slow progress to it, or of the expenses which have accrued and which they now seem unwilling to pay; great part of which has arisen from that want of energy in the federal constitution which I am complaining of, and which I wish to see given to it by a convention of the people, instead of hearing it remarked, that we have worked through an arduous contest with the powers congress already have (but which, by-the-by, have been gradually diminishing), why should they be invested with more?

To say nothing of the invisible workings of Providence, which has conducted us through difficulties where no human foresight could point the way, it will appear evident to a close examiner that there has been a concatenation of causes to produce this event, which in all probability at no time or under any circumstances will combine again. We deceive ourselves, therefore, by this mode of reasoning, and, what would be much worse, we may bring ruin upon ourselves by attempting to carry it into practice.

We are known by no other character among nations than as the United States. Massachusetts or Virginia is no better defined nor any more thought of by foreign powers than the county of Worcester in Massachusetts is by Virginia, or Gloucester County in Virginia is by Massachusetts (respectable as they are); and yet these counties with as much propriety might oppose themselves to the laws of the state in which they are, as an individual state can oppose itself to the federal government by which it is or ought to be bound. Each of these counties has, no doubt, its local policy and interests. These should be attended to and brought before their respective legislatures, with all the force their importance merits; but when they come in contact with the general interest of the state, when superior considerations preponderate in favor of the whole, their voices should be heard no more. So should it be with individual states when compared to the union. Otherwise I think it may properly be asked, For what purpose do we farcically pretend to be united? Why do congress spend months together in deliberating upon, debating, and digesting plans, which are made as palatable and as wholesome to the Constitution of this country as the nature of things will admit of, when some states will pay no attention to them, and others regard them but partially, by which means all those evils which proceed from delay are felt by the whole, while the compliant states are not only suffering by these neglects, but in many instances are injured most capitally by their own exertions, which are wasted for want of the united effort. A hundred thousand men coming one after another cannot move a ton weight, but the united strength of fifty would transport it with ease. So has it been with great part of the expense which has been incurred this war. In a word, I think the blood and treasure which have been spent on it have been lavished to little purpose unless we can be better cemented, and that is not to be effected while so little attention is paid to the recommendations of the sovereign power.

To me it would seem not more absurd to hear a traveller who was setting out on a long journey declare he would take no money in his pocket to defray the expenses of it, but rather depend upon chance and charity lest he should misapply it, than are the expressions of so much fear of the powers and means of congress. For heaven's sake who are congress? Are they not the creatures of the people, amenable to them for their conduct, and dependent from day to day on their breath? Where then can be the danger of giving them such powers as are adequate to the great ends of government and to all the general purposes of the confederation? (I repeat the word general, because I am no advocate for their having to do with the particular policy of any state, further than it concerns the union at large.) What may be the consequence if they have not these powers, I am at no loss to guess, and deprecate the worst; for sure I am, we shall in a little time be-come as contemptible in the great scale of politics as we now have it in our power to be respectable, and that when the band of union gets once broken, everything ruinous to our future prospects is to be apprehended. The best that can come of it, in my humble opinion, is, that we shall sink into obscurity, unless our civil broils should keep us in remembrance and fill the page of history with the direful consequences of them.

You say that congress lose time by pressing a mode that does not accord with the genius of the people, and will thereby endanger the union, and that it is the quantum they want. Permit me to ask if the quantum has not already been demanded? Whether it has been obtained? And whence proceed the accumulated evils and poignant distresses of many of the public creditors, particularly in the army?

For my own part I hesitate not a moment to confess that I see nothing wherein the union is endangered by the late requisition of that body, but a prospect of much good, justice, and propriety from the compliance with it. I know of no tax more convenient, none so agreeable as that which every man may pay, or let it alone as his convenience, abilities, or inclination shall prompt. I am, therefore, a warm friend to the impost.

I can only repeat to you that, whenever congress shall think proper to open the door of their archives to you, which can be best known and with more propriety discovered through the delegates of your own state, all my records and papers shall be unfolded to your view, and I shall be happy in your company at Mount Vernon while you are taking such extracts from them as you may find convenient.

It is a piece of respect which I think is due to the sovereign power to let it take the lead in this business (without any interference of mine), and another reason why I choose to withhold mine to this epoch is, that I am positive no history of the revolution can be perfect if the historiographer has not free access to that fund of information.

Mrs. Washington joins me in compliments to Mrs. Gordon.

Washington to George William Fairfax, State of New York, 10 July, 1783. Ex.

MY DEAR SIR: With very sincere pleasure I received your favor of the 26 March. It came to hand a few days ago only, and gave me the satisfaction of learning that you enjoyed good health and that Mrs. Fairfax had improved in hers. There was nothing wanting in this letter to give complete satisfaction to Mrs. Washington and myself, but some expression to induce us to believe you would once more become our neighbors. Your house at Belvoir, I am sorry to add, is no more, but mine (which is enlarged since you saw it) is most sincerely and heartily at your service till you could rebuild it.

As the path, after being closed by a long, arduous, and painful contest, is, to use an Indian metaphor, now opened and made smooth, I shall please myself with the hope of hearing from you frequently, and, till you forbid me to indulge the wish, I shall not despair of seeing you and Mrs. Fairfax once more the inhabitants of Belvoir, and greeting you both there, the intimate companions of our old age as you have been of our younger years.

I cannot sufficiently express my sensibility for your kind congratulations on the favorable termination of the war, and for the flattering manner in which you are pleased to speak of my instrumentality in effecting a revolution, which, I can truly aver, was not in the beginning premeditated, but the result of dire necessity, brought about by the persecuting spirit of the British government. This no man can speak to with more certainty or assert upon better grounds than myself, as I was a member of congress and in the councils of America till the affair at Bunker Hill, and was an attentive observer and witness to those interesting and painful struggles for accommodation and redress of grievances, in a constitutional way, which all the world saw and must have approved, except the ignorant, deluded, and designing.

I unite my prayers most fervently with yours for wisdom to these United States, and have no doubt after a little while all errors in the present form of their government will be corrected and a happy temper be diffused through the whole; but like young heirs, come a little prematurely perhaps to a large inheritance, it is more than probable they will riot for a while. But this, if it should happen, though it is a circumstance which is to be lamented (as I would have the national character of America be pure and immaculate), will work its own cure, as there is virtue at the bottom.

Oliver Ellsworth to Governor Trumbull, Princeton, 10 July, 1783. Ex.

How long congress will remain here is uncertain. They will hardly return to Philadelphia without some assurance of protection, or even then with the intention to stay longer than till accommodations shall be elsewhere prepared for a fixed residence.

But, sir, it will soon be of very little consequence where congress go, if they are not made respectable, as well as responsible; which can never be done without giving them a power to perform engagements, as well as make them. It was, indeed, intended to have given them this power in the confederation, by declaring their contracts and requisitions for the common defence sacredly binding on the states; but in practice it amounts to nothing. Most of the states recognise these contracts, and comply with the requisitions, so far only as suits their particular opinion and convenience. And they are the more disposed, at present, to go on in this way, from the inequalities it has already introduced, and a mistaken idea that the danger is over; not duly reflecting on the calamities of a disunion and anarchy, or their rapid approach to such a state.

There must, sir, be a revenue somehow established that can be relied on and applied for national purposes, as the exigencies arise, independent of the will or views of a single state, or it will be impossible to support national faith, or national existence. The powers of congress must be defined, but their means must be adequate to the purposes of their constitution. It is possible there may be abuses and misapplications; still, it is better to hazard something than to hazard all.

Vergennes to Luzerne, 21 July, 1783. Ex. Tr.

The representations that you have made to Mr. Morris, to prevent him from demanding of us new funds, have been fruitless. This superintendent of finance, abusing the facilities he has found on our part up to the present time, has so multiplied his drafts that they exceed by nearly two millions the six that the king has granted for the current year. It would have certainly been very agreeable to the king to assist by new succors the finances of the United States; but his majesty could not increase the burdens which weigh on his people for a nation which rejects, with unexampled obstinacy, every expedient thus far proposed to put an end to its distress. We have never founded our policy with regard to the United States on their gratitude; this sentiment is infinitely rare among sovereigns, and republics do not know it. Thus, sir, all that we have to do with regard to Americans is to let matters take their natural course, and for ourselves not to depart from the noble, frank, and disinterested march we' have kept up to the present time with regard to the Americans. And if we cannot direct them according to the great principles which serve for the base of our alliance with them, to take in season the necessary measures not to be the dupes of their ingratitude and of their mistaken policy. That, perhaps, which would suit us best, is that the United States may not assume the political consistency of which they are susceptible; because everything persuades me that their views and their affections will be very versatile, and that we could not count on them if ever there should happen new distractions with England. We are without the means of influencing the domestic arrangements of the United States; and, under all circumstances, we can but be tranquil spectators of the commotions that their constitution and their internal relations can meet with. As to the cession of the navigation of the Mississippi, England has given what did not belong to her any longer. I hear that Mr. Franklin has demanded his recall, but that congress has not decided on his demand. I wish it might reject it, at least for the present, for it would be impossible to give Mr. Franklin a successor so wise and so conciliating as himself; besides, I should be afraid lest they should leave us Mr. Jay; and this is the man with whom I should like least of all to treat of affairs. He is an egoist, and far too accessible to prejudices and humor.

We are much occupied with everything relative to our commerce with America, and we feel more than ever the necessity of granting it encouragements and favors.

Luzerne to Vergennes, 4 Aug., 1783. Ex. Tr.

These governments are as yet scarcely organized. In wishing to put them beyond danger from arbitrary power, their legislatures have gone beyond their object, and have formed constitutions without energy, without vigor, in which the powers are so balanced as to be without action, where the counterpoises, by their heaviness and by continual opposition of forces, keep it in permanent inactivity. These states by themselves are sheltered from a foreign invasion; but the government, though just, cannot be sure of being obeyed without having at its disposition the means of coercion; and there is nothing of it here for the great objects of administration. These observations on the powerlessness of the government do not prevent me from recognising that the people of this country are in general happy; that the tribunals have a sufficient authority; that there is room for all the world; that abundance reigns; that the most unlimited toleration does not engender the smallest religious dispute; that union and peace reign in families; and that the government is not faulty, except with regard to several great objects of internal administration and to those of foreign policy. The taxes, so poorly collected during the war, are yet worse collected at this time. The state of North Carolina has never paid anything; and nevertheless the governor, in a speech to the assembly, says that he hopes that the return of peace will permit congress to moderate the weight of the taxes. The state of Rhode Island has not even taken into consideration the address of congress for the establishment of a system of finances and the discharge of the debts. Every one is reduced to the necessity of waiting the result of the letter of General Washington; and more is hoped from the consideration of a single citizen than from the authority of the sovereign body. If I judge by what has happened up to this time, this letter will produce no great results.

Secretary Charles James Fox to Duke of Manchester, St. James's, 9 Aug., 1783. Ex.

By the despatch to Mr. Hartley which accompanies this, your grace will perceive that everything is done to prevent the American business being any longer a pretence for delay to M. de Vergennes. A definitive treaty with the United States is for reasons which I mentioned in my last despatch perfectly superfluous, but to prevent any pretence of dispute, I have sent Mr. Hartley a project for that purpose with authority to sign immediately. Under all these circumstances, I should hope there will be not much more delay in finishing the definetive treaties for which the public grows a little impatient; if there should, it will begin to be suspected there is some latent design on one side or other which is the cause of these delays, and it will be very material for Great Britain to show that this suspicion cannot fall upon her.

Fox to David Hartley, St. James's, 9 Aug., 1783. Ex.

SIR: With respect to the complaints made in the letter from the American commissioners to you and in the papers enclosed in that letter, I cannot make full answer until I am further informed upon some points into which I am now inquiring, but you may depend upon my answer very shortly; in the mean time, I cannot help being of opinion that Sir Guy Carleton's arguments, as related in the minute of the conversation between him and General Washington, seem to be solid and founded in equity. To have restored negroes, whom we had invited, seduced if you will, under a promise of liberty, to the tyranny and possibly to the vengeance of their former masters, would have been such an act as scarce any orders from his employers (and no such orders exist) could have induced a man of honor to execute; but upon all this I will write more fully when I shall be better informed.

Information respecting two American ships intended for the East Indies, 29 Aug., 1783.

A ship not yet named, but it is said will be called the Empress of China, of three hundred and fifty tons, built at Boston on the model of the Belisarius, is now coppering there, and will sail from thence about the 1st of October. She will carry eighteen 6- and 9-pounders, but is pierced for twenty-four; to be manned with about eighty very good seamen. The captain is not nominated, but it is said he will be a person who commanded one of the continental frigates during the war. Four or five of her officers have been in India, and a person who is pilot was with Captain Cook in his last voyage.

It is intended that the ship shall go directly from Boston round Cape Horn, from thence to coast along South America and touch at Lima and some other of the Spanish ports on that coast, and proceed as high as the latitude of 62°. From thence, at the proper season, to cross the Pacific Ocean and proceed to Canton in China, and from thence home by the Cape of Good Hope. It is expected she will perform this voyage in two years.

This ship is intended principally for a voyage of discovery, to examine the coast of California, and in what manner a trade may be best established in the South Seas and with India.

Major Shaw, aide-de-camp to Major-general Knox, a gentleman who has been in India, and has been bred to and is conversant in trade, goes in the above-mentioned ship.

It is intended to fit out another ship at Boston for India. This ship was late the continental frigate Deane, and is to sail by way of the Cape of Good Hope to Canton, in China. She is to carry out a quantity of dollars and ginseng, and is expected to arrive at Canton about the same time as the other ship.

Mr. Duer and several other persons of character and influence intend going in her.

The first ship is owned by Mr. Parker, Robert Moms, and three other merchants, of Boston and Philadelphia. They do not expect much profit by the voyage, but hope to establish a correspondence in India that may prove extremely advantageous in future.

They are not apprehensive of any interruption from the Spaniards, as they mean only to touch at some of their ports in the South Seas, and proceed to that part of the coast to which the Spaniards have no claim, and where they are to endeavor to establish a trade with the natives.

Jefferson to Madison, Monticello, 31 Aug., 1783. Ex.

Either here or in Philadelphia, I must ask a perusal of your congressional notes with leave to take notes from them, as they will better than anything else possess me of the business I am to enter on.

Report of Mr. Peters, Mr. McHenry, Mr. Izard, Mr. Duane, Mr. S. Huntington, on the concurrent resolutions of the assembly and council of New York of 21 and 22 July, 1782, for augmenting the powers of congress. Delivered 2 Sept., 1783. Entered. Read.

The committee to whom was referred a letter from the governor of the state of New York of the 4th of August, 1782, with sundry resolutions of the legislature of the said state therein referred to, report that it will be proper for congress to postpone the further consideration of the said resolutions until the effect of their resolution of the 18th day of April last, relating to revenue, shall be known.

James Madison to his father, Philadelphia, 8 Sept., 1783. Ex.

Honored Sir: On a view of all circumstances, I have judged it most prudent not to force Billey back to Virginia, even if it could be done; and have accordingly taken measures for his final separation from me, I am persuaded his mind is too thoroughly tainted to be a fit companion for fellow slaves in Virginia. The laws here do not admit of his being sold for more than seven years. I do not expect to get near the worth of him, but cannot think of punishing him by transportation merely for coveting that liberty for which we have paid the price of so much blood, and have proclaimed so often to be the right, and worthy the pursuit, of every human being.

Jay to R. It. Livingston, Passy, 12 Sept., 1783. Ex,.

General Washington's letter does him credit as a soldier, patriot, and Christian. I wish his advice may meet with the attention it merits.

Samuel Adams to   , of Connecticut, from the draft, Boston, 25 Sept., 1783.

SIR: I received very lately your letter of the 9th and continued to the 17th instant, wherein you express a wish to have my sentiments of a subject so much altercated in the state of Connecticut, the grant of half-pay to the officers of the army for life or a commutation thereof for full pay for the term of five years.

It is perfectly immaterial which of the states in congress voted in favor of the measure; two questions occur: whether congress had a right to make the grant, and whether it is founded in justice and sound policy. The first and great end the people of these states had in view in the appointment of congress was that the joint wisdom of the whole might be employed in the recovery of our just rights and liberties, which had been most violently infringed; and, finally, that the joint strength of the whole might be exerted in resisting the military power which the enemy sent to America to enforce their infringements on our rights. This brought us into a state of actual war, and an army became necessary. Congress was and ought to be the sole judge of the necessary means of supporting that army; and if, upon their own deliberate councils and the representations of the commander-in-chief of the army (whose prudence every one will acknowledge), they judged that the grant of half-pay was a measure absolutely necessary for the support and even the keeping a disciplined army, they had an undoubted right in the very nature of their appointment to make the grant; and, as it was made in behalf of the United States, each state is bound in justice to comply with it, even though it should seem to them to have been an ill-judged measure. States, as well as individual persons, are equally bound to fulfil their engagements, and it is one part of the description given to us in the sacred scriptures of an honest man, that, though "he sweareth (or promiseth) to his own hurt, he changeth not." It has been my constant opinion that it would have been impolitic to grant the half-pay for life, because in that case the officers must have kept up their uniform and military habit, and so far we should have had the appearance of a standing army in the time of peace; and I was besides apprehensive that while they kept that habit their manner of living and expenses must be conformable to it, and their half-pay would tend to beggar some, perhaps many of them; but I thought at the same time that, as their opportunities of acquiring even moderate fortunes or making such provision for their families as men generally wish to make were by no means equal to those of their fellow citizens at home, it would be but just and reasonable that an adequate compensation should be made them, at or as soon as conveniently might be after the end of the war. Commutation therefore, you will conclude, meets my former as it does my present views. It is a consideration whether the pay of five years is an adequate compensation. I am told that upon the most accurate calculation it is less than the amount of the half -pay for life; and if the officers are content with it, though less than they might judge adequate, for the sake of cultivating harmony and good humor among the citizens at large, should not others who may think it too much, or even that they should receive nothing, be glad to purchase those inestimable blessings on terms so easy?

Thaddeus Kosciuszko to Washington, Philadelphia, 26 Sept., 1783.

SIR: General Lincoln was pleased to recomend me to Congress, and requested them to promote me to the Ranck of Brygadier General which, by the date of the Commission I hold, he thought I was intitled to Long ago.

Your Excellency will forgive me the Liberty I take in troubling you in this affaire. Unacquainted as Congress may be of my services, by the different promotions already granted to many made me fearfull of puting me at last in the oblivion List of a General promotion. One word from your Excellency to Congress in my favor (if I can flater myself to obtain it:) will clear the doubt and rise my hope to certainty.

Thomas Paine to Robert Morris, Borden Town, 14 Oct., 1783. Ex.

People keep in the habit of wondering why the definitive treaty and treaty of commerce do not arrive, just as if foreign nations would be so foolish to pay respect to our confederated government when we set them the example of paying so little to it ourselves; for, if it has not authority enough to regulate a commercial tax, it cannot be important enough for a commercial treaty; and Britain, finding this out, will regulate our carrying trade by her own acts of Parliament.

Elias Boudinot to JR. B. Livingston, Princeton, 23 Oct., 1783. Ex.

Our public affairs are truly in a disagreeable situation. I am heartily tired of my station, and rejoice at my approach to obscurity. Congress, you have doubtless heard, lately [October 7] determined their place of residence to be near the Falls of Delaware. This mortified the southern members so much that they have manœuvred in such a manner as to take in the eastern members so completely as to get them (Mr. Gerry at their head) to conform entirely to their views, and, taking advantage of the absence of Pennsylvania, Jersey, and Delaware, hastily passed a vote for two places of residence, and fixed the other at or near Georgetown, on the Potomac, and their temporary residence alternately, near about at Annapolis and Trenton, till their buildings are erected. The president is to adjourn congress on the 12th of November to Annapolis.

Connecticut House of Representatives to Congress, 1 Nov., 1783. Ex.

This house is greatly alarmed at the construction put on the conderation, as appears in their address to the state of Rhode Island, which at one stroke vests congress with the power of sword and purse, and leaves nothing to the individual states but an empty name.

This house hold it as their indubitable right, and their constituents ever bound to contend for and maintain it, viz.: that of judging whether the requisitions of congress are founded in the confederation.

Read 13 Jan., 1784. Referred to Jefferson, Lee, Williamson.

Edward Bancroft to William Frazer, Philadelphia, 8 Nov., 1783. Ex.

Sir: Congress has lost a great deal of time, and a great part of its credit, in disputing about the places of its temporary and permanent residences.

The king's proclamation, respecting the trade between the British West India Islands and the United States, has very much surprised and alarmed the people of the latter, who, having formerly traded freely with those islands, confidently expected always to do it. But, though convinced that they are not injured by being deprived of the West India navigation, they know that their interests must greatly suffer thereby, and have, therefore, been forming projects to compel the British government to change its system. But these have generally been dictated rather by resentment than good policy. That which Mr. Robert Morris, and the most sensible men here, are inclined to adopt, is a duty on the tonnage of British shipping coming into the ports of the United States. But congress, from its own want of power, and the want of union among the different states, is afraid to adopt or advise any measure; nor will anything be attempted by that body, unless the different states should, by the complaints of the people, be induced to call for its interference; and in that case it is intended to call for new powers to congress, and particularly that of regulating foreign commerce. But the dispositions of the states must be very greatly changed before they will give that body any new power.

Should the confederation be dissolved, it is a question whether we shall have thirteen separate states in alliance, or whether the New England, the middle, and the southern states will form three new confederations. But, in either case, the public creditors will probably lose their rights, of which the people are now generally regardless; indeed, after having been excited to throw off obedience to the former government, they are but little inclined to submit to any; nor do I conceive it possible that the different states can ever be brought to agree in dividing and apportioning to each its share of public debt, and the federal expense, and much less to discharge it. Mr. Robert Morris is heartily tired of his situation, and determined to resign it, as soon as he can extricate some of his friends, who have been entangled by their confidence in him. This he is now endeavoring to do, by the money borrowing in Holland, but that resource will fail when the letters which Mr. Van Berckel is now writing thither shall be arrived.

The Empress of Russia's treatment of Mr. Dana has been resented by congress; and he is not only recalled, but blamed for his tameness under that treatment. The American ministers in Europe are, however, ordered to notify to the emperor the independency of the United

States, and their readiness to treat with him; this is done in consequence of an intimation of his wish for an opportunity to acknowledge their independency.

Multitudes of people are gone and going over the Alleghany mountains, to settle near the Ohio, and among them great numbers of disbanded officers and soldiers; and their leaders openly avow a determination soon to drive the Spaniards from West Florida. What relation they will hereafter maintain with the United States seems doubtful; but I think great disorder is to be expected from the licentious, ungovernable temper of all the interior inhabitants of America. Even in this state it has hitherto been found impossible to collect any taxes, within the back counties, since the revolution.

The importation of European goods has been so considerable, within the last six months, that the exportable produce of the states probably will not equal it in less than three years; the British are the only manufactures which have afforded any profit; the foreign have sold under prime cost, and there is hardly anything here to pay for them, except a very little Spanish silver, which is daily carried away, and will soon be all gone.

Washington to John Hancock, West Point, 15 Nov., 1788.

DEAR SIR: The very favorable opinion you are pleased to entertain of my public conduct, and the kind expressions of personal friendship you have had the goodness to repeat in your letter of the 15th ultimo, could not fail to receive my warmest acknowledgments had not the highest motives of esteem and attachment already riveted my affecttions to you. Accept my best thanks for the present testimony of your regard, which is made more acceptable by the happy occasion.

Actuated, as we are, by the same anxious concern for the interest, the dignity, and happiness of our country, I was extremely pleased with the patriotic sentiments contained in your excellency's speech at the opening of the present session of your legislature, as well as with the subsequent communication to them. Nor was I less satisfied with the happy effect of those sentiments in producing a compliance with the requisitions of congress; a measure strongly tending to revive the expiring reputation and credit of the nation. Would to heaven that the legislatures of all the states might be inspired by a similar rectitude in decision before it shall be too late.

Be persuaded, my dear sir, that my wishes and prayers will ever be most ardent for the health and happiness of your excellency, and for the prosperity of the commonwealth over which you preside.

Sir Guy Carleton to Lord North, New York, 21 Nov., 1783. Ex.

Great animosities subsist between the delegates from the eastern and southern states in congress, whose various embarrassments seem to increase. In New Hampshire they talk of following the example of Massachusetts in reviving their old claim of territory, and in Connecticut of demanding to have the question reconsidered, which congress had decided respecting their claims.

General Frederick Haldimand to the Secretary of War, Quebec, 27 Nov., 1783. Ex.

I beg leave to observe that in all probability this province,[1] when the posts in the upper country shall be evacuated, will lose much of its importance in a commercial light, and that it will be a matter of great doubt whether it would be right to expend much money for the preservation of it; or, at least, it would never be worth the while to go to war about it. From hence, it appears prudent to shun everything which might bring on a rupture with the bad neighbors which surround us.

Extract of instructions from the general assembly of Pennsylvania to their delegates in congress, dated 9 Dec., 1783.

This state, as a member of the republic of the United States, has ever considered its immediate interest, but in subordination to that of the great whole; and as national honor is of the first consideration, this house cannot be too solicitous that all engagements to the public creditors of every species, and particularly the army who have so distinguished a claim to our esteem and gratitude, should be faithfully performed. They are, therefore, of opinion that the requisitions of congress upon the states for funds, if yet insufficient, should be extended till they are fully commensurate to this object, and that the business of setting off the lands designed by congress for our line should be expedited, and the allotment of them in the vicinity of their other lands granted by this state requires your particular attention, it being considered by them as an essential point.

Certain measures now pursuing by some European states having a tendency materially to injure the general trade of America, the atten-

---

[1] This province: i.e., Upper Canada, opposite Detroit.

tion of this house is naturally turned to the affairs of commerce, and herein are struck with an apparent defect in the constitution of congress, for as the local exercise within the states of the powers of regulating and controlling trade can result only in discordant systems productive of internal jealousies and competitions, and illy calculated to oppose or counteract foreign measures, which are the effect of a unity of council, this house are clearly of opinion that the individual as well as general good will be best consulted by relinquishing to congress all these separate and independent powers.

And this house are willing and desirous on the part of Pennsylvania to concur in substantiating this idea by the necessary legal acts.

Another object of national consideration has been the establishment of a mint, and this house are desirous your abilities should be employed to carry that useful design into effect.

[Submitted by Thomas Mifflin, Annapolis, 5th February, 1784. Read February 6. Referred to Mr. Lee, Mr. Gerry, Mr. Read, Mr. Williamson, Mr. Chase.]

Jefferson to Madison, Annapolis, 11 Dec., 1783. Ex.

It is now above a fortnight since we should have met, and six states only appear. We have some hopes of Rhode Island coming in to-day, but when two more will be added seems as unsusceptible of calculation as when the next earthquake will happen. We have at length received the definitive treaty, with a joint letter from all our commissioners. Not a tittle is changed in the treaty but the preamble, and some small things which were of course. The commissioners write that the riot of Philadelphia and departure of congress thence made the most serious impressions in Europe, and have excited great doubts of the stability of our confederacy, and in what we shall end. The accounts were greatly exaggerated, and it is suspected that Great Britain wished to sign no treaty.

You have seen G. M. [George Mason] I hope, and had much conversation with him. What are his sentiments as to the amendment of our constitution?[1] What amendments would he approve? Is he determined to sleep on, or will he rouse and be active? I wish to hear from you on this subject, and at all times on any others which occupy your thoughts.

---

[1] Constitution of Virginia.

General Wayne to Washington, 14 Dec., 1783. Ex.

Permit me, sir, to assure you from my own knowledge that your address has had more influence upon their [Pennsylvania] councils than volumes from another quarter, and I fondly flatter myself that the same influence will shortly pervade the councils of every state in the confederation.

Extract of Letter from the Governor and Council at Cape Coast Castle, dated the 16 Dec., 1783.

One American, the first we have seen in this quarter, has slaved at this place, and is now nearly ready to sail. Having no orders touching ships or vessels of that state, we have been at a loss how to act; we have, however, cautiously avoided either giving offence or encouragement. We pray your orders as to any American vessels that may arrive here in future; how far they may be entitled to carry on a trade within our districts.

Joseph Jones to Jefferson, Richmond, 21 Dec., 1783. Ex.

We had passed a law empowering the congress to prohibit, if they thought fit, the entry of British vessels into our ports or to adopt any other mode they preferred, to counteract the designs of Great Britain on our commerce so long as they shall adhere to their present system. Your letter to the governor intimates your apprehensions, the business will not be speedily done by congress as they can only recommend. We meant by publishing our resolves on the subject to call the immediate attention of the states to it, that similar measures might be taken by them. The plan of counteracting the British policy I could wish should proceed from congress, in consequence of powers to be communicated for that purpose to exhibit to that nation an instance that the states are not so jealous of that body as to withhold powers that are necessary whenever the general welfare presents the occasion, and to convince them of their error that we cannot in this business act in concert; the transmission of our act to the executives of the several states with request that their attention may be immediately called to this great object, may produce similar acts on their part and expedite the plan of opposition.

Joseph Jones to Jefferson, Fredericksburg, 29 Dec., 1783. Ex.

The completing the cession and granting the impost may not improperly be called sacrifices by this state to the common good of the union, and will, it is to be hoped, lessen if not wholly suspend those illiberal censures heretofore cast upon us. Add to these the unanimity and spirit with which the legislature passed an act to empower congress to concert measures to counteract the designs of Great Britain on our commerce. All of them calculated to produce harmony, and strengthen the hands of the federal government. The impost, I assure you, was with some a bitter pill, but, finding it must be swallowed, they ceased at length to make opposition.

Franklin to Vergennes, Passy, 15 Dec., 1783.

I understand that the bishop or spiritual person who superintends or governs the Roman Catholic clergy in the United States of America resides in London, and is supposed to be under obligations to that court, and subject to be influenced by its ministers. This gives me some uneasiness, and I cannot but wish that one should be appointed to that office who is of this nation and who may reside here among our friends. I beg your Excellency to think a little of this matter, and to afford me your counsels upon it.

Richard Henry Lee to James Monroe, Chantilly, 5 Jan., 1784.

I have duly received the letter that you were pleased to favor me with on the 16th of December last, and I am very sensible of your kind sentiments respecting my health. I am indeed restored beyond my expectations, but yet very far from being so circumstanced as to promise hopes of being soon in a state to venture again on the stormy sea of politics and public business. Few, I believe, feel more sensibly than myself how much our unhappy country suffers, and is likely to suffer, from the want of those qualities and such conduct as is certainly indispensable to the success and well-being of society. It would seem that such feelings are natural to a man who has the misfortune to see his country likely to lose those blessings of liberty that he has so long and so strenuously labored to secure for it. You do me much honor in asking my poor opinion concerning the great congressional questions that are stated. They are of much consequence, no doubt, and I heartily wish that they may finally receive proper determinations. You are perfectly right, sir, in your observation concerning the consequence of a standing army, that it has constantly terminated in the destruction of liberty. It has not only been constantly so, but I think it clear, from the construction of human nature, that it will always *be* so, and it is really unfortunate for human freedom, safety, and happiness, that so many plausible arguments are ever at hand to support a system which both reason and experience prove to be productive of the greatest of human evils—slavery. But it may well be questioned, why, to avoid possible ills, should we adopt measures which in their nature produce the highest evil? The spirit of the fourth section of the sixth article of the confederation plainly discourages the idea of a standing army, by the special injunctions concerning a well-regulated militia, which is, indeed, the best defence and only proper security for a free people to venture upon. To guard our frontiers from Indian invasion, to prevent irregular settlements, and to secure the possessions of foreign powers from the encroachments of our people which may provoke foreign or Indian wars, seem to be the reasons assigned for the adoption of this mischief - working system, a standing military force. But surely it is the business of other powers to secure their own possessions and punish the violators of them, and it would be as new as it would be improper to keep a standing army to prevent the encroachments of our own citizens upon foreign states. It will ever be sufficient to disavow such proceedings and to give the culprits up to justice, or punish them ourselves. As to the protection of our own frontiers, it would seem best to leave it to the people themselves, as hath ever been the case, and if at any time the frontier men should be too hard pressed, they may be assisted by the midland militia. This will always secure to us a hardy set of men on the frontiers, used to arms, and ready to assist against invasions on other parts. Whereas, if they are protected by regulars, security will necessarily produce inattention to arms, and the whole of our people becoming disused to war, render the curse of a standing army necessary. In this light the Indians may be considered as a useful people, as it is surely fortunate for a free community to be under some necessity of keeping the whole body acquainted with the use of arms.

Should the fear of Indians in some measure check the settlement of that country, it can be no inconvenience to a people already inhabiting much too thinly the land that they possess. Irregular settlers, I think, may be kept away by timely and judicious proclamations of congress forbidding such settlements and declaring that no titles shall ever be given to such settlers, and, perhaps, also, by having a few persons near the scene authorized to give notice of this to all goers there upon their first appearance. If, at last, the horrid evil of a standing army must be encountered, it is clear to me that such forces had better be placed in fortifications judiciously chosen to give protection to our own commerce and that of foreigners. But I must confess that I would infinitely rather see this last valuable purpose effected by the more safe and more effectual measure of a navy, which I sincerely hope will be the constant, unremitting object of congressional attention. And both the building and manning of this navy should be, as much as possible, diffused throughout the thirteen states. With respect to trade, its combinations are so many and so various that it is not easy to say much with propriety on that subject hastily. One sentiment respecting it admits not of much doubt; it is, that the free nature and genius of commerce abhors and shuns restraint, and that in young commercial states to embarrass trade with heavy imposts or other clogs, is effectually to demolish it. How grievously do I lament that this is fully and fatally the case in our unfortunate country! In our actual circumstances it is difficult to meet and check effectually the illiberal commercial conduct of the European states, which seems to be by counter and similar restraints, but the want of men and vessels for the purpose of our own transportation renders this difficult if not impossible at present. A wise attention to the raising of seamen and building of ships may in time cause those states to repent their selfish policy. It appears to me that congress would do well to recommend strongly to the different legislatures the adoption of every legal means and encouragement for raising seamen. It is a most important object, and much too much neglected. Do you not think that it would be well for congress to regulate and bring to uniformity the business of weights and measures throughout the United States, and also to establish a uniformity in the value of coins of all sorts? Our country, in particular, is suffering great loss for want of the latter regulation. My respects, if you please, to your colleague Mr. Hardy, and tell him that I shall be very happy to receive a line from him now and then, when his leisure permits. I will thank you much for procuring for me the constitutions of the respective states as they are collected and published in one pocket volume.

R. R. Livingston to John Jay, New York, 25 Jan., 1784. Ex.

Our parties at present consist of three kinds: The tories, who still hope for power under the idea that all remembrance of what has passed should be lost, though they omit no occasion to show their attachment to Britain and their aversion to our government. The warm and hot headed whigs, who are for the expulsion of all the tories from the state, and who would wish even to render the more moderate whigs suspected in order to preserve in their own hands all the powers of government. The third are those who wish at present to suppress all violences, to soften the rigorous laws with respect to the tories by degrees.

Certain disqualifications in the election law passed before the evacuation have given those that are supposed to be the second of these parties the appointment of representative for this district.

Luzerne to Rayneval, Annapolis, 31 Jan., 1734. Ex. Tr.

Mr. Eden, formerly governor of this state, has returned since the peace to reclaim ancient possessions which the assembly of Maryland had confiscated during the war. He had some hopes of success until he destroyed them himself by an imprudence that can be called culpable. He had with him the old secretary and the seals of the old government. He made use of them to grant secretly to his partisans concessions of territory, and he has dated these acts from the epoch when he held the reins of this government. The fraud was soon discovered. The council testified to him its discontent at such conduct, and it is doubtful whether any one of his friends will dare to raise a voice in his favor, or in favor of Mr. Harford, heir of the house of Baltimore, who has also come here to reclaim the ancient patrimony of his family.

Luzerne to Rayneval, Annapolis, 13 Feb., 1784. Ex. Tr.

Scarcely had the treaty been ratified when several delegates who had come to Annapolis for that important act returned to their respecttive states. One was obliged to go home to take care of his sick child; another to marry; a third had very pressing personal business. I met one who told me that his wife called him back. It is thus that the federal assembly is scattered; and since the ratification has taken place, it has no longer been possible to form a congress of nine states; and yet that number is required to decide the most important affairs. The others are left to the decision of seven states, but there is often much difficulty in bringing them together; and when they do meet, they hardly do any business, because it is rarely that the seven states when present vote unanimously. In this way the time has passed since the month of June last. Almost no business has been done; and there is no prospect of a change for the better. Delegates truly attached to the public cause are in despair. Some wish congress to adjourn; others speak of a removal to Trenton; several regret Philadelphia. But this diversity of opinion hardly permits the hope that any one of the proposals will prevail; and congress appears to be condemned for some time longer to its present nullity. It is hard to imagine the reciprocal troubles of congress and those who follow them in a small town where no arrangements are made for their reception, and none are likely to be made, because at the next spring they may depart, never to return.

The Minister to Luzerne, Versailles, 15 Feb., 1784. Ex. Tr.

Certainly we ought to accord favors to the Americans in our islands, or they would engage in an illicit commerce which our colonists themselves would invite. But it is not easy to determine the nature and the extent of those favors. We have to take into consideration the interests of our national commerce as well as of our navigation; and we ought to sacrifice neither the one nor the other to please the Americans. The article which embarrasses us most is that of flour. We feel perfectly the interest that several American states have in furnishing us with it, as well as the abundance they would maintain in our isles; but we have to consider the exportation which several of our own provinces have made up to the present time, and the excess with which they would be menaced in case of competition. They utter loud cries, and the justice as well as the benevolence of the king will maturely weigh their representations.

We think that congress has acted wisely in recalling most of its agents in Europe; their character is too little conciliatory, and their head too much excited, to admit of their being useful to their country. The calmness and the prudence of Mr. Franklin are certainly grave faults in their eyes; but it is by those qualities that this minister has inspired us with confidence. I do not believe that the superior services which this minister has rendered to his country will be requited; I can say that it will be very difficult for congress to replace him.

Jefferson to Madison, Annapolis, 20 Feb., 1784. Ex.

DEAR SIR: I think I informed you in my last that an attempt had been made to ratify the definitive treaty by seven states only, and to impose this under the sanction of our seal (without letting our actual state appear) on the British court. Read, Williamson, and Lee were violent for this, and gave notice that when the question should be put they would call the yeas and nays, and show by whose fault the ratification of this important instrument should fail, if it should fail. I prepared the enclosed resolution by way of protest, and informed them I would place that also on the journals with the yeas and nays, as a justification of those who opposed the proposition. I believe this put a stop to it. They suffered the question to rest undecided till the 14th of January, when nine states appeared and ratified. Colonel Harmer and Colonel Franks were immediately despatched to take passage to Europe with copies of the ratification, but, by the extraordinary severity of the season, we know they had not sailed on the 7th inst. The ratification will not, therefore, arrive in time. Being persuaded I shall be misrepresented within my own state, if any difficulties should arise, I enclose you a copy of the protest containing my reasons. Had the question been put, there were but two states who would have voted for a ratification by seven. The others would have been in the negative or divided. I find congress every moment stopped by questions whether the most trifling money propositions are not above the powers of seven states as being appropriations of money. My idea is that the estimate for the year and requisition grounded on that, wherein the sums to be allowed to each department are stated, is the general appropriation which requires nine states, and that the detailing it out, provided they do not go beyond these sums, may be done by the subordinate officers of the federal government, or by a congress of seven states. I wish you to think of this and give me your thoughts on the subject. We have as yet no secretary of foreign affairs. Lee avows himself a candidate. The plan of foreign affairs likely to take place is to commission Adams, Franklin, and Jay to conclude treaties with the several European powers, and then to return, leaving the field to subordinate characters. Messrs. Adams and Jay have paid a visit to the court of London, unordered and uninvited. Their reception has been forbidding.

We cannot make up a congress at all. There are eight states in town, six of which are represented by two members only. Of these, two members of different states are confined by the gout, so that we cannot make a house. We have not sat above three days, I believe, in as many weeks. Admonition after admonition has been sent to the states to no effect. We have sent one to-day. If it fails, it seems as well we should all retire. There have never been nine states on the floor hut for the ratification of the treaty, and a day or two after Georgetown languishes. The smile is hardly covered now when the federal towns are spoken of. I fear that our chance is at this time desperate. Our object, therefore, must be, if we fail in an effort to remove to Georgetown, to endeavor then to get to some place off the waters of the Chesapeake where we may be ensured against congress considering themselves as fixed. My present expectations are, that as soon as we get a congress to do business, we shall attend to nothing but the most pressing matters, get through them and adjourn, not to meet again till November, leaving a committee of the states. That committee will be obliged to go immediately to Philadelphia, to examine the offices, and, of course, they will sit there till the meeting in November. Whether that meeting will be in Philadelphia or Trenton will be the question, and will, in my opinion, depend on the vote of New York.

Did not you once suppose in conversation with me that congress had no authority to decide any cases between two differing states except those of disputed territory? I think you did. If I am not mistaken in this, I should wish to know your sense of the words which describe those cases which may be submitted to a federal court. They seem to me to comprehend every cause of difference.

We have received the act of our assembly ceding the lands north of Ohio, and are about executing a deed for it. I think the territory will be laid out by passing a meridian through the north-western cape of the mouth of the Great Kanawha from the Ohio to Lake Erie, and another through the rapids of Ohio from the same river to Michigan, and crossing these by the parallels of latitude 37°, 39°, 41°, etc. Allowing to each state an extent of 2° from north to south, on the eastern side of the meridian of Kanawha, there will still be one new state, to wit, the territory lying between that meridian, Pennsylvania, the Ohio, and Lake Erie. We hope North Carolina will cede all beyond the same meridian of Kanawha, and Virginia also. For God's sake push this at the next session of assembly. We have transmitted a copy of a petition from the people of Kentucky to congress praying to be separated from Virginia. Congress took no notice of it. We sent the copy to the governor, desiring it to be laid before the assembly. Our view was to bring on the question. It is for the interest of Virginia to cede so far immediately, because the people beyond that will separate themselves, and they will be joined by all our settlements beyond the Alleghany, if they are the first movers. Whereas, if we draw the line, those at Kentucky, having their end, will not interest themselves for the people of Indiana, Greenbrier, etc., who will, of course, be left to our management, and I can with certainty almost say that congress would approve of the meridian of the mouth of Kanawha, and consider it as the ultimate point to be desired from Virginia. I form this opinion from conversation with many members. Should we not be the first movers, and the Indianans and Kentuckians take themselves off and claim to the Alleghany, I am afraid congress would secretly wish them well. Virginia is extremely interested to retain to that meridian: 1. Because the Great Kanawha runs from north to south across our whole country, forming by its waters a belt of fine land which will be thickly seated, and will form a strong barrier for us. 2. Because the country for one hundred and eighty miles beyond that is an absolute desert, barren, and mountainous, which can never be inhabited, and will, therefore, be a fine separation between us and the next state. 3. Because the government of Virginia is more convenient to the people on all the upper parts of Kanawha than any other which will be laid out. 4. Because our lead-mines are in that country. 5. Because the Kanawha is capable of being made navigable, and, therefore, gives entrance into the western waters to every part of our latitude. 6. Because it is not now navigable, and can only be made so by expensive works which require that we should own the soil on both sides. 7. Because the Ohio and its branches which head up against the Potomac afford the shortest water communication by five hundred miles of any which can ever be got between the western waters and Atlantic, and, of course, promises us almost a monopoly of the western and Indian trade. I think the opening this navigation is an object on which no time is to be lost. Pennsylvania is attending to the western commerce. She has had surveys made of the river Susquehanna, and of the grounds through which a canal must pass to go directly to Philadelphia. It is reported practicable at an expense of £200,000, and they have determined to open it. What an example this is! If we do not push this matter immediately, they will be beforehand with us, and get possession of the commerce. And it is difficult to turn it from a channel in which it is once established. Could not our assembly be induced to lay a particular tax which should bring in £5,000 or £10,000 a year, to be applied till the navigation of the Ohio and Potomac is opened, then James river, and so on through the whole successively? General Washington has that of the Potomac much at heart. The superintendence of it would be a noble amusement in his retirement, and leave a monument of him as long as the waters should flow. I am of opinion he would accept of the direction as long as the money should be to be employed on the Potomac, and the popularity of his name would carry it through the assembly. The portage between Yohogania and the north branch of Potomac is of forty or fifty miles. Cheat river is navigable far up. Its head is within ten miles of the head of the north branch of Potomac, and I am informed offers the shortest and best portage.

I wish in the next election of delegates for congress Short could be sent. His talents are great, and his weight in our state must ere long become principal. I see the best effects produced by sending our young statesmen here. They see the affairs of the confederacy from a high ground; they learn the importance of the union, and befriend federal measures when they return. Those who never come here see our affairs insulated, pursue a system of jealousy and self-interest, and distract the union as much as they can. General Gates would supply Short's place in the council very well, and would act. He is now here.

Among other legislative subjects, our distresses ask notice. I had been from home four months, and had expended twelve hundred dollars before I received one farthing. By the last post we received about seven weeks' allowance. In the mean time, some of us had had the mortification to have our horses turned out of the livery stable for want of money. There is really no standing this. The supply gives us no relief, because it was mortgaged. We are trying to get something more effectual from the treasury, having sent an express to inform them of our predicament. I shall endeavor to place as much in the Philadelphia bank as will repay your kindness, unless you should alter your mind and choose to take it in the Virginia treasury.

I have hunted out Chatellux's journal and had a reading of it. I had never so falsely estimated the character of a book. There are about six sentences of offensive bagatelles which are all of them publicly known, because having respected individual characters they were like carrion for the buzzard curiosity. All the rest of the book (and it is a 4to of 186 pages) is either entertaining or instructive, and would be highly flattering to the Americans. He has visited all the principal fields of battle, enquired minutely into the details of the actions, and has given what are probably the best accounts extant of them. He often finds occasion to criticise and to deny the British accounts from an inspection of the ground. I think to write to him and recommend the expurging the few exceptionable passages and publication of the rest.

I have had an opportunity here of examining Bynkershoek's works. There are about a fourth part of them which you would like to have. They are the following tracts: "Questiones Juris Publici," "De Lege Rhodia," "De Dominio Maris," "Du Juge competent des Ambassadeurs." This last, if not the rest, has been translated into French with notes by Barbeyrac. I have had a copy of Mussenbroeck's "Cours de Physique." It is certainly the most comprehensive and most accurate body of natural philosophy which has been ever published. I would recommend to you to get it, or I will get that and any other books you want.

I hope you have found access to my library. I beg you to make free use of it. Key, the steward, is living there now, and of course will be always in the way. Monroe is buying land almost adjoining me. Short will do the same. What would I not give could you fall into the circle! With such a society, I could once more venture home and lay myself up for the residue of life, quitting all its contentions, which grow daily more and more insupportable. Think of it. To render it practicable, only requires you to think it so. Life is of no value but as it brings us gratifications. Among the most valuable of these is rational society. It informs the mind, sweetens the temper, cheers our spirits, and promotes health. There is a little farm of one hundred and forty acres adjoining me and within two miles, all of good land, though old, with a small, indifferent house on it, the whole worth not more than £250. Such a one might be a farm of experiment, and support a little table and household. It is on the road to Orange, and so much nearer than I am. It is convenient enough for supplementary supplies from thence. Once more think of it, and adieu!

Washington to Jefferson, Mount Vernon, 3 March, 1784. Ex.

Has not congress received a memorial from Mr. De Witt, now or lately geographer to the northern army? The propositions contained in the copy which he has sent me seem founded in equity; and with respect to himself, I can assure you, he is extremely modest, sensible, sober, discreet, and deserving of favors. He is esteemed a very good mathematician.

Jefferson to Washington, Annapolis, 6 March, 1784.

DEAR SIR: Your favor of the 3d is this moment put into my hands, and as the post does not usually stay here above an hour, it leaves me time to scribble a few lines only, scarcely admitting them to be prefaced with an acknowledgment of the pleasure it will give me to be permitted to communicate with you occasionally. We received despatches from Europe yesterday by Captain Barney. There is no news but in one from Dr. Franklin of December 25th, and another from the Marquis Fayette of December 26th. The doctor tells us only of the movements of our ministers, that Mr. Laurens was about sailing from England for America, Mr. Adams about setting out from England for the Hague, and Mr. Jay at Bath; he gives a picture of the disposition of England toward us; he observes that though they have made peace with us, they are not reconciled to us, nor to the loss of us. He calls to our attention the numerous royal progeny to be provided for, the military education giving to some of them, the ideas in England of distraction among ourselves, that the people here are already fatigued with their new government, the possibility of circumstances arising on the continent of Europe which might countenance the wishes of Great Britain to recover us, and from thence inculcates a useful lesson to cement the friendships we possess in Europe. The marquis tells us the Turks and Russians will be kept apart for a while, probably for another year, but that they must in the end come to decision; that Mr. Fox and Lord North were both out of the ministry, and this by a manœuvre of the king's, who got them compromitted fairly with their East India bill, and contrived to get it rejected in the lords; and that Mr. Pitt and E. Temple would come in. The marquis himself will sail for America in the spring.

The present hurry forbids me to write to you on a subject I have much at heart, the approaching and opening the navigation of the Ohio and Potomac. I will trouble you by the next post.

De Witt's petition happens to be in my possession as member of a committee who have not yet reported on it. I was happy to learn from you something of the man.

Meriwether Smith to Monroe, Tappahannock, 6 March, 1784. Ex.

The arrangements that are making in Europe respecting commerce may no doubt have a tendency to depress these states, but are they not such as usage has established among all nations? Even right itself may justify their proceeding; upon what principle, then, are our united efforts to operate? I wish to have your sentiments concerning what we ought to insist on, and the manner of obtaining what we want.

I beg you to attend to one thing of importance to the prosperity of the Southern states; and that is the regulation of post-offices in those states. It is extremely odd that although peace has taken place, trade has commenced, and many obstacles are removed (perhaps all which have been alleged in excuse) which occasioned so great a neglect of us, not any alteration has taken place; and the rider still goes through the states in a straight line, neither turning to the right nor to the left. What think you of my going into the house of delegates next session? I am truly your friend.

Jefferson to Madison Annapolis, 16 March, 1784.

DEAR SIR: I received yesterday, by Mr. Maury, your favor of February 17th. That which you mention to have written by post a few days before is not yet come to hand. I am induced to this quick reply to the former by an alarming paragraph in it, which is that Mazzei is coming to Annapolis. I tremble at the idea. I know he will be worse to me than a return of my double quotidian headache. There is a resolution reported to congress by a committee that they will never appoint to the office of minister, charge des affaires, consul agent, etc. (describing the foreign employments), any but natives. To this I think there will not be a dissenting vote; and it will be taken up among the first things. Could you not, by making him acquainted with this, divert him from coming here? A consulate is his object, in which he will assuredly fail, but his coming will be attended with evil. He is the violent enemy of Franklin, having been some time at Paris. From my knowledge of the man, I am sure he will have employed himself in collecting on the spot facts true or false to impeach him. You know there are people here who on the first idea of this will take him to their bosom and turn all congress topsy-turvy. For God's sake, then, save us from this confusion if you can.

"We have eight states only, and seven of these represented by two members. Delaware and South Carolina we lost within these two days by the expiration of their powers. The other absent states are New York, Maryland, and Georgia. We have done nothing, and can do nothing in this condition, but waste our time, temper, and spirits in debating things for days or weeks, and then losing them by the negative of one or two individuals. Yours, affectionately.

Van Berckel to the States General, Philadelphia, 17 March, 1784.
Ex. Tr.

Shortly after the departure of my former letter, General Washington arrived in this city amid the jubilant shouts of the multitude and the ringing of all the bells. All the officers that had belonged to the army, and were then here, rode out on horseback to meet him to the distance of a league, and thus they accompanied him into the town; the corporation of merchants gave him a splendid banquet of three hundred covers and a ball, to which festivities the minister of your High Mightinesses as well as the French minister were invited, and at which they were present. At the general's departure, eight days after his arrival, the bells again were rung, and the same officers again escorted him the like distance out of the town.

A few days ago news arrived here from Charleston, South Carolina, that the Spaniards had awakened a considerable insurrection in Chili, which aimed at separation from Madrid and complete independence. The same news says, too, that the English were attempting to aid them, and had already sent them three ships with ammunition of war.

George Clinton to Haldimand, New York, 19 March, 1784.

SIR: I now do myself the honor to transmit to your Excellency the copy of a proclamation of the United States in congress assembled, announcing the ratification of the definitive treaty of peace between these states and his Britannic Majesty, and enjoining a due observance thereof.

Having no doubt that your Excellency will, as soon as the season admits, withdraw the British garrisons under your command from the places they now hold within the United States, agreeably to the seventh article of the treaty, it becomes a part of my duty to make the necessary provision for receiving the post of Niagara and the other posts within the limits of this state, and it is for that purpose I have now to request that your Excellency would give me every possible information of the time when those posts are to be delivered.

Lieutenant-Colonel Fish, who will have the honor to deliver this despatch, is instructed to confer with your Excellency, and to endeavor to make such arrangements for the transaction of this business as shall tend to promote mutual convenience and that harmony which it is the interest of both parties, and doubtless their desire, to establish.

Benjamin Walker to Washington, New York, 3 April, 1784.
Our legislature have been sitting here these three months and have done little or nothing, except the impost bill (which is horridly imperfect); they have passed no bill of any consequence. They had begun a bill to raise troops for their frontiers, but the two houses differed as to the number, and now I believe the matter rests till they hear from their delegates; they must by this time have arrived at congress.

The chief politics of the day here is whether the tories shall be sent away or not. I was in hopes these matters would have subsided by degrees, but I see little prospect of it; the tories have acted the most imprudent part possible. It never could be supposed that men who, during eight years, have been brought to consider those people as their greatest enemies, as the murderers of their friends, and as the worst of people, could drop their resentments in a day and receive them as their friends! Time and a proper conduct on their part could alone work such a change, and this would have done it. If the tories had kept themselves quiet and not interfered in public matters, all the liberal and judicious of the whigs would have been so far their friends as to have assisted in burying animosities, and, in the course of time, when their conduct had proved they might be trusted, they would have shared in the government with their fellow-citizens; but, instead of adopting such a conduct, they no sooner got over the first impresssion of fear than they laid claim to every attention, and very foolishly contested with the whigs of the church in the election of a rector, supporting with all their influence Mr. Moore against Mr. Provost, and such has their conduct continued. The consequence is such as might have been expected; resentments are rather heightened than decreased, and many of the most liberal of the whigs who came in with the most conciliating disposition are now their enemies. It has helped to carry the spirit of resentment against them into the legislature, and two bills are going through the house which, if passed, must drive great part of them away.

Rufus Putnam to General Washington, Rutland, 5 April, 1784. Ex.
The settlement of the Ohio country engrosses many of my thoughts, and much of my time since I left camp has been employed in inform-

ing myself and others with respect to the nature, situation, and circumstances of that country, and the practicability of removing ourselves there. And, if I am to form an opinion from what 1 have seen and heard on the subject, there are thousands in this quarter will emigrate to that country as soon as the honorable congress makes provision for granting lands there, and locations and settlements can be made with safety, unless such provision be too long delayed; I mean, till necessity turns their views another way, which is the case with some already, and must soon be the case with many more. You are sensible of the necessity as well as the propriety of both officers and soldiers fixing themselves in business somewhere as soon as possible, especially as many of them are unable to lie long on their oars waiting the decision of congress on our petition, and, therefore, must unavoidably fix themselves in some other quarter, which, when once done, the idea of removing to the Ohio country will probably be at an end with respect to most of them. Besides, the commonwealth of Massachusetts have come to a resolution to sell their eastern country for public securities, and, should their plan be formed and their proposition be made public before we hear anything from congress respecting our petition and the terms on which the lands petitioned for are to be obtained, it will undoubtedly operate much against the Ohio scheme.

From these circumstances, and many others that might be mentioned, we are growing very impatient to hear what our prospects are. Among others who have agreed to accompany me to the Ohio the moment the way is open are Brigadier-General Tupper, Lieutenant-Colonel Oliver, and Major Ashley.

I should have hinted these things to some members of congress, but the delegates from Massachusetts, although exceeding worthy men, and in general would wish to promote the Ohio settlement, yet if it should militate with the particular interest of this state by draining her of inhabitants, especially at a time when she is forming the plan of settling the eastern country, I doubt if they would be very warm advocates in our favor, and I dare not trust myself with any of the New York delegates, because that government are inviting the eastern people to settle in that state; and as to the delegates from the other states, I have no acquaintance with any of them.

These circumstances must apologize for my troubling your Excellency on this subject, and requesting the favor of a line to inform us what the prospects are with respect to our petition, and what measures have been already or are likely to be taken with regard to the Ohio country. I shall take it as a particular favor, sir, if you will be kind enough to recommend some character in congress acquainted with and attached to the Ohio cause with whom I may presume to open a correspondence.

Van Berckel to the States General, Philadelphia, 6 April, 1784. Ex. Tr.

Since the proclamation of the king of England prohibiting the carrying of the products of the British sugar islands to the United States in bottoms other than English, the merchants of several states have petitioned their respective state authorities to attempt reprisals. In the state of Pennsylvania the committee made their report on the 8th of last month, which resolves that a committee be appointed to bring in a bill by which the United States in congress assembled are authorized to prohibit, anywhere within the United States, the import of all products and manufactures of any of the British sugar islands in English bottoms as long as the present restriction on the part of Great Britain remains in force, with this proviso, however, that this act shall have no force until the other states of the union shall have adopted like laws,

I learned some time ago that a considerable trade was carried on as well from this place as from several other trading towns in North America with the West India islands, and especially with the colony Surinam. The traders did not content themselves with molasses and rum, which were the only products permitted to be exported by foreigners, but whole ship-loads of coffee, sugar, indigo, and cotton, to the disadvantage of the Dutch West India Company. I have certain information that some of these plantations, which are deepest in debt, have sent the above-mentioned products in American bottoms to the Philadelphia, Baltimore, and New York and other markets, and this trade is carried on with so much boldness that, at the unloading of the ships which come from the islands, the coffee and cotton bales still have the marks of the plantations whence the products were taken.

Secretary of State to Governor Haldimand, Whitehall, 8 April, 1784. Ex.

SIR: With regard to your refusing a compliance with the desire of Major-General Baron de Steuben for delivering up to him the posts within the limits of the United States, you are certainly justified in every part of your proceedings, even if you had been in possession of the definitive treaty of peace. The seventh article stipulates that they shall be evacuated with all convenient speed, but no certain time is fixed, and, as America has not, on her part, complied with even one article of the treaty, I think we may reconcile it in the present instance to delay the evacuation of those posts, at least until we are enabled to secure the traders in the interior country, and withdraw their property.

The management of the Indians requires great attention and address at this critical juncture, and I am persuaded that our retaining the possession of those posts will not even be detrimental to America, and may be the means of preventing mischiefs which are likely to happen should the posts be delivered up while the resentment of the Indians continues at so high a pitch. I hope the people of America will treat them with kindness; indeed, if they considered it for a moment, their own interest would prompt them so to do; but, if they should be determined to pursue a different conduct, you may assure those unfortunate people that they will find an asylum within his Majesty's dominions, should they be inclined to cross the lakes and put themselves under our protection.

The ship Lady Johnson is now loaded with a considerable cargo of articles for their use, and some implements for agriculture and tools for erecting habitations for the loyalists and their families who have taken refuge in the province of Quebec, which are to be divided among them according to your discretion upon an investigation of their wants. The offer made to you by Baron de Steuben for the purchase of the military stores and provisions in the different forts never can be consented to; there are many reasons exclusive of those you mention which operate very forcibly against it, and, therefore, you may conclude that, whenever you may receive the king's commands for evacuating them, you will be directed to remove every article of military stores, and anything else that might be useful for offensive operations.

I am really at a loss what instructions to convey to you at present respecting the conduct which you are to observe toward the people of the state of Vermont, as much will depend upon the reception their propositions shall meet with from congress. The language they have held to you has, to be sure, been somewhat extraordinary. I do not see how it is possible for us, consistently with the treaty of peace, openly to interfere in their disputes, and, on the other hand, I think it difficult to refuse to take them under our protection should they be determined to become subjects of Great Britain. The matter, in a great measure, must, therefore, be left to your judgment and discretion; but before you proceed to any final decision with those people, upon any material point, I should think it would be advisable for you to transmit their propositions to his Majesty's servants here, and receive their opinion upon the subject.

Governor Thomas Chittenden to Haldimand, Burlington, 15 April, 1784. Ex.

SIR: Since peace has taken place between Great Britain and America, and as in consequence thereof the British post on the island, now called the Heroes, in this state, named the Loyal Block House, will probably be evacuated some time this year, I shall esteem it a mark of your Excellency's favor if you would direct the commanding officer of the post to certify to me the time of its evacuation, that an officer from this state may take possession thereof. Such a favor will be gratefully acknowledged.

Luzerne to Rayneval, Mount Vernon, 12 April, 1784-. Ex. Tr.

The estate of General Washington not being more than fifteen leagues from Annapolis, I accepted an invitation that he gave me to go and pass several days there, and it is from his house that I have the honor to write to you. After having seen him on my arrival in this continent, in the midst of his camp and in the tumult of arms, I have the pleasure to see him a simple citizen, enjoying in the repose of his retreat the glory which he has so justly acquired. We have reciprocally congratulated ourselves that our task has been finished much sooner than we had dared to hope. The general has taken this occasion to make mention of all the obligations of the United States and their gratitude to his Majesty; and he has expressed himself with much sensibility relating to the service that the American cause has received from us. He did not seem to me wholly disinclined to make a journey to France; and he said to me that he should be very glad to go there if affairs of which ho desired to see the end would allow it.

He dresses in a gray coat like a Virginia farmer, and nothing about him recalls the recollection of the important part which he has played except the great number of foreigners who come to see him. His wife and his relations form his habitual society, and the happiness of the persons who surround him seems to be his principal occupation. Yet he is not without work, and, independent of the business which he has to finish in connection with his command, I am inclined to believe that he proposes to write memoirs, or to put in order materials relating to the grand events in which he has taken so important a part.

John Langdon to Tench Tilghman & Co., Portsmouth, 13 April, 1784.

GENTLEMEN: I am honored with your favor of the 1st January last, by which I see you have established a house at Baltimore. It would give me particular pleasure to keep up a correspondence with your house, and should any business (worth attending to) turn up, I am convinced it would be transacted by you on the best terms.

The enclosed letter from your Mr. Morris, my great and good friend, I have particularly attended to; wish I could see better prospects in commerce, but I despair of that until the several states can be prevailed on to give up this great object (which concerns the whole) to congress, their head; for, while thirteen different states, in thirteen different parts of the continent, undertake to regulate trade, it will not only destroy that social intercourse that ought to be cultivated between the states, but bring on the utmost confusion. However, I hope ere long we shall all see the necessity of leaving this business to congress, who only can, and ought to, regulate commerce. I am very respectfully, etc.

Luzerne to Rayneval, Annapolis, 21 April, 1784. Ex. Tr.

Without undertaking to predict what will happen in the interior countries, I believe they will be formed into free societies when they shall be sufficiently peopled to feel the want of a regular government; but I doubt very much if they are ever subject to congress. In a word, I see no gain in this except for the unhappy of Europe who may succeed in escaping from the countries where they are oppressed by the government and borne down by the weight of the public debt; and it appears to me that Germany and Great Britain are the countries most menaced by this emigration. Several ages will pass away before all the vacant places are filled; meantime the populations will flow without ceasing from the coasts toward the interior; when a family by increase shall find itself a little straitened in countries where estates touch each other, it will not fail to go where hands alone are wanting to till the land, and where man finds no limits to his industry. Meantime, the thirteen states will remain in a condition of weakness which, as far as I can see, will render chimerical the terrors of those who are alarmed over the destiny of our sugar colonies. If ever the government of these republicans are modified in such a way as to make them conquerors, the time is so distant that it ought to be permitted even to the policy which looks furthest into the future not to contemplate an epoch so remote.

Edmund Randolph to Jefferson, Richmond, 24 April, 1784. Ex.

I have not heard since the election, but I am confident from what reached me before, that our friend Madison will certainly be a member. His aid will be necessary to correct the extravagances of some plausible men who have many schemes of romance much at heart.

Jefferson to Madison, Annapolis, 25 April, 1784.

By the proposition to bound our country to the westward I meant no more than the passing an act declaring that that should be our boundary from the moment the people of the western country and congress should agree to it. The act of congress now enclosed to you will show you that they have agreed to it, because it extends not only to the territory ceded, but to be ceded, and shows how and when they shall be taken into the union. There is nobody, then, to consult but the people to be severed; if you will make your act final as to yourselves, so soon as those people shall have declared their assent in a certain manner to be pointed out by the act, the whole business is settled; for their assent will follow immediately. One of the conditions is that they pay their quota of the debts contracted. Of course, no difficulty need arise on this head, as no quota has been fixed on us unalterably. The minuter circumstances of selling the ungranted lands will be provided in an ordinance already prepared but not reported. You will observe two clauses struck out of the report: the first, respecting hereditary honors; the second, slavery. The first was done, not from an approbation of such honors, but because it was thought an improper place to encounter them. The second was lost by an individual vote only. Ten states were present. The four eastern states. New York, and Pennsylvania, were for the clause. Jersey would have been for it, but there were but two members, one of whom was sick in his chambers. South Carolina, Maryland, and! Virginia! voted against it. North Carolina was divided, as would have been Virginia, had not Mr. Monroe, one of its delegates, been sick in bed.

The place at which congress should meet in November has been the subject of discussion lately. Alexandria, Philadelphia, and Trenton, were proposed. The first was negatived easily. Trenton had the four eastern states. New York, New Jersey, and Pennsylvania. We expect Georgia and Delaware shortly, in which case it will become possible that Philadelphia may be determined on. The question is put off to be considered with the establishment of a committee of the states, which, to my astonishment, would have been negatived when first proposed had not the question been staved off. Some of the states, who were against the measure, I believe, because they had never reflected on the consequences of leaving a government without a head, seem to be come over.

Dr. Lee is appointed an Indian commissioner. He is not present, but is known to have sought it, and, of course, will accept. This vacates his seat here. I wish Short could be sent in his room. It is a good school for our young statesmen. It gives them impresssions friendly to the federal government, instead of those adverse, which too often take place in persons confined to the politics of our state.

I like the method you propose of settling at once with Maryland all matters relative to Potomac. To introduce this the more easily, I have conversed with Mr. Stone (one of their delegates) on the subject, and, finding him of the same opinion, have told him I would by letters bring the subject forward on our part. They will consider it, therefore, as originated by this conversation.

The more I have reflected on your proposition for printing the revisal, the more I have liked it. I am convinced, too, from late experiments, it cannot be passed in the detail. One of the eastern states had their laws revised, and then attempted to pass them through their legislature, but they got so mangled that all consistence was destroyed, and I believe they dropped them altogether. Should this be printed, I will ask you to send me half a dozen copies wherever I shall be.

You know that many gentlemen of this state had money in the hands of merchants in England. I am well informed that these merchants have uniformly refused to pay them interest, saying the money was always ready if they would have called for it. This adds another to the many good reasons we had before against paying interest during the war.

Congress hope to adjourn by the last of May. The estimate and requisitions for the year, the arrangements for the land office, and foreign treaties, are subjects they will endeavor to complete. Vermont is pressed on them by New York, and a day declared beyond which they will await no interposition, but assert their right of government. The Chevalier Luzerne has taken his leave of us. He makes a tour to the lakes before he leaves the continent. Marbois acts as chargé des affaires till the arrival of a successor.

April 30.—A London ship is arrived here which left that port the 25th March. Pitt was still in place, supported by the king, lords, and nation in general, the city of London enthusiastically in his favor. Still there was a majority of twelve in favor of Fox, who was supported by the Prince of Wales. It was thought the parliament would be dissolved. Congress has determined to adjourn on the 3d June to meet in November at Trenton. Adieu. Yours affectionately.

Fred. Haldimand to Secretary of State, Quebec, 26 April, 1784. Ex.

MY LORD: As this letter goes by land to New York, I cannot be very particular. It is, nevertheless, proper that your lordship should be apprised that I have not had the honor to receive any despatches of a later date than last August. I am very anxious for instructions with regard to the evacuation of the posts and garrisons in the upper countries which will be found without the limits assigned to this province by the definitive treaty of which I have not had any official information, though it has been many months printed in the American newspapers.

Van Berckel to the States General, Philadelphia, 2 May, 1784.. Ex. Tr.

The state of Massachusetts and of New York have passed a law whereby all the American refugees, who went over to the English, are forbidden to return. New Jersey seeks to take advantage of this policy of the two states. A great number of the most prominent inhabitants of New Jersey have passed several resolutions giving these refugees, and especially merchants from New York, every inducement to settle in that state.

News has arrived from Havana that there, at present, all care is taken to prevent the Americans from carrying on their trade henceforth.

Fred Haldimand to the, Secretary of State, Quebec, 12 May, 1784.
Ex. Tr.

MY LORD: At the same time that I transmit a duplicate of my letter of the 26th April I have the honor to acquaint your lordship that the American officer mentioned in it arrived at Quebec on the 7th May. He brought a letter from Governor Clinton, of which I enclose a copy, with my answer to it. Lieutenant-Colonel Fish was instructed by Governor Clinton, provided I had not received orders for the evacuation of the posts, to urge me to give a promise of giving notice, as soon as the order should arrive, of the time I thought the evacuation could take place. This I easily evaded by assuring him that I would scrupulously obey my orders, and that, uninstructed as I was by his Majesty's ministers in consequence of the definitive treaty of peace, I could come under no engagement of any kind relative to the measures to be adopted in carrying it into execution. But, however restrained I might be in my public answer to Governor Clinton's letter, I could not hesitate to declare to Lieutenant-Colonel Fish that, in my private opinion, the posts should not be evacuated until such time as the American states should carry into execution the article of the treaty in favor of the loyalists; that, in conformity to that article, I had given liberty to many of those unhappy people to go into the states in order to solicit the recovery of their estates and effects, but that they were glad to return without effecting anything, after having been insulted in the grossest manner; that, although in compliance with his Majesty's orders to shun everything which might tend to prevent a reconciliation between the two countries, I had made no public representations on that head, I could not be insensible to the sufferings of those who had a right to look up to me for protection, and that such conduct toward the loyalists was not a likely means to engage Great Britain to evacuate the posts, for in all my transactions I never use the words either of my delivering, or their receiving, the posts, for reasons mentioned in one of my former letters to your lordship. Lieutenant-Colonel Fish gave me the strongest assurances that the proceedings against the loyalists were disapproved by the leading men in the different states, and gave me a recent instance of Governor Clinton's having rescued Captain Muer of the 53d Regiment from the insolence of the mob in New York. Lieutenant-Colonel Fish set off on his return the 10th ult., and appeared sensible of the civility and politeness with which he had been received at Quebec and the different garrisons and posts through which he had passed.

The enclosure No. 3 is a copy of a letter which I received (though I could not learn how it was brought) from Governor Chittenden, relative to the time of my evacuating the post on Lake Champlain, which he claims as belonging to the state of Vermont. I have here to observe to your lordship that these people have not lately had much communication with me, and, from the manner in which I received their applications and communications last summer and fall, seem to have turned all their thoughts to establish their interest in the congress, at the same time that they are not neglectful of taking measures and steps which have the appearance of an approaching rupture with the state of New York. I have likewise to observe to your lordship that I think myself more justified in refusing the applications of the governors of New York and Vermont, as I apprehend that Great Britain has contracted the definitive treaty with the congress of the United States of America, and that, consequently, I am not bound to treat, except with persons authorized by congress, relative to carrying into execution the articles of that treaty; and it appears to me that the evacuation of the posts might be delayed as the means of obliging the congress to prolong the term of one year granted by the treaty for the loyalists to solicit the recovery of their estates, for, from the want of government and good order in the different states, it has not hitherto been safe for the loyalists to go among them for that purpose.

Vergennes to Luzerne, 12 May, 1784. Ex. Tr.

I have conferred with the nuncio on the project of establishing a bishop or apostolic vicar in America, and you will find annexed a letter that this prelate writes to you on the subject. You will see that we have not sufficient information to form a proper resolution.

The carelessness with which congress treats the debts which it has contracted to the king is inconceivable; and I do not conceal from you that his Majesty has testified his discontent. We do not press the Americans for reimbursement of the objects that we have furnished out of our own funds, but it is important for us that they should regularly attend to the sum that we have borrowed on their account in Holland, by furnishing with exactness the interest as well as the successive instalments of the capital as they become due. I pray you, sir, to speak of it seriously to Mr. Morris, inviting him to procure for you a satisfactory answer. I see that as yet no place is fixed for the residence of congress. A perpetually ambulatory condition of this body is as injurious to its dignity and its consideration as to the business of which the care is confided to it.

Wm. Short to Jefferson, Richmond, 11 May, 1784. Ex.

DEAR SIR: You will be pleased when I inform you of a conversation last evening between Mr. Henry, Mr. Madison, and Mr. Jones. I was left in the coffeehouse with these three. Mr. Henry told them he wished much to have a conference on a subject of importance. The event of it was that Mr. Jones and Mr. Madison should sketch out some plan for giving greater power to the federal government, and that Mr. Henry should support it on the floor. It was thought a bold example set by Virginia would have influence on the other states. Mr. Henry declared that was the only inducement he had for coming into the present assembly. He saw ruin inevitable unless something was done to give congress a compulsory process on delinquent states, etc. The assembly have not yet proceeded to active business. They have formed great hopes of Mr. Madison, and those who know him best think he will not disappoint their most sanguine expectations. A majority of this assembly are new members, and, consequently, we may expect new measures. Many officers of the late army and more young men compose this majority.

Edmund Randolph to Jefferson, Richmond, 15 May, 1784. Ex.

The great leaders of the assembly not having arrived, their business is stagnated. I am told, however, that Mr. Henry is in the neighborhood. The increase of new members has introduced some of the children of the revolution who labor to satisfy themselves, and disdain dependency on the dictum of any individual or faction. By this means we seem to have obtained another division of party in the assembly. It was manifest throughout the last session that Henry had one corps; R. H. Lee, though absent, another; and the speaker a third, founded on a riveted opposition to our late enemies and everything which concerned them. The first class, you know, has always been numerous, and will probably remain so. The second has never varied a single point either way for some years. The third is but a temporary bubble contrived to save the trouble of thinking on true national policy. I suspect, however, that these new legislative guests will want a general to enable them, to make head against those of the other parties, who will not fail to impeach them with an affectation of novelty when they only press the result of liberality and reflection. This renders it probable that our friend of Orange will step earlier into the heat of battle than his modesty would otherwise permit. For he is already resorted to as a general, of whom much has been pre-conceived to his advantage.

Luzerne to Rayneval, Philadelphia, 17 May, 1784. Ex. Tr.

I have already had the honor of speaking to you of Mr. Jefferson. He was nominated in 1781 one of the five plenipotentiaries to treat with England. He then refused; but, having lost his wife in 1782, he yielded to the entreaties of his friends. He was on the point of sailing for Europe when he learned that the provisional articles had been signed. He has been governor of Virginia; he quitted that place with the reputation of an enlightened, upright man, and of an excellent citizen; but incapable of holding the helm in stormy times. He loves the sciences and arts with passion, and he cultivates them with some success. He is full of sincerity; he loves much his own country; but he is far too much of a philosopher, and far too tranquil, to feel hatred or affection for any other nation, unless the interests of the United States are involved. His principle is that it is important for the happiness and the prosperity of the thirteen states to keep themselves as remote from England as the state of peace will permit; that as a consequence of this system it is for their advantage to keep up a particular attachment to France, and even congress ought, as far as it can, direct toward us the affection of the people in order to balance the inclination and the numerous causes which carry them continually toward England. He has, notwithstanding these principles, shown himself to be the protector and the support of the refugees. He regards several of their demands as founded in justice; he has employed his pen and his influence, but without great success, to ensure the passage of plans relative to the acquitment of the debts; and in almost all discussions, it should be remarked that he has been on the honorable side of the question. If Mr. Franklin should cease to be minister near the king while Mr. Jefferson should be in France or in Europe, I do not doubt that the choice will fall on him. In that case, you will soon perceive that Mr. Jefferson does not join to his theoretical knowledge much experience or habit of public affairs.

James Monroe to Thomas Jefferson, Annapolis, 20 May, 1784.

The committee, of which I am a member, appointed to view the country around Georgetown, under the Princeton engagement, set out this morning upon that business. I think with you that it will be proper to effect this business before the adjournment, and time may better be spared than the present. For four or five days past the qualification of the delegates from Rhode Island hath been the only subject before us. The question was, Shall a delegation retain its seat, or any particular member, the term of service having actually expired?

The gentlemen wait for me.

Jefferson to Monroe, Philadelphia, 21 May, 1784. Ex.

Is there a commission for an additional treaty with France? The instructions made this necessary, and without it we shall be at Paris but private citizens, unprotected by the laws of nations, and liable to the jurisdiction of the country. General Knox went on from hence two days ago to receive the orders of congress as to the western posts. The mouth of the Illinois is the interesting post for Virginia, because it will open a trade up the Missouri and Mississippi. The spot there is advantageous for defence according to Hutchins's pamphlet and General Washington's letter on the peace establishment, Michillimacinac is very important for the United States in general; it is interesting to Virginia on the expectation that she may open the navigation from Lake Erie to Potomac. Detroit is a place of consequence, but so strongly settled that I doubt whether any force need be kept there. The New Yorkers will wish a force at Niagara or Oswego. I should yield to them as far as necessity requires; but the further north that post is, the better for Virginia; were it even pushed to the intersection of the Cataraqui with the forty-fifth degree, it might then leave a possibility of drawing the six nations to Fort Pitt. Mr. Thompson's counsel on this subject will probably be useful, the interests of Pennsylvania and Virginia being united as to all these posts. We shall not begin to scramble for the trade till we have brought it to Fort Pitt. To the southward it would be our interest to have an agency kept up with the Overhill Cherokees, and Martin the agent. If South Carolina and Georgia would then be contented with one other agency, and could agree on its situation, it would be well. I had thought of the head of Mobile river, because there is a very short portage from there to the waters of the Tennessee which would give us access to it, but Mr. Reid thought it too distant from the inhabited country.

Hardy to Jefferson, Annapolis, 21 May, 1784.

Colonel Monroe, together with Mr. Lee and Mr. Gerry, sat out yesterday to Georgetown. We thought it expedient that the committee should proceed in order to turn the view of the continent to that place, as the spot where congress may, perhaps, ultimately fix.

Since your departure we have done nothing; congress have been involved in a scene of confusion greater than you can conceive. The Committee of Qualifications reported that the time of the delegates of Rhode Island had expired. To this report five states assented, two dissented, and three were divided. A question then arose whether, if the report was not agreed to by seven states, those gentlemen were deprived of their seats—or whether, when the right of a member to sit was questioned, it did not require seven states to establish that right.

It has produced great diversity of sentiment and more altercation than I have ever seen either in congress or any other place—so that I begin seriously to apprehend we shall be forced to adjourn, and confess to the world that the divisions of our councils have prevented the adoption of those measures which the interests of the union so loudly call for at our hands.

Ephraim Paine to R. R. Livingston, Annapolis, 24. May, 1784. Ex.

I expected in congress to find justice sit enthroned, supported by all the virtues. Judge, then, how great was ray disappointment when I found caballing, selfishness, and injustice reign almost perpetually: and in place of that good order and decency which ought to preside in all public bodies, especially in that august one, tumult and disorder prevail, even to the degree of challenging, in the house.

The Southern nabobs behave as though they viewed themselves a superior order of animals when compared with those of the other end of the confederacy; this, sir, you know, does not agree with the great spirits of the Northern gentry, and, unless a new disposition takes place, some important matters must either be left undone, or they will be ill done. Scarce any business of importance has been done in the house for about ten days upon the account that the right of the delegates from Rhode Island to sit in the house was called in question, and, the house being divided in opinion, those who were for expelling the Rhode Island members declared that they would attend to no business while they sat in the house.

The Southern members were opposed to having the loan office certificates inserted in the general statement as any part of the national debt, declaring that it was unjust for the Southern states to pay any part thereof, and prevailed so far as to have that debt struck out of the general statement; but a few days after, the other side of the house prevailed and had it inserted.

Various motions have been made on the part of the delegates of New York to get congress to declare the number of troops which our state may keep up for the purpose of garrisoning their frontier posts, and the utmost chicanery was urged in the house to prevent such motion being made; and when it could be no longer evaded, the motion was committed to the committee for arrangements for the frontier posts, and though we called upon that committee to report, cannot yet obtain it; and it appears to me evident that congress are unwelling that we should garrison Oswego and Niagara, as I believe the design is for congress to garrison these two posts, and that Massachusetts intends to cede a part of their country to the United States, preserving the rest for themselves; and I have reason to believe that it was with this view that a few days ago congress appeared almost determined to order the Massachusetts troops, which are now at West Point, to march, in order to garrison these posts as soon as they should be evacuated by the British troops; and the chagrin was very visible when congress were told plainly that New York would not suffer Massachusetts troops to march into that country.

A spirited memorial is presented to congress (agreeable to our instruction) respecting the New Hampshire grants; it is committed, the committee have been called upon to report, but as yet have not done it. It is a question with me whether there is a single state that would be for deciding in favor of New York; at the same time it is doubtful whether nine states will be for declaring Vermont a separate state. According to the present appearance, the New Hampshire grants will one day be acknowledged a separate state; if so, the sooner the better for New York, as they are daily increasing in numbers and extending their encroachments, and may, in a few years, get so strong as to dictate their own boundaries. It appears to me that New York had better raise the power of the state and crush them immediately, or else consent that congress shall declare them a separate state, and take them into the Federal union.

Monroe to Jefferson, Annapolis, 25 May, 1784.

My letter by the last post will inform you of the occasion which pointed that as the favorable moment for a trip to Georgetown, and of our availing ourselves of it; yesterday evening we returned; our report will be in favor of the Maryland side, and of a position near the town.[1] Upon our return we found that business hath been conducted as we expected; the affair of Rhode Island had not been settled till Monday (yesterday), and that in a very extraordinary way. I informed you whence the motion for inquiry originated, and I believe of the warmth with which it was conducted. I never saw more indecent conduct in any assembly before; the dispute was more pointed between Mercer and Howell.

What hath this business to do with Virginia, or Virginia with it, more than any other state in the United States, and wherefore is she brought so intemperately and actively in the field?

To day we resume (I am informed) the consideration of the western posts; what will be the result is uncertain. New York, I hear, will put restraint on every measure till she attains the object of her memorial or statement handed in before you left us; other states will be, perhaps, for doing nothing, and some persons who can not, perhaps, attain what they wish may attempt to mar the whole. We have only eight days before the adjournment, so that the prospect of effecting these or other objects before us is unfavorable.

I shall go instantly upon the business of your other commands, forward, if not yet gone, your instructions, etc., and will attempt giving you powers to negotiate with France if you have them not; but I supposed you had, for so I think it was reported, and I do not recollect that it was negative

It was certainly necessary something should be done respecting the restraint on tobacco in France, to extricate it from the monopoly of the Farmers General, contrary, in my opinion, to the spirit of the treaty; but I am not sufficiently at home on this subject to take it up, and wish your advice.

[1] This refers to the selection of the site of the seat of congress.

Edward Bancroft to William Frazer, Philadelphia, 28 May, 1184.

SIR: I did myself the honor of writing to you in November last, since which I have passed several months in South Carolina in endeavoring to obtain payment of considerable sums due from that state to the Prince of Luxembourg. Few events of any importance have occurred during my absence, and I believe none which you would not have expected from my preceding account of things here. It was not until the middle of January that, with much difficulty and special requisitions, the representatives of nine states were collected at Annapolis, so as to enable congress to ratify the definitive treaty; and some of these withdrew almost immediately after, and did not leave enough to enable that body to act on any matter of importance during the rest of the winter. This difficulty is, however, since removed, and congress, as you will have heard, has decided on a measure of great consequence— that of laying out ten new interior states. But it is necessary previously to purchase the soil from the aboriginal proprietors, and commissioners have been appointed to hold treaties with them for that purpose. At present, however, the intention of congress is only to purchase the country as far west and north as Lake Michigan, of which the propriety is claimed by about twenty-one Indian tribes. When this country shall have been purchased, it is intended to expose it to sale, and to receive in payment loan office certificates, and other government securities, now selling at one fourth part of their reduced nominal value; and it is imagined that almost the whole domestic debt may in this way be liquidated. Whether this will be the case or not, I am unable to say, but it is, I think, the only way in which there is any probability of its being ever discharged; for during this and the last year not one shilling even of the interest has been paid to any public creditor; and but a very trifling part of the taxes imposed for the year 1782 is as yet paid by any of the states, and not a penny by North Carolina, Delaware, or Georgia; and none of them have paid anything toward the quotas of any subsequent year. Indeed, the little paid by Pennsylvania, Massachusetts, South Carolina, etc., was almost wholly collected from the seaports and commercial towns, the interior counties having almost universally either refused or evaded all payment. But whatever congress may gain by selling the lands in the intended new states, it is not probable the purchasers will enjoy much of it, unless they actually remove and settle thereon, before other adventurers shall have usurped the possession. A great part of the country between the Alleghany mountains and the Ohio is already occupied by emigrants, who maintain that actual settlement and cultivation alone create a right to the soil, and laugh at every other title; and there will always be a majority of such settlers ready to support each other. Mr. De la Luzerne is, indeed, astonished at the policy, or rather impolicy, of congress in thus promoting the settlement of interior states, which will not only afford an asylum to all fugitives from their creditors, or from justice, but tend very much to diminish the value of landed property in the more settled states, and deprive them of their useful inhabitants, who after removing will never be made to contribute anything toward discharging the public debt, or supporting the confederation. Congress, however, feels the necessity of doing something toward satisfying the public creditors, and is, besides, convinced that the interior country, which has been constantly intended for that purpose, will never produce anything toward it, unless sold before it be usurped by lawless settlers.

Another step of importance taken by congress is that of sending Mr. Jefferson to join Dr. Franklin and Mr. Adams as commissioners to conclude commercial treaties with different European powers, and particularly with Great Britain. Indeed, a commercial treaty with your government is really, though not avowedly, the object which determined congress at this time to adopt this measure; it being imagined that the present administration will be more favorable to the commercial interests and wishes of the United States than the last. Whether this be the case or not, you may probably be glad to know that the obstacles which formerly were raised on the part of this country will subsist no longer; instead of contending for the right of carrying British West India produce to Great Britain, congress will now be glad of what was last year refused—the liberty of sharing in the carriage of American and West India produce between the United States and the British plantations, and that even in vessels of a limited burden, though endeavors will, I suppose, be previously made to obtain a little more. Toward this change of sentiments here I have, as I think, contributed in many ways. It is certain, however, that both the French and Spanish courts are determined to adhere to their former systems of monopolizing the commerce and productions of their several colonies, and making them subservient only to the interest of the parent countries respectively. St. Nicolas, on the Island of St. Domingo, will be the only port open to American vessels within the government of the Leeward Islands; and that only for such as are laden with lumber and a very few other articles. And the like restriction will be established in the government of the Windward Islands.

Mr. De la Luzerne tells me that if it had been possible to grant partial favors among the United States, the government of France would have admitted the vessels of North and South Carolina, and of Georgia, into all the French islands, as the productions of those states are not supposed to interfere with those of France. The president of congress has written to the Chevalier De la Luzerne that he shall be here the 7th of June, as that assembly is to adjourn on the 3d. Mr. Van Berckel, the Dutch Minister, has never once visited them since their removal to Annapolis. He has often privately expressed to me the most unfavorable opinions of men and things in this country, and I am confident that he has communicated them to the Dutch government—and, indeed, there is not one of the states in which committees or combinations of people do not frequently resist or oppose the legislative, executive, and judicial powers, and in which anarchy and confusion do not in some degree prevail. In Georgia the disorders which prevailed during the last winter, and I suppose yet prevail, were so atrocious that you would hardly believe any true account of them. One of the most extraordinary, but perhaps not one of the most mischievous of the evils there, is, that the whole state did not contain a single ecclesiastic or minister of any religious sect or community whatever.

In every one of the states government is too feeble to command either respect or obedience; and the powers of congress are still more inadequate to the support of the confederation. Of this, all reasonable men in the Middle states are now convinced; and Mr. Jefferson is just now informed, as he tells me, that the great leader of the Virginians, Mr. Patrick Henry, who has been violently opposed to every idea of increasing the powers of congress, is convinced of his error, and has within these few days pledged himself to Mr. Madison, Mr. Jones, and others, to support a plan which they are to prepare and propose to the legislature of Virginia, for amending the confederation by a further concession of powers to congress; but I do not believe that this or any other plan for this purpose will ever be adopted, even by a majority, much less by all the United States.

Respecting the five per cent duty, neither New York, North Carolina, Georgia, Connecticut, or Rhode Island has agreed to it, though it is expected that the four first of these states will adopt it by the end of this year, and that afterward Rhode Island singly will not long persist opposing the rest. The convention between France and the United States respecting consular jurisdiction is not yet concluded. The government of the former claims powers over the French in this country which congress is not willing to allow, though reciprocal powers are offered to congress over Americans in France. However, French consuls or vice-consuls are appointed in almost every one of the states, and they are particularly instructed to collect and transmit every kind of information requisite to increase the trade of France to this country, and especially to point out what changes or additions may be made in the various French manufactures, so as to render them more suitable to the habits, prejudices, or wants of this country. Mr. Jefferson sets out this day for Boston, where he intends to embark for France; and the Chevalier De la Luzerne, having obtained permission to return, and having hired a very fine ship to carry himself and suite to L'Orient, I have accepted the offer which he has repeatedly pressed upon me, of taking my passage with him, as it will shorten the distance by sea, and as I have some business in Paris, where I hope, however, not to stay more than a week. We expect to sail the 15th of June, and I hope to have the honor of seeing you in London early in August, and of informing you of some matters with which it is not expedient to trouble you at this time. I have the honor to be, etc.

Van Berckel to the States General, Philadelphia, 31 May, 1784.
Ex. Tr.

At the founding of the society of the Cincinnati it was determined that it should be hereditary, and that the right to it should descend from father to son; further, that the members of the society use their collective influence to support the government, and to cement, more and more, the union of the states; and, finally, that a fund should be established for the support of the officers and their families who might need assistance. A great part of the public is thoroughly displeased with the establishing of this society, and especially are many displeased concerning the three points just mentioned, fearing that the families in which such distinction should be hereditary would become powerful in time, and might wish to change the present government of the people into an aristocracy; that the funds which should be collected might be misused. To disabuse the public of this fear, a resolution was adopted in the general assembly of the society that the hereditary rights should be abolished, that none of their actions should have any political aim, and that the funds of the society should be put in the hands of the legislatures of each of the states, to be used under their oversight.

Monroe to Jefferson, Annapolis, 1 June, 1784. Ex.

Two points have been effected since my last—the putting the office of finance into commission, and establishment of the committee of the states, and appointment of the members; each state nominated its own member, and congress confirmed the preference. The committee consists of Mr. Blanchard, Dana, Ellery, Sherman, Dewitt, Dick, Hand, Chase, Hardy, Spaight, and Read; for the states not represented on the floor, any member who produces credentials may take his scat; the members also may relieve each other at pleasure; these resolutions were introduced by Mercer and supported by Read; by which the appointment, if this rule continues (longer than the present congress or rather committee), is taken out of the hands of congress, and vested in the delegation of each state, and of course gives it to whomever the chance of a popular vote may place at the head of a delegation; for those who pay a delicate attention to the sense of the state must take that sense from such evidence as appears to them. The powers of the committee are confined, so that no injury can be effected Sherman and Dana will necessarily govern it; Read and Spaight will be together; Hardy will perhaps be of the same society, and as the part they will act will perhaps be rather an intemperate one, they will have no weight themselves, and throw the indifferent states into the other scale. I intend also to put in execution the plan I had in view of visiting the western country if no difficulties arise.

Washington to Putnam, Mount Vernon, 2 June, 1784. Ex.

I wish it was in my power to give you a more favorable account of the officers' petition for lands on the Ohio and its waters than I am about to do. After this, and information respecting the establishment for peace, were my enquiries solely directed, as I passed through Annapolis on my way to Philadelphia, but I could not learn that anything decisive had been done in either. On the latter, congress are differing about their powers, but as they have accepted of the cession from Virginia, and have resolved to lay o& ten new states bounded by latitudes and longitudes, it should be supposed that they will determine something respecting the former before they adjourn, and yet I very much question it, as the latter event is to happen on the third of next month.

As the congress who are to meet in November next by adjournment will be composed from a new choice of delegates in each state, it is not in my power at this time to direct you to a proper correspondence in that body. I wish I could, for persuaded I am, that to some such causes as you have assigned, may be ascribed the delay which the petition has encountered; for surely, if justice and gratitude to the officers, and the general policy of the union, were to govern in this case, there would not be the smallest interruption in granting their request. I really feel for those gentlemen, who, by these delays, unaccountable by any other means than those which you have suggested are held in such an awkward and disagreeable state of suspense; and wish my endeavors could remove the obstacles. At Princeton (before congress left that place) I exerted every power I was master of, and dwelt upon the arguments you have used to show the propriety of a speedy decision. Every member with whom I conversed acquiesced in the justice of the petition; all yielded, or seemed to yield, to the policy of it, but pleaded the want of cession of the land to act upon; this is made, and accepted, and yet matters (as far as they have come to my knowledge) remain in status quo.

Knox to Washington, Annapolis, 4 June, 1784. Ex.

The president, who has just gone for Mount Vernon, will inform you of the state of public matters. Things are not well, and will probably be worse before they are better.

Hugh Williamson (of North Carolina) to James Duane, Annapolis, 8 June, 1784. Ex.

DEAR SIR: It is not to be supposed that a man who has assisted so long and to so much effect as yourself in the great council of the nation, can be indifferent to the progress of business in your absence. From the journals you will learn what is, and what is not done. The reason why, in many cases you are to guess at: In one or two instances I will try to cast some light on the question, viz., why certain things were not done! The affairs of your state have been very interesting. Massachusetts has, I think, fortunately, at length come out with her claim on your western country. I say fortunately, because the sooner it is determined the sooner peace will be restored, and I have understood that you courted and did not shun nor fear such enquiry. Had it been made years ago, I believe congress would have been saved from much perplexity during the last weeks of our late session. New York appeared jealous of the Massachusetts troops taking possession of the frontier posts, viz., Niagara and Oswego, lest they should hold them perforce, and under these circumstances our journals are sufficiently covered with yeas and nys. You know that some troops have long been kept in service with the view of taking possession of the posts which the British held in the jurisdiction of the United States. New York has asked for leave to raise a troop of five hundred men. You know that a peace establishment in the Eastern states is an unpleasing business; we could not easily obtain a vote for any troops in peace; in the meanwhile New York presses that we should say how many she is to keep. The business of the union was not determined. How many are the United States to keep? In this state of the question, the New York delegates refuse to agree to the United States raising a single man till we shall say how many is their state to raise. Others, thinking that the case of thirteen was full as important as that of one, refused to consider the demand of New York till the other question was determined. If the Eastern states really intend anything unfair, they think worse of Continental troops than I do; for I can not allow myself to believe that our troops will ever make themselves the tools of a state. The result is, the United States are not to raise any Continental troops—New York has no permission to raise any, except that militia are to be raised, of which part are to be raised in New York. You may guess whether the business was much forwarded by the assembly of New York telling us that they should raise troops, though the assent of congress was refused.

The affair of Vermont has been pushed as usual. The Eastern states, some of them, are solicitous for those insurgents. If Vermont must be independent, which I fear can not be prevented, I wish to see at least two Southern states formed at the same time. I think the Middle and Southern states will ever be the supporters of Federal measures, and I do not wish to see a phalanx of five dead votes against us on every interesting question till we are enabled to preserve the balance. The has been, I hope it will return, when the Southern states shall support or be supported by New York on Federal questions.

Washington to Sir Edward Newenham, 10 June, 1784. Ex.

This is an abounding country, and it is as fine as it is extensive. "With a little political wisdom it may become equally populous and happy. Some of the states, having been misled, ran rife for a while, but they are recovering a proper tone again, and I have no doubt but that our federal constitution will obtain more consistency and firmness every day. We have, indeed, so plain a road before us that it must be worse than ignorance if we miss it.

Luzerne to Rayneval, Philadelphia, 18 June, 1784. Ex.

Congress dispersed on the third of this month with great precipitation, leaving a vast amount of business in suspense, and a committee whose powers are extremely limited. This committee, composed of eleven members, will have cognizance only of affairs that congress could decide by a plurality of seven states. It scattered almost immediately, and I think it will not be easy to reassemble them. Behold, then, the body representing the sovereignty of the confederation without activity, and, so to say, annihilated, and the essential branch of the sovereign power retrenched at least for six months. Congress adjourned to Trenton for the month of next November. People think that different delegations will meet there punctually, and those who have seen so many times the uselessness of the efforts of congress flatter themselves that this assembly, after being withdrawn for six months from the sight of the public, will reappear with more energy and lus-tre, and that the people, who will feel the inconvenience of having been deprived of all head, will be disposed to give them more extend-ed powers. The army, which had but eight hundred men, has been reduced to a company of forty, destined to guard the magazines of West Point. The assembly, while it reduced the salary of its president and of its own officers, has given even to the last funds of which it was able to dispose to the foreign officers who have served the United States, and they have been recompensed with a generosity that could not have been expected from the decay of the finances and the parsimony of the people. In a word, on this matter and many others, it is not congress which is in fault for the disorder of the finances and public business; the evil comes from the people, and it would not be possible to display more zeal and consistency than congress has done in inspiring them with principles of honor and justice.

Vergennes to Luzerne, Versailles, 30 June, 1784. Ex. Tr.

I was not aware that Mr. Franklin had suffered drafts of Mr. Morris to be protested. I am not sorry, because that will serve as a lesson to the Americans. They think our resources inexhaustible for them, while they do not deign to take trouble about providing means for themselves, nor for the reimbursement of the advances that we have made to them, and procured for them. I think nothing of the loss of the subjects of the king for having placed confidence in American people. This article alone has done an almost irreparable injury to the reputation of the Americans. If congress cannot procure money to balance their account with us, it is important for us, at least in this moment, that it should put us in condition to meet the interest of the loan in Holland; but I confess to you that I do not flatter myself that they will do it, notwithstanding the letter which you sent the ninth of April last, and to which the king has given his approbation.

His Majesty has equally approved the journey that you have made to Mount Vernon, and has heard with sensibility all that General Washington has said to you of his attachment to France. You may assure this general officer that if he visits this country he will receive a welcome proportioned to his virtues, to his reputation, and to the signal services which he has rendered to his country.

Jefferson to Madison, Boston, 1 July, 1784.

DEAR SIR: After visiting the principal towns through Connecticut, Rhode Island, this state, and New Hampshire, in order to acquire what knowledge I could of their commerce and other circumstances, I am returned to this place, and shall sail the day after to-morrow in the Ceres, bound for London; but my purpose is to get on shore in some boat on the coast of France and proceed directly to Paris. My servant being to set off to-day, and much on hand to prepare for my voyage, I have no time for any particular communications. Indeed, there are few I should have to make, unless I were to enter into a detail, which would be lengthy, as to the country and people I have visited. The lower house of this state have passed a bill giving congress the powers over their commerce which they had asked. It has had two readings with the senate, and meets with no opposition. I find the conviction growing strongly that nothing can preserve our confederacy unless the band of union, their common council, be strengthened.

General Haldimand to Major-General Knox, Quebec, 13 July, 1784.

SIR: I have had the honor to receive your letter dated New York, thirteenth of last month, by Lieutenant-Colonel Hull, acquainting me that you was directed by congress, the sovereign authority of the United States, to write to me in order to ascertain the precise time when each of the posts within the United States, now occupied by the troops of his Britannic Majesty, shall be delivered agreeable to the definitive treaty of peace, and to propose, as a matter of mutual convenience, an exchange of certain cannon and stores now at these posts, for others to be delivered at West Point, upon Hudson's River, New York, or some other convenient place. I have the honor to enclose for your information copies of letters which passed between his Excellency Governor Clinton and me, upon the part of your proposition. Though I am now informed by his Majesty's ministers of the ratification of the definitive treaty of peace, I remain in other respects in the same situation I was then, not having received any orders to evacuate the posts, which are without the limits assigned by the treaty of peace to this province. It is therefore impossible for me to ascertain the time when the evacuation of these posts shall commence. I can only assure your Excellency that I shall lose no time in carrying into execution his Majesty's orders on that head, when I shall have the honor to receive them. In the mean time, I have to acquaint you that, however desirous I am to consult mutual convenience, I am not at present empowered (and have reason to think that I will not in future be empowered) to make the exchange of cannon and stores proposed by you, and for which Lieutenant-Colonel Hull was authorized to make the proper arrangements.

Kosciuszko to Robert Morris, New York, 17 July, 1784.

SIR: Your generous behavior toward me so entirely took hold of my heart, that, forgetting your uncommon delicate feelings, I am forced, by a great uneasiness of my mind, to present my warmest thanks to you before I quit this country; and to assure you that your kindness will be always fresh in my memory with the gratitude I owe you, and shall endeavor to put in practice what susceptibility now suggests the means to adopt. I am, sir, with perfect respect, your most humble and most obedient servant.

Monroe to Jefferson, King George, 20 July, 1784.

Mr. Madison, whom I saw lately at Richmond, will give you the proceedings of the assembly. Three important objects have, I find, employed their attention: the enlarging the powers of congress, regulation of the commerce of the state, and the recommendations of congress under the treaty. Their resolutions in the first instance I enclosed to you for Boston; in the second, they have established a port on each river, to which they have restricted the vessels of foreign nations, for the reception and unlading of their cargoes; they have deferred the commencement of the operation of this law to the expiration of two years. I fear a repeal will be attempted; I hope, however, it will fail, and that this is only a step to a more wise and mature system of policy. If so many parts are admitted, will the objects of the state be attained, or, on the contrary, will they not prove as subsidiary to Baltimore? It appears to me unwise to attempt erecting more than one great town at a time, since they will fail altogether while the exertion is beyond the means necessary to effect it. You will inform me, under the treaties which subsist, what regulations we may make that would at least make the advantages arising from our intercourse with those nations reciprocal.

You will be so kind as to give me every information upon these subjects you think necessary, for perhaps my enquiries may not extend to every subject upon which I should be informed. I beg of you also to turn my attention to those other great objects to which in your opinion it should be applied, for a variety of points may arise to you when you look back on our country, in which our policy may no doubt be much improved.

The day after to-morrow I set out upon the route through the western country. I have changed the direction, and shall commence for the westward upon the North river by Albany, etc. I shall pass through the lakes, visit the posts, and come down to the Ohio, and thence home. This route will necessarily take me all the time during the recess of congress.

I shall certainly be in Trenton on the thirtieth of October; in the trip

I shall take I may, perhaps, acquire a better knowledge of the posts which we should occupy, the cause of the delay of the evacuation by British troops, the temper of the Indians toward us, as well as of the soil, waters, and, in general, the natural view of the country.

Captain Denny, whom we saw at Annapolis, accompanies me. I am sensible of the fatigue I shall undergo, but am resolved to sustain it.

Secretary of State to Governor Haldimand, Whitehall, 2 August, 1784. Ex.

SIR: I very much approved of the answers which you have thought proper to return to the applications from Governor Clinton and Governor Chittenden for the evacuation of the posts within the limits of the United States remaining in our possession; and until you receive his Majesty's instructions for delivering them up, it will be advisable to avoid any decided refusal to the compliance with any future requisition that may be made to you on that subject as specially directed from hence.

Marhois to Rayneval, Philadelphia, 15 August, 1784. Ex. Tr.

The Catholics, always directed by the Jesuits in this country, have been ill-disposed to the revolution; they are not much better disposed toward us. But several persons of consideration have not the same prejudices. One of them, Mr. Carroll, the largest capitalist and the richest landholder in Maryland, has even spoken to me of the desire of the whole congregation to be directed by a bishop or apostolic vicar. He is a pious, wise, and prudent man, who feels the necessity of uniting under one chief the individuals of our religion scattered through Maryland and Pennsylvania; but he foresees great difficulties on account of their dispersion, and because there has never been a particular and regular correspondence between the Catholics of the two states. If we take any part in this matter, it ought to be with a great deal of reserve; and I, above all things, believe that we ought not to think of making the choice fall upon a French priest. The men of this country would make him prove all sorts of difficulties, and, respectable as might be his character and his conduct, there would be little probability of success in his apostolic labors. I sent to Mr. Carroll the letter of the nuncio for the oldest missionary, and I have the honor to address to you a copy of that which I wrote to him at the same time.

This prelate makes mention in his letter to M. de la Luzerne of the Abbé Carroll, one of the relations of him of whom I spoke to you. This priest, whose personal acquaintance I do not possess, enjoys a good reputation; and I believe that it would be desirable that the chief of the churches of Pennsylvania and Maryland should concur with the intention of his Holiness to raise him to the episcopal see.

George Clinton to James Monroe, Albany, 20 August, 1784.

DEAR SIR: I am favored with yours of yesterday. I have not received any intelligence since you left this to change my sentiments respecting the difficulties I was apprehensive you would meet with in passing the posts held by the British; on the contrary, some recent reports from Canada confirm me in the opinion that it is not their intention to evacuate them this season, or to encourage that free intercourse which ought to have taken place on the return of peace. Haldimand's ostensible reason for continuing to hold those posts after official information of the ratification of the definitive treaty—to wit: the want of orders—is a very absurd one, and it is most probable that secret orders to continue his garrisons is the real cause for this unjustifiable conduct. You may rely on the earliest advice of any information I may receive on this subject.

Marbois to Rayneval, Philadelphia, 24 August, 1784. Ex. Tr.

Mr. Jefferson is an upright, just man, who belongs to no party, and his representations will have the greatest weight on the general congress. This assembly desires sincerely to fulfil its engagements toward the king; but the obstacles come from the people, and congress has no means of coercion. From the superintendent we ought not to expect anything but that which he will not be able to prevent himself from doing. He is in the highest degree exasperated at the noise made about his dispute with Mr. Holker, and humbled at the proofs of avidity and injustice which have become public. The latter has told me that, in the warmth of discussions and in the presence of arbiters, the superintendent had allowed himself expressions which announced very little affection for France, and that, far from giving attention to the interests that the king may have in this suit, he thought nothing was more easy than to make the finances of his Majesty pay all the illegitimate profits that he had taken to himself, and of which he is unhappily in possession. I do not think Mr. Morris susceptible of affection or aversion for any power; but I have reason to believe that his avidity can make him capable of very reprehensible irregularities; and that, unless he is bound by the instructions of congress, he will take very little pains to fulfil the obligations of the United States toward his Majesty.

Additional Information from Dr. Bancroft, dated 26 August, 1784. Ex.

The congress and people of America had formed very extravagant opinions respecting the supposed importance of their commerce to the British and other European nations; and these opinions had produced the resolve of the thirtieth of April last, desiring to be invested by the several states, " for fifteen years, with power to prohibit any goods, wares, or merchandise from being imported into, or exported from, any of the states, in vessels belonging to or navigated by the subjects of any power with whom these states shall not have formed treaties of commerce," etc. Since that resolution passed, only three of the American legislatures had met, viz., those of Virginia, Massachusetts Bay, and Connecticut; of which the two first had complied with the desire of congress; but the assembly of Connecticut had separated without noticing it, because the resolution, as is said, had not been officially communicated. Perhaps it may be complied with by the remaining states before the end of the next winter, and in that case it is intended that the powers so given shall be employed by congress to stimulate or intimidate the nations of Europe not having commercial treaties with the United States into dispositions suited to such treaties; for which Mr. Jefferson has brought over no less than twenty-three commissions; and among them, two for concluding the treaties which I formerly mentioned, as projected with the governments of Denmark and Portugal. Congress is also very solicitous for a commercial treaty with Spain, which may grant American vessels admission to the Spanish colonies; but neither Dr. Franklin nor Mr. Jefferson had any expectation of obtaining it when I left Paris. But the proposed treaty with Great Britain is, as I lately mentioned, that for which congress is, of all others, the most anxious. Mr. Jefferson quitted America with strong expectations of obtaining it soon; but these were very much weakened when I left him in Paris, by the informations which had been given to him respecting the supposed disposetions of the government and people of the country. He and Dr. Franklin were then waiting for the arrival of Mr. Adams (whom I passed on the road), in order to determine respecting their future measures.

If no treaty should be concluded between Great Britain and the United States, and if congress should be invested with the powers required by the resolution of the thirtieth of April, that body will probably soon exclude British vessels from the ports of the United States, or at least prohibit them from carrying away any of the produce of the United States; which, as that produce consists chiefly of bulky raw material, it is supposed, will greatly diminish the British navigation, and soon induce the British government to allow the American vessels access to the British West Indies. How far this opinion is well founded I am not to decide; but I will venture to suggest that, if the views of his Majesty's ministers extend toward a recovery of the sovereignty of the now United States, or toward a dissolution of their confedera-tion, or of their present connection with France, these ends will be best promoted by an adherence to the system of excluding American vessels from the British plantations, and American shipping from the advantages of being sold and employed in this kingdom. Because, in fact, such exclusions will render the situation of many of the states, and particularly those of New England, in respect of commerce, much worse than it was while they were subject to the British crown and to the British navigation laws. Of this truth many persons in those states are already convinced; and it seems to me highly probable that, if such exclusions be continued, and a fixed determination to con-tinue them be manifested by this government, the people of New England, North Carolina, and, perhaps, some other states, will, in less than twelve months, loudly clamor against the confederation, and openly concert measures for entering into something like their former connections with Great Britain. But it may possibly be thought that such events, could they be certainly produced, would not be very interesting to Great Britain, and that, after what has happened, none but commercial advantages are to be expected from America. Should this be the case, it may, perhaps, be well to consider whether some facilities may not be advantageously given to the United States re-specting their former intercourse with the West Indies, and the sale of their shipping in Great Britain, not only to prevent those resentful measures which have been meditated against this country, but for the more reasonable purpose of enabling them to buy and pay or greater quantities of British manufactures than they can otherwise do.

General Greene to Washington, 29 August, 1784.

SIR: While I feel much for myself, I feel for you. You have had your troubles since you left public life. The clamor roused against the Cincinnati was far more extensive than I expected. I had no conception that it was so universal. I thought it had been confined to New England alone; but I found afterward our ministers abroad, and all the inhabitants, in general, throughout the United States, were opposed to the order, I am happy you did not listen to my advice. The measures you took seemed to silence all the jealousies on the subject; but I wish the seeds of discontent may not break out under some other form. However, it is hardly to be expected that perfect tranquillity can return at once, after so great a revolution, where the minds of the people have been so long accustomed to conflict and subjects of agitation. In this country many discontents prevail; committees are formed, and correspondencies going on, if not of a treasonable nature, highly derogatory to the dignity of government, as well as subversive of the tranquillity of the people. And I wish they may not break out into acts of violence and open rebellion against the authority of the state. Nor am I without some apprehensions that the situation of our public credit, at home and abroad, and the general discontent of the public creditors, may plunge us into new troubles. The obstinacy of Rhode Island, and the tardiness of some other states, seem to presage more mischief. However, I can but hope the good sense of the populace will correct our policy in time to avoid new convulsions. But many people secretly wish that every state should be completely independent; and that, as soon as our public debts are liquidated, congress should be no more—a plan that would be as fatal to our interest at home as ruinous to it abroad. I see by the Northern papers that the Marquis de la Fayette had arrived at New York, and set out for Mount Vernon. Doubtless you will have a happy meeting. "It will be the feast of reason, and the flow of soul." Present him my respectful compliments of congratulation upon his safe arrival in America, and my affectionate regards to Mrs. Washington.

William Gordon to Washington, Jamaica Plain, 30 August, 1784.

Your family, I judge, is increased by the presence of the Marquis. My most respectful compliments to him. You wished to get rid of all your negroes, and the Marquis wished that an end might be put to the slavery of all of them. I should rejoice beyond measure could your joint counsels and influence produce it, and thereby give the finishing stroke, and the last polish to your political characters. Could it not be contrived that the industrious among them might be turned into copy-holders on the lands of their present masters, and, by having a special interest in the produce of their labor, be made to yield more profit than at present? And would not this, in its consequences, excite the lazy to exertions that might prove highly beneficial? I am not for letting them all loose upon the public, but am for gradually releasing them and their posterity from bonds, and incorporating them so into the states that they may be a defence, and not a danger, upon any extraordinary occurrence.

Van Berckel to the States General, Philadelphia, 13 September, 1784. Ex.

During my absence, the state of Pennsylvania resolved to raise a corps of two hundred and fifty men from the militia of this state. This little corps enlisted for twelve months as the contingent of this state for the seven hundred men that congress has resolved to raise from the United States to take possession of the posts on the northwestern boundary.

A short time after the arrival of Jay, Henry Laurens arrived by the English packet-boat from London, and the following day the Marquis de Lafayette arrived by the French packet, and came a few days later to Philadelphia. He was met by the militia on horseback, and several other persons of distinction, some miles from here. The public have been busy guessing the purpose of his coming, imagining that he was charged with some important commission from the court of France; but this much is certain, that he has come with no other object than simply and solely to visit General Washington and some other distinguished officers, his old friends. The committee of states that was to regulate affairs during the adjournment of congress has resolved to separate and leave Annapolis, since nothing can be accomplished on account of the absence of many of the members, nor could they come to any resolve; so that now there are nowhere representatives of the thirteen United States in session, and its collective sovereignty is thus completely asleep, which state of affairs is to last till the thirtieth of October next, when a new congress is to assemble at Trenton, New Jersey.

Charles Thomson to Jefferson, Philadelphia, 1 October, 1784.

DEAR SIR: Though this invisibility of a federal head will have little effect on our affairs here, or on the minds of the citizens of the United States, who can easily reconcile themselves to it, and who will view it in no other light than the rising or dissolution of their several legislatures, to which they have been accustomed, yet I am apprehensive it will have an ill aspect in the eyes of European nations, and give them unfavorable impressions, which will require all your address and abilities to remove.

The messenger sent to Canada is returned, and has brought an answer from General Haldimand, of which I enclose a copy, and by which you will see that though he has received official information of the ratification of the definitive treaty of peace, yet no orders are sent to evacuate the posts within the United States; and there is a report that the garrisons are relieved and the posts supplied with near twelve months' provisions.

I leave you to draw conclusions from this conduct. What steps congress will take respecting this matter I know not. In the meanwhile, I am sorry to find that Rhode Island still continues obstinate, and refuses to grant the impost, which seems to be the only means of establishing national credit and reputation, and giving us weight with foreign nations. Howell and Ellery, it is said, got home just in time to prevent a change that was like to take place in their public councils, and to confirm their former obstinacy.

Van Berckel to the States General, Philadelphia, 12 October, 1784.
Ex. Tr.

I have the honor to announce to your H. M. that the state of New Jersey has passed an act declaring the ports of Burlington and Perth Amboy free ports for twenty-five years, from the first of October of this year. This is to repair the injury which these towns have suffered on account of the war, and to restore their injured trade. In the assembly of the state of Pennsylvania there have been debates for some time on the propriety of repealing the test laws. These test laws are laws that were made at the beginning of the revolution, and obliged every one of the inhabitants, within a certain limited time, to take the oath of allegiance to the state, or incur a penalty as an enemy, and the deprivation of the rights of citizenship. Many at that time refused to do this, but now they desire to return; but the time designated by the law has passed, and a return is refused them. In the mean time, on this point there were animated debates in the assembly of the state of Pennsylvania, which resulted in an irregular adjourning, and the assembly does not meet again until after the new elections. On this point several acts which were to be passed were untouched; one of them is said to have provided for the general security of foreign ministers.

Haldimand to the Secretary of State, Quebec, 2,. October, 1784. Ex.

MY LORD: Captain Joseph Brant arrived yesterday from Fort Stanwix; from him I have received information of the negotiations which had been carried on there between the commissioners from the United States and the deputies from the Indian nations, and between the state of New York and the latter. I have the satisfaction to find that nothing had been agitated there which could occasion hostilities between the American states and the Indians, or which could give encouragement to any attempt to dispossess his Majesty's troops of the forts in the upper country until such time as, in consequence of the definitive treaty, it shall please his Majesty to order the evacuation of them. I am nevertheless sorry to find that the western Indians have had some difference with the Americans, and that one Wilson, a trader of note from the states, has been put to death, and that some prisoners have been made by the Delaware and Shawanese Indians.

Washington to George Plater, Mount Vernon, 25 October, 1784.

To describe the usefulness of water transportation would be a mere waste of time. Every man who has considered the difference of expense between it and land transportation, and the prodigious saving in the article of draft cattle, requires no arguments in proof of it; and to point out the advantages which the back inhabitants of Virginia and Maryland would derive from an extension of the inland navigation of the river Potomac, even supposing our views did not extend beyond the Appalachian Mountains, would be equally nugatory.

But I consider the business in a far more extensive point of view; and the more I have revolved the subject, the more important it appears to me; not only as it respects our commerce, but our political interests, and the well-being and strength of the Union also.

Maryland, as it respects the navigation of the Potomac, stands upon similar ground with Virginia. Pennsylvania have it, I am told, in contemplation to open a communication between Toby's Creek (which empties into the Alleghany river ninety-five miles above Fort Pitt) and the west branch thereof, and to cut a canal between the latter— that is, the Susquehanna and the Schuylkill—the expense of which is not easy to be conceived, much less to be estimated or described. But a people possessed of the spirit of commerce, who see, and who will resolve to pursue advantages, may achieve almost anything. In the meanwhile, under the uncertainty of these undertakings, they are smoothing, as I have been informed, the roads, and paving the ways for the trade of that western world to their capital. That New York will do the same, so soon as the British garrisons are removed, which at present are an insuperable obstacle in their way, none who are as well acquainted with the genius and policy of the people as I am can harbor the smallest doubt, any more than they will of the difficulty of diverting trade, after connections are once formed, and it has flowed for any length, of time in one channel, to that of another.

I am not for discouraging any state to draw the commerce of the western country to its seaports; the more communications are open to it, the closer we bind that rising world (for indeed it may be so called) to our interests, and the greater strength shall we acquire by it. Those to whom nature affords the best communication will, if they are wise and politic, enjoy the greatest share of the trade. All I would be understood to mean, therefore, is that the gifts of Providence may not be neglected or slighted; and these, when considered on a commercial scale, are alone sufficient to excite our endeavors; but the political object of it, in my estimation, is immense.

I need not remark to you, sir, that the flanks and rear of the United Territory are possessed by other powers, and formidable ones, too; nor how necessary it is to apply the cement of interest to bind the several parts of it together; for what ties, let me ask, should we have upon those people, and how entirely unconnected must we be with them, if the Spaniards on their right, or Great Britain on their left, instead of throwing stumbling blocks in their way, as they now do, should invite their trade, and seek alliances with them? What, when they get strength, which will be sooner than is generally imagined (from the emigration of foreigners, who can have no predilection for us, as well as from the removal of our own citizens), may be the consequence of their having formed close connections with both or either of those powers in a commercial way, needs not the gift of prophecy to foretell.

The western settlers (I speak now from my own observation) stand, as it were, upon a pivot; the touch of a feather would almost incline them any way. They have looked down the Mississippi until the Spaniards (for themselves, very impoliticly, I think) threw difficulties in their way; and for no other reason, that I can conceive, but because they glided gently down the stream, without considering, perhaps, the tediousness of the voyage back, and the time necessary to perform it in; and because they had no other means of coming to us but by a long land transportation and unimproved roads.

These causes have hitherto checked the industry of the present settlers; for except the demand for provisions occasioned by the increase of population, and a little flour, which the necessities of the Spaniards have compelled them to buy, they have no excitements to labor. But open the road once, and make easy the way for them; and see what an influx of articles will be poured in upon us; how amazingly our exports will be increased by them, and how amply we shall be compensated for any trouble and expense we may encounter to effect it!

A combination of circumstances makes the present conjuncture more favorable than any other to fix these matters. The crusty and untoward disposition of the Spaniards on one side, and the private views of some individuals coinciding with the policy of the court of Great Britain on the other, to retain the posts of Oswego, Niagara, Detroit, etc, (which, though they are done under the letter of the treaty, is certainly an infraction of the spirit of it, and injurious to the union), may be improved to the greatest advantage by the states of Virginia and Maryland, if they would open their arms and embrace the means which are necessary to establish it. It wants but a beginning; the western inhabitants would do their part toward its execution. Weak as they are at present, they would meet us half way rather than be driven into the arms, or be dependent upon foreigners; the consequence of which would be a separation or a war. The way to avoid both, fortunately for us, is to do that which our most essential interest prompts us to; and which, at a very small comparative expense, is to be effected. I mean, to open a wide door to their commerce, and make the communication as easy as possible for them to use it.

Washington to Jacob Read, Member of Congress, Mount Vernon, 3 November, 1784. Ex.

My tour to the westward was less extensive than I intended. The Indians, from accounts, were in too dissatisfied a mood for me to expose myself to their insults, as I had no object in contemplation which could warrant any risk. You are pleased, my dear sir, to ask me to furnish you with such observations as I may have made in this tour, respecting the "western territory, posts, or, in general, on Indian affairs." With respect to the first and last, I saw and heard enough while I was in that country to convince me that the predictions of a letter which I wrote on the seventh of September, 1783, to a committee of congress (at their request), in part are already verified, and the rest, if the treaty which is now depending with the Indians does not avert them, are upon the verge of being so. And with respect to the posts, two other letters of mine, the first on the second of May last year, and the other of the eighth of September following—addressed (by desire) to the committee appointed to form a peace establishment for the union—contain my sentiments on that subject, fully and clearly.

As these letters were addressed to committees at their own request, 'tis possible the members of them only may have seen them; this must be my apology, therefore, for the reference, in preference to a recital. What may be the result of the Indian treaty, I know not; equally unacquainted am I with the instructions or powers given to the commissioners; but if a large cession of territory is expected from them, a disappointment, I think, will ensue; for the Indians, I have been told, will not yield to the proposal. Nor can I see wherein lies the advantage of it, if they would, at a first purchase, unless a number of states, though thinly inhabited, would be more than a counterpoise in the political scale for progressive and compact settlements. Such is the rage for speculating in and forestalling of lands on the north-west of the Ohio that scarce a valuable spot, within any tolerable distance of it, is left without a claimant. Men in these times talk with as much facility of fifty, an hundred, and even five hundred thousand acres, as a gentleman formerly would do of one thousand. In defiance of the proclamation of congress, they roam over the country, on the Indian side of the Ohio — mark out lands, survey, and even settle on them. This gives great discontent to the Indians, and will, unless measures are taken in time to prevent it, inevitably produce a war with the western tribes. To avoid which, there appears to me to be only these ways: purchase, if possible, as much land of them immediately back of us as would make one or two states, according to the extent congress design, or would wish to have them of, and which may be fully adequate to all our present purposes; fix such a price upon the lands so purchased as would not be too exorbitant and burthensome for real occupiers, but high enough to discourage monopolizers. Declare all steps heretofore taken to procure land on the north-west side of the Ohio contrary to the prohibition of congress to be null and void; and that any persons thereafter who shall presume to mark, survey, or settle on lands beyond the limits of the new states, or purchased lands, shall not only be considered as outlaws, but fit subjects for Indian vengeance.

If these or similar measures are adopted, I have no doubt of congress deriving a very considerable revenue from the western territory. But lands, like other commodities, rise or fall in proportion to the quantity at market; consequently, a higher price may be obtained by the acre for as much as will constitute one or two states than can be had if ten states were offered for sale at the same time; besides extending the benefits, and deriving all the advantages of law and government from them at once; neither of which can be done in sparse settlements, where nothing is thought of but scrambling for land, which may involve confusion and bloodshed.

It is much to be regretted that the slow determination of congress involves many evils; 'tis much easier to avoid mischiefs than to apply remedies when they have happened. Had congress paid an earlier attention to, or decided sooner on, Indian affairs, matters would have been in a more favorable train than they now are; and if they are longer delayed, they will grow worse. Twelve months ago, the Indians would have listened to propositions of any kind with more readiness than they will do now; the terms of the peace frightened them, and they were disgusted with Great Britain for making such. Bribery and every address which British art could dictate have been practised since to soothe them, to estrange them from us, and to secure their trade. To what other causes can be ascribed their holding our western posts so long after the ratification of the treaty, contrary to the spirit, though they do it under the letter of it? To remove their garrison and stores cannot be the work of a week; for, if report is true, they have only to shift them to the opposite side of the line. But it is now more than twelve months since I foretold what has happened; and I shall not be surprised if they leave us no posts to occupy, for if they mean to surrender them at all, they may fix upon a season, or appoint a short day, perhaps, for the evacuation, when no relief can be had, and congress having repeatedly called for an evacuation, will hardly know how to act, especially as they will be in no condition to take possession of the posts; for to do it properly requires time, as ordnance, stores, provisions, and other articles, as well as garrisons, are not to be established in a moment, even where boats and other conveniences—of which I question much whether you have any—are at hand. This being the case, there will be an interregnum, during which the works will be left without guards; and being obnoxious to our late enemy, now no doubt staunch friends with Indian prejudices in aid, will be the cause of accidental fires, or Indian drunkenness, in which the whole will end in conflagration, or I shall be mistaken.

There is a matter which, though it does not come before congress wholly, is, in my opinion, of great political importance, and ought to be attended to in time. It is to prevent the trade of the western territory from settling in the hands either of the Spaniards or British. If either of these happen there is a line of separation drawn between the eastern and western country at once, the consequences of which may be fatal. To tell any man of information how fast the latter is settling, how much more rapidly it will settle by means of foreign emigrants, who can have no particular predilection for us, of the vast fertility of the soil, and population the country is competent to, would be futile, and equally nugatory to observe that it is by the cement of interests alone we can be held together. If, then, the trade of that country should flow through the Mississippi or St. Lawrence—if the inhabitants thereof should form commercial connections, which lead, we know, to intercourses of other kinds—they would in a few years be as unconnected with us, indeed, more so than we are with South America, and entirely alienated from us.

It may be asked how we are to prevent this? Happily for us, the way is plain, and our immediate interests, as well as remote political advantages, point to it, while a combination of circumstances renders the present epoch more favorable than any other to accomplish them. Extend the inland navigation of the eastern waters—communicate them as near as possible with those which run to the westward—open these to the Ohio, and such others as extend from the Ohio toward Lake Erie, and we shall not only draw the produce of the western settlers, but the peltry and fur trade of the lakes also, to our posts, being the nearest and best, to the amazing increase of our exports, while we bind those people to us by a chain which never can be broken.

This is no Utopian scheme; it can be demonstrated as fully as facts can ascertain a thing, that not only the produce of the Ohio and its waters, at least to the falls, but those of the lakes, as far even as that of the Woods, may be brought to the seaports in the United States by routes shorter, easier, and less expensive than they can be carried to Montreal or New Orleans, if we would be at a little trouble and expense to open them. I will acknowledge that the most essential part of this business comes more properly before individual states than the United States. But there is one part of it which lies altogether with the latter; and that is to have actual surveys of the western territory, particularly of the rivers which empty into the Ohio on the north-west side, which have the easiest and best communication with Lake Erie; reporting the nature of these waters, the practicability of their navigation, and expense in opening them. This, in my opinion, is an important business, admitting of no delay. It would show the value of these lands more clearly; it would attract the attention of the settlers and trade, and fix ideas which are as floating as chaos.

You see, sir, I have obeyed your commands. My sentiments are delivered with freedom. The worst construction they admit of is, that they may be the errors of judgment, for sure I am I have no private views which can be promoted by the adoption of them. Mrs. Washington thanks you for your kind remembrance of her, and joins me in best respects.

I am, with esteem and regard, etc., etc.

Luzerne to Rayneval, 6 November, 1784. Ex. Tr.

The just, generous, and, I may say, novel conduct which his Majesty has pursued has smoothed all the difficulties which I had foreseen. It has been easy for me to cause his character to be respected, and himself personally to be cherished, since his benefactions and services exceeded the expectations and the demands of his allies. The independence of the United States is the work of the king; this is an established truth which the Americans do not seek to dissimulate, and it is, perhaps, the most memorable event which can honor the history of a nation or a reign. Its nature is indeed such that time, which diminishes the lustre of remarkable deeds in proportion as they grow old, ought continually to add to this a new importance. The population, agriculture, and commerce of the thirteen states will increase in a proportion of which Europe furnishes no examples, and of which it is difficult to form an idea.

This grand revolution will not be limited to the countries made free;

but, by a happy circumstance, independence given to this continent can but have happy consequences for humanity, even though the effects of the revolution should extend to other countries. Other parts of the world must insensibly participate in the advantages of this. Here is seen on a grand scale an experience of all the advantages which accompany tolerance and liberty.

Here too will be seen that if democracies are most fit to assure the individual liberty of each citizen, they are still less favorable to the arts which embellish life and contribute to the happiness of society; that they are deprived of the energy and activity which the situation of France makes necessary for its preservation and for its prosperity. While on the one side princes will be led to adopt principles of moderation and tolerance by the example of their happy effects, their subjects will be convinced that order and regularity, which assure tranquillity at home, energy and vigor which command respect abroad, are found united only in a well-ordered monarchy.

George Clinton to James Monroe, New York, 7 November, 1784.

DEAR SIR: I was on Long Island when your letter of the twenty-eighth ultimo was left at my house, which prevented my receiving it until yesterday. Previous to this I was informed that the commissioners had left this state without meeting with the difficulties you apprehended, so that any interference of mine became unnecessary, and I was relieved from determining on a point of no small degree of delicacy. I do not wish to animadvert on the general tenor of the conduct of those gentlemen in the execution of the business committed to them. This, I presume, must become a matter of public discussion; but as far as it respects myself, I consider it as having been so illiberal and ungenerous that I should not have been without apprehension that my interposition even to serve them might have been ascribed to unworthy motives.

I beg you at the same time to be assured that I esteem your letter as a singular favor, being persuaded it was dictated by a regard to the public good.

Thomas Jefferson to James Monroe, Paris, 11 November, 1784. Ex.

There is here some person, a Frenchman from Philadelphia (perhaps Perée), who has drawn up a visionary scheme of a settlement of French emigrants, five hundred in number, on the Ohio. He supposes congress, flattered by the prospect of such an addition to our numbers, will give them four hundred thousand acres of land, and permit them to continue French subjects. My opinion has been asked, and I have given it: that congress will make bargains with nobody; that they will lay down general rules to which all applicants must conform themselves by applying to the proper offices and not perplexing congress with their visions; that they are sufficiently assured that the land office will absorb all their certificates of public debt, beyond which they have no object but to provide that the new governments shall admit an easy and firm union with the old; and that, therefore, I did not think they would encourage a settlement in so large a body of strangers whose language, manners, and principles were so heterogeneous to ours.

We have taken some pains to find out the sums which the nations of Europe give to the Barbary states to purchase their peace. They will not tell this; yet from some glimmerings it appears to be very considerable; and I do expect that they would tax us at one, two, or perhaps three hundred thousand dollars a year. Surely our people will not give this. Would it not be better to offer them an equal treaty? If they refuse, why not go to war with them? Spain, Portugal, Naples, and Venice are now at war with them; every part of the Mediterranean, therefore, would offer us friendly ports. We ought to begin a naval power if we mean to carry on our own commerce. Can we begin it on a more honorable occasion, or with a weaker foe? I am of opinion Paul Jones, with half a dozen frigates, would totally destroy their commerce; not by attempting bombardments, as the Mediterranean states do, wherein they act against the whole Barbary force brought to a point, but by constant cruising and cutting them to pieces by piecemeal.

Jefferson to Madison, Paris, 11 November, 1784.

I am obliged to you for your information as to the prospects of the present year in our farms; it is a great satisfaction to know it, and yet it is a circumstance which few correspondents think worthy of mention. I am also much indebted for your very full observations on the navigation of the Mississippi. I had thought on the subject, and sketched the anatomy of a memorial on it, which will be much aided by your communications. You mention that my name is used by some speculators in western land jobbing, as if they were acting for me as well as for themselves. About the year 1776 or 1777 I consented to join Mr. Harvey and some others in an application for lands there; which scheme, however, I believe he dropped on the threshold, for I never after heard one syllable on the subject. In 1782 I joined some gentlemen in a project to obtain some lands in the western part of North Carolina, but in the winter of 1782-'83, while I was in expectation of going to Europe, and that the title to western lands might possibly come under the discussion of the ministers, I withdrew myself from this company. I am further assured that the members never prosecuted their views. These were the only occasions in which I ever took a single step for the acquisition of western lands, and in these I retracted at the threshold. I can with truth, therefore, declare to you, and wish you to repeat it on every proper occasion, that no person on earth is authorized to place my name in any adventure for lands on the western waters; that I am not engaged in any one speculation for that purpose at present, and never was engaged in any but the two before mentioned.

I am one of eight children to whom my father left his share in the Loyal company, whose interests, however, I never espoused, and they have long since received their quietus. Excepting these, I never was, nor am now, interested in one foot of land on earth off the waters of James river.

I shall subjoin the few books I have ventured to buy for you. I have been induced to do it by the combined circumstances of their utility and cheapness. I wish I had a catalogue of the books you would be willing to buy, because they are often to be met with on stalls very cheap, and I would get them as occasion should arise. The subscription for the Encyclopedia is still open. Whenever an opportunity offers of sending you what is published of that work (37 vols.), I shall subscribe for you and send it with the other books purchased for you. Whatever money I may lay out for you here in books, or in anything else which you may desire, may be replaced crown for crown (without bewildering ourselves in the exchange) in Virginia by making payments. Colonel Le Maire, whom you know, is the bearer of this; he comes to Virginia to obtain the two thousand acres of land given him for his services in procuring us arras, and what else he may be entitled to as having been an officer in our service; above all things, he wishes to obtain the Cincinnatus eagle, because it will procure him here the order of St. Louis, and of course a pension for life of one thousand livres; he is so extremely poor that another friend and myself furnish him money for his whole expenses from here to Virginia. There I am in hopes the hospitality of the country will be a resource for him till he can convert a part of his lands advantageously into money; but as he will want some small matter of money, if it should be convenient for you to furnish him with as much as ten guineas from time to time on my account, I will invest that sum in books or anything else you may want here by way of payment. He is honest and grateful, and you may be assured that no aid that you can give him in the forward-ing his claims will be misplaced.

The lamp of war is kindled here. England, I think, will remain neuter. Their hostility toward us has attained an incredible height. Notwithstanding the daily proofs of this, they expect to keep our trade and cabotage to themselves by the virtue of their proclamation. They have no idea that we can so far act in concert as to establish retaliating measures. Their Irish affairs will puzzle them extremely.

Monroe to Madison, Trenton, 15 November, 1784.

At Fort Stanwix you were necessarily acquainted with the variance which had taken place between the Indian Commissioners of the United States and those of New York. The land held by these Indians having never been ceded either by New York or Massachusetts, belongs not to the United States. The only point, then, in which New York can be reprehensible is, for preceding by a particular the general treaty. Will it not be most expedient in the present state of our affairs to form no decision thereon? I know no advantages to be derived from one. The variance which took place between the members of the committee of the states, which terminated in their abrupt dissolution by a secession on the part of some members, is also an affair which may come before us. But had we not also better keep this affair out of sight, and, while we lament they could not in that instance be calm and temperate, prevail on them if possible to be so in future? But the more interesting object is the variance between us and Great Britain, Indeed, the former derive their consequence principally from the weight they may have in forming her conduct with respect to us. If they are hastily disposed, these circumstances will tend to give them confidence. My letter to Governor Harrison gave you what had taken place in Canada. I am strongly impressed with the hostile disposition of that court toward us. Not only what I saw, but the information of all the American gentlemen lately from Great Britain confirm it, and particularly one of Maryland, one of Pennsylvania, and Mr. Laurens, who is now with us. The former two have lately returned to the continent. The minister whom we may order to that court to obtain an answer upon this head and cultivate its good wishes toward us will, we trust, inform us by the spring that the west posts will be given up, and the troops whom we may raise for that purpose will, of course, be applied to the garrisoning of them. Many of the west posts I have seen, and think twelve hundred the smallest number we should think of. But yet we have no congress, nor is the prospect better than when I wrote you last. All my associates are here except Grayson. I beg of you to write me weekly, and give me your opinion upon these and every other subject which you think worthy of attention. A motion will certainly be made, as soon as we have a congress, for its removal hence. To which shall we give the preference. New York or Philadelphia? We know not whom we shall have for president of congress. The rule heretofore adopted in the election of president will, I think, be deviated from; if this should be the case, it is not improbable Richard H. Lee may be elected.

Marhois to Rayneval, 17 November, 1784. Ex.

The fertility of the lands which border near the Mississippi will infallibly attract numerous colonists, and if they wish to penetrate to the Spanish colonies, or force the passage of the river to the Gulf of Mexico, it is not congress which will prevent it.

Marhois to Rayneval, 20 November, 1784.

A seat in congress is not desirable except for those who wish solely to devote themselves to public affairs, and there is scarce any one in that condition. You can judge of the extreme difficulty of having a congress well selected, or even of having a congress at all. The people, scarcely escaped from war, are already losing that public spirit which up to this time made good the want of energy in the government. There is neither congress, nor president, nor minister in any department. All matters, and especially those of finance, fall into a worse confusion than heretofore.

Beverly Randolph to Monroe, Chatsworth, 26 November, 1784. Ex.

MY DEAR MONROE: The only great point that has been discussed since the sitting of the assembly has been a motion for a general asessment upon more contracted grounds than I could ever have expected. The generals on the opposite sides were Henry and Madison. The former advocated with his usual art the establishment of the Christian religion in exclusion of all other denominations. By this I mean that Turks, Jews, and Infidels were to contribute to the support of a religion whose truth they did not acknowledge. Madison displayed great learning and ingenuity, with all the powers of a close reasoner; but was unsuccessful in the event, having a majority of seventeen against him. I am, however, inclined to think that the measure will not be adopted, as no bill has as yet been brought forward. The supporters of this holy system will certainly split whenever they come to enter upon the minute arrangements of the business.

Richard Henry Lee to Madison, 26 November, 1784. Postscript. Ex.

Apropos—it is by many here suggested as a very necessary step for congress to take, the calling on the states to form a convention for the sole purpose of revising the confederation so far as to enable congress to execute with more energy, effect, and vigor, the powers assigned to it than it appears by experience that they can do under the present state of things. It has been observed, Why do not congress recommend the necessary alterations to the states as is proposed in the confederation? The friends to convention answer, It has been already done in some instances, but in vain. It is proposed to let congress go on in the mean time as usual. I shall be glad of your opinion on this point, it being a very important one.

J. F. Mercer to Madison, Trenton, 26 November, 1784. Ex.

DEAR SIR: The gentlemen from the eastward have at length made their appearance, and I expect in a day or two a congress will be once more formed. This commencement, however, has discovered so great a relaxation in the confederal springs that I doubt the machine will not be long kept in motion unless great and effectual repairs be made. For my part, I have no hopes but in a convocation of the states. In this measure I yet see safety. It is the disposition of the people of America to place their confederal government on the most respectable basis, and the patriot fire is not yet extinguished; but I do not know how long it will last. There will be a motion made early in the ensu-ing congress for such a convention.

398   APPENDIX.

Van Berckel to the States General, 27 November, 1784.   Ex.

The delay of the English in evacuating the forts which they held in Canada, and along the river St. Lawrence, is great. It is feared that this conduct, whereby the commerce of this republic suffers considerably, will induce the Americans to adopt serious measures to effect the delivery of these forts, and that a longer postponement may have serious consequences. A difference has also arisen between this republic and the king of Spain, who desires to hinder the Americans from extending their navigation on the Mississippi river. Those who profit by this navigation are not inclined to relinquish it.

The French charge here has received news from his court regarding the measures which that court has made in respect to the trade between the United States and the island Mauritius. The Americans are allowed to proceed thither with their ships, to dispose of their cargoes there to the greatest advantage, or to exchange them for other goods. This measure is the more beneficial since the ships destined to India and China may now unload their cargoes at the islands whenever they find the markets there profitable.

General Greene to Washington, Newport, 2 December, 1784.   Ex.

I have not been at home long enough to learn the present temper of the people of this state. Many begin to be alarmed at the proposition of Connecticut[1] and I can but hope, if congress persist in the plan of finance, it will finally succeed. However, we are such a heterogeneous body that it is difficult to draw conclusions from any general principles which influence human conduct.

John Marshall to James Monroe, Richmond, 2 December, 1784.

DEAR SIR: Yours of the fourteenth of November I have just received. I congratulate you sincerely on your safe return to the Atlantic part of our world. I wish with you that our assembly had never passed those resolutions respecting the British debts which have been so much the subject of reprehension throughout the states. I wish it, because it affords a pretext to the British to retain possession of the forts on the lakes, but much more because I ever considered it as a measure tending to weaken the federal bands, which in my conception are too weak already. We are about, though reluctantly, to correct

---

[1] Connecticut proposed that the consent of twelve states should be sufficient to establish the impost — i. e., without Rhode Island.

the error. Some resolutions have passed a committee of the whole house, and been received by the house, on which a bill is to be brought in removing all impediments in the way of the treaty, and directing the payment of debts by instalments. The resolutions were introduced by your uncle. As the bill at present stands, there are to be seven annual payments, the first to commence in April, 1786. We have as yet done nothing finally. Not a bill of public importance, in which an individual was not particularly interested, has passed. The exclusive privilege given to Rumsey and his assigns to build and navigate his new invented boats is of as much, perhaps more, consequence than any other bill we have passed. We have rejected some which in my conception would have been advantageous to this country. Among these I rank the bill for encouraging intermarriages with the Indians. Our prejudices, however, oppose themselves to our interests, and operate too powerfully for them. The two subjects which now most engross the attention of the legislature are the general assessment and circuit court bills. I am apprehensive they will both be thrown out. When supported by all the oratory and influence of Mr. Henry, the former could scarcely gain admission into the house; and now, when he is about moving in a sphere of less real importance and power, his favorite measure must miscarry. I am sorry the members of council were appointed before your letter recommending Colonel Mercer had reached me. Had I known that that gentleman wished an appointment in the executive, I should certainly not have been unmindful of the debt I contracted with him on a former similar occasion. Mr. Jones supplies the vacancy made by the resignation of Mr. Short, and Mr. Roane and Mr. Selden take the places of our old friend Smith, and of Colonel Christian. I exerted myself, though ineffectually, for Carrington. He was excessively mortified at his disappointment, and the more as he was within one vote of Selden, and as that vote was lost by the carelessness of Colonel Jack Nicholas, who walked out just as we were about to ballot the last time, and did not return till it was too late to admit his ticket. I endeavored, too, to promote the interests of your friend Wilson Nicholas, who is just about to form a matrimonial connection with Miss Smith, of Baltimore; but he was distanced. I showed my father that part of your letter which respects the western country. He says he will render you every service of the kind you mention which is within his power with a great deal of pleasure. He says, though, that Mr. Humphrey Marshall, a cousin and brother of mine, is better acquainted with the lands, and would be better enabled to choose for your advantage than he would. If, however, you wish rather to depend on my father, I presume he may avail himself of the knowledge of his son-in-law. I do not know what to say to your scheme of selling out. If you can execute it, you will have made a very capital sum; if you can retain your lands, you will be poor during life, unless you remove to the western country, but you will have secured for posterity an immense fortune. I should prefer the selling business, and, if you adopt it, I think you have fixed on a very proper price. Adieu. May you be very happy is the wish of your J. Marshall.

Washington to Knox, Mount Vernon, 5 December, 1784. Ex.

DEAR SIR: Apologies are idle things; I will not trouble you with them. To whatever other causes my silence may be attributed, ascribe it not, I beseech you, to a want of friendship, for in this, neither time nor absence can occasion a diminution; and I regret that fortune has placed us in different states and distant climes, where an interchange of sentiments can only be by letter.

I am now endeavoring to stimulate my countrymen to the extension of the inland navigation of the rivers Potomac and James, thereby, of a short land transportation, to connect the western territory by strong commercial bonds with this. I hope I shall succeed, more on account of its political importance than the commercial advantages which would result from it, although the latter is an immense object; for if this country, which will settle faster than any other ever did (and chiefly by foreigners who can have no particular predilection for us), cannot by an easy communication be drawn this way, but are supposed to form commercial intercourses (which lead, we all know, to others) with the Spaniards on their right and rear, or the British on their left, they will become a distant people from us, have different views, different interests, and, instead of adding strength to the union, may, in case of a rupture with either of those powers, be a formidable and dangerous neighbor.

After much time spent (charity directs us to suppose in duly considering the matter), a treaty has at length been held with the six nations at Fort Stanwix; much to the advantage, it is said, of the United States, but to the great disquiet of that of New York; fruitlessly, it is added by some, who assert that the deputies on the part of the Indians were not properly authorized to treat. How true this may be I will not pretend to decide, but certain it is, in my opinion, that there is a kind of fatality attending all our public measures: incon-ceivable delays—particular states counteracting the plans of the United States when submitted to them, opposing each other upon all occasions, torn by internal disputes, or supinely negligent and inattentive to everything which is not local, and self-interests, and very often short-sighted in these, make up our system of conduct. Would to God our own countrymen, who are entrusted with the management of the po-litical machine, could view things by that large and extensive scale upon which it is measured by foreigners and by the statesmen of Eu-rope, who see what we might be, and predict what we shall come to. In fact, our federal government is a name without substance; no state is longer bound by its edicts than it suits present purposes without looking to the consequences. How, then, can we fail in a little time becoming the sport of European politics and the victims of our own folly?

I met the Marquis de La Fayette at Richmond—brought him to this place, conducted him to Annapolis, saw him on the road to Balti-more, and returned.

Monroe to Madison, Trenton, 6 December, 1784.

DEAR SIR: I enclose you a paper which will give you a state of the representation of the states, beside which little else hath taken place worthy your attention, Mr. Jay is here, and will, I understand, ac-cept the office of foreign affairs, upon condition congress will establish themselves at any one place. The conduct of Spain respecting the Mississippi, etc., requires the immediate attention of congress. The affair is before a committee. I think we shall leave this place and either remove to Philadelphia or New York, but to which is uncertain. I am very respectfully yours.

Jefferson to Madison, Paris, 8 December, 1784. Ex.

I thank you very much for the relation of the proceedings of assem-bly. It is the most grateful of all things to get those details when one is so distant from home. I like to see a disposition increasing to replenish the public coffers, and so far approve of the young stamp act; but would it not be better to simplify the system of taxation rather than to spread it over such a variety of subjects, and pass the money through so many new hands? Taxes should be proportioned to what may be annually spared by the individual, but I do not see that the sale of his land is an evidence of his ability to spare. One of my reasons for wishing to centre our commerce at Norfolk was that it might bring to a point the proper subjects of taxation and reduce the army of tax-gatherers almost to a single hand.

I still hope something will be done for Paine. He richly deserves it; and it will give a character of littleness to our state if they suffer themselves to be restrained from the compensation due for his services by the paltry consideration that he opposed our right to the western country. Who was there out of Virginia who did not oppose it? Place this circumstance in one scale, and the effect his writings produced in uniting us in independence in the other, and say which preponderates. Have we gained more by his advocation of independence than we lost by his opposition to our territorial right? pay him the balance only. I look anxiously to the approaching and improving the navigation of the Potomac and Ohio; the actual junction of that Big Beaver and Cuyahoga by a canal; as also that of Albemarle Sound and Elizabeth through the Dismal. These works will spread the field of our commerce westwardly and southwardly beyond anything ever yet done by man.

I once hinted to you the project of seating yourself in the neighborhood of Monticello, and my sanguine wishes made me look on your answer as not absolutely excluding the hope. Monroe is decided in settling there, and is actually engaged in the endeavor to purchase. Short is the same. Would you but make it a "partie quarrée," I should believe that life had still some happiness in store for me. Agreeable society is the first essential in constituting the happiness, and, of course, the value of our existence. And it is a circumstance worthy great attention when we are making first our choice of a residence. Weigh well the value of this against the difference in pecuniary interest, and ask yourself which will add most to the sum of your felicity through life. I think that, weighing them in this balance, your decision will be favorable to all our prayers. Looking back with fondness to the moment when I am again to be fixed in my own country, I view the prospect of this society as inestimable. I find you thought it worth while to pass the last summer in exploring the woods of America, and I think you were right. Do you not think the men and arts of this country would be worth another summer? You can come in April, pass the months of May, June, July, August, and most of September here, and still be back to the commencement of real business in the assembly following, which I would not have you absent from. You shall find with me a room, bed, and plate, if you will do me the favor to become one of the family; as you would be here only for the summer season, I think your outfit of clothes need not cost you more than fifty guineas, and perhaps the attendance on the theatres and public entertainments, with other small expenses, might be half a guinea or three quarters a day. Your passage backward and forward would, I suppose, be sixty or seventy guineas more. Say that the whole would be two hundred guineas. You will for that have purchased the knowledge of another world. I expect Monroe will come in the spring, and return to congress in the fall. If either this object, or the one preceding, for settling you near Monticello, can be at all promoted by the use of the money which the assembly have given me for my share in the revisal, make use of it freely, and be assured it can in no other way be applied so much to my gratification. The return of it may wait your perfect convenience,

Edward Bancroft to Lord Carmarthen, Paris, 8 Dec., 1784. Ex.

MY LORD: The commerce between this country and the United States seems totally suspended, to the great disappointment and dissatisfaction of people here. The Marquis de La Fayette is expected here from America in about three weeks.

The French government is highly dissatisfied with congress for having neglected to provide for paying the interests of the sum borrowed in Holland under the guaranty of France, and some strong representations are transmitted on the subject through the medium of Dr. Franklin as well as of Mr. Marhois,

Your lordship will probably have heard of the separation or dissolution of the committee of the United States, on the pretence that delegates of some of the New England states had been obliged to return home on account of their private affairs. I find, however, that, previous to this separation, a very serious disagreement had arisen between the members from the Northern and those from the Middle and Southern states respecting some plans for funding and providing for the federal debt, which congress had particularly recommended to the attention of the committee during the recess; that General Hand, the delegate of Pennsylvania, had, in a representation to the government of that state, charged the New England delegates with having improper views and designs; that this charge coming to their knowledge, they had insisted upon a formal retraction of it; and that this being refused, they had withdrawn themselves and returned home in resentment, thereby dissolving the only representative of the federal government then existing.

Van Berckel to the States General, Trenton, N. J., 12 Dec., 1784. Ex. Tr.

Congress of the United States, which is at present assembled here, on the second of this month chose as its president Richard Henry Lee, a delegate from the state of Virginia.

The Marquis de La Fayette is also here, and to-morrow he sets out for New York, whence he returns to France by a French man-of-war which has come to receive him. The distinguished proofs of affection with which he has been everywhere received have been extraordinary, and do no little honor to the character of the American nation, which at every opportunity exhibits its gratitude for his services.

Vergennes to Marhois, 14 Dec., 1784, Ex. Tr.

You have done well, sir, in recalling to the recollection of Mr. Morris the pecuniary engagements that congress has to fulfil toward us. "We hope that this superintendent will be faithful to the word which he has given us in relation to the interest to be paid in Holland, and we are persuaded that congress will be as exact in keeping its word as it has been ardent in soliciting the assistance of his Majesty. It appears, sir, that the American confederation has a great tendency toward dissolution. If this dissolution takes place, we shall soon see the Americans delivered up to intestine dissension and to troubles, of which it will be difficult to foresee the consequences. It is hoped that in this regard we have no obligation to fulfil nor interest to care for.

Monroe to Madison, Trenton, 14 Dec., 1184. Ex.

The business of importance is still before committee, or, if reported, not yet acted on. It seems to be the general sense of congress to appoint a minister to the court of London, and to give him instructions upon many subjects, and particularly those which arise in the conduct of both parties under the treaty; but whom they may appoint is uncertain; indeed, I fear that the difficulty of obtaining a vote for any person will obstruct this measure for a length of time. Franklin hath, through Mr. Laurens and the Marquis of Fayette, solicited permission to return home. This will, no doubt, be assented to as soon as taken up. An appointment must, therefore, be made in his place to that court. I think there will be little difficulty in obtaining it for Mr. Jefferson, for the opinion of all the members seems to concur in the propriety of it. The first question will be whether we shall or not add other ministers to those in office and annex them to the courts of London and Madrid, or depend on those for the management of all our business in Europe.

Connecticut hath, I hear, authorized congress to carry into effect the impost, with the assent of twelve states only. She hath also laid a duty of five per cent upon all goods imported from a neighboring state. This affects Rhode Island very sensibly. The question must soon be decided whether this state will accede to this measure or the other states recede from it, for it is said New York and Georgia will join in it.

Have you been able to carry the point in favor of the delivery of such citizens as may be guilty of the offences you describe to the power in whose territory and against whose subjects they are committed? This is certainly in strict conformity to the laws of nations, but, I believe, not to the common practice, except between those with whom particular treaties stipulate it.

Monroe to Jefferson, Trenton, 14 Dec., 1784. Ex.

It was late in November before we formed a congress, but at present we have nine states on the floor, with a member from all the states except Maryland, and in a few days we expect her delegation on. This is a respectable congress, and I am happy to inform you they have hitherto acted with perfect good temper and propriety, not only in the manner of conducting the business, but with a mind comprehensive of the interests of the union as well as an inclination upon the most general and liberal principles to promote it. I really promise great good to the union from this congress.

It seems to be an opinion generally given in to that a minister shall be appointed to the court of Britain; that one shall also be appointed to take the place of Franklin. Who the former will be is altogether uncertain, but I think it beyond a doubt you will be the latter.

Propositions for the arrangement of commerce to be handed to the states, requiring that they invest congress with the power of levying the duties upon imports and exports, are before them. I think recommendations to that effect will pass. A distinction will be made between the revenue and the regulation, the former, unless ceded by the state, to go to the state.

Thomas Stone to Monroe, Annapolis, 15 Dec., 1784.. Ex.

DEAR SIR: From every movement of the British court, I am satisfied their disposition is hostile toward America; and from this and other considerations I am anxious to do everything necessary to give weight and energy to the federal government. But the attention of most men is too much engaged by internal objects which appear near to admit a proper regard to those things which are of infinitely more importance, but appear remote because others are to be affected by them as well as ourselves. This cause, I fear, will keep the continental government weak and unsettled until the several members of the union feel severely for their remissness, and perhaps that which is the only remedy may unfortunately lead to ruin.

I have apprehensions from the temper New York seemed to be in when we were in congress, and from little good-will which some of her neighbors bear her, that their affairs will not be settled without some disturbance to the union. As you understand, and will impartially determine on these subjects, I pray you to attend to them with a watchful eye, and to guard against every measure which may have a tendency to excite civil war in America; for when once begun no bounds can be set to it, and this country, from the want of power in the common head and jealousy of the several parts of the union, is extremely liable to that greatest of all horrors which can befall mankind.

Our friend Gerry will be much uplifted by the approbation of his state to his attempt to deprive congress of the power of raising troops by requisition, and it is not impossible but that this idea, as it flatters the several states, will be adopted by others, and thus a weak and blamable desire of popular applause in members of congress may wrest from the federal government a power essential to the safety of the union. I have been made very uneasy by the conduct of members of congress upon this subject, because I am well satisfied that it will be found that government can neither be protected nor supported without the power, and that its being even questioned by leading men in America will render the exercise of it impracticable.

The proposed alteration of the eighth article of confederation has been unanimously agreed to, in a conference of both houses of our assembly, and I make no doubt will be adopted. A bill is prepared to give congress power over exports and imports agreeably to their recommendation of the thirteenth of April last, which will probably pass with some small amendments. And I think our assembly is well disposed to do everything necessary to give dignity and energy to the continental government; the only difficulty is to draw their attention from state objects to this, which, in my opinion, is much more important.

My best wishes attend you, etc.

Monroe to Madison, Trenton, 18 Dec., 1784. Ex.

R. H. Lee earnestly advocated the appointment of Jefferson to the court of Spain, only, in my opinion, to open those of Great Britain and France to himself and friends, among whom are R. R. Livingston and Arthur Lee. He reprehends highly the opposition the other delegates made to it; talks of the superior urgency of the affairs of Spain to us, etc. Fayette and Marbois assured me that Jefferson had been well received in the court of France, and that it was their wish he should succeed Franklin. R. H. Lee hath hitherto given all the opposition in his power to this appointment, and will continue to do it until opposetion will be vain, which I think will be the case. Arthur Lee is in nomination for the treasury board by Mr. Gerry; Mr. Mercer by a delegate from Georgia. In a late ballot, Osgood had six votes, Mercer five votes, and Arthur Lee two. Virginia votes for Mercer, and seems inclined to suffer Arthur Lee to retire from the public service, in the opinion it will be advantageous to the public.

It is proposed to recommend it to the states to invest congress with the power to regulate the commercial intercourse of the states with other powers, without which it is thought impracticable to comply with our engagements in treaties, or derive any advantage from them as a nation. To regulate the duties upon imports and exports (by which, if wise regulations are adopted, we may take some share in the carrying trade, by giving privileges to our own citizens in the exporttation which may encourage the merchants of the United States to employ natives as navigators, as well as the merchants of other countries to take in partnership those of the states), to enable us further to act in concert in the measures which may be found necessary to counteract the policy of the powers with whom we have not treaties of commerce—propositions to this effect are before a committee. The regulation and revenue are separated from each other; the latter will go to the states, unless conceded to the United States for particular purposes by each particular state. As a citizen, and a lawyer, I am pleased with the regulation taking place in the judicial department.

Samuel Adams to Richard H. Lee, Boston, 23 Dec., 1784.

By God's blessing on the councils and the arms of our country, we are now ranked with nations. May he keep us from exulting beyond measure. Great pains are yet to be taken, and much wisdom is requisite, that we may stand as a nation in the most respectable character. Better it would have been for us to have fallen in our highly famed struggle for our rights, or even to have remained in our ignoble state of bondage, expecting better times, than now to become a contemptble nation. The world has given us an exalted character, and thus have laid on us a heavy tax. They have raised expectations from us! How shall we meet these expectations? They have attributed to us wisdom! How shall we confirm them in their opinion of us?

Does not the true policy, the honor and safety of our country, greatly depend upon a national character, among other things consisting in simplicity and candor in all her public transactions; showing herself in reality friendly to those to whom she professes to be a friend; a constant regard to mutual benefit in commercial treaties, justly suspecting the honesty of those who refuse to deal with her upon equitable principles, and guarding her trade by wise commercial laws; an exact and punctilious fulfilment of obligations on her part to be performed by virtue of all treaties, and an unalterable determination to discharge her national debts with all possible speed?

Horatio Gates to Washington, Richmond, 24 Dec., 1784.

Believe me, sir, were I in health, fit to attend the committee this evening, I would on no account fail to do it; but I feel I must go to bed instead of going to Man's. You are so perfectly master of the business that my assent to your opinions is all I have to say upon the subject; this you may be sure of having whenever that is called for. When a vote must decide, I will get a coach and come at all hazards to Man's.

R. H. Lea to Washington, Trenton, 26 Dec., 1784. Ex.

DEAR SIR: I had the honor to receive your obliging letter of the 14th instant, seven days after its date, and I thank you, sir, for its friendly contents and sensible communications.

Much time hath been taken up in debate upon the permanent and temporary residence of congress, and finally it is determined that the former shall be on the banks of the Delaware, not exceeding eight miles above or below this place, and on either side of the river that may be fixed upon by commissioners to be appointed for the purpose of superintending the federal buildings.

New York is to be the temporary residence, and congress stands now adjourned to meet in that city on the 11th of January next, when I hope that we shall diligently put forward the public business. Spain seems determined to possess the exclusive navigation of the Mississippi, which, with the bickerings that appear already on that quarter, will oblige congress to send an able minister to Madrid. And one also to the court of London, that we may, if possible, negotiate commencing differences before they have proceeded too far. The western posts are withheld, and an encroachment already made on our north-eastern boundary. An ambiguity in the treaty, arising from there being two rivers named St. Croix that empty into Passamaquoddy Bay, has encouraged the British to settle the country between them, thus determining in their own favor the right to an extensive and valuable country. The fact is that the easternmost of these rivers is the true St. Croix, the same name having been of late date only applied to the westernmost of these waters. The very unfriendly commercial principles entertained by the British ministry, and the disputes concerning debts and removed negroes, are points of consequence also, which together form a field for able and ample negotiation.

Richard Henry Lee to Madison, Trenton, 27 Dec., 1784. Ex.

We have such momentous concerns with the courts of Madrid and London that we shall be obliged to send special ministers to each of them, or else a war may be the consequence of neglect. Mr. Madison has been nominated for Spain, and is much approved by the Southern states. The conversation concerning a continental convention has ceased for some time, so that, perhaps, it may not be revived again. The pointed manner in which Spain insists upon the exclusive navigation of the Mississippi renders it of more important consequence to explore and improve the navigation of the waters running through our states.

Washington to Knox, Mount Vernon, 5 Jan., 1785. Ex.

MY DEAR SIR: It is not the letters to my friends which give me trouble or add aught to my perplexity. I receive, them with pleasure, and pay as much attention to them as my avocations will permit. It is references of old matters with which I have nothing to do, applications which oftentimes cannot be complied with, enquiries which would employ the pen of a historian to satisfy, letters of compliment, as unmeaning, perhaps, as they are troublesome, but which must be attended to, and the commonplace business which employ my pen and my time, often disagreeably. Indeed, these, with company, deprive me of exercise, and, unless I can obtain relief, must be productive of disagreeable consequences. I already begin to feel the effect; heavy and painful oppressions of the head, and other disagreeable sensations often trouble me. I am determined, therefore, to employ some person who shall ease me of the drudgery of this business. At any rate, if the whole of it is thereby suspended, I am determined to use exercise. My private concerns also require infinitely more attention than I have given, or can give them under present circumstances. They can no longer be neglected without involving my ruin.

To correspond with those I love is among my highest gratifications, and I persuade myself you will not doubt my sincerity when I assure you I place you among the foremost of this class. Letters of friendship require no study. The communications are easy, and allowances are expected, and made. This is not the case with those which require researches—consideration, recollection, and the devil knows what, to prevent error, and to answer the end for which they are written.

In my last I informed you that I was endeavoring to stimulate my countrymen to the extension of the inland navigation of our rivers; and to the opening of the best and easiest communication for land transportation between them and the western waters. I am just returned from Annapolis, to which place I was requested to go by our assembly (with ray bosom friend, General Gates, who, being at Richmond, contrived to edge himself into the commission) for the purpose of arranging matters and framing a law which should be similar in both states so far as it respected the river Potomac, which separates them. I met the most perfect accordance in that legislature, and the matter is now reported to ours for its concurrence. To open at the public expense the communication with the western territory is a great political work.

Our amiable young friend, the Marquis de La Fayette, could not be otherwise than well pleased with his reception in America. Every testimony of respect, affection, and gratitude has been shown him wherever he went.

David Hartley to Lord Carmarthen, Bath, 9 Jan., 1785. Ex.

No treaty of commerce as yet existing between Great Britain and the American states, all commercial concessions and prohibitions are equally in the power of the respective parties. But I adduce them to show the great object which the American states have in view, viz.: to destroy the operation of all restrictive principles of commerce, which, having been systematically introduced among European nations, have by them been extended beyond the Atlantic to the Americans. This limited and restrictive system of European commerce has, at all times, given great discontent in America, as imposing great restraints upon their national industry and commercial profits. It is therefore now become their great object, as the first limits of their independence, to destroy all those commercial restraints which were formerly imposed upon them by European authority, by introducing general and unlimited freedom in every branch of intercourse.

The second point, which appears to me to be deserving of attention, respecting the immense cession of territory to the United States at the late peace, is a point which will, perhaps in a few years, become an unparalleled phenomenon in the political world. As soon as the national debt of the United States shall be discharged, by the sale of one portion of these lands, we shall then see the confederate republic in a new character—as a landlord or proprietor of lands, either for sale or to let out upon rents. While other nations may be struggling under national debts too enormous to be discharged, either by economy or taxation, and while they may be laboring to raise ordinary and necessary supplies by burdensome impositions upon their own persons and properties, here will be a nation possessed of a new and unheard-of financial organ of stupendous magnitude, and in the progress of time of unmeasured value, thrown into their lap as a fortuitous superfluity, and almost without being sought for. When such an organ of revenue begins to arise in produce and exertion, what public and national uses it may be applicable to, or to what abuses or perversions it may be rendered subservient, is far beyond the reach of probable discussion now. Such discussions would be merely visionary speculations. However, thus far is obvious and highly deserving of our attention, that it cannot fail becoming to the American states a most important instrument.

Marbois to Count Vergennes, Philadelphia, 17 Jan., 1785. Ex.

Here the resolution of congress to reside at New York, in spite of the pressing invitation of the assembly of Pennsylvania, has given much chagrin. On the other hand, at New York the arrival of congress causes lively satisfaction. New York, exhausted of money and ruined by the six years' occupation by the English, hopes that the residence of congress will help to restore its activity and lustre.

Knox to Washington, Boston, 31 Jan., 1785. Ex.

A neglect, in every state, of those principles which lead to union and national greatness—an adoption of local in preference to general measures—appears to actuate the greater part of the state politicians. We are entirely destitute of those traits which should stamp us *One Nation*, and the constitution of congress does not promise any capital alterations for the better. Great measures will not be carried in congress so much by the propriety, utility, and necessity of the thing, but as a matter of compromise for something else, which may be evil itself or have a tendency to evil. This, perhaps, is not so much the fault of the members as a defect of the confederation. Every state considers its representative in congress not so much the legislator of the whole union as its own immediate agent or ambassador, to negotiate and to endeavor to create in congress as great an influence as possible to favor particular views, etc. With a constitution productive of such dispositions, is it possible that the American can ever rival the Roman name?

General Lincoln and myself went to the eastern line of this state and found that the British had made excessive encroachments on our territories. There are three rivers in the bay of Passamaquoddy to which the British have, within twenty years past, with a view to confound the business, given the name of St, Croix. But the ancient St. Croix is the eastern river. The British have settled and built a considerable town called St. Andrews on the middle river, which has always sustained, among the people in that country, the Indian name Scudac. The proper St. Croix and the Scudac are only nine miles distant mouths. They run into the country about sixty miles, and they diverge from each other so much that, although at their mouths they are only nine miles apart, yet at their sources they are one hundred miles distant from each other, and it is from the source the north line to the mountains is to begin. The mountains are distant from the source about eighty or one hundred miles, so the difference to this state is one hundred miles square above the heads of the rivers and the land between the rivers, which must be sixty by fifty miles square. Our legislature have transmitted the report we made on this business to congress and the Governor of Nova Scotia. The matter has been involved designedly by the British in such a manner that it can now be settled only by commissioners mutually appointed for that purpose. I have seen a letter from Mr. John Adams, dated last October, which mentions that the river meant by the treaty of peace was decidedly the river next to St. John's river, westward, and there is plenty of proof that the ancient St. Croix was the next to St. John's. I have been particular, in this narration, that you may know the precise state of this affair, which it is probable will sooner or later occasion much conversation.

Rochambeau to Washington, Paris, 24 Feb., 1785. Ex.

You may believe that since the Marquis de La Fayette's coming back you are the main subject of our conversations. I have been ravished to learn that you was philosophically enjoying of the glory and of the general consideration that the part which you had in the most memorable revolution during eight years has so rightfully deserved to you from all your countrymen and from all the universe.

As soon as the shores of the Ohio will be peopled, that the lands will be covered with harvest, the opening of this water will engage your countrymen to force the barriers that the Spanish lay on their territory to all strange nations. I am very sorry that Mr. Le Jay has not settled this affair before his departure.

My respects, I beseech you, my dear general, to Madame Washington and to all your family. Madame de Rochambeau and the mine give thousand compliments, the most sincere, to you, and take part as much as me to your happiness and to all what can satisfy you.

414   APPENDIX.

Elbridge Gerry to Jefferson, Keio York, 25 Feb., 1785.   Ex.

Mr. Adams is appointed to the court of London, and a report for accepting Dr. Franklin's resignation is before congress, who will probably pass it, and appoint yourself to the court of Versailles. You will certainly have all the New England interest in your favor.

Marhois to Vergennes, New York, 25 Feb., 1785.   Ex.

Besides the public journal, the secretary of congress keeps private minutes of all secret affairs, reports of negotiations, and conferences with foreign ministers. He has also been charged with the custody of all the papers of foreign affairs down to the epoch when Mr. Jay entered upon the functions of that office. He has told me that he had taken advantage of the circumstance to prepare secret historical memoirs of everything which has not been inserted in the published journals; that his work had already more than a thousand pages in folio; and that it would complete the history of the revolution; but that, in thus preserving a great number of facts important as well to the confederation as to the alliance, he had taken measures to prevent them from being published before the death of those who have taken part in these great events.

Mr. Thomson is the oldest servant of congress, and there has been no one more constant in all the revolutions which have agitated this assembly. He is a man wise, uniform, and full of moderation. The confidence of congress in him has no limits; and, although he has not the right to speak in the debates of this assembly, he has often been consulted, because he has been present for the last ten years at everything which took place there, and he can contribute to maintain a uniform system better than the delegates who are continually changing, and who sometimes know nothing of the doings of their predecessors.

Instructions to the Delegates of Massachusetts in, Congress.

[The paper is in the handwriting of Samuel Adams, who is undoubtedly its author. It has no date, but is of 1785, and before March of that year.]

GENTLEMEN: Although the general court have lately instructed you concerning various matters of very great importance to this commonwealth, they cannot finish the business of the year until they have transmitted to you a further instruction which they have long had in contemplation, and which, if their most ardent wish could be obtained, might in its consequences extensively promote the happiness of man.

You are, therefore, hereby instructed and urged to move the United States in congress assembled to take into their deep and most serious consideration whether any measures can by them be used, through their influence with such of the nations in Europe with whom they are connected by treaties of amity or commerce, that national differences may be settled and determined without the necessity of war, in which the world has too long been deluged, to the destruction of human happiness and the disgrace of human reason and government.

If, after the most mature deliberation, it shall appear that no measures can be taken at present on this very interesting subject, it is conceived it would redound much to the honor of the United States, that it was attended to by their great representative in congress, and be ac-cepted as a testimony of gratitude for most signal favors granted to the said states by him who is the almighty and most gracious Father and friend of mankind.

And you are further instructed to move that the foregoing letter of instructions be entered on the journals of congress, if it may be thought proper, that so it may remain for the inspection of the delegates from this commonwealth, if necessary, in any future time.

Jacob Read to Washington, New York, 9 March, 1785.

From the want of a full congress, the great national questions still remain untouched, and will not be attempted till late in the spring, when it is hoped we may assemble the whole force of the union and try if we can act as a nation, which, by the by, I very much doubt, now the common tie of danger is removed.

James Duane to Washington, New York, 10 March, 1785. Ex.

Congress are fixed here for the present, apparently to their satisfaction. The five per cent requisition goes on heavily, and I am very apprehensive of its fate, even in this state, which once took the lead in every federal measure. The Rhode Island and other eastern publications against this grant have made a deep impression in the counties most exposed to their influence. A bill on this interesting subject is under commitment in the senate, and will be brought forward in a few days. It is to be lamented that even there it will meet with warm opposition.

Our legislature, I take it for granted, will in the course of this month pay into the continental treasury $110,000 in specie and

$37,000 in certificates in full of their arrears, which will be a present supply. A bill for this purpose has passed the senate.

William Grayson to Washington, New York, 10 March, 1785.   Ex.

DEAR SIR: Congress are engaged in a plan for opening their land office on the western waters, in recommending a plan for extending their powers in forming commercial treaties, in regulating the post-office, and in making a peace establishment. They have directed a treaty to be formed, if practicable, with the piratical states on the coast of Africa. I expect a minister will be appointed to the court of Spain after the arrival here of Don Diego Gardoqui, and one, I presume, will be appointed to Holland in the room of Mr. Adams, who goes to the court of St. James.

I have the honor to be, with the highest respect, your affectionate friend.

Washington to B. H. Lee, Mount Vernon, 15 March, 1785.   Ex.

The mission of congress will now be called upon to fix a medium price on these lands, and to point out the most advantageous mode of seating them; so as that law and good government may be administered, and the union strengthened and supported thereby. Progressive seating, in my opinion, is the only means by which this can be effected, and, unless in the scale of politics more than one new state is found necessary at this time, the unit, I believe, would be found more pregnant with advantages than the decies;[1] the latter, if I mistake not, will be more advancive of individual interest than the public welfare.

As you will have that untowardness, jealousy, and pride which are characteristic of the Spanish nation to contend with, it is more than probable that Mr. Gardoqui will give congress a good deal of trouble respecting the navigation of the Mississippi river.

To me it should seem that their true policy would lie in making New Orleans a free mart instead of shutting the port. But their ideas of trade are very limited.

---

[1] Washington had two years before proposed he colonization of Ohio with substantially its present boundaries and for the time being of that territory alone. The ordinance of Jefferson had provided for ten territories. Washington here renews to the president of congress, and through him to Grayson and to congress, his recommendation to proceed gradually in organizing territories, and to begin with Ohio alone rather than with the ten states as indirectly required by the terms of the Virginia cession and as proposed by Jefferson. Washington's advice prevailed even before Virginia modified its terms of cession.

LETTERS AND PAPERS. 417

Van Berckel to the States General, New York, 15 March, 1785. Ex.

The post from Philadelphia, which has just arrived, brings thence the news that the general assembly of the state of Pennsylvania has passed an act to issue £150,000 Pennsylvania money—that is, a million of Dutch florins in paper money—and to bring the same into circulation. I regard it as my duty to inform your High Mightinesses as soon as possible, since such must have a great influence on the trade of that state, for should they compel foreigners to receive this paper money in payment for their goods, it is easy to foresee that the commercial connections between that state and Europe will not only diminish, but will virtually be severed.

Motion of Rufus King, Wednesday, 16 March, 1785.

[From papers of old congress. No.31, p. 327. Reports of committees on clothing, commerce, etc., 1778 -'86. The following resolution is in the handwriting of Rufus King, and is endorsed in the handwriting of Charles Thomson: "Motion for preventing slavery in new states, 16 March, 1785. Referred to Mr. King, Mr. Howell, Mr. Ellery."]

A motion was made by Mr. King, seconded by Mr. Ellery, that the following proposition shall be committed:

Resolved, That there shall be neither slavery nor involuntary servitude in any of the states described in the resolve of congress of the twenty-third day of April, A. D. 1784, otherwise than in punishment of crimes whereof the party shall have been personally guilty.

And that this regulation shall be an article of compact, and remain a fundamental principle of the constitutions between the thirteen original states and each of the states described in the said resolve of the twenty-third day of April, 1784.[1]

---

[1] Mr. King no doubt wished to make his proposition as little disquieting to the South as possible ; so he wisely used Jefferson's words, and, as I infer from the circumstances, prepared the South for his motion, which was only a motion of reference. The choice of a committee exclusively of northern men was ominous. The relation of the two propositions to each other will appear best by placing them side by side :

The ordinance proposed by Jefferson, 1 Mar., 17S4. Ex.	A motion made by King, 16 Mar.,1785, that the following proposition he committed:
That after the year 1800 of the Christian aera there shall be neither slavery nor involuntary servitude in any of the said states, otherwise than in punishment of crimes, whereof the party shall have been duly convicted to have been personally guilty.	That there shall be neither slavery or involuntary servitude in any of the states described in the resolve of congress of the twenty-third day of April, a. d. 1784, otherwise than in punishment of crimes whereof the party shall have been personally guilty.
That the preceding articles shall be formed	That this regulation shall be an article of

Report of Rufus King, for the exclusion of slavery from the new states.

[The following report is in the handwriting of Rufus King. It is to be found in Vol. No. 31, p. 329, papers of old congress, and is endorsed in the handwriting of King : "Report of Mr. King's motion for the exclusion of slavery in the new states." And it is further endorsed in the handwriting of Charles Thomson: "Mr. King, Mr. Howell, Mr. Ellery. Entered 6 April, 1785, read. Thursday, 14 April, assigned for consideration."]

The committee, consisting of, etc., to whom was referred a motion from Mr. King for the exclusion of involuntary servitude in the states described in the resolve of congress of the twenty-third day of April, 1784, submit the following resolve:

Resolved, That after the year 1800 of the Christian aera there shall be neither slavery nor involuntary servitude in any of the states described in the resolve of congress of the twenty-third day of April, 1784, otherwise than in punishment of crimes whereof the party shall have been personally guilty; and that this regulation shall be an article of compact, and remain a fundamental principle of the constitutions between the thirteen original states, and each of the states described in the said resolve of congress of the twenty-third day of April, 1784, any implication or construction of the said resolve to the contrary notwithstanding. Provided always that upon the escape of any person into any of the states described in the said resolve of congress of the twenty-third day of April, 1784, from whom labor or service is lawfully claimed in any one of the thirteen original states, such fugitive may be lawfully reclaimed and carried back to the person claiming his labor or service as aforesaid, this resolve not-withstanding.

[A printed copy of this report of King follows on p. 331 of the same Vol. No. 31. It is identical with the foregoing, with the single exception of the substitution of the word "of" for "from" in the phrase "to whom was referred a motion from Mr. King."

into a charter of compact .... and shall stand as fundamentalconstitutions between the thirteen original states and those now newly described.	compact, and remain a fundamental principle of the constitutions between the thirteen original states and each of the states described in the said resolve of the twenty-third day of April, 1784.

Jefferson regarded King's motion of reference of 16 March, 1785, as "the same proposition" as his own of March, 1784. Jefferson, ix. 276. For the suggestion to King by Pickering of the immediate exclusion of slavery from the north-west territory, see Pickering's Pickering, i. 510. The report of King sent to Pickering, ibid., 511.

The printed report, printed exclusively for members of congress, is endorsed in the handwriting of Charles Thomson: "To prevent slavery in the new states; included in substance in the ordinance for a temporary government passed the thirteenth July, 1787."]

Jefferson to Madison, Paris, 18 March, 1785.

Your character of the Marquis de La Fayette is precisely agreeable to the idea I had formed of him. I take him to be of unbounded ambition, but that the means he uses are virtuous. He is returned fraught with affection to America, and disposed to render every possible service.

We hear nothing from England. This circumstance, with the passage of their Newfoundland bill through the house of commons, and the sending a consul to America (which we hear they have done), sufficiently proves a perseverance in the system of managing for us as well as for themselves in their connection with us. The administration of that country are governed by the people, and the people by their own interested wishes, without calculating whether they are just or capable of being effected. Nothing will bring them to reason but physical obstruction, applied to their bodily senses.

"We must show that we are capable of foregoing commerce with them before they will be capable of consenting to an equal commerce. We have all the world besides open to supply us with gewgaws, and all the world to buy our tobacco, for in such an event England must buy it from Amsterdam, L'Orient, or any other place at which we should think proper to deposit it for them. They allow our commodities to be taken from our own ports to the West Indies in their vessels only; let us allow their vessels to take them to no port. The transportation of our own produce is worth £750,000 sterling annually, will employ two hundred thousand tonnage of ships, and twelve thousand seamen constantly. It will be no misfortune that Great Britain obliges us to exclude her from a participation in this business. Our own shipping will grow fast under the exclusion, and till it is equal to the object the Dutch will supply us. The commerce with the English West Indies is valuable, and would be worth a sacrifice to us; but the commerce with the British dominions in Europe is a losing one, and deserves no sacrifice. Our tobacco they must have, from whatever place we make its deposit, because they can get no other whose quality so well suits the habits of their people. It is not a commodity like wheat, which will not bear a double voyage; were it so, the privilege of carrying it directly to England might be worth something. I know nothing which would act more powerfully as a sumptuary law with our people than an inhibition of commerce with England. They are habituated to the luxuries of that country, and will have them while they can get them. They are unacquainted with those of other countries, and, therefore, will not very soon bring them so far into fashion as that it shall be thought disreputable not to have them in one's house or on their table.

It is to be considered how far an exemption of Ireland from this inhibition would embarrass the councils of England on the one hand, and defeat the regulation itself on the other. I rather believe it would do more harm in the latter way than good in the former; in fact, a heavy aristocracy and corruption are two bridles in the mouths of the Irish, which will prevent them from making any effectual efforts against their masters.

Late letters tell us you are nominated for the court of Spain. I need not tell you how much I shall be pleased with such an event, yet it has its displeasing sides also. I want you in the Virginia assembly, and also in congress; yet we cannot have you everywhere; we must therefore be contented to have you present where you choose.

Adieu. Yours affectionately.

Marhois to Vergennes, Philadelphia, 27 March, 1785. Ex.

The enclosed packet for the priest, Doria Pamphili, has been addressed to me, and particularly recommended by Mr. Carroll, the superior of the missions. The holy see could not make a choice more agreeable to Catholics of the United States; and if circumstances permit his elevation to the episcopacy, I doubt not the general satisfaction. But all Catholics whose zeal is moderated by prudence desire that this measure should not be taken until the people shall have been sufficiently prepared for it. Nothing would be more easy for the ill-disposed than to spread an alarm touching the spiritual and temporal authority of the pope. Catholics have had seats in congress, and several members of the assembly of Maryland in like manner profess our religion; but it is only on the supposition that they are not dependent on any foreign power. The articles of the confederation do not permit any one of the officers of the United States to receive gifts, titles, or employments of any kind whatever from a king, prince, or foreign power. Republican jealousy would infallibly apply this prohibition to ecclesiastical officers; and without particular address in the management of this affair, religion would lose more than it would gain by the nomination of a bishop. Thus the holy see is sure to extend its progress in relaxing its jurisdiction as much as the good of the faith can permit; and a different practice would not fail to stop its own propagation and to augment the other sects on which the civil honors and authorities will devolve to the exclusion of the Catholics. The Anglicans themselves will prepare the bill for the introduction of the episcopate. They have never wished to receive a bishop before the revolution; but to-day they feel all the difficulties of having their ministers ordained in England. The laws accord to them the free exercise of their religion, and, consequently, everything which is necessary to this free exercise. They infer from it they have the right to have bishops; and they probably will soon have them. Then, my lord, it will appear odious to refuse the same advantage to the Catholics; but till then, I believe it is for the advantage of religion not to precipitate anything. His Holiness could nevertheless nominate in advance an apostolic vicar; and, when circumstances should be entirely favorable, raise him to the episcopacy. I cannot say if the choice ought to emanate purely and simply from the holy father, or if the churches of the different states ought to propose a candidate. This last form is undoubtedly most analogous to the spirit of this people. But the Catholics are not here united under a common chief; those of one state have no relation with those of another, and I do not see how they could have one at an election. It is one motive the more to raise by degrees to the episcopacy a person who has been for some time the chief, and whose nomination would, therefore, astonish no one. The first choice once made, it will be less difficult to organize our church than in its actual condition. The number of Catholics in the United States merits, in fact, the attention the holy see gives to it. There are in New England about 600; New York and New Jersey, 1,700; Pennsylvania and Delaware, 7,700; Maryland, freemen 12,000, slaves 8,000—20,000; in the states of the South, 2,500; at the Illinois, at Kaskaskia, and several other establishments purely French, on the Mississippi, 12,000: total, 44,500.

The Catholics of New York have no priest, but an Irish almoner from the ships of his Majesty, who has no permission to be absent from his convent. He has made a supposititious one which I have recognized to be false; yet he has obtained powers from Mr. Carroll, who was not informed of these circumstances. For the rest, the establishment of the chapel of the legation of New York gives to the Catholics of this city all the resources that they can desire.

Henry Hamilton to Lord Sydney, Quebec, 9 April, 1785. Ex.

MY LORD: The following particulars I have from Mr. Pond, which, perhaps, your lordship may think worth attention:

Two young men, Americans, educated at New Haven College (one of them named Woodroffe), were on board Captain Cook's ship when he prosecuted his discoveries on the western coast of North America; they had been seen at New York, and are actually gone to Boston to attend to the prosecution of an undertaking on foot for building two vessels designed for carrying on discoveries in those regions.

Mr. Pond assures me that seven thousand pounds are subscribed by but a small number of people in that country to support the expense of further discoveries.

Washington to James Duane, Mount Vernon, 10 April, 1785. Ex.

DEAR SIR: Enclosed you have my answer to the acts of your corporation, which I pray you to present.

I thank you for the arguments and judgment of the mayor's court of the city of New York in the cause between Elizabeth Rutgers and Joshua Waddington. I have read them with all the attention I could give the subject, and though I pretend not to be a competent judge of the law of nations, or the principle and policy of the statute upon which the action was founded, yet I must confess that reason seems very much in favor of the opinion given by the court, and my judgment yields a hearty assent to it.

It is painful to hear that a state which used to be foremost in acts of liberality, and its exertion to establish our federal system upon a broad bottom and solid ground, is contracting her ideas, and pointing them to local and independent measures; which, if persevered in, must sap the constitution of these states (already too weak), destroy our national character, and render us as contemptible in the eyes of Europe as we have it in our power to be respectable. It should seem as if the impost of five per cent would never take place; for no sooner does an obstinate state begin to relent, and adopt the recommendation of congress, but some other runs restive; as if there was a combination among them to defeat the measure.

The nations of Europe are rife for slavery. A thirst after riches, a promptitude to luxury, and a sinking into venality with their concomitants, untune them for manly exertions and virtuous sacrifices.

James Monroe to Thomas Jefferson, New York, 12 April, 1785. Ex.

I enclose you the report of a committee in favor of a change of the first paragraph of the ninth of the articles of the confederation, for the purpose of investing congress with almost the entire regulation of the commerce of the union, in exclusion of the particular states. I am inclined" to think it will be best also to postpone this for the present. Its adoption must depend on the several legislatures; and to carry it with them, the preferable way, perhaps, may be to let it stand as it now is. It hath been brought so far without a prejudice against it. If carried farther here, prejudices will take place; at least, I fear so; and those who oppose it here will in their states. The way, then, will be to present it to them in its present state, which may be effected by obtaining the permission of congress for each delegation to take copies for that purpose. If this should be its course, I shall have time for your answer and opinion on it.

I doubt much the advantage of forming treaties for the present with any of the powers with which you are authorized to treat (the piratical states excepted), for what advantages can we give here in consideration of advantages, or rather in consideration that they remove some of the restraints which now exist, which they do not at present possess, or possessing, that we can deprive them of? The more I investigate this subject, the more I am confirmed in this opinion; but all these embarrassments in the restrictions laid upon us by other powers will, I am persuaded, have a good effect; they will operate more powerfully than the utmost force of argument could do for the strengthening our government.

It is agreed to raise seven hundred men for purposes of guarding the public stores and giving security to the frontier settlements of the states. At Annapolis Mr. Gerry protested against the right of congress to require men in time of peace. His conduct was approved by his state, and the delegation instructed to oppose and protest upon all occasions against the exercise of the power. It is agreed by that requisition men cannot be raised upon a few states or less than the whole, but under particular circumstances of some, and then under a particular modification. It was thought in this instance necessary to have them in the field in a short time to protect the surveyors of the land, and as this consideration superseded the propriety of a requisition, on the whole it was agreed to recommend it to the states most contiguous to raise them.

I shall transmit you the journals of congress as far as they are printed; they will give you at least the resolutions which determine the erection of buildings at the falls of the Delaware, and our intermediate residence here; our dependence for their location at Georgetown had been on the Southern states. As soon as congress convened we found they had given it up; all further opposition we therefore considered useless. The conduct of our delegation at Trenton was founded upon an acquiescence with the voice of the majority of the union. We acted together, and voted unanimously upon every point respecting these measures. Grayson only was absent. I would wish no more movements until we take our final position.

I thank you for subscribing for me for the Encyclopedia; I have not at present the money, but will send it as soon as possible. I only wish it were in my power to join you this summer, but it is impossible. The next, I have it in contemplation, and shall then be under no necessity to hurry myself so quickly back; and I would wish to remain in Europe, if I ever visit it, at least twelve months.

I think congress should sit until our affairs with every foreign power were finally and most amicably settled, and until the commerce of the union is properly regulated; the confederacy might then stand secure, and not be exposed to injury or danger.

A Mr. Carbonneau, from the Kaskaskias, petitioned congress to take the people under their protection. A committee hath reported, which is so far adopted, that a commissioner be appointed to repair thither, instructed, etc. Mr. A. Lee is in nomination. The three commissioners of the treasury elected at Annapolis declined serving; in consequence of which, Gervais, Osgood, and Walter Livingston were elected. Gervais hath declined, and Mr. A. Lee, who hath upon every occasion been a candidate, is again in nomination. Mercer and himself were in nomination at Trenton, and we gave the former the preference. The fact is, we can get none better than Mr. Lee, and shall upon this occasion vote for him.

P. S. The alteration which this report proposes in the whole system of our government will be great; it is, in fact, a radical change of it. I beg of you to write your sentiments fully on it. If it is carried, it can only be by thorough investigation, and a conviction carried to the minds of every citizen that it is right; the slower it moves on, therefore, in my opinion, the better.

William Grayson to Washington, New York, 15 April, 1785.

DEAR SIR: I did myself the honor of writing to you by post the tenth of March last, in answer to your favor of the twenty-second of January; and I hope my letter has before this got safe to hand.

On my being appointed one of the committee for draughting the ordinance for ascertaining the mode of disposing of lands in the western territory, the president was kind enough to furnish me with an extract of your letter[1] to him on the subject of the back country, which now induces me to conclude it will be agreeable to you to be informed of the further progress of this important business. The ordinance was reported to congress three days ago, and ordered to be printed, and I now take the earliest opportunity of sending you a copy. The idea of a sale by public vendue, in such large quantities, appears at first view eccentric and objectionable. I shall therefore mention to you the reasons which those who are advocates for the measure offer in its support. They say this cannot be avoided without affording an undue advantage to those whose contiguity to the territory has given them an opportunity of investigating the qualities of the land; that there certainly must be a difference in the value of the lands in different parts of the country, and that this difference cannot be ascertained without an actual survey in the first instance, and a sale by competition in the next.

That with respect to the quantity of land offered for sale in a township, it will not have the effect of injuring the poorer class of people, or of establishing monopolies in speculators and engrossers; that experience is directly against the inference, for that the Eastern states, where lands are more equally divided than in any other part of the continent, were generally settled in that manner; that the idea of a township, with the temptation of a support for religion and education, holds forth an inducement for neighborhoods of the same religious sentiments to confederate for the purpose of purchasing and settling together; that the southern mode would defeat this end by introduceing the idea of indiscriminate locations and settlements, which would have a tendency to destroy all those inducements to emigration which

[1] Washington to R. H. Lee, 15 March, 1785.

are derived from friendships, religion, and relative connections; that the same consequence would result from sales in small quantities under the present plan.

That the advantages of an equal representation—the effect of laying off the country in this manner; the exemption from controversy on account of bounds to the latest ages; the fertility of the lands; the facilities of communication with the Atlantic through a variety of channels, as also with the British and Spaniards; the fur and peltry trade, and the right of forming free governments for themselves—must solicit emigrants from all parts of the world, and ensure a settlement of the country in the most rapid manner; that speculators and engrossers, if they purchase the lands in the first instance, cannot long retain them, on account of the high price they will be obliged to give, and the consequent loss of interest while remaining in their hands uncultivated.

That if they, however, should make money by engrossing, the great design of the land office is answered, which is revenue; and that this cannot affect any but European emigrants, or those who were not at hand to purchase in the first instance; that if it is an evil, it will cure itself, which has been the case in Lincoln county, Virginia, where the lands were first in the hands of monopolists, but who were forced to 23art with them from a regard to the general defence

That the expense and delay would be too great to divide the territory into fractional parts by actual surveys; and if this is not done, sales at public vendue cannot be made, as without a previous knowledge of the quality of the lands, no comparative estimate can be formed between different undivided moieties.

That the offering a small number of townships for sale at a time is an answer to the objection on account of delay, and at the same time it prevents the price from being diminished, on account of the markets being overstocked.

That the present plan excludes all the formalities of warrants, entries, locations, returns, and caveats, as the first and last process is a deed.

That it supersedes the necessity of courts for the determination of disputes, as well as that of creating new officers for carrying the plan into execution; that the mode of laying out the same in squares is attended with the least possible expense, there being only two sides of the square to run in almost all cases; that the expense will be repaid to the continent in a tenfold ratio, by preventing fraud in the surveyors.

That the drawing for the townships, and sending them on to the different states, is conformable to the principles of the government, one state having an equal right to the best lands at its market with the other; as also of disposing of its public securities in that way.

That if the country is to be settled out of the bowels of the Atlantic states, it is but fair the idea of each state's contributing its proportion of emigrants should be countenanced by measures operating for that purpose.

That if the plan should be found by experience to be wrong, it can easily be altered by reducing the quantities and multiplying the surveys.

These were the principal reasonings on the committee in favor of the measure, and on which it would give me great satisfaction to have your sentiments, as it involves consequences of the most extensive nature, and is still liable to be rejected altogether by congress, or to be so altered as to clear it of the exceptional parts. Perhaps the present draught might have been less objectionable if we had all have had the same views. Some gentlemen looked upon it as a matter of revenue only, and that it was true policy to get the money without parting with inhabitants to populate the country, and thereby prevent the lands in the original states from depreciating. Others (I think) were afraid of an interference with the lands now at market in the individual states. Part of the eastern gentlemen wish to have the lands sold in such a manner as to suit their own people who may choose to emigrate, of which I believe there will be great numbers, particularly from Connecticut. But others are apprehensive of the consequences which may result from the new states taking their position in the confederacy. They, perhaps, wish that this event may be delayed as long as possible. Seven hundred men are agreed on, in congress, to be raised for the purpose of protecting the settlers on the western frontiers and preventing unwarrantable intrusions on the public lands, and for guarding the public stores.

I must now apologize to you for the length of this letter. The subject appeared to me of the greatest consequence, and I was desirous you might have the fullest information thereon. As the communicating a report of a committee while under the deliberation of congress is against rule, I shall thank you to retain the possession of it yourself.

I have the honor to be, with the highest respect, your affectionate friend, etc.

Extracts of Letters from New York (enclosed by Chief Justice Smith to Lord Sydney), 18 April, 1785.

The legislature have refused to give the five per cent duty to congress. This has raised resentment from that quarter.

The grand jury in Georgia have presented their legislature. The eastern parts of Massachusetts have set up an independency in that quarter. New Jersey and Connecticut solicit emigration from this state. Pennsylvania is nearly equally divided upon the subject of the constitution; and the late attempt of their legislature to take away the charter to the bank, for refusing to give a credit to their last paper emission, has so shaken both public and private credit that an almost total stop is put to all traffic, foreign and domestic; and the bank have refused to discount. With us there is no trade. The tender laws are in daily practice, and people pay their debts with about four shillings in the pound. Last week Richard Morris, our chief justice, recovered against General Tryon, on the trespass act, for damage to his farm during the war, £5,000. The whole farm was never worth one third of the money. Our prospects are dark. I fear we have not seen the worst of our troubles.

New York, 1 May, 1785. — On Tuesday our legislature broke up without effecting anything for the loyalists, and the late election leaves no reason to expect a change of measures, as men of the most violent tempers are returned—William Duer, Malcolm, Sears, etc., etc. The moderate are turned out; of five thousand voters, but five hundred voted in this city. In the counties there are changes for the better, but not enough for essential alterations. God knows what will be the consequence.

Baron Montesquieu to Washington, Paris, 25 April, 1785. Ex.

Your Excellency's remembering me is that which flatters me the most. I shall never forget the favors which you have heaped upon me. I shall always recall with new pleasure the time that I passed near the greatest and the most virtuous man of his age. Let not your Excellency take this for flattery. It is nothing but the true expression of my heart. I have not renounced the hope of one day visiting America, and of going once more to admire its liberator.

At the end of the month of May I shall leave for Metz, where my regiment is stationed. I have already drank very often with the officers who dined with me to the health of your Excellency. All those who have been under your orders in America would with pleasure intoxicate themselves with drinking this toast. We all love you, and our respect for you is not less than our love. Such is the effect of virtue; it has an empire over all men, however corrupted they may be.

Extract of a Letter dated New York, 14 March, 1785. Sent to Lord Sydney by Ch. J. Smith, 25 April.—Though our legislature have been sitting six weeks, no step has yet been taken to repeal any of the hostile laws passed during the war, or since the peace. There will be no change of measure until there is a change of men; and this cannot happen until our eviction laws, which exclude many thousand citizens from voting, are repealed. Those in power, interested in the forfeited estates, have their fears that they will be restored, and the rather since very few of the moderate whigs and none of the loyalists became purchasers of such property, and reprobate the titles.

Those who rule affect to believe the state in a flourishing condition, and because they are adding house to house and farm to farm, treat with disdain the petitions of the distressed.

Thomas Jefferson to James Madison, London, 25 April, 1785. Ex.

DEAR SIR: Some of the objects of the joint commissions with which we were honored by congress called me to this place about six weeks ago. Tomorrow I set out on my return to Paris. With this nation, nothing is done; and it is now decided that they intended to do nothing with us. The king is against a change of measures; his ministers are against it, some from principle, others from attachments to their places; and the merchants and people are against it. They sufficiently value our commerce, but they are quite persuaded they shall enjoy it on their own terms. This political speculation fosters the warmest feeling of the king's heart—that is, his hatred to us. If ever he should be forced to make any terms with us, it will be by events which he does not foresee. He takes no pains at present to hide his aversion. Our commission expiring in a fortnight, there is an end of all further attempts on our part to arrange matters between the two countries.

The treaty of peace being yet unexecuted, it remains that each party conduct themselves as the combined considerations of justice and of caution require. We have had conversations on the subject of our debts with the chairman of the committee of American merchants here. He was anxious for arrangements. He was sensible that it was for the interest of the creditor as well as debtor to allow time for the payment of the debts due to this country, and did not seem to think the time taken by Virginia was more than enough; but we could not help agreeing with him, that the courts should be open to them immediately, judgments recoverable, the executions to be divided into so many equal and annual parts as will admit the whole to be paid by the year 1790, and that the payments should be in money, and not in anything else. If our law is not already on this footing, I wish extremely it were put on it. When we proceeded to discuss the sum which should be paid, we concurred in thinking that the principal and interest preceding and subsequent to the war should be paid. As to interest during the war, the chairman thought it justly demandable. We thought otherwise; I need not recapitulate to you the topics of argument on each side. He said the renunciation of this interest was a bitter pill which they could not swallow. Perhaps he would have agreed to say nothing about it, not expecting to receive it in most cases, yet willing to take the chance of it, where debtors or juries should happen to be favorably disposed. We should have insisted on an express declaration that this interest should not be demandable. These conferences were intended as preparatory to authoritative propositions; but the minister not condescending to meet us at all on the subject, they ended in nothing. I think the merchants here do not expect to recover interest during the war in general, though they are of opinion they are entitled to it.

Washington to William Grayson, Mount Vernon, 25 April, 1785.

DEAR SIR: I will not let your favor of the fifteenth, for which I thank you, go unacknowledged, though it is not in my power to give it the consideration I wish, to comply with the request you have made, being upon the eve of a journey to Richmond to a meeting of the Dismal Swamp Company, which by my own appointment is to take place on Monday next; and into that part of the country I am hurried by an express which is just arrived with the account of the deaths of the mother and brother of Mrs. Washington, in the last of whose hands (Mr. B. Dandridge) the embarrassed affairs of Mr. Custis had been placed, and call for immediate attention.

To be candid, I have had scarce time to give the report of the committee, which you did me the honor to send me, a reading, much less to consider the force and tendency of it. If experience has proven that the most advantageous way of disposing of land is by whole townships, there is no arguing against facts. Therefore, if I had had time, I should have said nothing on that head; but from the cursory reading I have given it, it strikes me that, by suffering each state to dispose of a proportionate part of the whole in the state, there may be state jobbing; in other words, that the citizens of each state may be favored at the expense of the union, while a reference of these matters to them has, in my opinion, a tendency to set up separate interests and to promote the independence of individual states upon the downfall of the federal government, which, in my opinion, is already too feeble, much too humiliated and tottering to be supported without props.

It is scarcely to be imagined that any man, or society of men, who may incline to possess a township, would make the purchase without viewing the land in person, or by an agent. Wherein, then, lies the great advantage of having the sale in each state, and by state officers? For, from the same parity of reasoning, there should be different places in each state for the accommodation of its citizens. Would not all the ostensible purposes be fully answered by sufficient promulgation in each state of the time and place of sale, to be holden at the nearest convenient place to the land, or at the seat of congress? Is it not highly probable that those who may incline to emigrate, or their agents, would attend at such time and place? And (there being no fixed prices for the land) would not the high or low sale of it depend upon the number of purchasers, and the competition occasioned thereby? and are not these more likely to be greater at one time and place than at thirteen? One place might draw the world to it if proper notice be given; but foreigners would scarcely know what to do with thirteen—to which or when to go to them.

These are first thoughts, perhaps incongruous ones, and such as I myself might reprobate upon more mature consideration. At present, however, I am impressed with them, and (under the rose) a penetrating eye and close observation will discover, through various disguises, a disinclination to add new states to the confederation westward of us; which must be the inevitable consequence of emigration to, and the population of, that territory. And as to restraining the citizens of the Atlantic states from transplanting themselves to that soil, when prompted thereto by interest or inclination—you might as well attempt, while our governments are free, to prevent the reflux of the tide when you had got it into your rivers.

As the report of the committee goes into minutiae, it is not minute enough, if I read it aright. It provides for the irregular lines, and parts of townships, occasioned by the interference with the Indian boundaries, but not for its interference with Lake Erie, the western boundary of Pennsylvania (if it is governed by the meanders of the Delaware), or the Ohio river, which separates the ceded lands from Virginia — all of which involve the same consequences. I thank you for the sentiments and information given me in your letter of the tenth of March respecting the Potomac navigation. My present determination is to hold the shares which this state has been pleased to present me, in trust for the use and benefit of it. This will subserve the plan, increase the public revenue, and not interfere with that line of conduct I had prescribed myself.

Van Berckel to the States General, 27 April, 1785. Ex.

The latest news from Boston which have arrived here announce that the merchants of that place are extremely dissatisfied; that a number of English factors and agents settling there have made a sort of monopoly of all the goods imported from England, whereby the trade of that town must fall entirely into English hands. The merchants have resolved to petition congress to adopt such measures regarding the trade of the United States as shall be advantageous; that, until the necessary resolutions shall be taken by congress, the merchants resolve solemnly to have no direct or indirect commercial relations with these factors or agents, and, for this object, neither to sell nor to rent houses or warehouses to them; further, they have resolved to address the supreme executive of each state to adopt the necessary measures to prevent the unloading of all goods on English account consigned to such factors or agents. It is certain that the English have the trade of these states almost wholly in their hands, whereby their influence must increase; and a constantly increasing scarcity of money begins to be felt, since no ship sails hence to England without large sums of money on board, especially the English packet-boats, which monthly take with them between forty and fifty thousand pounds sterling,

Monroe to Madison, New York, May, 1785. Ex.

An ordinance regulating the mode of survey and sale of the lands ceded by Virginia hath lately engaged the attention of congress. It hath not yet passed, but as all the points of variance seem at length accommodated, it will, perhaps in the course of the succeeding week. The original report admitted of the sale only of tracts containing thirty thousand acres, called townships; this was adhered to with great obstinacy by the eastern men, and as firmly opposed by the southern. At length, however, the eastern party gave up the point, at least so far as to meet on middle ground. As it now stands, it is to be surveyed in townships containing about twenty-six thousand acres each, each township marked on the plat into lots of one mile square, and one half the country sold only in townships and the other in lots. Thirteen surveyors are to be appointed for the purpose, to act under the control of the geographer, beginning with the first range of townships upon the Ohio and running north to the lakes, from the termination of the line which forms the southern boundary of the state of Pennsylvania, and so on westward with each range. As soon as five ranges shall be surveyed, the return will be made to the board of treasury, who are instructed to draw for them in the name of each state in the proportion of the requisition on each, and transmit its portion to the loan officer in each, for sale at public vendue, provided it is not, nor any part, sold for less than one dollar specie, or certifycates, the acre. Thus stands the ordinance at present.

William Grayson to Madison, New York, 1 May, 1785.

DEAR SIR: I am afraid my silence since I came to this place has given you some reason to suspect me to be impregnated with that *vis-inertiœ* which has been so often attributed to me; the only apology I have to make is, that I wished to have something to write to you worth your acceptance. However, as there would be some danger in risking a further delay, I shall give you what I have in the manner the New England delegates wish to sell the continental land—rough as it runs; what I miss in quality I will make up in quantity.

All our attentions here have been for some time turned toward the hostile preparations between the emperor and the Dutch, as it was thought the event might have a considerable influence on the affairs of the United States; the packet which arrived yesterday has brought different accounts of what is doing respecting this business; however, I take the following to be nearly the truth of the case: That the emperor has only made the opening the Schelde a pretext for marching his troops into the Low Countries while he has been underhandedly treating with the Elector of Bavaria for an exchange of his territories in the Low Countries for Bavaria; that France has not only been privy to the negotiations, but has actually countenanced them, while no other power has entertained the most distant suspicions of what was going forward; that the Prince de Deux Ponts, presumptive heir to Bavaria, on receiving the first notice of it, made application to the king of Prussia, supposing that old statesman would exert himself to the utmost to prevent Bavaria from becoming part of the domains of the house of Austria. It therefore seems to be probable that all those who wish to preserve the proper balance of power in the Germanic body will unite with the Prussian monarch against this accession of weight to the Austrian scale. Should this confederacy take place in its fullest extent, it will be very formidable, and in all likelyhood produce a bloody contest before the matter is finally decided. War, therefore, seems to be as probable as ever, although the ground of the contest may be altered. For my own part, I cannot clearly find out from any information.

I have had what have been the views of the court of France; they seem to have departed from their ancient principles in assisting the Austrian family to increase their power; 'tis true they adopted this system in the last reign, but then the French statesmen say that nothing done during that period ought to be quoted from their history. If the queen of France has drawn in the ministry to countenance the measures of her brother, it is an evidence of her great influence in the government; but from what appears at present, it is no proof of the wisdom of the public councils, as it is obvious if France keeps up large standing armies, she must neglect her marine, by which she will risk her foreign possessions whenever she happens to be engaged in a war with Great Britain.

The parliament has so lately sit that little has yet transpired; the minister is to bring forward a plan for a parliamentary reform which it is thought will require all his interest and ability to support.

The Wallachians, who were so oppressed as to be drove into a state of open resistance, are on the point of being subjugated; they are in number about seven hundred thousand; and I heartily wish they were all here. Congress are engaged in ascertaining a mode for the disposal of the western territory; I send you the first draught as reported by the grand committee, also a second edition, with amendments in congress; the matter is still under consideration, and other alterations will, no doubt, take effect. An amendment is now before the house for making the townships six miles square, and for dividing those townships, by actual surveys, into quarters of townships, making at every interval of a mile (in running the external lines of the quarters) corners for the sections of six hundred and forty acres. Then to sell every other township by sections. The reservation (instead of the four corner sections to be the central section of every quarter; that is to say, the inside lot, whose corner is not ascertained. Whether this will be carried or not I cannot tell, the eastern people being amazingly attached to their own customs, and unreasonably anxious to have everything regulated according to their own pleasure.

The construction of the deed of cession from Virginia has taken up four days, and at length it is agreed not to sell any land between the Little Miami and Scioto until the conditions respecting the officers and soldiers are complied with. Some members of congress think they have a right to have the land laid off for the officers and soldiers in such manner as they please, and by their own surveyors, provided they give good land and square figures; others are willing it shall be laid off in the same manner as the rest, and the officers and soldiers to choose by sections. If the state insists on the right of surveying agreeable to their own laws, I should suppose that congress could have no objection to appointing commissioners for deciding that question, as well as all others that might arise respecting the compact.

Mr. King, of Massachusetts, has a resolution ready drawn, which he reserves till the ordinance is passed for preventing slavery in the new state. I expect seven states may be found liberal enough to adopt it.

Seven hundred men are voted for protecting the settlers on the frontiers, for guarding the public stores, and for preventing unwarrantable intrusions on the lands of the United States.

I enclose you a plan for altering the ninth article of the confederation; also a newspaper informing what the people of Boston are about. The requisition for the present year is before congress; one article—to wit, thirty thousand dollars for federal buildings at Trenton—I objected to, and was supported by the delegates of Maryland, Delaware, and New Hampshire. North Carolina was divided. Unfortunately for me, the rest of the delegates for our state do not think as I do. This is *entre nous*.

I shall, notwithstanding, do everything in my power to frustrate the measure. We shall, in all probability, get it struck out of the requisition, because nine states will not vote for it. I understand, however, that it is intended to get seven states to vote for the sum out of the loans in Holland, supposing that as a hundred thousand dollars was voted at Trenton by nine states, generally that seven can direct the particular appropriation. This matter I have not yet considered, neither do I know how it will turn out on investigation; however, I hope I shall find means to avoid it for the present year, and I hope by the next the Southern states will understand their interests better.

Congress have refused to let the state discount any part of the moneys paid for the western territory out of the requisitions for the present year, and I believe if they don't help themselves they will never find congress willing to discount. In the mean time, they will sell the lands. A treaty is directed to be held with the Barbary states to purchase their friendship. Treaties are also to be held with the Cherokees, Chickasaws, etc., also with the western Indians, shortly. I am sure you are surfeited, therefore conclude with great sincerity.

Your affectionate friend and most obedient servant, etc.

Jefferson to Monroe, Paris, 11 May, 1785. Ex.

DEAR SIR: This will be delivered you by young Mr. Adams, whom I beg leave to introduce to your acquaintance, and recommend as worthy of your friendship. He possesses abilities, learning, application, and the best of dispositions. Considering his age, too, you will find him more improved by travel than could have been expected.

No change of disposition begins yet to show itself in England. The probability of the impost, the concurrence of all the states in the resolutions of April, 1784, the measures for making congress the head of our confederacy in commerce as well as in war, will probably begin to make them see a possibility of our acting as a nation. The spirit which has appeared in our legislatures and newspapers lately will, I think, dispose them to lend a more favorable ear, and form a favorable ground-work for Mr. Adams to take his stand on. His going to London will at any rate produce a decision of some sort.

Since writing so far I have received the appointment of congress to succeed Dr. Franklin here. I give them my sincere thanks for this mark of their favor. I wish I were as able to render services which would justify their choice as I am zealous to do it. I am sure I shall often do wrong, and though it will be a good excuse for me that my intentions were good, it will be but a barren consolation to my country.

What measures have you taken for establishing yourself near Monticello? Nothing in this world will keep me long from that spot of ultimate repose for me. I keep my eye on yourself and Short for society, and do not despair of Madison.

Jefferson to Madison, Paris, 11 May, 1785. Ex.

DEAR SIR: Your favor of ninth January came to my hands on the thirteenth of April. The very full and satisfactory detail of the proceedings of assembly which it contained gave me the highest pleasure. The value of these communications cannot be calculated at a shorter distance than the breadth of the Atlantic.

They yesterday finished printing my Notes. I had two hundred copies printed, but do not put them out of my own hands, except two or three copies here, and two which I shall send to America, to yourself and Colonel Monroe, if they can be ready this evening, as promised. I beg you to peruse it carefully, because I ask your advice on it, and ask nobody's else. I wish to put it into the hands of the young men at the college, as well on account of the political as physical parts; but there are sentiments on some subjects which I apprehend might be displeasing to the country, perhaps to the assembly, or to some who lead it. I do not wish to be exposed to their censure, nor do I know how far their influence, if exerted, might effect a misapplication of law to such a publication, were it made. Communicate it, then, in confidence, to those whose judgments and information you would pay respect to, and, if you think it will give no offence, I will send a copy to each of the students of William and Mary College, and some others to my friends and to your disposal. Otherwise I shall only send over a very few copies to very particular friends, in confidence, and burn the rest. Answer me soon, and without reserve. Do not view me as an author, and attached to what he has written. I am neither. They were at first intended only for Marbois. When I had enlarged them, I thought first of giving copies to three or four friends. I have since supposed they might set our young students into a useful train of thought, and in no event do I propose to admit them to go to the public at large.

R. H. Lee to J. Madison, New York, 30 May, 1785. Ex.

DEAR SIR: When I was in our assembly, it appeared to me rather to be the wish, than otherwise, that Kentucky should apply for separation, and I should suppose that if, when they found themselves competent to the business of self-government, they properly applied to our assembly, no good objection could be made to a separation. For they have, and will remain for a long time, if not always, more expense than profit to the rest of the country.

We have, after much debate indeed, and great waste of time, at last passed an ordinance for disposing of such part of the lands north-west of the Ohio as belongs to the United States and has been purchased of the Indians. If this proves agreeable to the public, it will extinguish about ten millions of the public debt; and the remaining lands, going southward to the Mississippi, will nearly discharge all the domestic debt; besides the probable prospect that we have of considerable cessions from North and South Carolina and Georgia. This source does indeed deserve our warmest cultivation, as it seems to be almost the only one that we have for discharging our oppressive debt.

The American enterprise has been well marked by a short and successful voyage made from hence to Canton, in China. The Chinese were kind to our people, and glad to see a new source of commerce opened to them from a new people, as they called us. The Europeans there were civil, but astonished at the rapidity of our movements, especially the English, I fear that our countrymen will overdo this business, for now there appears everywhere a rage for East India voyages.

R. R. Livingston to Lafayette, Claremont, 1 June, 1785, Ex.

The imposts laid by particular states have been extremely productive; had the general system been established, it would have rendered it easy to fund our debt, which is all that ought to be wished in our present situation. I have reason to think that, had it not been for the mistaken policy of New York, which rejected them, the recommendations of congress on this subject would have been complied with in a few months, even by Rhode Island.

Intelligence from New York, 4 June, 1785. Received 15 July from Mr. Smith. Ex.

There is no trade with any but the British, who alone give the credit they want, and draw off all the bullion they can collect. They see no prospect of clothing themselves, unless they had the circuitous commerce they formerly enjoyed in connection with Great Britain, which many think a vain expectation, now they are no part of the empire. The scarcity of money makes the produce of the country cheap, to the disappointment of the farmers and the discouragement of husbandry. Thus the two classes of merchants and farmers, that divide nearly all America, are discontented and distressed. Some great change is approaching.

Washington to William Carmichael, Mount Vernon, 10 June, 1785. Ex.

I feel myself under singular obligation to you, sir, as the means of procuring two jacks of the first race, to be sent me; but my gratitude for so condescending a mark of esteem from one of the first crowned heads in Europe calls for a better expression than I have, to make suitable acknowledgments to his Catholic Majesty; especially, too, as his Majesty's very valuable present was accompanied by a sentiment of approbation.

Great Britain, viewing with eyes of chagrin and jealousy the situation of this country, will not, for some time yet, if ever, pursue a liberal policy toward it; but, unfortunately for her, the conduct of her ministers defeats their own ends; their restriction of our trade with them will facilitate the enlargement of congressional powers in commercial matters more than half a century would otherwise have effected, The mercantile interests of this country are uniting as one man to vest the federal government with ample powers to regulate trade, and to counteract the selfish views of other nations. This may be considered as another proof that this country will ever unite in opposition to unjust or ungenerous measures, whensoever or from whomsoever they are offered.

Monroe to Jefferson, New York, 16 June, 1785. Ex.

DEAR SIR: By Colonel Smith, secretary to the London legation, I wrote you in April last very fully upon our transactions previous to that date. I also enclosed you the journals that were then printed, with the copy of a report upon the first paragraph of the ninth of the articles of confederation, proposing a change in it, and the absolute investment of the United States with the control of commerce. I now enclose you a copy of the journals, as well those sent by Colonel Smith as those since printed; likewise an ordinance for surveying and disposing of the lands beyond the Ohio.

The report upon the ninth article hath not been taken up. The importance of the subject, and the deep and radical change it will create in the bond of the union, together with the conviction that something must be done, seems to create an aversion, or rather a fear, of acting on it. If the report should ultimately be adopted, it will certainly form the most permanent and powerful principle in the confederation. At present the alliance is little more than an offensive and defensive one, and, if the right to raise troops at pleasure is denied, merely a defensive one. The political economy of each state is entirely within its own direction, and to carry into effect its regulation with other powers, to attain any substantial ends to the state, they must apply as well to the states of the union as other powers, and such a course as this will produce very mischievous effects. On the other hand, the effect of this report will be to put the commercial economy of every state entirely under the hands of the union. The means necessary to obtain the carrying trade, to encourage domestic by a tax on foreign industry, or any other ends which in the changes of things become necessary, will depend entirely on the union. In short, you will perceive that this will give the union an authority upon the states respectively, which will last with it and hold it together in its present form longer than any other principle it now contains will effect. I think the expediency, in a great degree, of the measure turns on one point (especially to the Southern states), whether the obtainment of the carrying trade and the extension of our national resources is an object, and this depends entirely upon the prospect of our connection with other powers. If, like the empire of China, we were separated and perfectly independent of them, it might perhaps be unnecessary; but even in that event a question arises which may be of consequence, "whether the giving our own citizens a share in the carrying trade will not otherwise be advantageous to them than as it obtains the particular objects which the regulations necessary to effect it have in view; whether it will not in effect increase the value of land, the number of inhabitants, the proportion of circulating medium, and be the foundation upon which all those regulations which are necessary to turn what is called 'the balance of trade' in our favor, must he formed." A preference to our own citizens is the foundation of the carrying trade, and upon it, I suspect, will depend all these consequences. Yet an opinion seems to be entertained by the late commercial writers, and particularly a Mr. Smith on the wealth of nations, that the doctrine of the "balance of trade" is a chimera, in pursuit of which Great Britain hath exposed herself to great injury. The subject is of great magnitude, and I very earnestly wish to hear from you on it before it obtains its fate.

There seems in congress an earnest disposition to wind up our affairs as they respect foreign nations, exclude their interests totally from our councils, and, preserving our faith with the utmost punctuality with those to whom it is plighted, make such regulations as will effectually promote our interests. Information, and a knowledge in what it consists, are the only points in which they are defective.

I have never seen a body of men collected in which there was less party, for there is not the shadow of it here. I think there will be no adjournment, and I sincerely wish there may not be, for I fear it will not be easy to collect men from the states with more upright intentions.

That you may have in view whatever is in agitation respecting the western country, to judge of the system if there is one, I enclose you the copy of a report now before congress, which comprehends whatever is proposed to be done respecting it, for the present; upon the report of the Indian commissioners the matter will again be taken up, and then it will be determined what authority congress will exercise over the people who may settle within the bounds of either of the new states previous to the establishment of a temporary government, where they will leave them to themselves or appoint magistrates over them. I think the enclosed report will be adopted; it hath been several times before congress, and each time there were eight states; to-morrow, it is believed, there will be nine.

The plan of a requisition is before congress. The states have failed essentially during the last year in making their payments. Virginia hath paid, I believe, more than all the rest; the present plan is the passage of the requisition of eight millions, as was that of the last year. The amount necessary for the current year, about three millions: first, for the interest upon the foreign debt, and expenses of government, and, second, the domestic debt. For the latter purpose facilities are proposed to be admitted. I must confess I doubt the propriety of pressing old requisitions, and think it would be better to ascertan what had been paid by the several states upon that requisition, and upon the apportionment under it; what claims those paying most had on the others, and then begin anew, making also a new apportionment; this would be more simple and better understood. I am also rather doubtful of the propriety of doing anything whatever in the domestic debt. Several of the states, Pennsylvania in particular, hath appropriated her money to her own citizens only; from her, and the other states taking the same course, we shall have no support. It appears, then, better to recommend it to the states to take on themselves the debts of the United States to their citizens, respectively; let them be paid by state operations, and then, after liquidating the whole, and the quota of each is ascertained, of the proportion of expense of the late war, let the balance which either shall have advanced beyond its proportion be paid it by the union.

This is a new idea, nor do I know that I shall suggest it further; but perhaps may hereafter, more especially if it shall appear founded in justice and expedience.

During the recess of congress last year, North Carolina made a cession of territory to the United States, authorizing her delegates to make the deed; before congress convened she repealed it. The people within the said territory had separated themselves from the state and declared themselves an independent state, under the name of Franklin. Their agent was also here at the time upon that subject. He received no countenance whatever, and all that was done relative to it was to renew the recommendation to the state to make a second cession.

Jefferson to Monroe, Paris, 17 June, 1785. Ex.

If it is better for the states that congress should regulate their commerce, it is proper that they should form treaties with all nations with whom they may possibly trade. You see that my primary object in the formation of treaties is to take the commerce of the states out of the hands of the states, and to place it under the superintendence of congress, so far as the imperfect provisions of our constitutions will admit, and until the states shall, by new compact, make them more perfect. I would say, then, to every nation on earth, by treaty your people shall trade freely with us, and ours with you, paying no more than the most favored nation, in order to put an end to the right of individual states, acting by fits and starts, to interrupt our commerce, or to embroil us with any nation. As to the terms of these treaties, the question becomes more difficult,

Washington to Grayson, Mount Vernon, 22 June, 1785. Ex.

DEAR SIR: I am very glad to find you have passed an ordinance of congress respecting the sale of the western lands. I am too well acquainted with the local politics of individual states not to have foreseen the difficulties you met with in this business; these things are to be regretted, but not to be altered until liberality of sentiment is more universal. Fixing the seat of empire at any spot on the Delaware is, in my humble opinion, demonstrably wrong; to incur an expense for what may be called the permanent seat of congress, at this time, is, I conceive, evidently impolitic; for, without the gift of prophecy, I will venture to predict that, under any circumstance of confederation, it will not remain so far to the eastward long; and that, until the public is in better circumstances, it ought not to be built at all. Time, too powerful for sophistry, will point out the place, and disarm localities of their power. In the meanwhile let the widow, the orphan, and the suffering soldier, who are crying to you for their dues, receive that which can very well be rendered to them.

There is nothing new in this quarter of an interesting nature to communicate, unless you should not have been informed that the Potomac navigation proceeds under favorable auspices. At the general meeting of the subscribers in May last, it appeared that upward of four hundred of the five hundred shares had been engaged. Many more have been subscribed since. A board of directors have been chosen; proper characters and laborers advertised for, to commence the work in the least difficult parts of the river, till a skilful engineer can be engaged to undertake those which are more so; and it is expected the work will be begun by the tenth of next month.

Washington to Hon. George W. Fairfax, Mount Vernon, 30 June, 1785. Ex.

MY DEAR SIR: The information which you have given of the disposition of a certain court coincides precisely with the sentiments I had formed of it from my own observations upon many late occurrences, and from a combination of circumstances. With respect to ourselves, I wish I could add that as much wisdom had pervaded our councils as reason and common policy most evidently dictated; but the truth is, the people must feel before they will see; consequently are brought slowly into measures of public utility. Past experience, or the admonitions of a few, have but little weight where ignorance, selfishness, and design possess the major part; but evils of this nature work their own cure, though the remedy comes slower than those who foresee, or think they foresee, the danger, attempt to effect. With respect to the commercial system which Great Britain is pursuing with this country, the ministers in this, as in other matters, are defeating their own ends by facilitating those powers in congress which will produce a counteraction of their plans, and which half a century without would not have invested that body with. The restrictions of our trade, and the additional duties which are imposed upon many of our staple commodities, have put the commercial people of this country in motion; they now see the indispensable necessity of a general controlling power, and are addressing their respective assemblies to grant this to congress. Before this, every state thought itself competent to regulate its own trade, and were verifying the observations of Lord Sheffield, who supposed we never could agree upon any general plan; but those who will go a little deeper into matters than his lordship seems to have done, will readily perceive that in any measure where the federal interest is touched, however wide apart the politics of individual states may be, yet, as soon as it is discovered, they will always unite to effect a common good.

Samuel Adams to John Adams, Boston, July, 1785. Ex.

DEAR SIR: Our merchants are complaining bitterly that Great Britain is ruining their trade, and there is great reason to complain; but I think much greater to complain of too many of the citizens through the commonwealth who are imitating the Britons in every idle amusement and expensive foppery which it is in their power to invent for destruction of a young country. Before this reaches you, you will have heard of the change in our chief magistrate.[1] I confess it is what I have earnestly wished for. Our new governor has issued a proclamation for the promoting of piety, virtue, education, and manners, and suppressing of vice, which, with the good example of a first magistrate and others, may, perhaps, restore our virtue.

[1] The election of James Bowdoin.

Monroe to Jefferson, New York, 15 July, 1785.

The report respecting the treaty with western Indians hath been adopted, except in the change of the place at which it will be held, being the mouth of the Big Miami, or the falls of the Ohio, instead of post Vincent; and the article respecting the people of the Kaskaskia, and neighboring villages, which, although first adopted, was afterward repealed, from an apprehension it would create too great an expense. The report of proposing a change in the first paragraph of the ninth of the articles of confederation hath been before congress in a committee of the whole for two days past; the house are to take it up again on Monday in the same manner; it hath been fully discussed, and, in my opinion, the reasons in favor of it are conclusive; the opposition, however, is respectable in point of numbers, as well as talents, in one or two instances; from our state you will readily conjecture the sentiments of one; Hardy is for it, Grayson doubtful, but I think rather in favor of it.

Some gentlemen have inveterate prejudices against any attempts to increase the powers of congress; others see the necessity, but fear the consequences. It is proposed by the latter and former classes that congress form and recommend a navigation act to the states, to continue in force for a limited time. What will or will not be done ultimately in this business is uncertain. The report also upon the instructions hath been before congress, and is referred to the consideration of some day next week. It will not probably be adopted.

I have it in contemplation, after a few weeks, to set out for the Ohio to attend the treaty above mentioned; this will complete my tour through the western country.

R. H. Lee to Washington, 23 July, 1785. Ex.

Is it possible that a plan can be formed for issuing a larger sum of paper money by the next assembly? I do verily believe that the greatest foes we have in the world could not devise a more effectual plan for ruining Virginia. I should suppose that every friend to his country, every honest and sober man, would join heartily to reprobate so nefarious a plan of speculation.

Monroe to Madison, New York, 26 July, 1785. Ex.

DEAR SIR: Since my last, a report, proposing a change in the first paragraph of the ninth of the articles of confederation, hath been taken up and acted on two days, in a committee of the whole. It proposes to invest congress with power to regulate trade externally and internally. Those in favor of it were of opinion that the exercise of this power, in the hands of each state, would be less advantageous to its particular interests than in those of the union, because if, in the regulation of trade, it was sought: 1, to encourage domestic industry in any line by a tax upon foreign, which, however remote at present, may hereafter be the case; 2, if to obtain reciprocity in its commercial intercourse with foreign nations, either with or without treaties; 3, if to establish a commercial interest within, in contradistinction to a foreign one, and thereby keep its councils independent of foreign influence; 4, or to raise a naval strength for the public safety—all these ends might be obtained more effectually by the exercise of the power in the hands of the union than of each state; for, unless they act in concert in every instance, instead of counteracting the regulations of other powers, they will become instrumental in their hands to impede and defeat each other; that there was but one alternative, either to act together or against each other; that the latter plan established deep-rooted jealousies and enmities between them, at the same time that it would be unsuccessful; greater under its operation for any length of time than they would have against other powers, since being more convenient and better able to frustrate each other's measures, their restrictions must be more severe and pointed against each other than against other powers; that such a course tended to throw them apart, and weaken the present rights of the confederacy; that their interests were nearly similar, being all exporting and importing states; that it was of little consequence whether they exported the same or different materials, since the restrictions which tended to restrain exportation would injure the whole, and they were all equally interested in getting their admission upon the best terms into the ports of foreign powers; that they imported nearly the same materials, and of course had the same interest in that line; that if there were different interests in every instance, the restriction of every measure to eleven states, the number proposed, with the revenues to each state, would form a sufficient security. On the other side it was argued: 1. That it was dangerous to concentrate power, since it might be turned to mischievous purposes; that, independent of the immediate danger of intoxication in those entrusted with it, and their attempts on the government, it put us more in the power of other nations.

2. That the interests of the different parts of the union were different from each other, and that the regulations which suited the one would not the other part; that eight states were of a particular interest whose business it would be to combine to shackle and fetter the others. 3. That all attacks upon the confederation were dangerous, and calculated, even if they did not succeed, to weaken it. These, I think, were the principal arguments on either side, though they were carried out into great extent. I think Colonel Grayson informed me, some time since, he had transmitted to you the report; otherwise I should now do it. I wish very much your sentiments on the subject. Mr. Gardoqui is here. Congress have authorized the secretary of foreign affairs to treat with him upon the subject of his mission.

Van Berckel to the States General, 1 August, 1785. Ex. Tr.

In my letter of the twenty-seventh of April I had the honor to inform your H. M. that the state of Massachusetts was about to adopt measures for the purpose of putting their commerce and navigation on such a footing that it should be out of the hands of the English, into which it had seemed more and more to come, to the great injury of the Americans, and, as they feared, to their inevitable ruin. I am now to inform your H. M. that the same state has passed an act whereby their commerce and navigation is regulated, imposing such restrictions and burdens on foreign nations that all prospect of any advantage in their ports is entirely lost, and they consequently are obliged to relinquish all commerce with this state so long as this act is in force. This act appears to me of the utmost importance, and I have the honor to send a copy of it enclosed, and to refer most humbly to its contents. In a conversation which I have had with the secretary of foreign affairs on this subject, I invited him to observe what injurious consequences, according to my opinion, must result, and how impossible it appeared to me that such an act should be looked upon in Europe favorably, since the object of this is nothing other than to destroy entirely the shipping of foreign nations, and to require them to carry their European goods in American bottoms to this country, and, in like manner, the American products to Europe. All the answer I received was, that, this act being passed by a single state, congress could not oppose it, because every state, by reason of its independent sovereignty, possesses the power of adopting such measures for itself as it judges best. Mr. Leertower, consul of your H. M. for the states of New Hampshire and Massachusetts, who has arrived in Boston, announces to me that he finds himself in a very unpleasant situation, because several ships are expected from Holland, consigned to him, which could not have been informed of this law before they left Holland, and they will experience considerable loss on their arrival at the port. The majority of the thirteen states have resolved to grant complete power to congress to regulate their commerce and navigation; but as long as this resolution has not been adopted by all the states, affairs will remain in their present situation. Every state caring for its own par-ticular interest, it is to be feared that the different states will take measures wholly opposing each other.

Washington to E. Randolph, Mount Vernon, 13 August, 1785. Ex.

DEAR SIR: The great object for the accomplishment of which I wish to see the inland navigation of the rivers Potomac and James improved and extended is to connect the western territory with the Atlantic states. All others with me are secondary; though I am clearly of opinion that it will greatly increase our commerce, and be an immense saving in the article of transportation and draft cattle to the planters and farmers who are in a situation to have the produce of their labor water-borne. These being my sentiments, I wish to see the undertaking progress equally in both rivers; and but for my local situation and numerous avocations, my attention to each should be alike. What little I do for the advancement of the enterprise in this river is done, as it were, en passant, and because I think the difficult-ties greater than in the other, and not because I give it the preference. For both, in my opinion, have their advantages, without much, if any, interference with each other. The advantages arising from my patron-age of either are probably more ideal than real; but, such as they are, I wish them to be thought equally distributed. My contribution to the works shall be the same. I have already subscribed five shares to the Potomac navigation; and enclosed I give you a power to put my name down for five shares to that of James river.

Monroe to Madison, New York, 14 August, 1785. Ex.

The report upon the ninth of the articles of confederation will not, I believe, be finally determined until the winter. It will, however, probably be taken up merely for the sake of investigation, and to be committed to the journals for public inspection. You have, I understand, copy, and I wish much your sentiments on it. A navigation act by recommendation hath been proposed in conversation and debate, but not submitted to the inspection and consideration of congress. This is the other plan, and should not be adopted but in the ultimate decision that it is improper the power should rest in congress. If this should be the decision, it might be well to collect better information from the merchants of each state than congress now possess on the subject; indeed, with or without the power, this information should be obtained, or we may err in the act. If this report should be adopted, it gives a tie to the confederacy which it hath not at present, nor can have without it. It gives the states something to act on, the means by which they may bring about certain ends. Without it, God knows what object they have before them, or how each state will move, so as to move securely, with respect to federal or state objects.

Monroe to Jefferson, New York, 15 August, 1785. Ex.
The report proposing to invest congress with the power to regulate commerce hath been twice before congress, in committee of the whole. It met with no opponent except the president[1]; by this I do not mean that there were no others opposed to it, for the contrary is the case. They, however, said but little, or rather committed their side of the question to his care.

In favor of it there were but few speakers also. The committee came to no conclusion, but desired leave to sit again. A second plan hath been proposed, a navigation act, digested here and recommended to the states; this hath not been presented, but probably will be. One would expect in a particular quarter of the union perfect concert in this business, yet this is not altogether the case. The second plan, above alluded to, takes its origin with MacHenry.

The eastern people wish something more lasting, and will, of course, in the first instance, not agree to it; they must therefore come in with that proposed in the report. You will ask me why they hesitate. To be candid, I believe it arises from the real magnitude of the subject, for I have the most confidential communications with them, and am satisfied they act ingenuously. They fear the consequences that may possibly result from it. The longer it is delayed, the more certain is its passage through the several states ultimately. Their minds will then be better informed by evidences within their views of the

[1] R. H. Lee,

necessity of committing the power to congress. The commerce of the union is daily declining. The merchants of this town own, I am told, not more than two ships. I wish much to hear from you upon this subject. I expect it will be brought on again shortly. If for the purpose of committing it to the journals, it may then be delayed for some time, until we may obtain full information on it. The report changing the instructions for forming commercial treaties will, I believe, be adopted. It changes the principle, and puts an end to that of the right of the most favored nation.

Mr. Adams seems to suppose the principal object in his mission to the court of London was the relation of a treaty, but the contrary was certainly the case; it was merely to conciliate, and prevent a variance which seemed to threaten at that time. He might, however, readily make this mistake under the present instructions. A treaty is not expected, and I am satisfied the majority here wish all propositions on that head to cease; at least for the present, and until our restrictions on their commerce have effected a different disposition. Mr. Jay is authorized to treat with Mr. Gardoqui upon the subjects arising between the two parties. He is to lay every proposition before congress before he enters into any engagement with him; as yet we have heard nothing from him. The consulate convention lately formed with France is universally disapproved.

John Page to Jefferson, Rosewell, 23 August, 1785. Ex.

MY DEAR SIR: To add to my employments, I am a deputy to the general convention of the members of the American Episcopal church, which is to meet next month at Philadelphia. I have enclosed you a copy of the proceedings of the convention at Richmond. You will find we were liberal, and I think we shall reform the Episcopal church so as to make it truly respectable.

Indeed, this sect was always the most liberal I ever heard of, not only with respect to religious opinions, but, I think, with respect to political matters too—at least, they have showed themselves such in America; for they took an open and decided part in support of our late glorious revolution, though at the risk of the certain destruction of their establishment and importance. Such disinterestedness entitles them to respect; and the liberality of their religious sentiments is such as is sufficient to make any one of a liberal way of thinking lament that this sect is declining daily, while some others, the most bigoted and illiberal, are gaining ground. Fontaine has been almost starved; Andrews has quitted his gown, he says, to avoid starving.

Nothing but a general assessment can prevent the state from being divided between immorality and enthusiastic bigotry. We have endeavored eight years in vain to support the rational sects by voluntary contributions.

I think I begin to see a mischief arising out of the dependence of the teachers of the Christian religion on their individual followers, which may not only be destructive to morality, but to government itself. The needy, dependent preacher not only cannot boldly reprove the vicious practices of his friends and benefactors, his only support, but he must, to keep well with them, fall into their opinions, and support their views and interests; so that, instead of being bound by the strongest ties of interest to discountenance vice, and support and strengthen the hands of government, they may be supporting the jarring interests of the enemies to all government. Some may preach up the true doctrine of   , which may prove more fatal to some states in America than it did to some in Germany; while others, furthering the views of the rich, proud, and aristocratical gentry, may, amid tumult and anarchy, offer their services to restore order and stability to government, fixing on the basis of a pure aristocracy.

I have said the more on this subject because I have just read an outrageous piece against the assessment, in which your opinion is quoted, and referred to as authority against the arguments for an assessment, and because I have heard that you had altered your opinion, having found that the most rational sects bear up with difficulty under the unequal burden of supporting their teachers.

Monroe to Jefferson, New York, 25 August, 1785.

DEAR SIR: Since my last, nothing very material hath taken place here. I leave this merely to inform you of my departure hence for the Indian treaty on the Ohio, which will be in about two hours. The two commercial propositions are as they were. Although congress will, I believe, not adjourn yet, I apprehend the business of consequence will be postponed for the present, perhaps till the winter. There is but a thin representation of the states, and, of course, not the ability, if the inclination, to act on these subjects. I intend to take within my view the country lying between Lake Erie and the Ohio, the Ohio and the Potomac or James river, as it may suit me to return by the northern or southern part of the state. I pass through Lancaster and Carlisle, at the latter of which posts I join General Butler. The people of Kentucky intend, I hear, to petition the legislature for a separation. I must confess I am one of those who doubt the policy of this measure (for I make no doubt it will be granted), either upon state or federal principles. My opinion is: we could so model our regulations as to accommodate our government to their convenience; and, unquestionably, the more we diminish the state, the less consequence she will have in the union. On the part of the union, or rather the states upon the Atlantic, it is, in my opinion, their policy to keep a prevailing influence upon the Ohio or to the westward. What unites us to them or they to us when the Mississippi shall be open? Removed at a distance from whatever may affect us beyond the water, they will necessarily be but little interested in whatever respects us; besides, they will outnumber us in congress, unless we confine their number as much as possible. In my opinion, this matter should be well investigated before any measure is hastily adopted. I direct your letters to be forwarded to me to Fredericksburg. So soon as I shall return to the settled country, I shall advise you of it, and am, your affectionate friend and servant, etc.

Jacob Read to James Madison, Chamber of Congress, New York, Monday, 29 August, 1785. Ex.

SIR: An opinion prevails in South Carolina that the principal holders of slaves in your state wish to divest themselves of that kind of property, and that tolerably good purchases might be made on good security being given for payments by instalments, with a regular discharge of the interest.

Under the impression of this opinion, the Hon. Mr. J. Rutledge, of South Carolina, has addressed a letter to me wishing to become engaged in any purchase I may be able to make, and to make a joint concern. You know his validity, and I do not mean to deceive you when I say I am possessed of a property that will fully authorize me to engage in a considerable purchase. My present application to you is to request you to inform me if you know of any such persons as may wish to sell a gang of hands, and the terms on which they might be had. On receiving intelligence of the name and residence of the party, I'd write myself to such person more particularly.

Congress is thin, and I am sorry to say the states seem averse to any act that has in prospect to assert the dignity of the federal government. We debate, make, and hear long and often spirited speeches, hut when the moment arrives for a vote we adjourn, and thus the feelings of individuals and the welfare of the union is trifled with. We have not yet got through a requisition for the expenses of the current year; our treasury is exceedingly low; we have, in short, nothing pleasing in prospect, and if in a short time the states do not enable congress to act with some vigor and put the power of compulsion into the hand of the union, I am free to confess I think it almost time to give over the form of what I cannot consider as an efficient government. We want! greatly want!! the assistance of your abilities and experience in congress. I would not be thought to derogate from the merits or abilities of the present delegation, but one cannot help drawing comparisons between the language of 1783 and 1785.

Washington to Doctor Cochran, Mount Vernon, 31 August, 1785. Ex.

I persuade myself you are too well convinced, my dear Doctor, of my friendship and of my inclination to promote your interest or wishes to doubt my ready compliance with the request of your letter (respecting the office of continental treasurer), if it comported with the line of conduct which I had prescribed for my government. But from my knowledge of the composition of congress—the state politics of its members, and their endeavors to fill every civil office with a citizen from their own state, if not altogether, at least by a compromise—I took up an early determination not to hazard the mortification of a refusal, or of the passing by my application, by not asking anything from it; and to this resolution I was further prompted by the numberless applications with which it was impracticable, and, in many instances, would have been improper for me to comply. Except in a single one, and that not pointed to any office directly, I have never gone beyond the general recommendation which accompanied my resignation, nor do I believe I ever shall.

Washington to David Humphreys, Mount Vernon, 1 Sept., 1785.

DEAR HUMPHREYS: The times are dull with us. The assemblies are in their recess, and the merchants are preparing petitions to them, respectively, to enlarge the powers of congress for commercial purposes. In congress I understand diversity of opinion prevails respecting the extent of these powers. They are also deliberating on the establishment of a mint for the coinage of gold, silver, and copper, but nothing final is yet resolved on respecting either.

Washington to Lafayette, Mount Vernon, 1 Sept., 1785. Ex.

MY DEAR MARQUIS: My best wishes will always accompany your undertakings, but remember, my dear friend, it is a part of the military art to reconnoitre and feel your way before you engage too deeply. More is oftentimes effected by regular approaches than by an open assault; from the first, too, you may make a good retreat; from the latter (in case of repulse) it rarely happens.

It is to be hoped that Mr. Adams will bring the British ministry to some explanation respecting the western posts. Nothing else can, I conceive, disturb the tranquillity of these states; but, if I am mistaken in this conjecture, you know my sentiments of, and friendship for, you too well to doubt my inclination to serve you to the utmost of your wishes and my powers.

Washington to the Marquis de Chastellux, Mount Vernon, 5 Sept., 1785. Ex.

DEAR SIR: My first wish is to see the blessings of peace diffused through all countries, and among all ranks in every country, and that we should consider ourselves as the children of a common parent, and be disposed to acts of brotherly kindness toward one another. In that case, all restrictions of trade would vanish; we should take your wines, your fruits, and surplusage of other articles, and give you, in return, our oils, our fish, tobacco, naval stores, etc.; and, in like manner, we should exchange produce with other countries, to our reciprocal advantage. The globe is large enough. Why, then, need we wrangle for a small spot of it? If one country cannot contain us, another should open its arms to us. But these halcyon days, if they ever did exist, are now no more. A wise Providence, I presume, has ordered it otherwise, and we must go on in the old way, disputing, and now and then fighting, until the globe itself is dissolved.

E. Gerry to Samuel Adams, New York, 5 Sept., 1785.

MY DEAR SIR: I am much obliged to you for your favor of the twenty-seventh of August, enclosing the proceedings of the legislature respecting the institution of the Cincinnati. Congress have been ever tender of the reputation of their military officers, and, as far as I could collect the sentiments of the members at Annapolis, were in expectation of a voluntary abolition of the institution. It was then conceived that all the officers might have been mistaken with respect to its fatal tendency, and that many certainly were, but that, seeing the sense of their fellow-citizens and of some of the legislatures on the subject, no time would be lost in putting a period to so obnoxious a measure. In this congress have been mistaken, for so far have the Cincinnati congress been from an abolition that, in my opinion, the plan is worse on the last establishment than it was on the first. My reason is this, that in the first case it was too glaring to escape the observation of any one, and, in the last, it may lull some into a security until the Cincinnati nobility have so established their influence as to control our republican governments, and then they may reassume their first shape and bid defiance to opposition. I am not sure that congress will take the matter up; but sure I am that, if the delegates of Massachusetts retain their health and seats in congress, they will put on the journals some propositions that will sound a federal alarm, being firmly persuaded this institution must be abolished soon, or it will destroy our liberties.

We have by this post given his Excellency, Governor Bowdoin, our reasons for suspending a delivery of his despatches for a general revision of the confederation, which I presume he will officially communicate to his council, and I wish to have your sentiments on the subject.

My compliments to your lady, and be assured I am, sir, on every occasion, your friend and very humble servant, etc.

Washington to his Excellency Chevalier de la Luzerne, Mount Vernon, 5 Sept., 1785.

SIR: The mercantile interest, feeling the necessity of giving a controlling power to congress to regulate the trade of this country, have prepared, and are now preparing, addresses to their respective assemblies for this purpose. They are now clearly convinced that this power cannot be exercised with propriety, unless one system pervades the whole union, and is made competent to the ends. It has happened in this instance, as in the revolution itself, that the means which Great Britain pursues to obtain advantages defeat her own ends; for I am certain that if she had forborne to tax our trade with those resttricttions and imposts which are laid on it by acts of parliament, or orders of the king in council, half a century would not have produced those powers in congress which more than probably will be given to them in a few months, and by which equal restrictions and duties may be laid; and in the interim, sorry I am to add, she would have monopolized in a very great degree the commerce of the United States.

At length congress have adopted a mode for disposing of the western lands; but I confess it does not strike me as a very eligible one; however, mine is only an opinion, and I wish to be mistaken in it, as the fund would be very productive, and afford great relief to the public creditors, if the lands meet with a ready sale.

Treaty has been holden with the western Indians at Fort McIntosh, on the Ohio (twenty-five miles below Pittsburgh), and advantageous terms entered into with those who met, for they ceded without any compensation as large a district north-west of that river as we have any occasion for at present; but it should seem as if others of their resepecttive tribes are dissatisfied, and keep the settlers of the western territory in a state of disquietude. This, I am persuaded, will be the case while the British retain the posts within the American lines, and when they will be surrendered is not for me to decide.

From the last European accounts we have reason to hope that the clouds which seemed to be gathering in your hemisphere will yield to a tranquil sky, and peace, with all its blessings, will spread its mantle over the threatened lands. My first wish is to see the sons and daughters of the world mixing as one family, enjoying the sweets of social intercourse and reciprocal advantages. The earth certainly is sufficient to contain us all, and affords everything necessary to our wants, if we would be friendly and endeavor to accommodate one another. Why, then, should we wrangle, and why should we attempt to infringe the rights and properties of our neighbors? But, lest you should suppose that I am about to turn preacher, I will only add that, with the highest esteem and consideration, I have the honor to be, etc,

Washington to the Count de Rochamheau, Mount Vernon, 7 Sept., 1785. Ex.

MY DEAR COUNT: Every occasion that assures me of your health increases my happiness, as I have a sincere respect and an affectionate regard for you. My time now, as the Marquis de La Fayette might have informed you, is spent in rural employments, and in contemplation of those friendships which the revolution enabled me to form with so many worthy characters of your nation, through whose assistance I can now sit down in my calm retreat, and, under my own vine and my own fig-tree, enjoy those pleasures which are here felt with less alloy than upon a larger theatre and in the more busy scenes of life.

I hope the storms which rumbled about you all the winter, and which seemed to portend so much mischief, are dispersed, and that a tranquil sky has succeeded. Although it is against the profession of arms, I wish to see all the world in peace; how long this blessing may be dispensed to us I know not. The British still hold the posts upon the lakes, within the territory of the United States, and discover no inclination (that has come to my knowledge) to give them up. With respect to the Spaniards, I do not think the navigation of the Mississippi is an object of great importance to us at present; and when the banks of the Ohio and the fertile plains of the western country get thickly inhabited, the people will embrace the advantages which nature affords them, in spite of all opposition.

Samuel Adams to E. Gerry, Boston, 19 Sept., 1785. Ex.

MY DEAR SIR: I intended in my last, of the fifteenth, to have reminded you of the approaching period to which your continuing to hold a seat in congress is limited. Those who may take your places may not happen to be of your sentiments respecting the Cincinnati, and in that case they will overrule Mr. King and prevent your good intentions.

A general revision of the confederation appears to me to be a dangerous measure to be adopted at this time, nor do I think it necessary. Our government at present has liberty for its object. It is to be feared that, by the artifices of a few designing men, and a general inattention of the many, the principle may be lost, or, at least, a new confederation may be expressed in such ambiguous terms as will admit of a construction unfavorable to liberty. It is much to be wished that congress may be vested with sufficient power to regulate the trade of the states with foreigners. This commonwealth suffers for want of it. Cannot this power, properly guarded, be given to congress without endangering the principles of the confederation by a general revision? I said this commonwealth suffers for want of such a power in congress. By our late acts we have tied our own hands. Vessels from foreign countries have come into our ports and gone out again with the cargoes they brought, perhaps to the state of Rhode Island or Connecticut, neither of which passed similar acts. Thus Massachusetts and New Hampshire are suffering by their own honest exertions for the general interest. The arrival of Stanhope at Nova Scotia with fresh provisions cheered the spirits of the half-starved inhabitants. The number of inhabitants there was seven thousand before the arrival of the refugees, and they never could supply themselves with provisions without aid from these states. The refugees have added many thousands to their numbers. I am informed, by an intelligent gentleman who lately left Halifax, that the governor, supposing the neighboring states had joined in our measures, had determined to issue a proclamation for admitting provisions in American bottoms, but an arrival of a vessel from Connecticut prevented it. Our governor has written a circular letter to the governors of the other states, urging the necessity and, to us, the justice of coming into our measures. If they do not, and I fear Connecticut and Rhode Island will not, we must repeal our acts, and the trade of the whole must suffer all the injury and our country all that indignity which Britain shall please to impose upon it. Would not a strong recommendation from congress to those states to afford their aid to Massachusetts and New Hampshire, who are voluntarily suffering in the common cause, have the desired effect? I write in haste, and can only give you the hint. I wish you would think of it. Adieu.

Governor William Moultrie, of South Carolina, to Governor Bowdoin, of Massachusetts, 20 Sept., 1785.

I have to acknowledge the honor of your favor of the twenty-eighth of July, 1785, enclosing two resolves of the commonwealth of Massachusetts of the eighteenth and twenty-third of June last, and likewise an "act for the regulating of navigation and commerce."

I shall take the earliest opportunity of laying the same before the legislature of this state, and have no doubt but that similar modes will be adopted so as to further a work which has now become equally essential to all.

The state of South Carolina is in general impressed with the propriety of investing congress with proper and full powers for the regulating the trade and commerce of the union; and until that body can have such powers, it must remain with individual states to guard against and counteract the machinations that are contriving and putting in practice to ruin our credit at home and abroad.

I flatter myself that as no state in the confederation can doubt the fatal tendency of the British navigation act, they will not, from local situation or any narrow and ill-grounded prejudice, be so far assistant to British policy as to decline approving the only measures that can be used to support our dignity and character as a trading nation, either by investing congress with full and sufficient powers to regulate and support the trade and commerce of the union, or by similar resolves with those of the commonwealth of Massachusetts.

I trust that this state, with every other in the confederation, are well convinced their existence as a nation depends on the strength of the union. Cemented together in one common interest they are invincible: but ruined when divided, and must fall a sacrifice to internal dissensions and foreign usurpations. I shall do myself the honor of communicating to your Excellency the result of the legislature on this subject, and shall continue to communicate to you such other acts of the state as may concern the particular interest of the commonwealth of Massachusetts, or that of the union.

Washington to J. Trumbull, Mount Vernon, 1 Oct., 1785.

MY DEAR SIR: You know too well the sincere respect and regard I entertained for your venerable father's public and private character to require assurances of the concern I felt for his death, or of that sympathy in your feelings for the loss of him which is prompted by friendship. Under it, however, great as your pangs may have been at the first shock, you have everything to console you. A long and well-spent life in the service of his country justly entitled him to the first place among patriots. In the social duties he yielded to none; and his lamp, from the common course of nature, being nearly extinguished and worn down with age and cares, but retaining his mental faculties in full vigor, are blessings which rarely attend advanced life; all these combining have secured to him universal respect and love here, and no doubt immeasurable happiness hereafter.

My principal pursuits are of a rural nature, in which I have great delight, especially as I am blessed with the enjoyment of good health. Mrs. Washington, on the contrary, is scarcely ever well, but thankful for your kind remembrance of her, and joins me in every good wish for you, Mrs. Trumbull, and your family.

Van Berckel to the States General, New York, 4 Oct., 1785. Ex.

The state of Rhode Island, at the last sitting of its assembly, passed an act regulating its navigation, and putting it for the most part on the same footing as in Massachusetts.

An act has passed in the state of Pennsylvania for the encouragement of their manufactures by a high tariff to be assessed at once on all foreign ships, except those of nations with which congress has a treaty of commerce.

Otto to Vergennes, New York, 8 Oct., 1785.   Ex.

The hostilities which the Barbary pirates practise on the Americans begin to disquiet them. The laws which they propose to pass for the extension of their navigation will only serve to deprive them of their commodities, which would have been secure on board of European vessels. Mr. Jay, whom congress instructed to make a report on this subject, proposed to arm privateers and to suppress force by force, but congress has felt the inadequateness of this means, and perceives that the United States cannot have the ambition to subjugate barbarians whom so many powerful nations have not been able to hinder from carrying on their piracies. The conviction prevails universally that it will be much better to negotiate with them, and to pay them annually a tribute in tobacco, or in naval stores, of which they have great need. I have reason to believe that Mr. Jefferson will receive instructions to beseech the intervention of his Majesty to conclude at the earliest possible moment a treaty with the Barbary powers.

Washington's Diary for 10 Oct., 1785.   Ex.

A Mr. McLane, on his way to Bishop Seabury for ordination, called and dined here; could not give him more than a general certificate, founded upon information respecting his character, having no acquaintance with him, nor any desire to open a correspondence with the new ordained bishop.

R. H. Lee to Washington, New York, 11 Oct., 1785.   Ex.

DEAR SIR: The advantage that I received to my health from relaxation, and the medical power of the springs I visited, has been very flattering, and will, I hope, furnish me with a stock of health sufficient to finish my presidential year with some degree of comfort. I hear with singular pleasure that the very important business of opening the navigation of Potomac goes on so well. I well know how much the community will be obliged for success in this useful work to your exertions. By a letter lately received from the Hon. Colonel Monroe, who is at Pittsburg and intends to be at the Indian treaty this month at the mouth of Great Miami, we learn that the temper of the great Indian nations, as nations, is not unfriendly to the United States, and promising success as well to the coming treaty as to the execution of the plan for surveying and disposing of territory beyond the Ohio for payment of the public debt. Colonel Monroe represents the intending settlers north-west of Ohio to be very few in number, and they disposed to obey quietly the orders of congress. The negotiation with Mr. Gardoqui proceeds so slowly, and as yet so ineffectually, that I fancy the free navigation of Mississippi is a point that, we may take it for granted, will not hastily be concluded upon, so that mischiefs from that source are probably postponed to a distant day.

R. H. Lee to Monroe, New York, 17 Oct., 1785. Ex.

DEAR SIR: It is most clear to me, from Mr. Adams's account of what passed between him and the secretary of state concerning the British debts, that, if our assemblies do not irritate by throwing obstructions in the way of the treaty of peace, we shall obtain every reasonable wish concerning time for payment. He seems to be apprehensive of violence, for he says: "It cannot be too strongly recommended to let persons and property be held sacred." You will find that the business of facilities, insultive as it is to us who have few or none, has been forced upon us as contended for when you were here. It is to me most plainly proper that our assembly should tax our people only for federal purposes what will suffice to pay our quota of the foreign interest and the expenses of the federal government; and not admit any facilities to be received in discharge of the taxes but such as have originated with our own citizens. This last will disappoint the plan of purchasing our produce with the certificates of these Northern states, which will pay the domestic creditors in these states whilst our own go unpaid—and thus we shall really give a bribe to prevent the settlement of our accounts, and consequently prevent the payment of our own citizens, who are at least as large creditors of the United States as the citizens of any other state.

R. H. Lee to Samuel Adams, New York, 17 Oct., 1785. Ex.

We do not find that the civil appearances about the court of London have as yet produced any solid, good effects, for still they hold the posts, still they encroach on our eastern boundary, and still their commercial regulations continue crabbed, and hurtful to themselves and to us. Perhaps time may heal the wound that yet rankles in the national breast. I fear it is too true that the Algerines, those *hostes humani generis*, have commenced war upon our commerce, and if we are not lucky enough to purchase a peace from these barbarians before they taste the sweets of plundering our commerce, it may be long before we can quiet them, and be most difficult to accomplish.

Minute of Conversation with Mr. Adams, 20 Oct., 1785.

Mr. Adams began the conversation by recapitulating the complaints of the United States on the subject of the posts not being yet evacuated, and no satisfaction having been given for the negroes who were carried away. He observed that Mr. Pitt had suggested the non-payment of the debts due to British subjects as a motive for not having settled either of these matters. On my observing to him that it was naturally to be expected that the payment of those debts was the first step necessary to any communications between the two countries, he replied the public were not obliged, either by treaty or otherwise, to discharge the debts of individuals; all that was stipulated by congress being merely a promise of leaving the matter open to such legal remedies as might be thought necessary, and throwing no obstructions in their way.

He then went to the subject of the fisheries, and stated the probability of France entirely running away with that valuable article, both from England and America, unless some regulations were made between the two countries to prevent the French from supplying their own West India islands, and rendering it unnecessary for the states to enter into the views of France on that head.

He referred to the readiness expressed by his Majesty to promote the friendship of the two countries whenever America should manifest a preference in favor of England over the rest of Europe. This preference, he insisted, was already apparent from the conduct of America toward this country, in respect to commerce, ever since the peace; that they wished to continue that preference in every article of trade, unless, by our backwardness to meet them on terms of fair and friendly reciprocity, they should find it necessary to enter into stipulations, with France or other powers, detrimental to the commerce and manufactures of this country.

Jefferson to Madison, Fontainebleau, 28 Oct., 1785.

DEAR SIR: Seven o'clock and retired to my fireside, I have determined to enter into conversation with you. This is a village of about five thousand inhabitants when the court is not here, and twenty thousand when they are, occupying a valley through which runs a brook, and on each side of it a ridge of small mountains, most of which are naked rock. The king comes here in the fall always to hunt. His court attend him, as do also the foreign diplomatic corps; but as this is not indispensably required, and my finances do not admit the expense of a continued residence here, I propose to come occasionally to attend the king's levees, returning again to Paris, distant forty miles. This being the first trip, I set out yesterday morning to take a view of the place. For this purpose, I shaped ray course toward the highest of the mountains in sight, to the top of which was about a league. As soon as I had got clear of the town, I fell in with a poor woman walking at the same rate with myself, and going the same course. Wishing to know the condition of the laboring poor, I entered into conversation with her, which I began by enquiries for the path which would lead me into the mountain, and hence proceeded to enquiries into her vocation, condition, and circumstances. She told me she was a day-laborer, at eight sous, or fourpence sterling, the day; that she had two children to maintain, and to pay a rent of thirty livres for her house (which would consume the hire of seventy-five days); that often she could get no employment, and, of course, was without bread. As we had walked together near a mile, and she had so far served me as a guide, I gave her, on parting, twenty-four sons. She burst into tears of a gratitude which I could perceive was unfeigned, because she was unable to utter a word. She had probably never before received so great an aid. This little attendrissement, with the solitude of my walk, led me into a train of reflections on that unequal division of property which occasions the numberless instances of wretchedness which I had observed in this country, and is to be observed all over Europe. The property of this country is absolutely concentred in a very few hands, having revenues of from half a million of guineas a year downward. These employ the flower of the country as servants, some of them having as many as two hundred domestics, not laboring. They employ also a great number of manufacturers and tradesmen, and lastly the class of laboring husbandmen; but after all these comes the most numerous of all the classes—that is, the poor who cannot find work. I asked myself what could be the reason that so many should be permitted to beg, who are willing to work, in a country where there is a very considerable portion of uncultivated lands. These lands are kept idle mostly for the sake of game. It should seem, then, that it must be because of the enormous wealth of the proprietors, which places them above attention to the increase of their revenues by permitting these lands to be labored. I am conscious that an equal division of property is impracticable; but, the consequences of this enormous inequality producing so much misery to the bulk of mankind, legislators cannot invent too many devices for subdividing property, only taking care to let their subdivisions go hand in hand with the natural affections of the human mind. The descent of property of every kind, therefore, to all the children, or to all the brothers and sisters or other relations, in equal degree, is a politic measure, and a practicable one. Another means of silently lessening the inequality of property is to exempt all from taxation below a certain point, and to tax the higher portions of property in geometrical progression as they rise. Wherever there are in any country uncultivated lands and unemployed poor, it is clear that the laws of property have been so far extended as to violate natural right. The earth is given as a common stock for man to labor and live on; if, for the encouragement of Industry, we allow it to be appropriated, we must take care that other employment be furnished to those excluded from the appropriation. If we do not, the fundamental right to labor the earth returns to the unemployed. It is too soon yet in our country to say that every man who cannot find employment, but who can find uncultivated land, shall be at liberty to cultivate it, paying a moderate rent; but it is not too soon to provide by every possible means that as few as possible shall be without a little portion of land. The small landholders are the most precious part of a state.

The next object which struck my attention in my walk was the deer, with which the wood abounded; they were of the kind called "cerfs," and are certainly of the same species with ours. They are blackish indeed under the belly, and not white as ours, and they are more of the chestnut-red; but these are such small differences as would be sure to happen in two races from the same stock, breeding separately a number of ages. Their hares are totally different from the animals we call by that name, but their rabbit is almost exactly like him; the only difference is in their manners—the land on which I walked for some time being absolutely reduced to a honey-comb by their burrowing. I think there is no instance of ours burrowing. After descending the hill again, I saw a man cutting fern. I went to him under pretence of asking the shortest road to the town, and afterward asked for what use he was cutting fern. He told me that this part of the country furnished a great deal of fruit to Paris; that when packed in straw it acquired an ill taste, but that dry fern preserved it perfectly, without communicating any taste at all. I treasured this observation for the preservation of my apples on my return to my own country. They have no apple here to compare to our Newtown pippin. They have nothing which deserves the name of a peach, there being not sun enough to ripen the plum-peach, and the best of their soft peaches being like our autumn peaches. Their cherries and strawberries are fair, but I think less flavored. Their plums, I think, are better; so, also, the gooseberries, and the pears infinitely beyond anything we possess. They have no grape better than our Sweet-water; but they have a succession of as good from very early in the summer till frost. I am tomorrow to go to Mr. Malsherbes (an uncle of the Chevalier Luzerne's), about seven leagues from hence, who is the most curious man in France as to his trees. He is making for me a collection of the vines from which the Burgundy, Champagne, Bordeaux, Frontignac, and the other most valuable wines of this country are made. Another gentleman is collecting for me the best eating grapes, includeing what we call the raisin. I propose, also, to endeavor to colonize their hare, rabbit, red and gray partridge, pheasants of different kinds, and some other birds; but I find that I am wandering beyond the limits of my walk, and will therefore bid you adieu.

The French Minister to Jefferson, Fontainebleau, 30 Oct., 1785.   Ex.

But the king has advised me at the same time, sir, of the slight regard had in America to the rule of reciprocity, and how they are disposed there to swerve from the principles which have served as a foundation to the connections which have subsisted between France and the United States. We are in fact informed, sir, that in several states regulations of navigation and trade have been made injurious to the French commerce, and hurtful and contrary to the spirit of the treaty of the sixth of February, 1778. Congress is too enlightened not to perceive how greatly these proceedings would affect us, and too prudent and far-sighted not to be impressed with the necessity of maintaining affairs on the footing of reciprocity on which they have been since France became the ally of the United States. Without this precaution, it is impossible that the mutual trade of the two nations should be able to prosper, and even to exist, and the king will find himself obliged, in spite of himself, to seek suitable expedients for placing this affair on a perfect equality, by making respecting the Americans regulations similar to those which have been adopted, or may be adopted in the future, respecting France.

Washington to Doctor Price, Mount Vernon, Nov., 1785.

G. Washington presents his most respectful compliments to Dr. Price. With much thankfulness he has received, and with the highest gratification he has read, the doctor's excellent observations on the importance of the American revolution, and the means of making it a benefit to the world. Most devoutly is it to be wished that reasoning so sound should take deep root in the minds of the revolutionists. But there is cause to apprehend that the inconveniences resulting from ill-founded jealousies and local politics must be felt ere a more liberal system of federal government is adopted. The latter I am persuaded will happen, but its progress may be slow—unless, as the revolution itself was, it should be precipitated by the all-grasping hand of——, or the illiberal and mistaken policy of other nations.

For the honorable notice of me in your address, I pray you to receive my warmest acknowledgments, and the assurances of the sincere esteem and respect which I entertain for you.

Elbridge Gerry and Rufus King to Governor Bowdoin, New York, 2 Nov., 1785.

SIR: We are honored with your Excellency's letter of the twenty-fourth of October, enclosing two others for his Excellency the president of congress, which we have carefully delivered him.

We observe your Excellency is of opinion "that, if in the union there is the operation of such discordant principles as make it hazardous to entrust congress with powers necessary to its well-being, the union cannot long subsist." This opinion is perfectly coincident with our own, and we flatter ourselves it does not militate with the ideas expressed in our letters of the tenth of August and third of September, for we still have reason to conceive that the best and surest mode of obtaining such an addition to the powers of congress as is necessary to the well-being of the union is, to make the powers temporary, in the first instance, and, when approved by experience, to adopt them as part of the confederation; and we likewise conceive that, if a convention of the states is necessary on this occasion, the members thereof should be limited in their authority, and confined to the revision of such parts of the confederation as are supposed defective, and not entrusted with a general revision of the articles, and a right to report a plan of federal government essentially different from the republican form now administered.

Otto to Vergennes, New York, 7 Nov., 1785. Ex.

MY LORD: Mr. Richard Lee, who has occupied the chair of president of congress for a year, has just set out for Virginia, and congress will proceed at once to the election of a new president. Mr. Lee is universally missed by that body. By his prudent and moderate conduct he has been able to conciliate the friendship and respect of all the delegations; by his personal talents and his just principles with regard to European powers, he has also merited the favor of the foreigners accredited to congress. Easy in his manners, but resolute and decided in his principles, uniting to very extensive knowledge a long experience in affairs, versed as deeply as possible at such a great distance in the political relations of the different powers of Europe, he was as well qualified as any private individual of this continent to fill the office of the first magistrate. But that which has chiefly distinguished Mr. Lee from the other presidents is, that in the grand committees of the whole house he won votes by his eloquence and the force of his arguments. We particularly lose in Mr. Lee a man who felt perfectly all the obligations which the United States have to France. Mr. Lee has often spoken to me with ardor of the necessity of zealously drawing the two nations nearer together, and, as far as possible, causing our commerce in America to flourish. He especially desires that we should carry on, without any restriction, the tobacco trade with Virginia, and that the Farmers General should take, in that state, no measures prejudicial to the interests of individuals. In regard to this commerce he has the same principles as those of the other Virginians with whom I have had opportunity to converse. He sees with regret that our tobaccos are paid for by letters of exchange, and in the commodities of England instead of our manufactured goods, and he desires that private individuals may not be discouraged by the contracts which the Farmers General are in a position to make by the wholesale. I have already had the honor of stating these principles to you in my despatch No. 10, and what I have learned since only confirms me in my opinion upon this subject.

Mason to Washington, Gunston Hall, 9 Nov., 1785.

DEAR SIR: The bearer waits on you with a side of venison (the first we have killed this season), which I beg your acceptance of.

I have heard nothing from the assembly except vague reports of their being resolved to issue a paper currency; upon what principles or funds I know not; perhaps upon the old threadbare security of pledging solemnly the public credit. I believe such an experiment would prove similar to the old vulgar adage of carrying a horse to the water. They may pass a law to issue it, but twenty laws will not make people receive it.

I intended to go down to Richmond about the fifteenth of this month to have reported the compact with the Maryland commissioners, but I have lately had so severe a fit of the convulsive colic, or the gout, in my stomach, that I dare not venture far from home; it held me from Sunday evening till Tuesday morning, and has left me so weak that I am hardly able to walk across the floor.

We hope to hear that you, your lady, and family are well; to whom Mrs. Mason and the family here present their best compliments, with those of, dear sir, your affectionate and obedient servant, etc.

David Stuart to Washington, Richmond, 16 Nov., 1785. Ex.

The inhabitants of Kentucky have sent in their petition by their delegates, praying a separation. It is so sensible, respectful, and modest, that it seems to produce conviction on every mind of the propriety of the measure. The members nominated to congress in lieu of Mercer and Handy are Colonel Lee and Colonel Carrington. There were several other candidates for these places, who were not ashamed openly to solicit votes. Indeed, I am sorry to observe that Richmond abounds with people watching for places, and who omit no opportunity of paying court to the very honorable members.

Your letter to the governor has been read in the house, and a bill is brought in repealing the former law, according to your petition; and giving you full power to appropriate to any purposes you may think fit the donations of the assembly. It will, I suppose, be transmitted to you by order of the house as soon as it is passed. I have heard much approbation and satisfaction expressed at your declining those donations. I enclose to you a bill, now under the consideration of the house, giving powers to congress to regulate our trade. Its fate will not be decided till Friday week. If, therefore, any amendment occurs to you, I shall receive it with pleasure.

Archibald Gary to Washington, Senate Chamber, 25 Nov., 1785. Ex.

MY DEAR SIR: It will always give me pleasure to show every mark of civility to any gentleman[1] who is honored with your notice. The gentleman[1] has solicited and obtained an act for securing to the authors of literary works an exclusive property therein for a limited time, which I think just.

I omitted to mention a bill which has passed both houses founded on your letter respecting James and Potomac rivers, in which your request is fully complied with.

I am really fearful we shall not rise before March. I am sure, if they go through the new code of laws, it will employ them near that time. Nothing determined yet as to the assessment, but judge it will be rejected. A petition for a general emancipation has met justly that fate.

Washington to David Stuart, Mount Vernon, 30 Nov., 1785. Ex.

DEAR SIR: The resolutions which were published for consideration, vesting congress with powers to regulate the commerce of the union, have, I hope, been acceded to. If the states individually were to attempt this, an abortion, or a many-headed monster, would be the issue. If we consider ourselves, or wish to be considered by others, as a united people, why not adopt the measures which are characteristic of it, and support the honor and dignity of one? If we are afraid to trust one another under qualified powers, there is an end of the union. Why, then, need we be solicitous to keep up the farce of it? It gives me pleasure to hear that there is such an accordance of sentiments between the eastern and western parts of this state. My opinion of the separation has always been to meet them upon fair and just grounds, and part like friends disposed to acts of brotherly kindness thereafter. I wish you had mentioned the territorial line between us.

[1] Noah Webster

Edmund Randolph to Washington, Richmond, 3 Dec., 1785. Ex.

A lengthy and earnest debate has been held on the propriety of vesting congress with a control of commerce. But the advocates for the measure will scarcely succeed, so strong are the apprehensions, in some minds, of an abuse of the power.

I am, my dear sir, with the greatest esteem and respect, your affecttionate friend and servant.

Washington to Alexander Hamilton, Mount Vernon, 11 Dec., 1785. Ex.

DEAR SIR: I have been favored with your letter of the twenty-fifth of November, by Major Farlie. Sincerely do I wish that the several state societies had or would adopt the alterations which were made and recommended by the general meeting in May, 1784. I then thought, and I have had no cause since to change my opinion, that if the society of the Cincinnati mean to live in peace with the rest of their fellow-citizens they must subscribe to the alterations which were at that time adopted. That the jealousies of, and prejudices against, this society were carried to an unwarrantable length, I will readily grant; and that less than was done ought to have removed the fears which had been imbibed, I am as clear in as I am that it would not have done it. But it is a matter of little moment whether the alarm which seized the public mind was the result of foresight, envy, jealousy, or a disordered imagination, the effect of perseverance would have been the same; and wherein would have been found an equivalent for the separation of interests which, from my best information (not from one state only, but many), would have inevitably taken place? The fears of the people are not yet removed—they only sleep, and a very little matter will set them afloat again.

Had it not been for the predicament in which we stand, with respect to the foreign officers and the charitable part of the institution, I should on that occasion, as far as my voice would have gone, have endeavored to convince the narrow-minded part of our countrymen that the *amor patriæ* was much stronger in our breasts than in theirs, and that our conduct through the whole of this business was actuated by nobler and more generous sentiments than was apprehended by abolishing the society at once, with a declaration of the causes and the purity of its intention; but the latter may be interesting to many, and the former is an insuperable bar to such a step.

Jefferson to Monroe, Paris, 11 Dec., 1785.   Ex.

How goes on the disposition to confer the regulation of our commerce on congress? On this side the Atlantic we are viewed as objects of commerce only, and as little to be relied on, even for this purpose, while its regulation is so disjointed.

Robert Pleasants to Washington, Cayles, 11 12th month, 1785.

P. S. I herewith send thee a small pamphlet on the subject of slavery, said to be wrote by John Dickinson, which, if thou hast not before seen, I doubt not will afford pleasure in the perusal.

David Stuart to Washington, Richmond, 18 Dec., 1785.   Ex.

DEAR SIR: An act has just passed for paying in hard money the interest due on money put into the continental loan office. I send you the act, lest you might not attend to it in the papers. If you have any business of this sort to be transacted, I shall be happy to serve you in it. But you will observe the time will be soon elapsed. It did not occur to me before that you might have money in the office, or I should have given you earlier notice of it.

You will have seen from the journals that nothing is yet done on the subject of trade. I doubt much if anything effectual will be done. If there is, it may be ascribed to a letter from the legislature of Maryland, requesting an appointment of commissioners by each state to fix on a similarity of restrictions.

The consideration of British debts is now before us, and from the opposition made by Mr. Smith [the motion for] for leave to bring in a bill on that subject, I have my fears about the success of it. I expect to get the bill you transmitted passed the ensuing week, as it is reported reasonable by the committee to whom it was referred.

Monroe to Madison, New York, 19 Dec., 1785.   Ex.

DEAR SIR: The conduct of the legislature in complying with the requisition of congress, in the opinion of all here, does the highest honor to the state, and, at the same time that it evinces a regard for public justice and a mind superior to little resentments, gives an additional assurance of the strength and permanence of the federal government.

We earnestly wish to have the result of the deliberations of the house upon the commercial propositions.

I find the most enlightened members here fully impressed with the expedience of putting an end to the dismemberment of the old states, doubtful of the propriety of admitting a single new one into the confederacy, and well inclined to a revision of the compact between the United States and Virginia respecting the division of the country beyond the Ohio.

Otto to Vergennes, New York, 20 Dec., 1785. Ex.

The negotiations of Mr. Gardoqui with Mr. Jay make no progress whatever, my lord; it appears that the navigation of the Mississippi is not the chief obstacle to the conclusion of a commercial treaty. Mr. Gardoqui has told me confidentially that he regards that navigation as a matter of great indifference to his court, and that, whatever may be the pretensions of the inhabitants of Kentucky, they could never gain great advantages from their expeditions upon the Mississippi. Indeed, he continued, what profit will they be able to receive from a river which they can ascend only at great expense and with extreme difficulty? To carry on a profitable trade there is need of means to make return voyages. Every one knows that it requires several months to ascend the Mississippi as far as the Ohio, that a season and a special time is necessary in order not to run aground, and that the profits of this navigation can never compensate for its dangers. It is not, therefore, the Mississippi which causes us the greatest embarrassment, but it is the incontestable principle of reciprocity, which ought to form the basis of every commercial treaty, and which they have refused to adopt so far as we are concerned. If we concede to the United States an unrestricted right of entering our ports, we wish to enjoy the same privilege in theirs. They reply to me that we have no manufactured goods to ship to them; granted. Still, we may, in the course of time, have the means for them, and we insist, at least, upon the right of shipping our commodities to them. We know very well that the balance of trade is against us in all the countries of the world; but we hope that it will not always be so, and we are unwilling to renounce the hope of stimulating our commerce and of making it active as soon as circumstances will permit. For the rest, we are not urged to conclude a commercial treaty with the United States, and we have no interest in hastening the measure by founding it upon unfavorable principles. Mr. Gardoqui is himself well versed in commercial affairs, and however intelligent the Americans may be in that science, it will be difficult for them to seduce that minister by false concessions. For the rest, he has never spoken to me of the support of France, and it appears in general that the court of Madrid takes but a moderate interest in its connections with this country.

Mr. Temple does everything in his power, my lord, to acquire popularity here. At first he was attacked in some of the newspapers; but seeing the little impression that these pasquinades made upon the public, they were abandoned. This consul-general has the misfortune to be very deaf; but it is suspected that he exaggerates this defect a little, in order to reassure everybody, and the better to hear that which is said of him. I have certainly noticed that there are moments when he is less deaf than at others. He makes especial attempts to draw near to the minister of Holland; he overwhelms him with protestations of friendship, and assures him positively that in a little time he will learn that the former connection between Holland and England has been renewed in the most solid manner, and that, independently of the proposed marriage between the Prince of Wales and the Princess of Orange, they are at work in England upon a political alliance of infinite advantage to the two nations. Mr. Van Berckel distrusts greatly all these demonstrations of friendship, and he has spoken to me with an air of incredulity which leads me to believe that he sincerely desires that the reports of Mr. Temple may not be true.

Otto to Vergennes, New York, 25 Dec., 1785. Ex.

MY LORD: The jealousy of the Americans in regard to their representatives in congress produces many bad effects, as I now have the honor of reporting to you. By the constitution of the various states, delegates holding a seat in congress are not permitted to remain there longer than three years. Some, indeed, cannot remain longer than one year. It follows that it is impossible, through the withdrawal of the different members, that that body should not lose at least two months of the year in dissolving and reforming, and that the choice of the citizens should not very often fall upon those less capable of occupying themselves with the larger interests of the republic. A man, through talent and patriotism worthy of sitting in the senate of the United States, hesitates to accept a place whose short duration can oblige him to neglect his private affairs. Scarcely has he the time to acquaint himself with the business when the rule established by his state forces him to return to private life. Young men of great talent, but of little experience, begin to seek places in congress, which ought to be for them a school of politics, but which cannot gain much stability through the presence of these delegates. Of this, my lord, a very great indifference is the result. The delegates absent themselves for the most trifling reasons, and it is difficult to assemble seven states, which form the number required to transact the least important business; but even in this case it is difficult for seven states to unite in opinion, and it cannot be seen without astonishment that an object of so little importance as the appointment of an American minister to Holland has been postponed for six months.

The little stability of congress, my lord, insensibly gives to the ministers of the different departments a power incompatible with the spirit of liberty and of jealousy which prevails in this country. There is an unwillingness that the members of congress should hold their seats longer than three years, but the secretaries of state can be removed only for bad conduct. It follows that these ministers, being perfectly acquainted with current affairs, enjoy a great superiority over the delegates whom chance has assembled from all parts of the continent, and who are for the most part strangers to their task. Mr. Jay especially has acquired a peculiar ascendancy over the members of congress. All important business passes through his hands. He makes his report on it, and congress seldom has an opinion different from his Instead of appointing committees, they will insensibly become accustomed to seeing only through the eyes of Mr. Jay, and, although that minister may be as capable as possible of conducting wisely the measures of the United States, this influence necessarily is hurtful to the freedom and impartiality which ought to prevail in the national senate.

The continual rotation of the members of congress produces another effect very prejudicial to the despatch of business. After having debated an important subject for several weeks, the arrival of some new deputies causes a new discussion, as diffuse as the first, and precious time is lost in constantly recurring to the same subjects.

Whatever the influence of Mr. Jay may be, he has not succeeded in bringing about the adoption of his report in regard to the Algerines. This minister has seriously proposed making war upon them. He is positive that the United States are in a condition to keep the Barbary pirates in awe, without coming to the disgrace of paying them a tribute. I should not be sorry, he said to me, among other things, if the Algerines were to come and burn some of our maritime towns, in order to bring back to the United States their former energy, which peace and commerce have almost destroyed. War alone will bring the different states nearer together, and give a new importance to congress; we shall not lack means, but we do lack that republican and national spirit which alone can give vigor to our operations. We have more need of soldiers than of traders, of patriotism than of foreign manufactures, of citizens than of rich ship-owners. War, and war alone, will give us soldiers, patriotism, and citizens. Commerce has already separated the interests of the various states; war will make them identical. I wish the New Englanders to strike for the flour, tobacco, and rice of the people of the South, and the Carolinians to pour out to the last drop their blood for the fisheries of Massachusetts. The majority of congress perceive very clearly, my lord, that war would serve as a bond to the confederation, but they cannot conceal the lack of means which they possess to carry it on with advantage. It is hoped that the agents whom Mr. Jefferson has sent to Algiers to negotiate a treaty of amity will succeed in obtaining desirable terms, but the resolution is firm to make war rather than subscribe to hard conditions.

Monroe to Madison, New York, 26 Dec., 1785.

DEAR SIR: I am perfectly satisfied that the more fully the subject is investigated, and the better the interests of the states severally are understood, the more obvious will appear the necessity of committing to the United States permanently the power of regulating their trade. Whether it will be expedient to accept it for a limited time only, it is difficult to determine. If it is expedient for a day, while the states bear the same relation they do to each other, and to other powers, or rather while they adjoin each other and are bounded by the ocean, it will still be so; whether, then, will it be expedient to avail ourselves of the present disposition, so far only as to try an experiment, the success of which, as such, must depend upon a variety of circumstances, or if to delay any remedy until, under the pressure of the present difficulties, it may be made complete. As an experiment, in what light will it be conceived, and how treated by the foreign powers? Will they not all wish to defeat it, and, of course, avoid those stipulations in our favor which may hereafter furnish arguments for its renewal? We may, with propriety, also take into consideration the diversity of interest which will arise in the admission of western states into the confederacy. In a government also so fluctuating there will never be energy or calculation on it, either at home or abroad; everything will be in a state of uncertainty; the states severally will be at a loss how to act under it (in their respective delegations); they will fear to take those decisive measures with respect to other powers which might be necessary, lest their vigorous operation may prevent its renewal; but whether these or any other consideration may be of sufficient weight to induce us to seek only a permanent change, is what I have not absolutely determined on.

I beg of you to give me your sentiments thereon, as well as of the course you think I may, with propriety, take here, provided the state should confide it only for a limited time.

Is it not strange, in this situation, that we should be disputing whether we shall act together, or cement and strengthen the union?

Van Berckel to the States General, New York, 1 Jan., 1786. Ex.

I have to announce to your High Mightinesses that the navigation act passed last year in the state of Massachusetts is repealed, but remains in full force in regard to the English nation. The same state has given a bounty for the encouragement of their fisheries.

The general assembly of Pennsylvania has now under consideration a bill, by virtue of which all those who, at the beginning of the war, did not take the oath of allegiance to the state, and thereby forfeited their rights to citizenship, may be allowed to take this oath, at the same time swearing that they have not aided the English with any inimical design against the United States since the declaration of independence in any respect.

A considerable number of citizens of the state of Maryland have presented a memorial to their assembly asking for paper money; yet it is very uncertain whether this will be taken up.

Otto to Vergennes, New York, 2 Jan., 1786.

All Christian sects enjoy in America an entire liberty. The Jews have the exercise of their religion only; but they make efforts to enter into the legislative assemblies. It would be very remarkable if this people, after having suffered the contempt of all ages and nations, should succeed in America in taking part in the affairs of government. But this revolution is not yet ripe; and although, according to the terms of several of the constitutions, it is enough to recognise a God to enter the assembly, prejudices are still too strong to enable the

Jews to enjoy the privileges accorded to all their fellow-citizens. But whatever may be the tolerance of the different states in the United States, religious zeal awakens so soon as one sect dares to take the lead over another. The Presbyterians of Pennsylvania and Massachusetts have not yet been reconciled to the Anglicans; and when a preacher announces some exaggerated pretensions, it is enough to inflame the opposite party. The small number of Catholics has not yet given umbrage; but it is believed here, as in England, that this religion is contrary to political liberty; and, if it is augmented by the aid of any foreign power, they will not fail to oppose its increase with vivacity. Moreover, we are essentially interested that there should not be in America a French church, since it would be one motive the more to excite the subjects of his Majesty to emigrate. Mr. de la Valinière assembles the French who are in his house. He preaches regularly to them every Sunday, and he assured me that he is persuaded that, if there were a French church here, it would, without doubt, attract a great number of his countrymen.

Temple to Lord Carmarthen, New York, 5 Jan., 1786. Ex.

The trade and navigation of these states appear to me to be now, in a great measure, at a stand; the exclusion of their ships and vessels from his Majesty's sugar islands greatly deranged and decreased what commerce they had been accustomed to; and a dread of the Barbary rovers hath of late struck a palsy into what remained of their trade to Spain, Portugal, and the Mediterranean. The mercantile part of the people, in consequence thereof, begin to have their eyes open to what they ought to have seen immediately upon the restoration of peace to their country—that Great Britain hath undoubtedly many commercial favors to grant, if she pleases, to these states, while they, in return, have scarce a single favor or advantage to offer; the vast debt owing to the British merchants who unwisely gave too much credit, together with high taxes, poverty, and other concurring circumstances, have been the means of bringing the commercial part of these states, in some measure, to their reason, but the landed people still continue to hold high notions of their rising importance among the nations of the earth.

Count de Rochambeau to Washington, Paris, 7 Jan., 1786.

MY DEAR GENERAL: I but receive now the letter which you honored me with on September the seventh ultimo. I send at once to

Captain Pusignan your answer, and I hope you will be henceforth got clear from all those troublesome askings.

I am enchanted of the continuance of your good health, of the calm that you are enjoying in the bosom of your family, and under the shadow of your laurels.

The storms which threatened us on the account of Holland are entirely dissipated, and the France as yet played, on this occasion, the fine part of moderatrix. The troubles for the succession of Bavaria shall yet threaten us at the death of the elector of Bavaria, or at that of the king of Prussia, of whom the health is old and reeling. He is at the head of a formidable confederation to hinder the exchange, to which the emperor has not renounced where the circumstances will permit it to him.

Our neighbors, the English, retrieve their finances; the young Pitt gets every day a great majority, and a great confidence in his nation, by a good and wise administration and economy. The against part has lost one of its chief members by the nomination of Mr. Eden in the station of commissary to make a treaty of commerce with the France, and they believe that the settlement of Ireland will be consolidated this winter.

I have seen Cornwallis last summer at Calais. He was sent by the king of England to wait on the Duke of York, his son, to the instructive camps of the king of Prussia. I gave him a supper in little committee; he was very polite, but, as you may believe, I could not drink with him your health in toast.

The English treat us very politely, but I think in the bosom of their hearts they do not love us more than they do the Americans. I have many invitations from them to go to London, but I am not hurry to profit of it, and I like better to see them on my hearths than to go and see them on their own. They pretend by their public papers that they wait only for the construction of some new forts upon their limits to deliver up to you those which they have on yours. It is a pretence that you can, better than anybody, judge of the value.

I am very glad that the respectable and old Doctor Franklin has received in his country the honors that they owe to his services.

I beg of you, my dear General, to present my respects, and give my best compliments, to Madame Washington, and to all your family, and be well persuaded of my eternal attachment, and of the respect with which I have the honor to be, my dear General, etc.

Otto to Vergennes, New York, 10 Jan., 1786. Ex.

The political importance of Mr. Jay increases daily. Congress seems to me to be guided only by his directions, and it is as difficult to obtain anything without the co-operation of that minister as to bring about the rejection of a measure proposed by him. The indolence of the majority of the members of congress and the ignorance of most of the others cause his superiority. It is found much easier in current business to ask the opinion of the minister of foreign affairs than to form into committee; hence the prejudices and passions of Mr. Jay insensibly become those of congress, which does not perceive that it ceases to be anything more than the organ of its chief minister. Happily, Mr. Jay is a patriot, and in general well disposed, but his grievances against France render him as obstinate as possible in regard to our demands the most just. I have already had the honor of informing you that Mr. Marbois has not for nearly a year received any response to the various memorials which he has presented; nor have I. The minister always says to me that congress is too much occupied to take them into consideration, but I know that that assembly has not for a long time had anything of importance to decide, and that these delays are due solely to the ill-will of Mr. Jay. I would not complain of this if I had no reason to apprehend that the long silence of congress might be attributed to my inactivity, but I am pained to see that in the most simple affairs, and those demanding but two hours' discussion, he delays his reply for many months.

I cannot constantly importune Mr. Jay, for his reply is ever ready, that he will seize the first opportunity to lay this business before congress. The minister has furthermore the character, with which the Quakers are reproached, of never replying directly to any question. As he never discloses his opinion, it is impossible to rectify it, and, although he inspires the majority of the resolutions of congress, he always seems to defer to the judgment of that body in all the explanations asked of him. It is very unfortunate for us that for a place so important the choice of congress should have fallen upon the very man who does not love us. The affair of the fisheries still lies heavy upon his heart. For the rest, whatever the prejudices of this minister toward us may be, I cannot deny that there are few men in America better able to fill the place which he occupies. The veneration with which he has inspired almost all the members of congress proves, more than anything else, that even the jealousy so inseparable from the American character, has not prevailed against him, and that he is as prudent in his conduct as he is firm and resolute in his political principles and in his coolness toward France.

I am very glad to see a restoration of confidence between the delegation of Massachusetts and our court. Massachusetts will for a long time play the principal part in the national congress. She is almost constantly represented by four or five delegates, all men of merit and laborious, while the other states are rarely represented by two. That state furthermore distinguishes herself by her inviolable attachment to certain principles which she never gives up, and by virtue of perseverance and resolution she is always sure of success. She has the advantage of laying down the law, so to speak, to New Hampshire, Rhode Island, and Connecticut, and those four states, almost always in accord, rarely fail to carry the vote.

Monroe to Jefferson, New York, 19 Jan., 1786. Ex.

DEAR SIR: My last advised you of my departure hence on the twenty-fourth of August last for the westward, with intention to take a view of the Indian treaty to be held at the mouth of the Big Miami and of the country lying between Lake Erie and the head waters of James or Potomac rivers, with those which empty from either side into the Ohio; thence to attend the federal court on the fifteenth of November at Williamsburg; but the danger from the Indians made it imprudent for me to pass the river, and the delay at Fort Pitt, and upon the Ohio, the water being low, consumed so much of the time allotted for this excursion that I was forced to leave the commissioners at Limestone and take my course directly through the Kentucky settlements and the wilderness to Richmond, so that I was neither gratified with a view of the treaty nor to such a degree with that of the country as I had proposed.

Mr. Franklin was here a few days since upon some private business, and was so kind as to favor me frequently with his company. I have also been much pleased with an acquaintance with Mr. Otto; he hath made an impression here very flattering to himself and favorable to the idea you entertain of him.

My several routes westward, with the knowledge of the country I have thereby obtained, have impressed me fully with a conviction of the impolicy of our measures respecting it. I speak not in this instance of the ordinance for the survey and disposal of it, but of those which became necessary and were founded upon the act of cession from the state of Virginia.

I am clearly of opinion that to many of the most important objects of a federal government their interests, if not opposed, will be but little connected with ours; instead of weakening theirs and making it subservient to our purposes, we have given it all the possible strength we could; weaken it we might also, and at the same time (I mean by reducing the number of the states) render them substantial service. A great part of the territory is miserably poor, especially that near Lakes Michigan and Erie; and that upon the Mississippi and the Illinois consists of extensive plains which have not had, from appearances, and will not have, a single bush on them for ages. The districts, therefore, within which these fall, will, perhaps, never contain a sufficient number of inhabitants to entitle them to membership in the confederacy, and in the mean time the people who may settle within them will be governed by the resolutions of congress, in which they will not be represented.

The tendency which at present prevails for a dismemberment of the old states not only increases their strength, but will also add to the diversity of interest. At the instance of which of the states hath the right to the navigation of the Mississippi been carried thus far? And if you lop off the western parts of those states by whom it was brought about, will you not necessarily draw them from that pursuit? Whatever shall be done or attempted on this subject I will transmit you. The subject of the mint was taken up last summer and determined that the unit should be a dollar; it was afterward postponed. It will be taken up again so soon as we shall have nine or ten states (for at present we have but seven). The proposition for recommending it to the states to vest the United States [with power] to regulate their trade is still before congress. What will be its fate is uncertain.

Accept my acknowledgments for your book, which I have read with pleasure and improvement, and be assured I will keep it as private as you might wish until you shall consent to its publication, which I hope will be the case. I should suppose the observations you have made on the subjects you allude to would have a very favorable effect, since no considerations would induce them but a love for the rights of Indians and for your country. Whether I shall be able to visit you is still doubtful. My dependence is almost altogether on the bar. By my late absence left the I have door open to others; the sooner I therefore return to it, the better it will be for me. I feel myself returning to the same train of thoughts upon this subject as when I had finished my studies. I am thinking of settling at Richmond, building a house, etc. Will you be so kind as to transmit me a plan? Suppose the house when finished to cost $3,000 or $4,000 (a part to be finished only at first). I shall, I believe, commence it as soon as I receive it.

John Adams to Samuel Adams, Grosvenor Square, 26 Jan., 1786. Ex.

DEAR SIR: Congress has hitherto been studiously kept out of sight by the king, ministry, and opposition. They are afraid of raising in American minds ideas of their importance. Russia, Denmark, and England would not form a balance to Bourbon and Holland, if congress should be joined. Indeed, if the United States should be neutral, the balance would not be exact. In my humble opinion we must be neutral, or join the French and Dutch

I have endeavored to convince them that neutrality is in our power, but with little success; indeed, they really do not think us of much consequence. We have no navy, and are awkward in uniting in anything. Some of them indeed agree that we shall grow, both in union, dignity, and power. It is really of more moment to this country to secure the neutrality of the United States than the alliance of Russia, and the time will come when it will be seen and felt. But the nation is too much inflamed and embittered to reflect coolly upon anything respecting America.

Our path is plain. We must make navigation acts and take care of ourselves, preserve our neutrality as long as we can, and when we must part with it get the best price for it we can.

It is much to be desired that our commerce with all other nations may be increased, especially France and Holland, and lessened with England as much as possible, until she shall put it on a more liberal footing. The political friendship, too, of France, Spain, and Holland should be cultivated as much as possible without involving us too far. With great esteem and affection, yours, etc.

Lieutenant-Governor Henry Hope to the Commissioners of American Claims at Halifax, Quebec, 29 Jan., 1786. Ex.

By the muster rolls of loyalists settled in this province, taken in the months of August, September, and October last, the total numbers are about six thousand three hundred, exclusive of about five hundred settled in Chaleur and Gaspe bays in the lieutenant-government of Gaspé.

The heads of families are about two thousand five hundred, who are distributed nearly as follows:

Near Niagara and Detroit	300
From Johnstown to Cataraqui and its vicinity	1,800
About Sorel and in all the Lower Canada	200
Chaleur Bay and Gaspé	200
	2,500

Van Berckel to the States General, New York, 31 Jan., 1786. Ex.

The legislature of this state assembled on the sixth of this month, being called together by a proclamation of the governor. There is a rumor current that in this session an act will be passed for issuing paper money to the amount of four hundred thousand pounds (two million four hundred thousand Dutch guilders). There are now lying here, ready for sailing, two ships destined for Canton, in China, in one of which Mr. Shaw and Mr. Randall are to sail, the former as consul, the latter as vice-consul, of the United States near the emperor of China. The owners of both these ships had addressed me to obtain letters of recommendation, but I concluded that I could not fulfil their wish.

Monroe to Madison, New York, 11 Feb., 1786. Ex.

DEAR SIR: In my last I mentioned to you the subject of the impost was revived, and that a report of a committee had given place to a motion of Mr. Pinckney, the latter being still before the house. The report and motion, with a report from the board of treasury to the same effect, have since been committed, in which state the business now lies. I enclose you a paper containing the report. It is doubted whether in any event this state will adopt it. Those members elected in opposition to such as were turned out for their opposition to this measure have, I hear, imbibed their sentiments, and act under them. They are, it is said, possessed to a great amount (I mean the leaders of the party) of public securities, and, doubtful of their payment by federal exertion, seem inclined to pursue the course Pennsylvania latterly did and provide for it by establishing state funds. The more extensive the funds of the state, and the more fully they exclude the citizens of other states and foreigners from such provision, the better, of course, for the party.

If you visit this place shortly, I will present you to a young lady who will be adopted a citizen of Virginia in the course of this week.

From Sir Guy Carleton relative to the Military Force to he kept up in Canada, 20 Feb., 1786. Ex.

The number of British subjects in North America, compared with the inhabitants of the revolted provinces, may be considered in the proportion of one to something between ten and fifteen. The weakness occasioned by such unequal numbers is increased by a disadvantageous frontier, where the communication, even from its centre, is at all times tedious, and for a great part of the year 'tis impracticable; while from the United States, almost at all seasons, there is an easy approach into the midst of Canada.

Lord Carmarthen to Mr. Temple, St. James's, 28 Feb., 1786. Ex.

I am also to desire you will procure and transmit to me, with as much expedition as possible, copies of all acts of congress, and of all acts of the legislatures of the several provinces of the said United States, any ways relating to or affecting the commerce or shipping of his Majesty's dominions, with such information or observations as may in your judgment throw any light there upon.

Count de Rochambeau to General Washington, Paris, 9 March, 1786.

MY DEAR GENERAL: It comes to have in the parliament of England a scene of a great concern. The question was to know if they should fortify the harbors of the kingdom, having at their head M. Pitt and the Duke of Richmond that were for the affirmative. The house of parliament has been divided, and the voice of the speaker has decided for the negative. So much the worse, I believe, because the enormous sums that they should have spent at this fortifications, having the Lord Richmond at the head of this kind of works, whereof he is a virtuoso—this sums, I say, instead of being needless spent there, shall turn to the benefit of their navy and clearing of their debts.

Lord Cornwallis comes to be appointed general governor of the Bengal. His taste for travelling shall not be disputed to him, and this last voyage will be more lucrative than that of America, though

I believe he will behave with much more honor than any of his predecessors.

I have successively received, my dear General, your letters of the seventh of September and of the first of December, ultimo. I think, as you, that the Doctor Franklin has undertaken too hasty and ungrateful a task for his old age; and your existence is much more noble than his own, and without title you enjoy of all the consideration owing to your person, and so much deserved by the distinguished services that you have rendered to your country, which ought never forget them.

The health of the king of Prussia has been very weak all this winter, but, if Germany comes to lose him, I do not believe that event will bring war. He has prepared everything, that his successor may be able to make revive him. They do already his epitaph in Latin, that I find handsome by its laconism, *hic cineres, ubique nomen*; that is all what remains to the greatest men, my dear General, but what is to last as long as I live is the inviolable and respectful attachment with which I have the honor to be, etc.

Daniel Carroll to Madison, Annapolis, 13 March, 1786.

DEAR SIR: Our general assembly adjourned this day after a session of four months. The proposition from your assembly for a meeting of commissioners from all the states to adjust a general commercial system reached us not long before the conclusion of the session. Our house of delegates proposed commissioners for that purpose. The measure appeared to the senate, though undoubtedly adopted by your assembly with the best intentions, to have a tendency to weaken the authority of congress, on which the union and, consequently, the liberty and safety of all the states depend. I shall only observe that sound policy, if not the spirit of the confederation, dictates that all matters of a general tendency should be in the representative body of the whole, or under its authority.

Our assembly have granted the five per cent completely on twelve states complying, including Maryland, and have granted ten shillings on every hundred pounds property for twenty-five years for our proportion of the internal fund required.

Otto to Vergennes, New York, 17 March, 1786. Ex.

While the different states are active in granting the requisition of last September, and also a duty of five per cent upon all importations, congress has been informed that New Jersey had suddenly recalled the powers which it had already given, and that it had refused to levy its contingent for the expenses of the confederation. The motive for this revolting conduct was jealousy, on the part of New Jersey, of New York, which by its position enjoys an advantage in carrying on a great part of its commerce, and which, by means of its customs duties, levies a sort of impost upon New Jersey and Connecticut. New York, not having acceded to the resolutions of congress, derives a great advantage from its customs, and obliges its neighbors, which have no large commercial towns, to pay a part of the expenses of its government. Congress on this occasion thought proper to take a step which could only be taken in the most urgent circumstances. It appointed a deputation composed of three of its members to represent to the legislature of New Jersey, in the most solemn manner, the deplorable consequences of its action. This embassy was received with the respect due to the members of the sovereign body. The legislature granted them a public audience. Mr. Pinckney, delegate from South Carolina, the head of the deputation, made a speech. He began by setting forth the means, the views, and the resources of the confederation. He made it evident that the individual states ought to be impressed with the idea of their weakness as separate governments; that their prosperity and their political existence depended wholly on their union; that it was with this salutary view that the confederation had been formed; that congress alone was the centre of all the powers which are the basis of their national strength; that it alone had the right to make war or peace, to conclude treaties or alliances, to equip fleets, to raise armies, to make laws in the name and on the account of the United States, and to fix the contingent of each member of the union for the common expenses of the government; but that these contingents had been hitherto insufficient, and that the project of a general impost throughout the United States was the only effective means that congress had been able to devise to meet its numerous engagements; that if New Jersey had manifested its resentment against the state of New York by laying extraordinary duties upon all goods imported from that state, and by opening a free port even opposite the city 'of New York, all the members of the union would have applauded. Its present conduct in refusing the constitutional demands of congress, and in plunging all its companion states into an abyss from which they could only emerge with great difficulty, would divert the attention of the confederation, and would cause the criminal obstinacy of New York to be forgotten. For what inconsistency would it not be in congress, to be severe against that state, while it should allow another member of the union to refuse with impunity its consent to federal measures? Mr. Pinckney added to these arguments very long details on the finances of the United States and upon the necessity of sustaining the confederation. Another deputy,[1] more animated than he, and indignant that the less important states should continue to oppose national measures, exclaimed, among other things, "What is your object in hastening the dissolution of a confederation which has cost us so dear? That compact was the result of necessity; but do you suppose that in a new system of government you would be allowed the importance that you have had hitherto? Do you think that Virginia, South Carolina, Pennsylvania, and Massachusetts would be willing to stand on an equal footing with the handful of citizens which inhabit your state? Although greatly inferior to those powerful republics, you have had an equal part in the deliberations of congress; but in a new confederation you will be put in your proper place." These vigorous words produced a good effect. The assembly of New Jersey has just repealed its resolutions; and, to force New York to submit to the wish of congress, it establishes a free port at Paulus Hook, lying to the west of the mouth of the North river, opposite New York. This port can do great damage to the commerce of that state, and it is hoped that a measure so decisive, the appeals of all the members of the union, and the activity of congress, seated in that city, will finally prevail in changing its system. All the other states have been struck with the deplorable situation of the finances. Maryland, Georgia, and Rhode Island, which had not as yet granted the impost of five per cent, have recently assented to it unanimously. As to New Jersey, it has merely recalled the resolution which it had taken against the impost, but it has not yet done anything toward its adoption, and its legislature dissolved without adjournment. The mania for paper money, which prevails more than ever in America, has caused great divisions in that state. The governor, who opposed it, was hung in effigy, and it is believed that all the members who were unfavorable to this measure will not be re-elected at the next elections.

Even this method of paying their debts, however dishonest, does not satisfy the people of New Jersey; they desire to pass a law of

[1] William Grayson

which the two Carolinas have furnished the first example. By this unjust law, an insolvent debtor has the right of giving up to his creditor any portion whatever of land according to the appraisement of his neighbors, and after this cession of land the creditor has no further means of proceeding against his debtor. The latter is careful to choose the worst of his lands, on which he induces his neighbors, who are themselves debtors and therefore interested in favoring themselves by an exorbitant valuation, to place any price whatever, and after this formality he forces his creditor to accept his land, and even at times to pay him an imagined excess. By this unworthy means a debt of three thousand pounds sterling has often been expunged by land not worth two hundred, and the English merchants have been ruined in Carolina.

Honest people cannot refrain from comparing this conduct with that of the people of Rome; they demanded, at least without subterfuge, and often with arms in their hands, the abolition of debts, while the Americans endeavor to give to the most crying injustice an air of equity, of which no one can be the dupe. They call this law of Carolina the Barren Land Law, and their creditors take good care not to press them, fearing to acquire land which they do not want. It is believed that New Jersey will imitate this fine legislation; the paper money which it demands so urgently will, besides, be very favorable to it, and will furnish to the unjust debtor great facilities for discharging his debts legally,

Monroe to Madison, New York; 19 March, 1786. Ex.

DEAR SIR: Jersey having taken into consideration the late requisition, the house of delegates resolved that, having entered into the confederation upon terms highly disadvantageous to that state, from the necessity of public affairs at the time, and a confidence that those points in which they were aggrieved would be remedied, and finding this was not the case, and a compact founded in such unequal principles, likely, by their acquiescence, to be fettered on them, they would not therefore comply with the same until their grievances were redressed. In the course of their reasoning they mention the failure of some states to comply with the impost, and seem to rest themselves on that ground in such manner as to intimate that, if they should comply, their objections would be nearly removed. This resolution being brought before congress gave great uneasiness. It is to be observed that here is no express act of the legislature, but merely the negative of a proposition to comply with the requisition in the branch in which it should originate; they, therefore, are in a less direct opposetion to the confederation than if it were the act of the legislature, but being in a high degree reprehensible, congress resolved that a committee be appointed to attend the legislature and endeavor to prevail on them to rescind the resolution and accede to the measure. The committee were Pinckney, Gorham, and Grayson. They left us immediately, and have not since returned. We have in the papers an act stated to be of Rhode Island passing the impost in the full latitude recommended by congress; it is believed to be the case; in that event this state will most probably pass it also; it is also said that Georgia hath passed it. A report, urging in very pointed terms a compliance with the recommendation for changing as therein proposed the eighth of the articles of confederation, is before congress; it will most probably pass, although some gentlemen in the eastern states would willingly throw it aside. The better disposed and better informed are aware of the impolicy of an opposition to it, even if injurious to those states (which is not admitted), while they seek a more important alteration in the extension of the powers of congress in the regulation of trade.

Franklin to Jefferson, Philadelphia, 20 March, 1786. Ex.

The disposition to furnish congress with ample powers augments daily, as people become more enlightened; and I do not remember ever to have seen during my long life more signs of public felicity than appear at present throughout these states, the cultivators of the earth, who make the bulk of our nation, having had good crops, which are paid for at high prices with ready money; the artisans, too, receive high wages, and the value of all real estate is augmented greatly. Merchants and shopkeepers, indeed, complain that there is not business enough, but this is evidently not owing to the fewness of buyers, but to the too great number of sellers; for the consumption of goods was never greater, as appears by the dress, furniture, and manner of living of all ranks of the people.

William Grayson to Madison, New York, 22 March, 1786.

DEAR SIR: I should have done myself the pleasure of writing to you sooner, but really nothing occurred here of sufficient consequence to communicate. Congress, from the small number of states that have come forward, have remained in a kind of political torpor. They have, of course, taken no active steps till lately that they have addressed the states on the subject of commerce. They were not long since a good deal alarmed at the conduct of sister Jersey; the house of delegates of that state, in a moody fit, declared that they would not only not comply with the requisition of 1785, but with no other requisition, until the five-per-cent impost was adopted. The state, by this act, having declared independence, congress thought it was a matter that merited some attention; they therefore ordered a committee to go to Trenton and expostulate with the house on the impropriety of their conduct. The committee was heard, and the house was so complaisant as to rescind the resolution; but they have passed no legislative act in affirmation of the requisition, and I very much doubt whether they will. It may, however, have this effect, that other states will not be deterred (by her conduct in an absolute refusal) from passing the requisition. There is at present a greater prospect of the impost than has been ever known; Georgia and Rhode Island have come into the measure, and it remains only with New York to give her consent to make it productive. The legislature is now sitting and deliberating on this subject, but I doubt extremely whether the result will be favorable.

Our foreign affairs are very little altered one way or other since I had the pleasure of seeing you. Mr. Adams has done nothing with the British ministry, and Mr. Jay has done very little more with Mr. Gardoqui. The commissioners in Europe have despatched Mr. Barclay, Mr. Franks, Mr. Lamb, and Mr. Randal, to negotiate with the Barbary powers, and we understand that Mr. Barclay has actually arrived at the court of the emperor of Morocco. I am very apprehensive that no good will come of all this. These potentates are the most greedy and rapacious in the whole world, and yet we offer nothing worth their acceptance. In addition to this it is shrewdly to be suspected that the maritime powers will underhandedly counteract all our measures. They cannot but be pleased to see American vessels (in addition to the dearness of labor) tottering under the accumulated, pressure of corsair insurance. Some people are seriously of opinion that we should turn Algerines ourselves; they must surely be out of their senses; however, not more so than some others who thought it for the interest of the United States to keep constantly at war with them. This latter sentiment, which proceeds from our secretary of foreign affairs, comes fully up to the idea of fighting for nothing and finding ourselves.

There has been a great contest in Jersey for the *argent papier*; but, though it went triumphantly through the lower house, it was lost in the council, eight to five. Some of the members, who were adverse to it, have been burnt in effigy—in particular Colonel Ogden, at or near Elizabethtown; the old governor was drawn up to the stake, but pardoned on account of his having been the first magistrate. This same Jersey bill was one of the most iniquitous things I ever saw in my life. Their money was a tender; if it was refused, the debt was suspended for twelve years. In the mean time the act of limitation ran, of course, which in effect destroyed it. Jersey has not been singular in her attempts at cheating; in this place a bill is depending of the same purport as that of Jersey, and which it is probable will pass, although it is violently opposed by the upright and respectable part of the community. The ancients were surely men of more candor than we are; they contended openly for an abolition of debts in so many words, while we strive as hard for the same thing under the decent and specious pretence of a circulating medium. Montesquieu was not wrong when he said that the democratical might be as tyrannical as the despotic; for where is there a greater act of despotism than that of issuing paper to depreciate for the purpose of paying debts on easy terms? If Lord Effingham is right, that an act against the constitution is void, surely paper money with a tender annexed to it is void, for is it not an attack upon property, the security of which is made a fundamental in every state in the union?

There have been some serious thoughts in the minds of some of the members of congress to recommend to the states the meeting of a general convention, to consider of an alteration of the confederation, and there is a motion to this effect now under consideration. It is contended that the present confederation is utterly inefficient, and that, if it remains much longer in its present state of imbecility, we shall be one of the most contemptible nations on the face of the earth. For my own part, I have not yet made up my mind on the subject; I am doubtful whether it is not better to bear those ills we have than fly to others that we know not of. I am, however, in no doubt about the weakness of the federal government; if it was weaker notwithstanding, it would answer, if the states had power, as in the United Netherlands. The federal government is weak, but the individual states are strong. It is no wonder our government should not work well, being formed on the Dutch model, where circumstances are so materially different. Your friend, Colonel Monroe, has taken to himself a wife out of the house of Kortright. Mr. King is to be married in a few days to Miss Alsop. Mr. Gerry is already married to Miss Thomson. Mr. Houston is to be married to Miss Mary Bayard. Many more manœuvres are going forward among the members of congress which seem to portend a conjunction copulative. In short, I think we have got into Calypso's island. I heartily wish you were here, as I have a great desire to see you figure in the character of a married man.

I tried to get you the book respecting canals, but all were sold but one, which, at General Washington's desire, I sent to him. All I could do was to employ the bookseller to import some. This will be done with all convenient speed; out of the importation I have engaged five copies—two for you, two for myself, and one for the Potowmack people. I remain, with the greatest friendship, etc.

Van Berckel to the States General, New York, 3 April, 1786. Ex.

Although at the time of the revolution, as well as later, the sad and ruinous effects of paper money were tasted, yet there is an inclination in New York to make another trial of it, and the assembly, as well as the senate, have voted to bring into circulation two hundred thousand pounds of this money. This has so astounded the best intentioned and most intelligent of the citizens that every effort is made to stop the dangerous procedure, and, for this purpose, they seek to induce the council of revision to withhold their assent to this act; in which case the matter must again be deliberated upon, and cannot be concluded except with a majority of two thirds in both houses. So soon as this matter shall be decided, I shall not neglect to inform your High Mightinesses in regard to it, because it appears to me of very great importance, as having immediate relation to the foreign credit of America. In this same light it appears to the majority of merchants here.

Lord Sydney to Joseph Brant, Whitehall, 6 April, 1786.

SIR: The king has had under his royal consideration the two letters which you delivered to me on the fourth of January last, in the presence of Colonel Johnson and other officers of the Indian department, the first of them representing the claims of the Mohawks for losses sustained by them and other tribes of Indians from the depredations committed on their lands by the Americans during the late war, and the second expressing the desire of the Indian confederacy to be informed what assistance they might expect from this country in case they should be engaged in disputes with the Americans relative to their lands situated within the territory to which his Majesty has relinquished his sovereignty.

Were the right of individuals to compensation for losses sustained by the depredations of an enemy to be admitted, no country, however opulent it might be, could support itself under such a burden, especially when the contest happens to have taken an unfavorable turn; his Majesty upon this ground conceives that, consistently with every principle of justice, he might withhold his royal concurrence to the liquidation of those demands. But his Majesty, in consideration of the zealous and hearty exertions of his Indian allies in the support of his cause, and as a proof of his most friendly disposition toward them, has been graciously pleased to consent that the losses already certified by his superintendent-general shall be made good, that a favorable attention shall also be shown to the claims of others who have pursued the same system of conduct, and that Sir Guy Carleton, his governor-general of his American dominions, shall take measures for carrying his royal commands into execution immediately after his arrival at Quebec.

This liberal conduct on the part of his Majesty, he trusts, will not leave a doubt upon the minds of his Indian allies that he shall at all times be ready to attend to their future welfare, and that he shall be anxious upon every occasion, wherein their interests and happiness may be concerned, to give them such further testimonies of his royal favor and countenance as can, consistently with a due regard to the national faith, and the honor and dignity of his crown, be afforded to them.

His Majesty recommends to his Indian allies to continue united in their councils, and that their measures may be conducted with temper and moderation, from which, added to a peaceable demeanor on their part, they must experience many essential benefits, and be most likely to secure to themselves the possession of those rights and privileges which their ancestors have heretofore enjoyed. I am, etc.

Sydney to Lieutenant-Governor Hope, Whitehall, 6 April, 1786. Ex.

SIR: His Majesty's ministers observe that the meeting between the deputies from the several tribes and the deputies from congress will take place sometime this spring, though probably not till after the arrival of Joseph Brant, and much will depend upon the turn which matters will then take. His Majesty's ministers rather imagine that no disputes will arise at this meeting, but that the Americans will leave them in the possession of their hunting-grounds until a more favorable opportunity shall hereafter offer for effecting the purposes which it is supposed that congress have ultimately in view, and, if that should be the case, no difficulties will immediately occur; but if, contrary to their expectations, the Indians should not accede to any proposals that may be made to them by the American deputies, or cannot be prevailed upon peaceably to accept of the asylum already directed to be offered to them within the province of Quebec, our situation will in some degree become embarrassing. To afford them open and avowed assistance, should hostilities commence, must, at all events, in the present state of this country, be avoided. But his Majesty's ministers, at the same time, do not think it either consistent with justice or good policy entirely to abandon them and leave them to the mercy of the Americans, as from motives of resentment it is not unlikely that they might hereafter be led to interrupt the peace and prosperity of the province of Quebec. It is utterly impracticable for his Majesty's ministers to prescribe any direct line for your conduct should matters be driven to the extremity, and much will depend upon your judgment and discretion in the management of a business so delicate and interesting, in which you must be governed by a variety of circumstances which cannot at this moment be foreseen.

The enclosed copy of a letter to Joseph Brant, in answer to his representation, will explain to you the extent of the engagements entered into on this side of the water, with which he will proceed in the course of a few days to meet his brethren; and, from his professions of attachment to this country, his Majesty's ministers are led to expect that he will from time to time furnish you with the earliest notice of anything material that may occur, which you will communicate to me in the most expeditious way for his Majesty's information, that instructions may be transmitted to you for your guidance upon such measures as it may be judged advisable to adopt. I am, etc.

Temple to Lord Carmarthen, New York, 9 April, 1786. Ex.

The idea of confining my appointment of consul-general in these states merely to matters of trade and navigation, I have no doubt was suggested to congress by their self-sufficient, uncourtly minister in London, who, enviously apprehending, and perhaps truly apprehending, that, if I could enter upon business in general with congress, I might possibly ripen matters to a tolerably good understanding between his Majesty's ministers and these states much sooner than it is probable that he, with his mulish obstinacy, will be able to do it in London.

Otto to Vergennes, New York, 9 April, 1786. Ex.

The states continue to make laws to hamper the commerce of Great Britain. Massachusetts and Rhode Island have already excluded English shipping from their ports. New Hampshire will presently follow the same way. North Carolina has just published an act by which the ships of all nations which shall not have made a commercial treaty with the United States are to pay double duties. Virginia has laid upon English vessels a discriminating impost of five shillings a ton. To give greater consistency to the commercial measures of the continent, it has appointed eight commissioners to regulate, with the delegates of the other states, in an assembly called for that purpose, the commerce of the United States; and to make their report of it, in order to enable congress to construct a general act of navigation for the whole extent of the United States. This measure appears indispensable to enlighten that body in regard to the real interests of its constituents. The majority of the members of congress are either lawyers or farmers, and therefore little versed in the affairs of commerce. A work of this importance will require time and great prudence and impartiality, and perhaps another year will pass before all the states will be able to agree upon a uniform plan. Meantime several legislatures have appointed delegates to confer with those of Virginia. More and more is the necessity felt of laying restrictions on the commerce of Europe, and efforts are making to establish in America, as far as possible, manufactures of articles of the first necessity. There is one of them in New Hampshire which promises great success in the manufacture of common cloths, and General Sullivan is doing everything in his power in favor of a law prohibiting the importation of foreign cloths.

On the other hand, the Americans are encouraging, by all sorts of means, the commerce with the Indies. Since the peace they have despatched twelve ships to China and the Cape of Good Hope. The Chevalier de la Luzerne granted to the captains of the first two expeditions circular letters to recommend them, in case of distress, to our officers commanding in India. I have been requested to give similar letters to the last vessels departing since my arrival. I thought it so much the less my duty to refuse in this case, as I saw by a letter of the commandant at Pondicherry that he was not sorry to see the Americans arriving there. Mr. Jay and several persons of distinction have assured me that the freedom from jealousy that we have shown thus far in the Indies, and the cordiality with which we have received there the ships of the United States, had produced an excellent effect; that they perceived, not only in private conversations, but also through letters addressed to them from the different parts of the continent, that their countrymen could not enough admire the disinterestedness of France in admitting into the ports of the Indies the flag of the United States. If, however, this admission is contrary to recent regulations, of which I have no knowledge, my letters of recommendation can have no possible ill effect, since they suppose cases of distress, where humanity prescribes the behavior and attentions toward all nations. I restrict myself to the observation that the United States cannot forego the merchandise of the Indies; that their natural disposition will never permit them to receive these commodities at second hand; that ginseng, which grows in great abundance in the interior of the country, gives them great facilities in trading with China, and that they export it even to the Cape of Good Hope, to which they give the preference over the Isle of France, either because they find there a greater market, or because the voyage offers less difficulties.

The different state governments have for some time given special attention to this commerce. New York particularly is engaged in introducing the culture of ginseng on lands less exposed to the devastations of the savages.

Congress itself begins to be interested in this new market for American products; they have just appointed a consul and a vice-consul for Canton. These two officers have already departed for their destination. The former[1] is a man of well-known talent, and will infallibly aid in cementing the connections between China and this country.

The want of specie, and the desire to speculate in the public funds, cause in all the different states a fermentation the more dangerous,

---

[1] Samuel Shaw

since it tends to overturn the foundations of the social system, credit, and public confidence. The debtors, who form the majority of the citizens, desire above all things the emission of a new paper money. This measure, adopted in many of the states, has for three weeks engaged the legislature of New York. It has finally resolved to make a new emission for the sum of two million six hundred thousand livres tournois. The most enlightened members of this assembly have in vain portrayed the present discredit of American commerce, that this would only serve to augment the difficulties of the republic, would only establish between the citizens a secret war, and would give to dishonest debtors, in case of depreciation, the means to pay their creditors in nominal sums; in spite of all the arguments and opposition of the chamber of commerce, the paper money law was passed by both branches of the legislature, and is at present under the consideration of the council of revision. In North Carolina, paper began to depreciate from the first week; in several other states it has only a precarious existence. The council of New Jersey having rejected this measure, the people thronged together, and the most violent proposed to abolish all the courts, in order to prevent the suits of their creditors. Fortunately, this effervescence had no result whatever. It is true that no further tender law has been made, as during the war; nevertheless, a debtor, after having made a genuine tender in paper money before witnesses, can no longer be compelled to pay.

Virginia has recently passed an act eventually recognising the sovereignty of the state of Kentucky. It now rests with congress to determine whether this district ought to be admitted as a member of the confederation.

This body, having in vain endeavored to secure a permanent revenue by a general impost of five per cent on imports, has finally published the resolution of which I enclose a copy. This document is the result of the deliberations which have followed the repeated demands of the public creditors, and it contains in part the remarks of the bureau of the treasury on my note of the thirtieth of November of last year. It proves clearly that the destitute condition of the exchequer is beyond remedy, and that it is necessary either to dissolve the confederation or to give to congress means proportioned to its wants. Its patience is pushed to the extreme, and it expresses itself with that nobleness which has always characterized its measures. It calls upon the states for the last time to act as one nation; it affords them a glimpse of the fatal and inevitable consequences of a bankruptcy; and it declares to the whole world that it is not to blame for the violation of the engagements which it has made in the name of its constituents. All its resources are exhausted; the payment of taxes diminishes daily, and scarcely suffices for the moderate expenses of the government. The state of New York is the only member of the union which opposes the five per cent impost. The motive for its pertinacity is, that, by levying this duty, it collects a kind of impost from the states of New Jersey and Connecticut, which, not having large towns, have their chief market in the city of New York. The reading of the enclosed resolution will acquaint you more fully with the present distress of the United States than all that I might say on this subject.

The present crisis concerns solely the existence of congress and of the confederation; the individual states continue to prosper, and to increase their population and their industry.

Otto to Vergennes, New York, 23 April, 1786. Ex.

MY LORD: For several weeks a rumor has been current that Louisiana was to be exchanged for a French possession in some other part of the world. Several delegates from the southern states have come to testify to me their satisfaction with such an arrangement. They maintain that if Louisiana belonged to France, she would put a complete stop to the plans of conquest which the new states of the union have for the western bank of the Mississippi, and that the United States will become a powerful nation only in so far as they shall no longer have the facility of extending toward the west. They take it for granted, furthermore, that France would not fail to make New Orleans a free port, and to promote the commerce of the interior, which will have the greatest need of this outlet. This opinion is general here. Although I have ever maintained profound silence upon this subject, I could not refrain from informing myself as to the point of view from which the Americans would regard an arrangement of this nature if it should take place.

A resolution was passed during the same session to exclude forever from the right of suffrage, and from the power of filling public offices, not only those persons who have borne arms against the United States, but also every person who, during the revolution, took the oath of allegiance to the crown and parliament of England, aided in any manner the armies and fleets of his Britannic Majesty, or directly or indirectly refused to submit to the authority of congress. This measure, adopted in almost all of the states, has preserved hitherto the principles of the revolution in all their purity, and has kept the reins of government in the hands of the whigs. If any enthusiastic tories still flatter themselves with a change in this system, these proceedings must dispel their hopes.

The eyes of the whole confederation have for some time been fixed upon the state of New York; all the other states having granted the impost of five per cent, it was hoped that this state would offer no obstacle. The assembly has indeed recently acceded to this system, but in a manner so incomplete that congress cannot be satisfied with it. It declares that this impost shall be levied by the officers of the state and not by those of congress, and it further permits it to be paid in paper money. The two provisions render this concession wholly illusory, and it is impossible to foresee the end of the present difficulties. Connecticut and New Jersey appear disposed to cramp the commerce of New York by prohibiting all importations from that state. It is surprising that, under these circumstances, the measures of the legislature are absolutely contrary to the wish of the majority of the citizens, and that a single intriguing member has found means to carry the vote. The government itself is of the party of the opposition. The hope must arise, however, that the present crisis will produce a change in the legislature at the next election.

Thomas Rodney's Report of Debates in Congress.   Ex.

New York, in Congress, 2 May, 1786.—A report was read respecting a proposed peace with the Algerines and Barbary states.

Mr. Pinckney said that the sum of eighty thousand dollars, heretofore appropriated to the purchasing peace with those states, was insufficient; that it was necessary to send a larger sum; that congress ought to address the states and let them know our situation, that they might provide; that we ought to send a sufficient sum, and a person of talents and integrity to negotiate a treaty; that Mr. Lamb, the person now there, is not a sober man, but of a loose character, unfit for that purpose; that he was surprised congress appointed such a person, etc.

Mr. Grayson said the sum was contemptible; that even the great maritime states of Europe were obliged to buy peace of those pirates, and that they at least winked at the depredations on our trade; that probably Great Britain would give them a larger sum than we had sent, to continue those depredations; and that, if we expected peace, we must outbid them, etc.

Almost every member in congress rose on this occasion, and the general sentiment respecting this matter singly was to the same purpose. But the consideration how money was to be procured drew into argument the whole affairs of the United States. So it was postponed till Monday.

Wednesday, 3 May, 1786.—Mr. Pinckney, of South Carolina, moved that a grand committee be appointed, to take into consideration the affairs of the nation.

Said our situation was such that it was necessary to inform the states thereof; that it was necessary that congress should be invested with greater powers, and therefore it was necessary to appoint a convention for that purpose, or that congress should call on them by requisition for such powers as were necessary to enable them to administer the federal government, or it must fall; that the confederation was deficient in powers of commerce, in raising troops, and in the means of executing those powers that were given, etc.

Mr. Monroe, of Virginia, alleged that congress had full power to raise troops, and that they had a right to compel a compliance in every case where they acted agreeable to the powers given them by the confederation; that all the states but New York had invested them with commercial powers (a member informed that New York passed an act for that purpose yesterday), therefore he saw no occasion for a convention, etc.

Much was said pro and con on this subject to the same purpose on one side or the other, and then the matter was referred to a committee of the whole on Tuesday next.

Thursday, 4 May, 1786.—The report respecting the cession of Connecticut to the United States (to wit, of all that country to the westward of a line running parallel with the western bounds of Pennsylvania, and one hundred and twenty miles distant therefrom).

Mr. Johnson, to show the right of Connecticut to this country, gave a well-digested historical account of the charters of New England, Virginia, New York, and Pennsylvania, and of the disputes that had arisen about them, and the decisions of the king and council in several instances, and then made many judicious observations thereon.

He said one of three things must be done: 1, congress must accept the cession; or, 2, contest their claim; or, 3, admit Connecticut to settle the lands. That the only objections he had heard were: that Connecticut, by agreement with New York, had fixed their western boundary; that their title had been tried in a court of law (in the dispute with Pennsylvania), and the decision was against them; and that the territory they offer to cede is already ceded by New York and Virginia; and these he endeavored to answer.

Mr. Grayson, of Virginia, opposed the cession, and asked the gentleman of Connecticut if he remembered the Canada, or Quebec, bill or act, passed in 1T74, limiting the western boundary of all the colonies. Did Connecticut put in her claim on that occasion, or remonstrate against that bill? Did she ever claim the western territory before the revolution? The Quebec act took in all that country, and Virginia had a right to what she conquered with her own arms, and the United States had a right to all the rest of that country by conquest.

That the crown did no more with respect to the Quebec bill than they did in the grants of New York and Pennsylvania, by taking away what had been granted before; therefore, the Canada bill having fixed the rights in the crown, the land belongs to the United States by conquest, etc.

Van Berckel to the States General, 6 May, 1786.

The hope that I had when I wrote last, that the council of revision would oppose the emission of paper money in this state, has entirely vanished; for the time having elapsed within which their objections might have availed, this act has received the force of a law, and they are busy in preparing the paper, which, as is thought, will be in circulation within two or three months.

Extract of a Letter from Major Ancrum, commanding at Detroit, 8 May, 1786.

The Indians, from everything that I can learn, are all very much attached to our interest, and very much incensed against the Americans, particularly against Clark and the other commissioners joined with him to treat with the Indians—and they have been for that purpose at the mouth of the Great Miami ever since the first of October last till very lately. Clark himself is gone, I understand, toward

Post St. Vincent, to treat with the Wabash Indians, and the other commissioners are returned home.

I have lately heard that several parties of Indians of different nations have gone out to war against the frontiers of the American states. I do not think that the Indians will ever suffer the Americans to draw their boundary lines or survey or settle any part of their country.

Monroe to Jefferson, New York, 11 May, 1786. Ex.

DEAR SIR: Since my last I have received yours of eleventh December and twenty-seventh January last. Until lately we have had so thin a congress that few acts of consequence have passed, a very pointed recommendation to those states who have hitherto declined to accede to the recommendation respecting a revenue system only excepted; since which Rhode Island and Georgia have acceded to the impost fully, so that it now depends on New York, who has also granted it, but under restrictions as to the officers to carry it into effect, and Pennsylvania and Delaware, who have limited the operation of that part which respects the impost to the adoption of the other or supplementary funds by all the states, having adopted both themselves. I am inclined to believe this measure will pass the union in the course of the year, so as to be carried into operation. We have now eleven states present, and a member from the other two; it is expected we shall have the thirteen shortly. The commissioners for treating with the western and southern Indians have concluded treaties in both instances with the principal tribes, and returned a statement lately of their proceedings to congress. The object for which these commissions was instituted seems to be now fully obtained, and as further management of those tribes, so as to regulate the trade and keep up a good understanding with them, is to be effected by some permanent arrangement, I apprehend these commissions will be annulled and such system adopted. The subject is now before a committee.

In my last I mentioned to you that the propriety of the acts of congress founded on the condition of the acts of cession from the states, fixing the limits of the states westward, was questioned. A proposition, or rather a report, is before congress, recommending it to Virginia and Massachusetts to revise their acts as to that condition, so as to leave it to the United States to make what division of the same future circumstances may make necessary, subject to this proviso: "that the said territory be divided into not less than two and not more than five states." The plan of a temporary government, to be instituted by congress and preserved over such district until they shall be admitted into congress, is also reported. The outlines are as follows:

Congress are to appoint, soon as any of the lands shall be sold, a governor, council, judges, secretary to the council, and some other officers; the governor and council to have certain powers until they have a certain number of inhabitants, at which they are to elect representatives to form a general assembly, to consist of the governor and council and said house of representatives. It is, in effect, to be a colonial government, similar to that which prevailed in these states previous to the revolution, with this remarkable and important difference: that, when such districts shall contain the number of the least numerous of the "thirteen original states for the time being," they shall be admitted into the confederacy. The most important principles of the act at Annapolis are, you observe, preserved in this report. It is generally approved of, but has not yet been taken up. The treaty with Prussia will be shortly ratified, and forwarded for exchange.

Upon the subject of commerce I have nothing new to give you. The plan of a convention at Annapolis, which I believe will be carried into effect, has taken the subject from before congress. As it originated with our state, we think it our duty to promote its object by all the means in our power. Of its success I must confess I have some hopes. The investigation of the subject will always be of advantage, since truth and sound state policy in every instance will urge the commission of the power to the United States.

You will be surprised to hear that I have formed the most interesting connection in human life with a young lady in this town, as you know my plan was to visit you before I settled myself; but having formed an attachment to this young lady (a Miss Kortright, the daughter of a gentleman of respectable character and connections in this state, though injured in his fortunes by the late war), I have found that I must relinquish all other objects not connected with her. We were married about three months since. I remain here until the fall, at which time we remove to Fredericksburg, in Virginia, where I shall settle for the present, in a house prepared for me by Mr. Jones, to enter into the practice of the law. I intended to have made you a remittance by this packet to replace the money you have advanced for the Encyclopedia, but have been unable. I shall not neglect this.

Otto to Vergennes, New York, 20 May, 1786. Ex.

The encouragement which his Majesty's council has given to our fisheries by the order of the eighteenth of September of last year has caused a new disaffection of the northern states against us. They obstinately regard as acts of hostility all regulations prejudicial to their navigation and their fisheries; and Mr. King, the principal delegate from Massachusetts bay, has recently spoken of it to me with much bitterness. He said to me, among other things, that he regretted infinitely that congress had not sufficient powers to regulate commerce; that he would propose at once retaliatory measures; that his opinion was, that every extraordinary duty on American products imported to the islands should be counterbalanced by an equivalent duty on the merchandise of the kingdom imported into America. It is not necessary for me to send to you the arguments of which I made use to convince Mr. King how contrary such a measure would be to the principles established by our treaty of commerce. To soften a little his first assertions, that delegate said to me that he was persuaded that, in making some sacrifices to the islands in favor of the United States, we should induce congress to exclude entirely the commerce of England from all the ports of the continent, and to grant favors to our merchants. This opinion is not peculiar to Mr. King. The most prominent delegates, and especially those of Virginia and of South Carolina, have spoken to me on the subject with great warmth. Their hatred of England increases daily, and, perhaps, it would not be difficult to profit by these dispositions; but they would probably put so high a price on the favors which they might grant us that it would be impossible for us to accept them.

However that may be, Mr. King has found means imperceptibly to postpone the ratification of our consular convention, and during this interval congress, which for fifteen days was composed of eleven states, has been reduced to eight, a number inadequate for affairs of this nature. Mr. Jay, who himself is only the echo of the delegates of Massachusetts bay, discovers all sorts of pretexts to justify this new delay.

Grayson to Madison, 28 May, 1786.

DEAR SIR: Your letter has come safely to hand, and I should have wrote to you sooner, but could not find anything to communicate worth your acceptance. Till lately congress has been perfectly inactive; for about a fortnight past we have had a tolerably full representation. However, Delaware has grown uneasy, and left us; and Connecticut, having prevailed on congress to accept her cession, moves off to-morrow. It is a practice with many states in the union to come forward and be very assiduous till they have carried some state job, and then decamp with precipitation, leaving the public business to shift for itself.

The delegation of our state was very much embarrassed with the Connecticut business, as it was said it was but neighbor's fare that Connecticut should be treated as we had been before with respect to our cession; and that cessions of claims conveyed no right by implication to the territory not ceded. We, however, after some consideration, took a hostile position toward her, and voted against the acceptance in every stage of it; it appeared to the delegation that the only proper claim was already vested in congress by the cession of our state; and that their cession was nothing but a state juggle contrived by old Roger Sherman to get a side-wind confirmation to a thing they had no right to. Some of the states, particularly Pennsylvania, voted for them on the same principle that the powers of Europe give money to the Algerines. The advocates for the acceptance have, however, some plausible reasons for their opinion, such as the tranquillity of the union; the procuring a clear title to the residue of the continental lands; the forming a barrier against the British as well as the Indians; the appreciating the value of the adjacent territory, and facilitating the settlement thereof.

The assembly of Connecticut now sitting mean immediately to open a land office for the one hundred and twenty miles westward of the Pennsylvania line, which they have reserved; and I don't see what is to prevent them from keeping it always, as the federal constitution does not give a court in this instance; and a war with them would cost more than the six millions of acres are worth.

Mr. Adams has just informed congress that he has made a demand of the posts, and has been refused; the Marquis of Carmarthen states in substance as a reason for the refusal that several of the states in the union have violated the treaty with respect to the debts; that, whenever the states show a disposition to fulfil the treaty on their part, the king will perform his engagements according to good faith. The states which are not included in the accusation are Rhode Island, Connecticut, New Hampshire, New Jersey, and Delaware.

The charge against Massachusetts is only this: that she has passed a law preventing executions from issuing for interest until the judgment of congress should be had thereon. The only charge against Maryland that I recollect is her having received large sums of money (the property of British subjects) during the war from their debtors. The charges against New York are heavy and numerous. With respect to Virginia, I think she may at least be speciously justified for what has passed; the proclamation of Governor Harrison is not imputable to her, as it was not done by any authority from the legislature; and, if I am rightly informed, it was disapproved of as soon as they met. As to the instalment act, it never did pass into a law, and the British committee of merchants had no right to mention it in their report; but the state of Virginia has not repealed her prohibitory laws on that subject. To this it may be answered that no such repeal was necessary, for that the definitive treaty, as soon as it was ratified by the contracting parties, became the law of the land in every state; if it became the law of the land, it, of course (by repealing anterior obstructions), opened the courts of justice to all those creditors who came within its description. This principle, no doubt, will subject the debtor who has paid into the public treasury. But where is the hardship of this if the public are liable to the debtor for such payment? From this it must result that the British have no right to complain, until the courts of justice refuse to take cognizance of their claims on the principle of prohibitory laws. Should the legislature view this business in as serious a light as I do, and wish to preserve the honor of the state with as much decency as the nature of the case will admit of, I submit it to your consideration whether it would not be proper for them to enact.

That the late treaty of peace now is, and ever has been since its ratification by the contracting parties, the law of the land in each state, and of course has repealed all lawful impediments to the recovery of any British debts therein described, any law, custom, or usage to the contrary notwithstanding. I am not certain I am right in my positions on the ground of the law of nations as applying to a federal government of separate sovereignties. Though I have understood this was the opinion of Count de Vergennes as it respected the treaty with France, at all events, if it is doubtful ground it is plausible ground; and I know of no other principle that will save the honor of the state. If it is said the British have first violated the treaty with respect to the negroes, they acknowledge the fact and agree to make satisfaction. What more can be desired? As to the interest, it is a subject of negotiation; if the point is gained, it will conduce to the benefit of Virginia as well as every other state; and, in the mean time, where is the danger of submitting the point to a jury composed of American citizens? There is, no doubt, one great difficulty in the matter: if the state of Virginia adopts this or some other system confirmatory of the treaty, she then complies on her part, while at the same time, if the other states adhere to their refusal, she leaves Great Britain at liberty to act as she pleases with respect to the negroes and the posts. Perhaps a proper attention to this difficulty may lead to the striking impropriety of the interference of states as to the construction of a treaty in any case whatever. Your sentiments on this matter will greatly oblige me. The treaty with the king of Prussia has been confirmed in congress; it is, in my opinion, as far as it respects commercial objects, of no great importance. Mr. Monroe, I know, has informed you that a day is assigned for congress to go into a committee of the whole on the state of the nation; also for what purposes this is intended.

I am apprehensive this will produce nothing, and that congress will never be able to agree on the proper amendments even among themselves. The eastern people mean nothing more than to carry the commercial point. There they intend to stop, and would not agree, if it rested with them, that congress should have the power of preventing the states from cheating one another as well as their own citizens by means of paper money.

Mr. Pinckney, who brought forward the motion, will be astounded when he meets with a proposition to prevent the states from importing any more of the seed of Cain. New York and Pennsylvania will feel themselves indisposed when they hear it proposed that it shall become a national compact that the sessions shall always be held in the centre of the empire. How will Delaware, Rhode Island, Jersey, and some others like to vote (with respect to any new powers granted to congress) according to their real and not their supposed importance in the union? I am of opinion our affairs are not arrived at such a crisis as to ensure success to a reformation on proper principles; a partial reformation will be fatal; things had better remain as they are than not to probe them to the bottom. If particular states gain their own particular objects, it will place other grievances, perhaps of equal importance, at a greater distance. If all are brought forward at the same time, one object will facilitate the passage of another, and, by a general compromise, perhaps a good government may be procured. Under these impressions I cannot say I think it will be for the advantage of the union that the convention at Annapolis produce anything decisive, as in this event nothing more is to be expected from Massachusetts, etc. The state of Virginia having gone thus far, it is matter of great doubt with me whether she had not better go farther and propose to the other states to augment the powers of the delegates so as to comprehend all the grievances of the union, and to combine the commercial arrangements with them and make them dependent on each other; in this case her own objects ought not to be pretermitted, among which a proper and liberal mode of settling the public accounts ought not to be forgotten.

Some alterations have lately been made in the land ordinance. The surveyors are liberated from all kind of connection with the stars, and are now allowed to survey by the magnetic meridian, and are limited to the territory lying southward of the east and west line as described in the said ordinance. The navigable waters, and the carrying places between them, are made common highways forever, and free to the citizens of the Atlantic states as well as those of the new states, without any tax or impost whatever. An attempt was made to change the system altogether, and was negatived. Indeed, the eastern and some other states are so much attached to it that I am satisfied no material alteration can be effected. The geographer and surveyors will set out, it is supposed, immediately, to carry the ordinance into execution, provided the Indians will permit them, of which, however, I have very great doubts. I beg leave to inform you confidentially that there does not appear at present the most distant prospect of forming treaties with Spain or Great Britain. That the treaty with Portugal, now carrying on in London, is in an apparently proper train. That peace can certainly be obtained from Tripoli and Tunis for thirty-three thousand guineas each, and probably from Morocco and Algiers for double that sum, respectively, provided money can be loaned in Holland for that purpose; and (which being the only resource) will be attempted.

That Mr. Jefferson has lately informed congress that he has applied to the court of France to destroy the monopoly of the Farmers General respecting tobacco. His reasoning and calculations on this subject do him the highest honor; he has proved incontestably that it is the undoubted interest of both nations that this injurious monopoly should be destroyed.

I shall not make any observations on this subject, as I am satisfied you must have long since fully considered it in all its relations. I only beg leave to submit to you the propriety of the states of Virginia and Maryland, through congress, representing to the court of France, in strong but affectionate language, the fatal consequences of an adherence to this measure.

This representation, when added to the commercial interest of France, and joined by the natural enemies of the Farmers General, will possibly shake this ruinous system.

The delegation have lately received a letter from the governor, stating the depredations and murders of the Wabash Indians on the Kentucky settlements. These Indians refused to come to the treaty last year—i.e., they gave no answer, and are now at war with the citizens of the United States. They have, therefore, left no alternative to them but hostilities. The delegation intend to move to-morrow that Colonel Harman, with four hundred continental troops, and such a number of Kentucky militia as may be necessary, march to their towns and destroy them if they do not make concessions, and deliver hostages as security for their good behavior in future. They will also press for the arrangement of a standing Indian department. In all this, however, they expect opposition from the circumscribed states, who, being themselves in no danger, will reluctantly yield assistance to those who are exposed.

I have, with pleasure, understood from Colonel Monroe that you intend paying this place a visit in the course of the summer. I hope you will do it in such a seasonable manner as to preclude the necessity of an immediate return, as was the case last year.

I remain, with great sincerity, your affectionate friend and most obedient servant, etc.

Monroe to Jefferson, New York, 16 June, 1786.

DEAR SIR: Since my last, but little hath been done in congress. We have had generally not more than seven states present; the only time that nine were, their time was employed upon the subject of the

Connecticut cession, which ultimately was accepted, whereby she cedes all the land lying westward of a line to be drawn westward of the Pennsylvania line parallel with the same. Our state voted against it, but were in sentiment for it. It is hoped it will terminate the variance respecting the Wyoming settlement by enabling Connecticut to give the claimants other land in lieu, and thereby establish the government of Pennsylvania in the benefit of the decree of Trenton. Other reasons there are which apply to the geographic position of the land, and the influence that consideration may have in the councils of Connecticut. We voted against it, under the sentiment upon which our state hath acted of her right to the north-west line from the northern extremity of her charter limits, which we supposed should be regarded even after the right was given to the United States by the delegation. What shall finally be done with Spain respecting the Mississippi? becomes an interesting question, and one pressing on us for a decision. Gardoqui has been long laboring its occlusion with Jay. For some time past I have been perfectly satisfied the latter required no arguments to bring him to the same sentiment. The proposition is that it be shut for thirty years, in consideration for which Spain will admit us into her ports upon a footing with her own subjects, we reciprocating. This, you may recollect, was rejected at Annapolis upon its own merits only. It is, however, magnified here as a great advantage, and equivalent to the consideration required. We are also threatened with the project of a treaty between Spain (in case this fails) and Britain; yet I cannot comprehend upon what principle it can take effect. Jay stated difficulties in the management of this business with the minister, and proposed, without bringing any of these circumstances to view, that a committee be appointed with powers to control all circumstances respecting the treaty, with a view of evading his instructions and concluding the treaty before they were known; but, as they were known to some who had marked the progress of the business, each proposition was discussed on its own particular merits in the first instance. A committee was appointed to report. Jay attended it. Of this I was a member. To us he would make no communication we did not already know, so that the plan failed in not carrying a committee in the first instance for the purpose. This was a fortnight past, and as yet we have made no report.

I have given circumstantially the state of this business as it has appeared to me, not on evidence absolutely, presumptive only.

Otto to Vergennes, New York, 17 June, 1786. Ex.

MY LORD : The low condition into which congress has fallen since the peace begins to excite the attention of true patriots. They see that the federal government cannot remain in its present inaction without endangering the reputation of the United States, and even their independence. The most urgent recommendations of that body are treated by a majority of the states with an indifference which causes lamentations from those who are least susceptible of an interest in public affairs. The department of finance has never been so destitute as at this moment, and one of the commissioners has assured me that he has not the means of meeting current expenses. The most important members of congress are doing all in their power to add to the act of confederation some articles which the present situation of affairs appears to render indispensable. They propose to give to congress executive powers, and the right to make exclusively emissions of paper money and of regulating commerce. They desire, further, the division of that body into two chambers, to prevent an eloquent and ill-intentioned member from carrying away the majority. As to the executive power, the confederation will always be unstable until congress shall have carried this important point. The inconsistency of the idea of a sovereign body which has no right but to deliberate and to recommend, in spite of the jealousy of a large number of individuals in America, cannot be concealed. The constant rotation of members of congress is another disadvantage, whose fatal effects are felt more and more; it is difficult for men who merely travel from one end of the continent to the other, and who remain but a few weeks in New York, to master the course of affairs.

Be this as it may, it will require much time and negotiations to correct these defects, and it is impossible to foresee the end of the present embarrassments.

The king of England having renewed, by an order in council of the twenty-fourth of March, the former prohibitions in regard to the importation of American commodities into the British West Indies in American ships, the hopes which were founded on the negotiations of Mr. Adams have vanished. Powerful declamations are the only response to this order, which is here termed a new hostility; and, without remembering the deplorable state of the public treasury and the exhaustion of the finances, there is already talk of arming troops and of seizing by force the posts on the lakes, as if the United States in the present condition of affairs could find the means for such an armament.

Count de Rochamheau to General Washington, Calais, 28 June, 1786.

I come, my dear general, to read in the public papers your letter to the general assembly of Virginia by which you refuse the fifty shares that have been by it offered to you. There I have well known again your character and your virtues, and I am very glad to see in a corrupted age how they make still a great account of this rare example of generosity. I come, my dear general, to make a turn in Holland. This republic and yours are not much alike. In Holland they have done, as God, of a heap of dirt the finest world that can be, by strength of art and industry. Your country, on the contrary, has received all the most generous natural gifts; but it remains yet to be done many things by the art to improve it, which should not require a long time with arms and under the direction of my dear general, if it would follow them. Furthermore, that republic of the seven united provinces is at present in a great crisis between the patriot party and that of the stadtholder, which has still strength and credit.

My neighbors, the Englishmen, begin to restore themselves of their loss, and are governed by a wise man, who sets their finances in good order. Our sovereign has gone to visit the harbor of Cherbourg. He enjoys always in Europe of the consideration that his firm and moderate character inspire with generally. The king of Prussia is at the death; but he shall have a successor that will continue him in all. Europe appears to be quiet, and likely will not be disturbed, but after the death of the elector of Bavaria; and it appears that all the politic prepares itself at that event.

Give me news of you, my dear general, and be persuaded of the tender interest that I take of, and of the eternal and inviolable attachment with which I have the honor to be, my dear general, etc.

INDEX TO LETTERS AND PAPERS.

	PAGE
Adams, John, to Samuel Adams, 26 Jan., 1786	482
from Samuel Adams, July, 1785	444
minute of conversation with, 20 Oct., 1785	462
Adams, Samuel, to , 25 Sept., 1783	329
to John Adams, July, 1785	444
to E. Gerry, 19 Sept., 1785	
to R. H. Lee, 23 Dec, 1784	408
from John Adams, 26 Jan., 1786	482
from E. Gerry, 5 Sept., 1785	454
from R. H. Lee, 17 Oct., 1785	461
Ancrum, Major, commanding at Detroit, 8 May, 1786	501
Armstrong, John, to Washington, 22 April, 1783	308
from Horatio Gates, 22 June, 1783	318
Bancroft, Edward, to Lord Carmarthen, 8 Dec, 1784	403
to William Frazer, 8 Nov., 1783	331
to William Frazer, 28 May, 1784	367
information from, 26 Aug., 1784	380
Bland, Theodorick, from Washington, 4 April, 1783	302
Boudinot, Elias, to R. R, Livingston, 23 Oct., 1783	331
Boudinot, Elisha, from Washington, 10 May, 1783	311
Bowdoin, Governor, from E. Gerry and R. King, 2 Nov., 1785	466

	PAGE
Bowdoin, Governor, from Governor William Moultrie, 20 Sept., 1785	458
Brant, Joseph, from Lord Sidney, 6 April, 1786	492
Carleton, Sir Guy, to the English Secretary, 20 Feb., 1786	484
to Lord North, 17 June, 1783	318
to Lord North, 21 Nov., 1783	334
to Secretary Townshend, 8 Jan., 1783	293
from Lord North, 15 June, 1783	314
Carmarthen, Lord, to Mr. Temple, 28 eb., 1786	484
from Edward Bancroft, 8 Dec, 1784	403
from David Hartley, 9 Jan., 1785	411
from Temple, 5 Jan., 1786	477
from Temple, 9 April, 1786	495
Carmichael, William, from Washington, 10 June, 1785	439
Carroll, Daniel, to Madison, 13 March, 1786	485
Gary, Archibald, to Washington, 25 Nov., 1785	469
Chastellux, Marquis de, from Washington, 5 Sept., 1785	454
Chittenden, Governor Thomas, to Haldimand, 15 April, 1784	354
Clinton, George, to Haldimand, 19 March, 1784	349
to James Monroe, 20 Aug., 1784	379
to James Monroe, 7 Nov., 1784	392
Cochran, Dr. John, from Washington, 31 Aug., 1785	453
Commissioners of American Claims	

514   INDEX TO LETTERS AND PAPERS.

	PAGE
from Lieutenant-Governor Henry Hope, 29 Jan., 1786	482
Duane, James, to Washington, 29 Jan., 1781	283
to Washington, 10 March, 1785	415
from Washington, 20 Dec., 1780	283
from Washington, 19 Feb., 1781	284
from Washington, 10 April, 1785	422
from Hugh Williamson, of North Carolina, 8 June, 1784	373
Ellsworth, Oliver, to Governor Trumbull, 10 July, 1783	324
Fairfax, George William, from Washington, 10 July, 1783	323
from Washington, 30 June, 1785	443
Fitz-Herbert, Alleyne, to Lord Grantham, 13 March, 1783	300
Fox, Charles J. to David Hartley, 9 Aug., 1783	327
to Duke of Manchester, 9 Aug., 1783	326
Franklin, Benjamin, to Jefferson, 20 March, 1786	489
to Vergennes, 15 Dec, 1783	337
from Jefferson, 5 Oct., 1781	288
Frazer, William from Edward Bancroft, 8 Nov., 1783	331
from Bancroft, 28 May, 1784	367
Gates, Horatio, to John Armstrong, Jr., 23 June, 1783	318
to Washington, 24 Dec, 1784	408
George, the King, to the Earl of Shelburne, 10 Nov., 1783	293
to the Earl of Shelburne, 8 Dec, 1783	292
Germain, Secretary, to General Haldimand, Governor of Quebec, 2 Jan., 1782	289
Gerry, Elbridge, to Samuel Adams, 5 Sept., 1785	454
and Rufus King, to Governor Bowdoin, 3 Nov., 1785	466
to Jefferson, 35 Feb., 1785	414
from Samuel Adams, 19 Sept., 1785	457
Gordon, William, to Washington, 30 Aug., 1784	383
from Washington, 8 July, 1783	330
Governor and Council at Cape Coast Castle, 16 Dec, 1783	336

	PAGE
Grantham, Secretary, from Alleyne Fitz-Herbert, 13 March, 1783	300
Grayson, William, to Madison, 1 May, 1785	433
to Madison, 22 March, 1786	489
to Madison, 28 May, 1786	504
to Washington, 10 March, 1785	416
to Washington, 15 April, 1785	435
from Washington, 25 April, 1785	430
From Washington, 33 June, 1785	443
Greene, General, to Washington, 29 Aug., 1784	382
to Washington, 3 Dec, 1784	398
Haldimand, General Frederick, to Major-General Knox, 3 July, 1784	376
to Secretary of State, 26 April, 1784	358
to Secretary of State, 13 May, 1784	359
to Secretary of State, 24 Oct., 1784	385
to Secretary of War, 27 Nov., 1783	334
Haldimand, Governor of Quebec, from Governor Thomas Chittenden, 15 April, 1784	354
from George Clinton, 19 March, 1784	349
from Secretary George Germain, 2 Jan., 1782	289
from Secretary of State, 8 April, 1784	352
from Secretary of State, 2 Aug., 1784	378
Hamilton, Alexander, from Washington, 11 Dec, 1785	470
Hamilton, Henry, Lord Sidney, 9 April, 1785	423
Hancock, John, from Washington, 15 Nov., 1783	333
Hand, General Edward, to General Irvine, 19 April, 1788	307
Hardy to Jefferson, 21 May, 1784	364
Harrison, Benjamin, Governo of Virginia to G. Washington, 31 March, 1783	301
from Washington, 30 April, 1783	309
Hartley, David, to Lord Carmarthen, 9 Jan., 1785	411
from C. J. Fox, 9 Aug., 1783	327

INDEX TO LETTERS AND PAPERS. 515

	PAGE
Hope, Lieutenant-Governor, to the Commissioners of American Claims, 29 Jan., 1786	482
from Sidney, 6 April, 1786	494
Humphreys, David, from Washington, 1 Sept., 1785	453
Irvine, General, from Edward Hand, 19 April, 1783	307
Jay, John, to R. R. Livingston, 12 Sept., 1783	329
to Washington, 6 April, 1783	307
from R. R. Livingston, 25 Jan., 1784	339
Jefferson, Thomas, to Benjamin Franklin, 5 Oct., 1781	288
to James Madison, 14 Feb., 1783	295
to Madison, 14 Feb., 1783	296
to Madison, 15 Feb., 1783	296
to Madison, 7 May, 1783	310
to Madison, 1 June, 1783	311
to Madison, 17 June, 1783	317
to Madison, 31 Aug., 1783	328
to Madison, 11 Dec, 1783	335
to Madison, 20 Feb., 1784	341
to Madison, 16 March, 1784	348
to Madison, 25 April, 1784	356
to Madison, 1 July, 1784	375
to Madison, 11 Nov., 1784	393
to Madison, 8 Dec, 1784	401
to Madison, 18 March, 1785	419
to Madison, 25 April, 1785	429
to Madison, 11 May, 1785	437
to Madison, 28 Oct., 1785	463
to Monroe, 21 May, 1784	363
to Monroe, 11 Nov., 1784	392
to Monroe, 11 May, 1785	436
to Monroe, 17 June, 1785	442
to Monroe, 11 Dec, 1785	471
to Washington, 6 March, 1784	347
from Benjamin Franklin, 20 March, 1786	489
from Elbridge Gerry, 25 Feb., 1785	414
from Hardy, 21 May, 1784	364
from Joseph Jones, 21 Dec, 1783	336
from Jones, 29 Dec, 1783	336
from James Monroe, 20 May, 1784	363
from Monroe, 25 May, 1784	366
from Monroe, 1 June, 1784	371

	PAGE
Jefferson, Thomas, from Monroe, 20 July, 1784	377
from Monroe, 14 Dec, 1784	405
from Monroe, 12 April, 1785	423
from Monroe, 16 June, 1785	439
from Monroe, 15 July, 1785	445
from Monroe, 15 Aug., 1785	449
from Monroe, 25 Aug., 1785	451
from Monroe, 19 Jan., 1786	480
from Monroe, 11 May, 1786	502
from Monroe, 16 June, 1786	509
from John Page, 23 Aug., 1785	450
from Edmund Randolph, 24 April, 1784	356
from Edmund Randolph, 15 May, 1784	361
from William Short, 14 May, 1784	361
From Charles Thomson, 1 Oct., 1784	384
from Vergennes, 30 Oct., 1785	465
from Washington, 3 March, 1784	346
Jones, Joseph, to Jefferson, 21 Dec, 1783	336
to Jefferson, 29 Dec, 1783	336
from Washington, 24 March, 1781	285
King, Rufus, and Elbridge Gerry, to Governor Bowdoin, 2 Nov., 1785	466
Knox, Henry, to Washington, 4 June, 1784	372
to Washington, 31 Jan., 1785	412
from Haldimand, 13 July, 1784	376
from Washington, 5 Dec, 1784	400
from Washington, 5 Jan., 1785	410
Kosciuszko, Thaddeus, to Robert Morris, 17 July, 1784	376
to Washington, 26 Sept., 1783	330
Lafayette from R. R. Livingston, 1 June, 1785	438
from Washington, 1 Sept., 1785	454
Langdon, John, to Tench Tilghman & Co., 13 April, 1784	355
Lee, Richard Henry to Samuel Adams, 17 Oct., 1785	461
to Madison, 26 Nov., 1784	397
to Madison, 27 Dec, 1784	409
to Madison, 30 May, 1785	438
to J. Monroe, 5 Jan., 1784	337
to J. Monroe, 17 Oct., 1785	461

516 INDEX TO LETTERS AND PAPERS.

	PAGE
Lee, Richard Henry, to Washington, 26 Dec, 1784	409
to Washington, 23 July, 1785	445
to Washington, 11 Oct., 1785	460
to William Whipple, 1 July, 1783	318
from Samuel Adams, 23 Dec, 1784	408
from Washington, 15 March, 1785	416
Livingston, R. R., to John Jay, 25 Jan., 1784	389
to Lafayette, 1 June, 1785	438
from Elias Boudinot, 23 Oct., 1783	331
from Jay, 12 Sept., 1783	329
from Ephraim Paine, 4 May, 1784	364
Luzerne to Rayneval, 31 Jan., 1784	340
to Rayneval, 13 Feb., 1784	340
to Rayneval, 12 April, 1784	354
to Rayneval, 21 April, 1784	355
to Rayneval, 17 May, 1784	362
to Rayneval, 18 June, 1784	374
to Rayneval, Nov., 1784	391
to Vergennes, 6 Feb., 1783	293
to Vergennes, 29 March, 1783	301
to Vergennes, 4 Aug., 1783	325
from Vergennes, 21 Dec., 1782	293
from Vergennes, 27 Feb., 1783	297
from Vergennes, 21 July, 1783	324
from Vergennes, 15 Feb., 1784	341
from Vergennes, 12 May, 1784	360
from Vergennes, 30 June, 1784	375
from Washington, 5 Sept., 1785	455
Madison, James, to his father, 8 Sept., 1783	328
from Daniel Carroll, 13 March, 1786	485
from William Grayson, 1 May, 1785	433
from Grayson, 22 March, 1786	489
from Grayson, 28 May, 1786	504
from Thomas Jefferson, 14 Feb., 1783	295
from Jefferson, 14 Feb., 1783	296
from Jefferson, 15 Feb., 1783	296
from Jefferson, 7 May, 1783	310
from Jefferson, 1 June, 1783	311
from Jefferson, 17 June, 1783	317
from Jefferson, 31 Aug., 1783	328
from Jefferson, 11 Dec, 1783	335

	PAGE
Madison, James, from Jefferson, 20 Feb., 1784	341
from Jefferson, 16 March, 1784	348
from Jefferson, 25 April, 1784	356
from Jefferson, 1 July, 1784	375
from Jefferson, 11 Nov., 1784	393
from Jefferson, 8 Dec, 1784	401
from Jefferson, 18 March, 1785	419
from Jefferson, 25 April, 1785	429
from Jefferson, 11 May, 1785	437
from Jefferson, 28 Oct., 1785	463
from R. H. Lee, 26 Nov., 1784	397
from R. H. Lee, 27 Dec, 1784	409
from R. H. Lee, 30 May, 1785	438
from J. F. Mercer, 26 Nov., 1784	397
from Monroe, 15 Nov., 1784	395
from Monroe, 6 Dec, 1784	401
from Monroe, 14 Dec, 1784	404
from Monroe, 18 Dec, 1784	407
from Monroe, May, 1785	433
from Monroe, 26 July, 1785	445
from Monroe, 14 Aug., 1785	448
from Monroe, 19 Dec, 1785	471
from Monroe, 26 Dec, 1785	475
from Monroe, 11 Feb., 1786	483
from Monroe, 19 March. 1786	488
from Jacob Read, 29 Aug., 1785	452
Manchester, Duke of, from Charles James Fox, 9 Aug., 783	326
Marbois to Rayneval, 15 Aug., 1784	378
to Rayneval, 24 Aug., 1784	379
to Rayneval, 17 Nov., 1784	396
to Rayneval, 20 Nov., 1784	396
to Vergennes, 17 Jan., 1785	412
to Vergennes, 25 Feb., 1785	414
to Vergennes, 27 March, 1785	420
from Vergennes, 14 Dec, 1784	404
Marshall, John, to James Monroe, 2 Dec, 1784	398
Mason to Washington, 9 Nov., 1785	468
from Washington, 27 March, 1779	281
Mercer, J. F., to Madison, 26 Nov., 1784	397
Monroe, James, to Thomas Jefferson, 20 May, 1784	363
to Jefferson, 25 May, 1784	366
to Jefferson, 1 June, 1784	371
to Jefferson, 20 July, 1784	377
to Jefferson, 14 Dec, 1784	405
to Jefferson, 12 April, 1785	423

INDEX TO LETTERS AND PAPERS. 517

	PAGE
Monroe, James, to Jefferson, 16 June, 1785	439
to Jefferson, 15 July, 1785	445
to Jefferson, 15 Aug., 1785	449
to Jefferson 25 Aug., 1785	451
to Jefferson, 19 Jan., 1786	480
to Jefferson, 11 May, 1786	502
to Jefferson, 16 June, 1786	509
to Madison, 15 Nov., 1784	395
to Madison, 6 Dec, 1784	401
to Madison, 14 Dec, 1784	404
to Madison, 18 Dec, 1784	407
to Madison, May, 1785	433
to Madison, 26 July, 1785	445
to Madison, 14 Aug., 1785	448
to Madison, 19 Dec, 1785	471
to Madison, 26 Dec, 1785	475
to Madison, 11 Feb., 1786	483
to Madison, 19 March, 1786	488
from George Clinton, 20 Aug., 1784	379
from George Clinton, 7 Nov., 1784	392
from Jefferson, 21 May, 1784	363
from Jefferson, 11 Nov., 1784	392
from Jefferson, 11 May, 1785	436
from Jefferson, 17 June, 1785	442
from Jefferson, 11 Dec, 1785	471
from R. H. Lee, 5 Jan., 1784	337
from R. H. Lee, 17 Oct., 1785	461
from John Marshall, 2 Dec, 1784	398
from Beverly Randolph, 26 Nov., 1784	396
from Meriwether Smith, 6 March, 1784	347
from Thomas Stone, 15 Dec, 1784	406
Montesquieu, Baron, to Washington, 25 April, 1785	428
Montmorin, Count de, to Vergennes, 11 Jan., 1782	289
to Vergennes, 25 Jan., 1782	290
to Vergennes, 30 March, 1782	291
to Vergennes, 5 May, 1782	291
to Vergennes, 8 June, 1782	292
Morris, Robert, from Kosciuszko, 17 July, 1784	376
from Thomas Paine, 14 Oct., 1783	331
from Tench Tilghman, 24 June, 1781	285
Morris, Robert, from Washington, 3 June, 1783	311
Moultrie, Governor William, to Governor Bowdoin, 20 Sept., 1785	458
Newenham, Sir Edward, from Washington, 0 June, 1784	374
North Lord, to Sir Guy Carleton, 15 June, 1783	314
from Sir Guy Carleton, 17 June, 1783	318
from Sir Guy Carleton, 21 Nov., 1783	334
Otto to Vergennes, 8 Oct., 1785	460
to Vergennes, 7 Nov., 1785	467
to Vergennes, 20 Dec, 1785	472
to Vergennes, 25 Dec, 1785	473
to Vergennes, 2 Jan., 1786	476
to Vergennes, 10 Jan., 1786	479
to Vergennes, 17 March, 1786	485
to Vergennes, 9 April, 1786	495
to Vergennes, 23 April, 1786	498
to Vergennes, 20 May, 1786	504
to Vergennes, 17 June, 1786	511
Page, John, to Jefferson, 23 Aug., 1785	450
Paine, Ephraim, to R. R. Livingston, 24 May, 1784	364
Paine, Thomas, to Robert Morris, 14 Oct., 1783	331
Plater, George, from Washington, 25 Oct., 1784	385
Pleasants, Robert, to Washington, 11 Dec, 1785	471
Price, Richard, from Washington, Nov., 1785	466
Putnam, Rufus, to Washington, 5 April, 1784	350
from Washington, 2 June, 1784	371
Randolph, Beverly, to Monroe, 26 Nov., 1784	396
Randolph, Edmund, to Jefferson, 24 April, 1784	356
to Jefferson, 15 May, 1784	361
to Washington, 3 Dec, 1785	470
from Washington, 13 Aug., 1785	448
Rayneval, from Luzerne, 31 Jan., 1784	340
from Luzerne, 13 Feb., 1784	340
from Luzerne, 12 April, 1784	354
from Luzerne, 21 April, 1784	355
from Luzerne, 17 May, 1784	362

INDEX TO LETTERS AND PAPERS.

	PAGE
Rayneval, from Luzerne, 18 June, 1784	374
from Luzerne, 6 Nov., 1784	391
from Marbois, 15 Aug., 1784	378
from Marbois, 24 Aug., 1784	379
from Marbois, 17 Nov., 1784	396
from Marbois, 20 Nov., 1784	396
Read, Jacob, to James Madison, 29 Aug., 1785	452
to Washington, 9 March, 1785	415
from Washington, 3 Nov., 1784	387
Rochambeau to Washington, 24 Feb., 1785	413
to Washington, 7 Jan., 1786	477
to Washington, 9 March, 1786	484
to Washington, 28 June, 1786	512
from Washington, 7 Sept., 1785	456
Secretary of State to Governor Haldimand, 8 April, 1784	352
to Haldimand, 2 Aug., 1784	378
from Haldimand, 26 April, 1784	358
from Haldimand, 12 May, 1784	359
from Haldimand, 24 Oct., 1784	385
Secretary of War from Haldimand, 27 Nov., 1783	334
Shelburne, Earl of, from George the King, 10 Nov., 1782	292
from George the King, 8 Dec, 1782	292
Short, Wm., to Jefferson, 14 May, 1784	361
Sidney, Lord, to Joseph Brant, 6 April, 1786	492
to Lieutenant-Governor Hope, 6 April, 1786	494
from Henry Hamilton, 9 April, 1785	422
Smith, Meriwether, to Monroe, 6 March, 1784	347
Stone, Thomas, to Monroe, 15 Dec, 1784	406
States General from Van Berckel, 17 March, 1784	349
from Van Berckel, 6 April, 1784	352
from Van Berckel, 2 May, 1784	358
from Van Berckel, 31 May, 1784	370
from Van Berckel, 13 Sept., 1784	383
from Van Berckel, 12 Oct., 1784	384
from Van Berckel, 27 Nov., 1784	398
from Van Berckel, 12 Dec, 1784	404
from Van Berckel, 15 March, 1785	417
States General from Van Berckel, 27 April, 1785	432
from Van Berckel, 1 Aug., 1785	447
from Van Berckel, 4 Oct., 1785	459
from Van Berckel, 1 Jan., 1786	476
from Van Berckel, 31 Jan., 1786	483
from Van Berckel, 3 April, 1786	492
from Van Berckel, 6 May, 1786	501
Stuart, David, to Washington, 16 Nov., 1785	468
to Washington, 18 Dec, 1785	471
from Washington, 30 Nov., 1785	469
Temple to Lord Carmarthen, 5 Jan., 1786	477
to Lord Carmarthen, 9 April, 1786	495
from Lord Carmarthen, 28 Feb., 1786	484
Thomson, Charles, to Jefferson, 1 Oct., 1784	384
Tilghman, Tench, to Robert Morris, 24 June, 1781	285
Tilghman, Tench, & Co., from John Langdon, 13 April, 1784	355
from Washington, 24 April, 1783	308
Townshend, Secretary, from Sir Guy Carleton, 18 Jan., 1783	293
Trumbull, Jonathan, to Washington, 10 June, 1783	314
from Washington, 1 Oct., 1785	459
Trumbull, Governor, from Oliver Ellsworth, 10 July, 1783	324
Van Berckel to the States General, 17 March, 1784	349
to the States General, 6 April, 1784	352
to the States General, 3 May, 1784	358
to the States General, 31 May, 1784	370
to the States General, 13 Sept., 1784	383
to the States General, 12 Oct., 1784	384
to the States General, 27 Nov., 1784	398
to the States General, 12 Dec., 1784	404
to the States General, 15 March, 1785	417

INDEX TO LETTERS AND PAPERS. 519

	PAGE
Van Berckel to the States General, 27 April, 1785	432
to the States General, 1 Aug., 1785	447
to the States General, 4 Oct., 1785	459
to the States General, 1 Jan., 1786	476
to the States General, 31 Jan., 1786	483
to the States General, 3 April, 1786	492
To the States General, 6 May, 1786	501
Van Dyke, Nicholas, to Washington, 2 July, 1783	319
Vergennes to Jefferson, 30 Oct., 1785	465
to Luzerne, 21 Dec, 1782	293
to Luzerne, 27 Feb., 1783	297
to Luzerne, 21 July, 1783	324
to Luzerne, 15 Feb., 1784	341
to Luzerne, 12 May, 1784	360
to Luzerne, 30 June, 1784	375
to Marbois, 14 Dec, 1784	404
to Marbois, 17 Jan., 1785	412
from Franklin, 15 Dec, 1783	337
from Luzerne, 6 Feb., 1783	293
from Luzerne, 29 March, 1783	301
from Luzerne, 4 Aug., 1783	325
from Marbois, 25 Feb., 1785	414
from Marbois, 27 March, 1785	420
from Count de Montmorin, 11 Jan., 1782	289
From Count de Montmorin, 25 Jan., 1782	290
from Count de Montmorin, 30 March, 1782	291
from Count de Montmorin, 5 May, 1782	291
from Count de Montmorin, 8 June, 1782	292
from Otto, 8 Oct., 1785	460
from: Otto, 7 Nov., 1785	467
from Otto, 20 Dec, 1785	472
from Otto, 25 Dec, 1785	473
from Otto, 2 Jan., 1786	476
from Otto, 10 Jan., 1786	479
from Otto, 17 March, 1786	485
from Otto, 9 April, 1786	495
from Otto, 23 April, 1786	498
from Otto, 20 May, 1786	504

	PAGE
Vergennes, from Otto, 17 June, 1786	511
Walker, Benjamin, to Washington, 3 April, 1784	350
Washington to Theodorick Bland, 4 April, 1783	302
to Elisha Boudinot, 10 May, 1783	511
to William Carmichael, 10 June, 1785	439
to Marquis de Chastellux, 5 Sept., 1785	454
to Doctor Cochran, 31 Aug., 1785	453
in Diary, for 10 Oct., 1785	460
to James Duane, 20 Dec, 1780	283
to Duane, 19 Feb., 1781	284
to Duane, 10 April, 1785	422
to George William Fairfax, 10 July, 1783	323
to Fairfax, 30 June, 1785	443
to Dr. William Gordon, 8 July, 1783	320
to William Grayson, 25 April, 1785	430
to Grayson, 22 June, 1785	443
to Governor Harrison, 30 April, 1783	309
to Alexander Hamilton, 11 Dec, 1785	470
to John Hancock, 15 Nov., 1783	333
to David Humphreys, 1 Sept., 1785	453
to Jefferson, 3 March, 1784	346
to Joseph Jones, 24 March, 1781	285
to Knox, 5 Dec, 1784	400
to Knox, 5 Jan., 1785	410
to Lafayette, 1 Sept., 1785	454
to R. H. Lee, 15 March, 1785	416
to Chevalier la Luzerne, 5 Sept., 1785	455
to George Mason, 27 March, 1779	281
to Robert Morris, 3 June, 1783	311
to Sir Edward Newenham, 10 June, 1784	374
to George Plater, 25 Oct., 1784	385
to President of Congress, 17 June, 1783	315
to Richard Price, Nov., 1785	466

INDEX TO LETTERS AND PAPERS.

	PAGE
Washington to Rufus Putnam, 2 June, 1784	371
to E. Randolph, 13 Aug., 1785	448
to Jacob Read, 3 Nov., 1784	387
to Count de Rochambeau, 7 Sept., 1785	456
to David Stuart, 30 Nov., 1785	469
to T. Tilghman, 24 April, 1783	308
to J. Trumbull, 1 Oct., 1785	459
from J. Armstrong, 22 April, 1788	308
from A. Gary, 25 Nov., 1785	469
from J. Duane, 29 Jan., 1781	283
from J. Duane, 10 March, 1785	415
from H. Gates, 24 Dec, 1784	408
from W. Grayson, 10 March, 1785	416
from W. Grayson, 15 April, 1785	425
from N. Greene, 29 Aug., 1784	382
from N. Greene, 2 Dec, 1784	398
from W. Gordon, 30 Aug., 1784	382
from Benjamin Harrison, Gov. of Va., 31 March, 1783	301
from John Jay, 6 April, 1783	307
from Jefferson, 6 March, 1784	347
from Knox, 4 June, 1784	372
from Knox, 31 Jan., 1785	412
from Thaddeus Kosciuszko, 26 Sept., 1783	330
from R. H. Lee, 26 Dec, 1784	409
from R. H. Lee, 23 July, 1785	445
from R. H. Lee, 11 Oct., 1785	460
from G. Mason, 9 Nov., 1785	468
from Baron Montesquieu, 25 April, 1785	428
from R. Pleasants, 11 Dec, 1785	471
from R. Putnam, 5 April, 1784	350
from E. Randolph, 3 Dec, 1785	470
from Jacob Read, 9 March, 1785	415
from Rochambeau, 24 Feb., 1785	413
from Rochambeau, 7 Jan., 1786	477
from Rochambeau, 9 March, 1786	484
from Rochambeau, 28 June, 1786	512
from D. Stuart, 16 Nov., 1785	468

	PAGE
Washington, from D. Stuart, 18 Dec, 1785	471
from J. Trumbull, 10 June, 1783	314
from Gov. Nicholas Van Dyke of Delaware, 2 July, 1783	319
from B. Walker, 3 April, 1784	350
Wayne, A., to Washington, 14 Dec, 1783	336
Whipple, W., from Richard Henry Lee, 1 July, 1783	318
Williamson, H., to J. Duane, 8 June, 1784	372

MISCELLANEOUS.

	PAGE
Articles of Confederation, report on, 22 Aug., 1781	283
2 Sept., 1783	328
7 Aug., 1786. See Vol. II.	
British Ministry, information for, Feb., 1783	296
March, 1783	297
Aug., 1783	327
Aug., 1784	380
April, 1785	428
April, 1785	429
June, 1785	439
Congress, motion in, by T. Bland, 5 June, 1783	
Petition to, from army officers, 16 June, 1783	314
Letter to, from Connecticut, 1 Nov., 1783	331
Instructions to Pennsylvania delegates in, 9 Dec, 1783	334
Instructions to Massachusetts delegates in, 1785	414
Motion in, by R. King, for excluding slavery from new States, 16 March, 1785	417
Report to, by R. King, 6 April, 1785	418
Thomas Rodney's report of debates in, 2-4 May, 1786	499
Conversation in Paris relative to America, April, 1783	302

THE END OF VOLUME I.

Made in the USA
Las Vegas, NV
23 December 2021